D0810133

CLINICIAN'S GUIDE TO NEUROPSYCHOLOGICAL ASSESSMENT

CLINICIAN'S GUIDE TO NEUROPSYCHOLOGICAL ASSESSMENT

Edited by

RODNEY D. VANDERPLOEG

James A. Haley Veterans' Hospital, Tampa, Florida
University of South Florida

LEA LAWRENCE ERLBAUM ASSOCIATES, PUBLISHERS
1994 Hillsdale, New Jersey   Hove, UK

Copyright © 1994 by Lawrence Erlbaum Associates, Inc.
All rights reserved. No part of this book may be reproduced in
any form, by photostat, microfilm, retrieval system, or any other
means, without the prior written permission of the publisher.

Lawrence Erlbaum Associates, Inc., Publishers
365 Broadway
Hillsdale, New Jersey 07642

Library of Congress Cataloging-in-Publication Data

Clinician's guide to neuropsychological assessment / edited by Rodney D.
Vanderploeg.
     p.   cm.
    Includes bibliographical references and index.
    ISBN 0-8058-1253-9 (c). − ISBN 0-8058-1254-7 (p)
    1. Clinical neuropsychology. 2. Neuropsychological tests.
I. Vanderploeg, Rodney D.
    [DNLM: 1. Neuropsychology. 2. Neuropsychological tests. WL 103
G946 1993]
RC386.6.N48G85 1993
616.8 '0475 − dc20
DNLM/DLC
for Library of Congress   93-14115
                                  CIP

Books published by Lawrence Erlbaum Associates are printed on acid-free
paper, and their bindings are chosen for strength and durability.

Printed in the United States of America
10 9 8 7 6 5 4 3 2 1

616.80475
c G4

96-3271
30907489

Contents

PREFACE   ix

**1 INTERVIEW AND TESTING:
THE DATA-COLLECTION PHASE OF
NEUROPSYCHOLOGICAL EVALUATIONS**   1
Rodney D. Vanderploeg

Testing Versus Assessment   *2*
The Nature and Purpose of the Evaluation:
     Clarifying the Evaluation Question(s)   *3*
Interview, Case History, and Behavioral Observations   *6*
Neuropsychological Testing   *17*
Summary   *38*

**2 ESTIMATING PREMORBID LEVEL
OF FUNCTIONING**   43
Rodney D. Vanderploeg

Intraindividual Variability Across Cognitive Abilities   *44*
Premorbid Estimation Methods   *49*
Premorbid Estimation Recommendations   *63*

**3 PRINCIPLES OF NEUROPSYCHOLOGICAL
INTERPRETATION**   69
Cynthia R. Cimino

Importance of a Conceptual Model
     of Brain-Behavior Relationships   *70*
Influence of Subject-Specific Variables   *79*

Determining When a Difference Is a True
  and Meaningful Difference   *84*
Effects of the Interaction of Different
  Cognitive Domains   *88*
Evaluating the Consistency
  of Neuropsychological Data   *93*
Distinguishing Neurologic, Psychiatric,
  and Test-Taking Conditions That May Overlap   *99*
Avoiding Erroneous Assumptions and Inferences   *103*
Summary   *107*

4 APPLICATION OF NEUROPSYCHOLOGICAL
ASSESSMENT RESULTS   113

Bruce Crosson

Properties of Neuropsychological Tests   *114*
Diagnostic Context   *121*
Rehabilitation Context   *132*
Forensic Context   *143*
Giving Feedback to Patients and Families   *152*
Conclusions   *158*

5 ISSUES IN CHILD
NEUROPSYCHOLOGICAL ASSESSMENT   165

Eileen B. Fennell

General Issues in Assessing Children   *166*
Approaches in Child Neuropsychology   *170*
A Model for Neuropsychological
  Assessment of Children   *172*
Measurement Issues in Child
  Neuropsychological Assessment   *177*
Future Directions in Child Neuropsychological
  Assessment   *180*

6 NEUROPSYCHOMETRIC ISSUES
AND PROBLEMS   185

Paul D. Retzlaff and Michael Gibertini

Traditional Psychometrics: Concepts
  and Applications   *187*

Neuropsychometrics: Putting the Classics
   in Perspective   *194*
Operating Characteristics and Sampling:
   Toward Useful Validities   *199*
Summary   *208*

**7   THE COGNITIVE–METRIC, FIXED
     BATTERY APPROACH TO
     NEUROPSYCHOLOGICAL ASSESSMENT**   **211**
Elbert W. Russell

History of Neuropsychological Battery
   Assessment Methods   *211*
Foundations of the Cognitive–Metric Approach   *214*
Requirements for a Cognitive–Metric Set
   of Tests   *229*
Chapter Summary and Conclusions   *252*

**8   THE FLEXIBLE BATTERY
     APPROACH TO
     NEUROPSYCHOLOGICAL ASSESSMENT**   **259**
Russell M. Bauer

Distinguishing "Fixed" and "Flexible" Batteries   *262*
An Intermediate Approach: Multiple
   Fixed Batteries   *268*
Three Flexible Approaches   *272*
Skills Required of the Flexible Battery
   Clinician   *280*
Advantages and Limitations of the
   Flexible Battery Approach   *284*
Summary and Conclusions   *286*

AUTHOR INDEX   **291**

SUBJECT INDEX   **301**

Preface

Neuropsychological assessment is a difficult and complicated process. Often clinicians fail to attend to fundamental issues of assessment or are unaware of many of the potential sources of error. Given that formal test data on the surface appear unambiguous and objective, neuropsychologists may fall into the practice of overemphasizing tests and their scores and underemphasizing the less formal aspects of assessment, including all of the prerequisite factors that affect the validity, reliability, and interpretability of test data. Interpretation is far from straightforward, and a pragmatic application of assessment results requires attention to a multitude of issues and concerns.

Clinician's Guide to Neuropsychological Assessment is a text focusing on the clinical practice of neuropsychology. It is intended to serve as a graduate-level textbook for courses in neuropsychological assessment. With its focus on clinical practice, this volume also is designed to serve as a handbook for interns and professionals who engage in the practice or teaching of clinical neuropsychological assessment. Individuals practicing in forensic settings where the evaluation of brain damage or cognitive impairment is relevant also will find this a useful reference. This volume does not cover the academic and research background in neuroanatomy and functional neuroanatomy, neurological and medical diseases, or neuropsychology. Because cognizance of these topics is essential to competent neuropsychological practice, either prior knowledge or a companion text covering them would be necessary.

Neuropsychological assessment typically begins with a consultation request and proceeds to the examination of the patient. Evaluation results are then interpreted and conveyed to the referral source, patients, and others in a manner designed to clarify diagnostic, treatment, prognostic, and functional capacity issues. For the purposes of this text, the assessment process is divided into stages, which in clinical practice typically overlap significantly. The initial four chapters of this text take the reader through these stages of the neuropsychological evaluation: data collection, estimation of premorbid functioning, interpretation, and application of results.

The first phase of any assessment process is data collection. It begins with clarification of the nature and purpose of the evaluation, proceeds to the gathering of relevant data through a variety of methods, and typically includes the scoring of the tests administered. This phase is the focus of chapter 1. Chapter 2 covers the estimation of premorbid functioning, an intermediate and necessary prerequisite process that is essential for accurate interpretation. Chapter 3 focuses on the next major phase of neuropsychological assessment, integration and interpretation of data. Data collected from a variety of sources (past history, behavioral observations, reports of patients and others, and neuropsychological tests) must be integrated and analyzed for consistency. This includes consistency across sources, within sources, and with possible diagnostic conditions. Interpretation of these data involves the consideration of possible reasons for findings and a determination of the most likely explanation. Diligent interpretation takes not only observed behavior and test results into account but views them in the larger context of each patient's history and current psychological, social, and vocational milieu. In reality, the interpretation phase of assessment goes hand-in-hand with the next phase, application. Chapter 4 explores application issues relevant to different clinical contexts: diagnostic, rehabilitation, forensic, and feedback to patients and families.

The middle segment of this text addresses special problems unique to pediatric assessment (chapter 5) and psychometric properties of neuropsychological tests (chapter 6). The final two chapters discuss two approaches to neuropsychological assessment, the fixed battery (chapter 7) and the flexible battery (chapter 8). These two approaches, broadly defined, capture current clinical practice. However, as both chapter authors note, most competent neuropsychologists utilize aspects of both approaches in their clinical practice.

Contributors to this volume are all engaged in the clinical practice of neuropsychological assessment, as well as in teaching and research. Thus, they are very familiar with common misconceptions, practice errors, and methodological problems and are able to integrate both academic and practical aspects of neuropsychological assessment.

An edited work such as this increases the difficulty in appropriately acknowledging all those who contributed to its successful completion. I would like to convey my gratitude and appreciation to chapter authors for their thoughtful and articulate contributions to this volume. I am grateful also to Chava Reyna Casper, PhD, Kathryn M. Scornavacca, and Lawrence Erlbaum Associates for their encouragement, support, and deadline extensions. On behalf of myself and the other authors, I express our gratitude to our families who have endured late evenings of work with patience, support, and understanding. Finally, we owe a debt of gratitude to our colleagues, patients, and students who have contributed in various ways to the formulation of the ideas conveyed in this text.

—Rodney D. Vanderploeg

Interview and Testing: The Data-Collection Phase of Neuropsychological Evaluations

Rodney D. Vanderploeg
James A. Haley Veterans' Hospital
Tampa, Florida
and
University of South Florida

Since the 1970s, the clinical assessment of brain–behavior relationships has advanced from the use of single tests of "organicity" to a complex, multifaceted process. Alternative approaches to assessment have been developed. One approach is to utilize carefully constructed, well-validated batteries; another is to adapt each examination to the specific questions and clinical needs of individual patients; and others lie in between. Regardless of the structure of the evaluation, the process neither begins nor ends with testing (i.e., the administration, scoring, and comparison of test results with cutoff scores or normative data). The competent neuropsychologist interprets evaluation findings and integrates them with historical data, unique aspects of individual performance, and the life situation of each patient. The neuropsychological assessment process has multiple phases. The first stage of that process is the gathering of meaningful and interpretable data; this is the focus of this chapter.

Multiple issues require the attention of the neuropsychologist within this initial phase. For the purposes of presentation and discussion, these have been broken into four general areas: (a) neuropsychological testing versus assessment; (b) clarification of the evaluation and referral questions; (c) the interview, case history, and behavioral observations; and (d) issues of neuropsychological test selection, administration, and session structure. Of course, during the actual evaluation the neuropsychologist will be carrying out activities of hypothesis testing, test administration, and behavioral observation simultaneously, and making adjustments in approach and methodology as dictated by each patient's unique needs. This chapter identifies assessment principles that can help guide the clinical neuropsychologist. However, competent practice requires the thoughtful consideration of how these assessment issues differentially impact each case. There is no "cook book" approach.

TESTING VERSUS ASSESSMENT

A *psychological test* is a sample of behavior obtained under controlled conditions (Anastasi, 1988; Maloney & Ward, 1976). It involves the measurement of differences between individuals, or within the same individual across time utilizing objective, standardized, and quantified data-collection procedures. In and of itself, testing is not capable of answering questions and requires minimal clinical expertise other than the correct administration and scoring of test instruments. Testing is a tool that may be utilized during a neuropsychological assessment as one source of information. However, a proper evaluation ultimately rests on much more than test results.

Psychological assessment differs from testing in purpose, goals, and methodologies (Maloney & Ward, 1976; Matarazzo, 1990). Psychological assessment, or in this case, neuropsychological assessment, involves a *process* of solving problems or answering questions. In conducting a neuropsychological assessment, the clinician must first be able to define and clarify the question(s) that need to be answered to meet particular clinical needs. Formulation of the examination questions (and later interpretation of the obtained data; see chapter 3) is based in part on knowledge of a variety of content areas. Lezak (1983) suggested that mastery of four areas is essential: (a) clinical psychological practice, (b) psychometrics, (c) neuroanatomy and functional neuroanatomy, and (d) neuropathologies and their behavioral effects. A fifth knowledge area that is also essential is a theoretical understanding of how the four content areas just listed inter-relate and interact. This latter knowledge area might best be viewed as an overarching model or knowledge of brain–behavior relationships that is applicable across clinical settings and diagnoses.

Once the evaluation questions of interest have been clarified, the neuropsychologist must determine what information needs to be collected and how best to obtain it. In this regard, testing would be only one of several methods that might be utilized. Other methods include the case history, the clinical interview, the mental status examination, general behavioral observations, and information from other people who are involved with the patient (spouse, children, friends, employer, and other professionals such as nursing staff). If testing is to be conducted, issues of test selection must be competently addressed. Structuring the testing session, administration procedures, and scoring and clerical issues are also important factors in the overall competent completion of the data-collection phase of the evaluation process.

Returning for a moment to psychological testing, within classical test theory reliability refers to how consistent test scores are across various conditions, whereas validity is the extent to which tests assess what they were designed to measure. Apart from factors unique to the test instruments themselves, both reliability and validity can be adversely impacted by population-specific variables (Sattler, 1988). These include factors such as test-taking skill, guessing, misleading or misunderstood instructions, illness, daydreaming, motivation, anxiety, performance speed, examiner–examinee rapport, physical handicaps, and distractibility. Although psychometric issues are addressed in greater detail in chapter 6, it is important to be cognizant of data-collection variables that can adversely impact the reliability and validity of data.

THE NATURE AND PURPOSE OF THE EVALUATION: CLARIFYING THE EVALUATION QUESTION(S)

Neuropsychological evaluations traditionally have been undertaken for three reasons: diagnosis, patient care, and research (Lezak, 1983). Given the nature of the current text, assessments for research purposes are not discussed. Regarding clinical assessments, I strongly believe that a neuropsychological evaluation should not be undertaken unless it is likely to make a relevant difference in a patient's treatment, quality of life, vocational or educational plans, placement/disposition planning, or patient/family education or counseling. Helping in the diagnostic process at times certainly falls within this pragmatic framework as well. Often a correct diagnosis is essential in educating patients, their families, and their treatment staff about prognosis, and in helping to develop a treatment plan. The one exception to this rule would be performing an evaluation for professional training purposes, as long as the patient is willing and realizes the potential benefits or lack of benefits that might occur. Table 1.1 lists a variety of common and potentially important reasons for conducting an evaluation.

Requests for evaluation arise from a variety of sources: medical professionals, psychologists or other mental health professionals, various rehabilitation treatment staff, attorneys, patients, and patients' families. In practice, all too often the relevant clinical questions for the evaluation are unclear, both to the referral source and to the neuropsychologist. The referral source may be aware that this patient appears different from those

TABLE 1.1
Potentially Useful Reasons for Conducting a Neuropsychological Evaluation

1. Diagnosis
   a. Identifying the presence of a neurological condition
   b. Discrimination between behaviorally similar neurological diagnoses
   c. Discriminating between neurologic versus psychiatric diagnoses
   d. Identifying possible neuroanatomic correlates
   e. Prognostication
2. Descriptive assessment of cognitive–emotional–psychological strengths and weaknesses
   a. Baseline or pretreatment evaluation
   b. Posttreatment or follow-up evaluations
   c. Help in designing a treatment plan
3. Goal Setting
   a. Realistic treatment planning
   b. Educational planning needs and potential
   c. Vocational planning and potential
4. Discharge/placement planning
5. Establishment of impairment for disability compensation
6. Personal injury (forensic) compensation
7. Competency evaluation
8. Other forensic issues (e.g., diminished capacity)
9. Research
10. Training of others

with whom he or she typically works. For example, in a psychiatric setting, the patient may exhibit atypical psychiatric symptoms, and "organicity" is suspected. Or, there may simply be a history of an incident that suggests the possibility that a brain injury may have occurred. In medical settings, the staff may wonder if the patient's subjective complaints can be objectively verified or whether symptom patterns can be identified that suggest a particular diagnostic condition. Alternatively, family members may observe some difficulty with memory and suspect dementia. Yet in each case, the relevant clinical questions remain somewhat unclear.

The training axiom of clarifying the referral question(s) with the referral source in practice may not be as easy as it sounds. Apart from the obvious problems of the time and energy this requires and the potential unavailability of the referring professional, referral sources may be unclear in their own minds regarding exactly what they want or need to know. In fact, their clinical questions may change, based in part on the results of the neuropsychological evaluation, yet follow-up evaluation is impractical. Therefore, these additional consultative questions need to be anticipated and addressed at the time of the evaluation, if at all possible.

How then does the neuropsychologist clarify the evaluation question(s)? This, as with the entire evaluation, is a process that will vary across cases and settings. If actual referral questions are asked, a starting point is provided. If not, the referral information furnished likely provides clues. At times, it is indeed practical and helpful to talk with the referring professional or with other staff who work with the patient. It is also frequently useful to ask the patient and/or his or her family their understanding of why the evaluation was requested and what questions or concerns they have. The history and clinical interview may suggest questions that appear relevant and potentially important. Finally, the observations and results obtained during the evaluation will likely raise questions in the examiner's mind, the answers to which the referring professional and patient may also find useful. By imagining what it is you would want and need to know, if you were responsible for the patient's care (or if you were the patient), it is possible to develop meaningful evaluation questions and begin to structure a useful evaluation. The neuropsychologist should answer not only the referral questions that were asked, but also those that should have been asked.

For example, a typical referral might be: "Please evaluate this 57-year-old male with complaints of memory problems for the past year. Patient also appears depressed." This referral suggests the following series of questions:

- Does this man have an amnestic disorder, or is he demented, depressed, or some combination of these conditions?
- Regardless of the underlying diagnosis, does this man have impaired cognitive abilities?
- If cognitively impaired, what is the likely etiology: prior stroke, anoxia, Alzheimer's disease, Pick's disease, multiinfarct dementia, psychiatric disorder, or other?
- If demented/impaired, what is the severity of the dementia/impairment?
- If demented, what other cognitive problems exist in addition to memory problems?
- Even if organically impaired, is there a functional component to any identified cognitive difficulties (e.g., depressed and anxious because of a realization of his difficulties)?
- If cognitively impaired, what is the interaction between his personality/psychological characteristics and his impaired cognitive functioning?
- If demented/impaired, what are the implications of the evaluation results for everyday life: ability to work, manage personal finances, live independently, and so on?
- Is this man still competent?

- What recommendations can be offered to help him manage or cope with his cognitive problems?
- What is the prognosis?
- What treatment or life-planning recommendations can be offered?
- What education needs to be provided to his family and what recommendations can be offered to them?

INTERVIEW, CASE HISTORY, AND BEHAVIORAL OBSERVATIONS

The Clinical Interview

The clinical interview and behavioral observations occur prior to any test-based assessment. These preliminary, less formal aspects of assessment yield an essential database and qualitative information that may drastically alter the interpretation of subsequent formal test data (Lezak, 1983; Luria, 1980). In fact, they result in the determination of whether it is even possible to pursue formal testing.

For example, a referral is received to rule out dementia on an elderly psychiatric inpatient who is confused, disoriented, has a variable level of arousal, and appears to be hallucinating during the initial interview. Based on these observations, it is likely that this patient is delirious, psychotic, or both. The patient is not capable of concentrating on or cooperating with standardized testing. Therefore, formal neuropsychological testing is not likely to provide any meaningful data about the nature and extent of any possible underlying dementia. In this case, testing should be rescheduled after the acute psychosis or delirium has cleared.

The clinical interview is part of the process by which a case history is developed and integrated with presenting complaints and behavioral observations. This information then can be used to help generate hypotheses about the etiological bases for symptomatology. Such hypotheses, in turn, serve to guide the ongoing interview and the overall evaluation plan. Although such a hypothesis-testing approach is an excellent interview strategy, it is important for the clinician to be aware of "confirmatory bias"; that is, the tendency to seek and value evidence in support of a working hypothesis whereas ignoring or minimizing contradictory evidence (Greenwald, Pratkanis, Leippe, & Baumgardner, 1986). An example is a neuropsychologist who suspects memory problems and consistently probes for subjective complaints and examples while failing to recognize evidence of intact memory processes. A patient's rich descriptive examples of memory problems are seen as confirmatory, when alternatively they can be viewed as evidence of *intact recall* of some phenomena that the patient is interpreting as memory dysfunction. If the neuropsychologist focuses on evidence consistent with working hypotheses and minimizes contradictory data, hypotheses will always be confirmed, whether correct or not. The corrective measure to confirmatory bias is to systematically list both confirmatory and disconfirmatory information and to consider alternative explanations for observed behaviors.

For patients (e.g., demented elderly) or children who have difficulty providing important background information, an interview with family or friends is often critical. In other cases, patients, from their perspective, may be able to provide a reliable history but lack insight into or awareness of problems that is quite apparent to others who know or live with them.

Maloney and Ward (1976) suggested one way to proceed with the interview. They recommended beginning with minimal structure and becoming progressively more structured to clarify details and inconsistencies. An examiner would begin with an open-ended question regarding the presenting complaints or patients' understanding of why they are being evaluated and what they hope to gain from the results. By starting with open-ended questions, the examiner can begin to evaluate clients' speech, language, thought processes, affective behavior, and ability to identify and structure their presentation of relevant information. This is one of the few unstructured times during a neuropsychological evaluation and affords an opportunity to observe how clients handle ambiguity. Subsequent interventions or comments by the examiner are generally designed to have a facilitative effect on the client's self-report. Questions at this stage continue to be rather open-ended: "Can you tell me more about that?," or "What else did you notice?"

Gradually, more specific questions are introduced to help clarify aspects of the patient's self-report. As patients report various symptoms, the onset and course should be noted. Typically, this will be followed up later in the interview with detailed medical, psychiatric, substance use, educational, vocational, and family histories. It is important to clarify patients' reports of their symptoms. At times their subjective labels do not correspond to objective findings and yet represent a significant clinical concern. For example, patients commonly report memory problems when the underlying deficit is in attentional rather than memory processes. By asking for specific examples rather than descriptive labels, the exact deficit usually can be identified.

Typically, contradictions in a patient's self-report are noted by the examiner. These can be pointed out to the patient (a process often called "confrontation") to see how they explain or account for such inconsistencies. Discrepancies commonly arise between what patients may report and what is known from the medical record or reports of others. Alternatively, there may be inconsistencies in the information provided by the patient. Two other types of inconsistencies may occur: between the content of what patients say and the affect they display, or between different desires or affective states (e.g., feeling disabled at the same time that they do not want to be perceived as disabled). These latter two types of contradictions may be more important in general mental health settings during psychological and personality evaluation but also may be important considerations during neuropsychological evaluations.

Toward the end of the clinical interview, the examiner may ask direct questions about other factors not previously covered. These might include basic demographic information and elements of the case history that have not been covered but that the examiner believes may be relevant to the overall evaluation. When clarifying aspects of the history, it may be important to ask the same question in a variety of ways. The context of the question can result in different answers. For example, patients may deny having had problems in school but admit to placement in special classes, failed courses, repetitions of academic grade levels, or school suspensions.

The Case History

The patient's report of symptomatology and the problems identified in the referral provide the rationale and serve as the starting point for gathering a more detailed case history. Neurologists commonly teach their residents that the history and clinical exam provide approximately 90% of the information necessary to make a correct diagnosis. Regardless of actual percentages, more often than not a careful history will inform the neuropsychologist about the nature and general severity of cognitive and emotional problems, as well as the likely underlying diagnostic condition(s). For both the neurologist and the neuropsychologist, additional tests (medical procedures or neuropsychological tests, respectively) can be used to confirm or disconfirm clinical questions developed as a result of the interview and case history. Similarly, when formal test results are confusing and do not appear to fit any diagnostic pattern, the case history and informal behavioral observations can often clarify the situation. Hampton, Harrison, Mitchell, Pritchard, and Seymour (1975) stated: "Extra time on the history is likely to be more profitable than extra time spent on the examination" (p. 489). For the clinical neuropsychologist, the important historical data are whether a history of cognitive, affective, or behavioral symptoms can be identified and traced that suggest particular neurologic, medical, or psychiatric conditions.

Table 1.2 lists significant content areas to explore in history gathering, whereas Table 1.3 covers important issues that the history can help address. These content areas may suggest particular diagnostic conditions or may reveal factors that could influence the performance on and interpretation of formal test data. Space does not permit covering these issues in detail. However, the following examples provide some indication of the importance and potential use of historical information in the assessment process.

TABLE 1.2
Areas to Explore in Neuropsychological Assessment History Taking

1. Presenting problems and concerns (symptom onset and course)
2. Basic demographic information
   a. Age
   b. Gender
   c. Handedness and family history of handedness
3. Developmental history
   a. Congenital abnormalities
   b. Pregnancy and delivery history including complications and problems
   c. Developmental disorders
      1) ADD (with or without hyperactivity)
      2) Developmental learning problems
      3) Childhood illnesses with sustained high fevers
4. Educational history and achievement performance
   a. Average grades obtained
   b. Best and worst subjects
   c. Failed courses or grades
   d. Placement in special education classes
   e. Learning disabilities
   f. Emotional, social, and peer adjustment
   g. Factors that may affect academic performance
      1) Cultural background
      2) Parental interest in education and parental educational levels
      3) Interest in education versus sports versus peer relationships
      4) Drug or alcohol usage
5. Vocational history
   a. Performance and stability
   b. Reasons for job terminations
6. Psychiatric history and current symptoms/problems
   a. Past and present symptoms and diagnoses
   b. Past and present treatment (medication and/or ECT)
7. Substance abuse history and current usage
8. Medical history
   a. High fevers
   b. Head injuries
   c. Loss of consciousness
   d. Seizures

(Continued)

TABLE 1.2
(Continued)

---

   e. Cerebral vascular accidents
   f. Infectious processes (encephalitis or meningitis)
   g. Cardiovascular problems
   h. Anoxia/Hypoxia
   i. Pulmonary problems
   j. Arthritis
   k. Injuries affecting the extremities
   l. Peripheral neuropathies
   m. Other sensory or motor problems
   n. Cancer
 9. Current medication
10. Current general medical and health status
11. Current functioning in day-to-day living
12. How a typical day is spent
13. Hobbies and interests (avocational activities)
14. Legal history and current problems, pending or anticipated legal suits
15. Current life situation (factors that might suggest possibility of secondary gain or malingering)
16. Family history
   a. Academic and vocational achievement
   b. Medical/Neurologic
      1) Alzheimer's disease
      2) Huntington's disease
      3) Parkinson's disease
      4) Vascular disease (cardiac and cerebral)
      5) "Senility"
      6) Cancer/Tumors
   c. Psychiatric
      1) Depression
      2) Anxiety disorders
      3) Psychotic conditions
      4) Substance abuse

Sometimes careful questioning will reveal that prior intellectual or neuropsychological testing has been conducted. If this was prior to the development of the current symptomatology, such data would be invaluable for premorbid comparative purposes; if conducted postonset, it would help in evaluating the course of a patient's problems. When no prior test data is available, academic achievement and vocational history, in conjunction with basic demographic information, may prove useful in estimating premorbid levels of functioning. Careful questioning will reveal premorbid patterns of cognitive strengths and weaknesses. Certain occupations may have been selected because of innate patterns of cognitive abilities. In addition, once embarked upon, occupational endeavors may differentially enhance particular skills and abilities and consequently affect performance on related tests. One might hypothesize, for ex-

TABLE 1.3
Issues That the History Can Help Address

1. Premorbid functioning
   a. General level of ability
   b. Patterns of cognitive strengths and weaknesses
   c. Personality and psychological characteristics or problems
2. Pre-existing conditions that may account for or interact with current findings
   a. Developmental problems
   b. Learning disabilities
   c. Attention deficit disorder (ADD) or attention deficit hyperactivity disorder (ADHD)
   d. Psychiatric conditions
   e. Prior CNS injuries or neurological conditions
   f. Current or past medical problems (current medication)
3. Motivational considerations
   a. Family/marital/social issues of secondary gain
   b. Pending legal or disability concerns
   c. Financial gain
   d. Malingering
   e. Problems with authority or with being evaluated
4. Current lifestyle factors that may influence test performance
   a. Drinking
   b. Substance abuse
   c. Eating disorder
5. Onset of current problems
6. Course of current symptoms and problems
   a. Worsening
   b. Stable
   c. Improving
7. Family history of similar problems and their presumed etiology

ample, that artists, designers, and mechanics would perform better on visuospatial tasks because of the visuospatial, constructional, and psychomotor activities entailed in their work. Similarly, an avid tennis player may show unusual patterns of performance on psychomotor measures (e.g., an average level of performance on nondominant hand motor tasks, e.g., grip strength), with dominant hand performances at the 90th percentile.

A careful history may reveal a repetitive pattern of cognitive symptoms and complaints that emerge and resolve concomitant with psychiatric conditions that referring clinicians have interpreted as evidence of brain damage. Alternatively, a positive family history of dementia may never have been diagnosed and yet be revealed by a careful family medical history. Such information would be very useful in dementia evaluations, particularly in cases where subjective complaints are present and test performance is in the average range, but the individual premorbidly would be expected to have high-average range abilities. In such a case the history, in conjunction with a somewhat lower level of achievement than expected, would lead one to the consideration of a possible mild dementia.

This is not to say that all points outlined in Table 1.2 must be explored fully in every assessment. Clinical interviews and history taking will be shortened and tailored to the presenting complaints and referral question(s). However, failure to obtain relevant historical data results in a lack of information that may be essential in test selection and subsequent interpretation.

Obtaining the Case History

There are several ways in which a case history may be obtained. One way is as part of the initial clinical interview, as already discussed. If this approach is used, examiners will typically develop some type of guide or outline to ensure that they cover all potentially important aspects of the history. The outline contained in Table 1.2 could be used. A second but not mutually exclusive approach is to utilize symptom checklists and history questionnaires. Several such questionnaires are commercially available for use. These include the Neuropsychological Questionnaires developed by Melendez (1978); one form is available for children, another for adults. Schinka (1983) developed the Neuropsychological Status Examination, which consists of two parts. One part is the Neuropsychological Symptom Checklist, a 93-item form that may be completed by the patient, someone who knows the patient well, or the examiner in an interview format. The second part is the Neuropsychological Status Examination. It may be used as a guide for structuring and planning the evaluation, a recording form during the clinical interview, and an outline for drafting the final report.

It is important to note that these instruments are not tests with normative data available. Rather, they are means of collecting potentially valuable historical and background information that must be evaluated and interpreted by the examiner and integrated with the rest of the evaluation data (clinical interview, behavioral observations, and test results). Typically, the skilled examiner will quickly review completed forms or questionnaires with the patient (or a family member) and obtain more details and clarifying information about items that appear relevant to the evaluation questions and issues.

The Cognitive Behavior Rating Scale (CBRS; Williams, 1987) is a similar symptom questionnaire that was developed to be completed by a family member or close friend of individuals undergoing dementia evaluations. It is mentioned separately here because the items are grouped into nine subscales that can be plotted out on a profile sheet with T scores and percentile norms available for comparison with nondemented elderly. In this sense the CBRS is more akin to formal psychometric tests than to the other history-gathering forms described previously.

Use and Review of the Medical Records

Reviewing the medical records is often the first thing a neuropsychologist will do after receiving a consultation referral. The medical record provides an important source of historical information, as well as details of current symptoms, their onset and course, and recent and ongoing evaluative workups and treatments. It will frequently help clarify why a patient has been referred, the questions and issues that should be addressed in the evaluation, and what historical data need to be explored further in the interview and history.

Mastering a thorough yet expeditious review of medical records takes practice, familiarity with its layout (which varies from facility to facility), and awareness of what information is potentially available in them. Phay, Gainer, and Goldstein (1986) suggested developing a systematic plan of search and standard format for recording pertinent information. The neuropsychologist will be interested both in various medical diagnostic procedures that are being undertaken as well as any other information about suspected diagnostic conditions (e.g., clinical findings, symptom history, history of past neurologic conditions, and family history of heritable medical/neurological diseases). Note should be made of the presence of a variety of medical conditions that have been shown to have an adverse impact on aspects of cognition. These would include not only those with known CNS involvement, such as AIDS, epilepsy, multiple sclerosis, and cerebral vascular disease, but also conditions such as hypertension, diabetes, chronic obstructive pulmonary disease (COPD), systemic lupus erythematosus, thyroid disease, and metabolic and nutritional disorders. There is increasing evidence that these latter conditions do have an adverse effect on brain function and cognitive status (e.g., Denburg, Carotte, & Denburg, 1987; Skenazy & Bigler, 1984; Tarter, Van Thiel, & Edwards, 1988; Vanderploeg, Goldman, & Kleinman, 1987).

A typical record review might begin with a careful consideration of the admitting history and examination (and discharge summary if already completed), followed by a review of various medical and diagnostic workups that have been undertaken. These are often grouped together in the medical record in sections labeled *Laboratory Findings, X-rays,* and *Consults.* The consult section of a medical record will contain the evaluations of other professionals who were consulted by the primary physician. Depending on the setting, there might be reports from various medical specialists, clinical psychologists, social workers, speech therapists, occupational therapists, and physical therapists. For the neuropsychologist the diagnostic procedures of interest include the CT and MRI scans, PET or SPECT scans, EEG, Event-Related Potentials (ERPs), cerebral spinal tap results, and other laboratory data, particularly tests that would determine the presence of infectious processes, metabolic disturbances, or nutritional abnormalities. Occasionally, there will be data from previous psychological examinations as well. Finally, a review of the *Progress Notes* will often provide information about a patient's day-to-day functioning and problems noted by direct caretakers that have not been described elsewhere in the record.

Behavioral Observations

A mental status examination (MSE) "checklist" may or may not be conducted as part of the ongoing interview and case history, especially because neuropsychological testing can be viewed as an extensive and standardized mental status examination. However, covering the MSE content areas in some manner is essential in making various differential diagnoses. The MSE may serve as a rapid cognitive screen and as a method for organizing information. Table 1.4 covers MSE content areas and the ranges of behaviors relevant to each. Of equal importance are observations about patients' test-taking manner and variables that might influence performance. For instance, physical problems may interfere with individuals' ability to take certain tests. Psychological states such as anxiety, depression, or psychosis may have similar adverse affects.

Some observations appear pathognomonic of underlying neurological problems: a differential arm or leg size suggestive of atrophy, or confusion in response to an apparently straightforward question suggestive of dementia. However, such observations may well have other nonneurologically based explanations (e.g., previous broken limbs or a psychiatric disorder, respectively). Therefore, unusual observations should always be noted but interpreted in the overall context of history, environmental situation, and test performance. Certainly, any time a behavioral observation is noted that is abnormal or unusual, alternative explanations should be explored in the history before arriving at the conclusion of brain impairment.

Naturalistic observation or reports of the same may provide an invaluable adjunct to other data-collection techniques. For example, during a forensic evaluation of a patient with severe memory complaints and very impaired performance on memory testing, observations of intact ability to independently arrive at the appointment on time and follow oral directions to a nearby restaurant for a lunch break certainly call into question the apparent memory difficulties. Similarly, rehabilitation nursing staff may report excellent functional day-to-day independent living skills in a head-injured patient who has severe difficulty on formal testing. In this

TABLE 1.4
Mental Status Examination

I. Appearance
   A. Clothing (neat–messy, casual–formal, clean–dirty, appropriate–inappropriate)
   B. Personal hygiene (clean–dirty; body odor; grooming)
   C. Physical handicaps (presence or absence)
   D. Unusual features
II. Behavior
   A. Verbal
      1. Speech pattern (fluency, paraphasias, articulation/dysarthria)
      2. Prosody
      3. General flow (rapid–slow, pressured–controlled, hesitant)
      4. Voice tone
      5. Speech impediments or accents
      6. Apparent conversational comprehension
   B. Nonverbal
      1. Ambulation (limp, weakness, speed, agility, balance, gait)
      2. Motor activity (fidgety, restless, slow, lethargic, tics)
      3. Facial expression(s)
   C. Interpersonal
      1. Cooperative
      2. Friendly, unfriendly, or overly friendly
      3. Establishes eye contact
      4. Anxious
      5. Suspicious
      6. Submissive versus dominant
      7. Dependent versus aggressive
   D. Unusual behaviors: excessive or inappropriate laughing, crying, shouting, motor movement, talking
III. Orientation
   A. Person (awareness of who they are and what the examiner's role is)
   B. Place (awareness of present physical location and location of their home)
   C. Time (awareness of current year, month, date, day, time of day)
   D. (Situation): some clinicians assess clients' awareness of what is transpiring (the evaluation) and why they are being evaluated
IV. Memory
   A. Immediate (within interview)
   B. Recent (recent life events)
   C. Remote (past historical information)
V. Sensorium/level of alertness
   A. Alert/attentive
   B. Lethargic (sleepy but arousable)
   C. Obtunded (clouding of consciousness, reduced alertness)
   D. Stuporous (unresponsive and only briefly arousable)
   E. Comatose (nonresponsive, nonarousable, nonreactive to stimuli)
VI. Mood and affect: Emotional state (angry, irritable, happy, anxious, afraid, suspicious, depressed/sad, apathetic)
   A. Mood: Predominant emotion observed
   B. Affect: Range of emotions displayed in facial expression or voice tone and content
   C. Appropriateness: Appropriate to situational context and/or content of interview

---

(Continued)

TABLE 1.4
(Continued)

VII. Intellectual functioning: Estimate of level of functioning based on behavioral obser-
vation, vocabulary usage, historical information, organization of thought processes
VIII. Perceptual processes: Accurate perception of the world, presence of hallucinations
(visual, auditory, tactile, olfactory, gustatory)
IX. Thought content
    A. Focus of thoughts and concerns
    B. Presence of delusional material
    C. Obsessive thoughts or ideas
    D. Report of compulsive actions
    E. Fears or phobias
    F. Sense of unreality or depersonalization
X. Thought process
    A. Organization (organized and sensible progression, or rambling)
    B. Productivity (minimal material presented, normal amount, or excessive)
    C. Flow (fluid, stopping or blocking, loss of train of thought)
    D. Focus (flight of ideas, loosening of associations, circumstantial, tangential)
XI. Insight: Recognition of present status and problems, psychological mindedness, self-
awareness
XII. Judgment
    A. Level of decision-making abilities (current and historical)
    B. Nature of problem-solving approach: Rational, impulsive, methodical, respon-
sible–irresponsible

---

latter case the patient may have developed compensatory strategies that
cannot be utilized in formal test situations.

Summary

Clinical interviewing, history gathering, and observation of behavior can
and should be a dynamic and interactive process. Observing unusual or
unexpected behaviors should lead to questions about why this might be
so. Many observations that suggest the possibility of brain damage or impairment have unrelated, yet easily ascertained, causes. One should never
fail to ask about observations, problems, or deficits that appear to have
an obvious brain-injury-related explanation. All too often the obvious is
not the truth. Failure to utilize observations, follow-up questions, and
the history to explore alternative explanations periodically will result in
an incorrect "finding" of brain impairment. The opposite is also true.
Some observations appear to have obvious nonbrain-injury-related explanations (e.g., questionable memory problems in a moderately
depressed and anxious 50-year-old man) and yet are indicative of neurological problems (beginning stage of Alzheimer's disease). In these cases,
a careful history and tracing of symptom onset and development will help
clarify the clinical picture.

NEUROPSYCHOLOGICAL TESTING

Test Selection

Different Approaches to Testing

There are several neuropsychological schools of thought with some-what differing approaches to the neuropsychological assessment process. Differences arise along two continuums: "fixed" versus "flexible" battery approaches to data collection and "quantitative/normative-based" versus "qualitative/process-based" approaches to data interpretation. The traditional Halstead–Reitan would be an example of a fixed battery, quantitative/normative approach. On the other end of both continuums would be clinicians utilizing a clinically oriented process approach, a flexible battery with qualitative/process analyses of the results. In a recent survey of randomly selected neuropsychologists (Butler, Retzlaff, & Vanderploeg, 1991), 34% of the respondents described their theoretical orientation as eclectic; many of these also checked other orientations. Thirty-one percent affirmed a hypothesis-testing approach, 25% a process approach, 20% a Halstead–Reitan approach, 3% a Benton orientation, and 2% a Luria orientation. In reality, most neuropsychologists combine some fixed set of tests with a flexible use of additional measures and integrate quantitative and qualitative information during test interpretation. Regardless of whether one takes a battery or nonbattery approach to assessment, some decisions must be made regarding what tests to administer.

Selecting Tests

A wide variety of cognitive and intellectual abilities are typically assessed during a *comprehensive* neuropsychological evaluation: attention and concentration; sensory–perceptual abilities; speech and language abilities; visuospatial and visuoconstructional skills; learning and memory; general intellectual competence; "executive functions" (such as abstraction; reasoning; problem solving; behavioral self-monitoring; response discrimination, selection, and inhibition; and mental processing efficiency and flexibility); and psychomotor speed, strength, and coordination. Included are measures of sensory–perceptual input, the two major central processing systems (verbal/language and nonverbal/visuospatial), executive organization and planning, and response output (motor abilities). Interacting with these processing networks would be memory systems; underlying them all are attention, concentration, arousal, and motivation. Although this list of cognitive functions might be organized or labeled differently by various neuropsychological schools of thought, these behaviors are commonly assessed during neuropsychological evaluations. Frequently, aspects of psychological functioning (psychopathology, behavioral adjustment, and interpersonal issues) also are assessed in a neuropsychological evaluation. Whether selecting a standard battery, choosing a unique set of tests for a particular assessment, or combining these two approaches, a variety of issues are important to consider:

1. Selected measures should cover all relevant behavioral domains of interest, both for that individual's particular referral question(s) and for the potential neurologic, medical, and/or psychiatric conditions suspected. The use of general screening measures for organicity fails to take into account the variety and complexity of possible brain-related behavioral patterns.

2. Both lower level (domain specific) abilities and higher level more general, diffuse, or interactive cognitive functions should be covered. The former includes basic sensory–perceptual and psychomotor abilities, whereas the latter involves not only higher order language and visuospatial abilities but also complex cross-modal reasoning, problem solving, and abstraction.

3. If one desires to analyze quantitatively a particular patient's performance, the use of tests with good normative data for a comparable population would be essential. As an example, the Peabody Picture Vocabulary Test-Revised (Dunn & Dunn, 1981) is an excellent measure of receptive vocabulary for certain populations, but no normative data is available for individuals over 40 years of age.

4. Use tests with an appropriate level of difficulty for the patient under study. Tests that are too easy or too hard for a patient result in ceiling or floor effects, reducing possible performance variability, and consequently reducing reliability. Even within adult tests, some measures may be too easy for highly intelligent individuals, whereas others may be too difficult for those of borderline or lower intellectual functioning.

5. Avoid tests where patterns of brain–behavior relationships have not been established or tests that have face validity but no empirically validated brain–behavior relationship correlate. A related axiom is that tests of brain damage are always measures of some aspect of cognitive ability, but measures of cognitive abilities are not necessarily tests of brain damage. Select test measures that have established validity for the assessment of the cognitive ability and associated anatomical functioning that you plan to evaluate.

For example, from a functional anatomical perspective, it is reasonable to anticipate that the right temporal lobe would be important in the processing of musical patterns or rhythmic sequences. Thus, tests with similar processing requirements would logically be assumed to reflect the integrity of these brain regions. Some clinicians assume that the Seashore Rhythm Test reflects right temporal functioning, and clinical guides suggest this interpretation (Golden, Osmon, Moses, & Berg, 1981; Jarvis & Barth, 1984). However, empirical studies consistently fail to support this interpretation of impaired performance. Instead, the Seashore Rhythm Test appears to be a sensitive but nonspecific measure of brain impairment, possibly because of its high attentional requirements (Milner, 1962; Reitan & Wolfson, 1989; Sherer, Parson, Nixon, & Adams, 1991).

6. Many neuropsychologists advocate using several measures within each cognitive domain (e.g., several memory measures) to look for convergence or divergence of findings. This can provide a stronger base for claims of impaired or intact abilities. However, when selecting additional measures, one should be cautious about the use of tests that are highly correlated with each other. This results in redundancy of measurement and limited utility for purposes of clarification. Ideally, multiple measures within a cognitive domain would have low correlations with each other but strong positive correlations with the criterion ability. This increases the likelihood that convergent findings are related to the actual ability rather than being an artifact.

Standardization Issues

Standardized Administration

Standardized testing consists of uniform administration and scoring procedures. Those procedures are developed and described by test developers and publishers for the purpose of ensuring that all administrations of a test are comparable (Anastasi, 1988). Standardized procedures typically include specific phrases used to instruct examinees, specific directions regarding test material that may be involved and time limits allowed, and explicit scoring criteria for item responses. Calibration procedures for test instruments are standardized as well. Under standard conditions, results can be compared across administrations, across examiners, and with the test normative database. However, following test manual standardized procedures carefully does not ensure that other subtle factors will not influence test performance. Anastasi (1988) reviewed a variety of factors that have been shown to influence test performance: testing environment, examiner–examinee rapport, oral presentation style and rate, similarity or familiarity between the personal characteristics of examiner and examinee, supportive or encouraging gestures and comments, and test-taking anxiety.

Standardized conditions are generally designed to help examinees attain their maximal level of performance. Thus, in the ideal testing situation, standard conditions are also optimal conditions for the patient under study (Lezak, 1983). However, during many neuropsychological evaluations, those conditions necessary to help patients engage the task effectively differ substantially from standard conditions. This raises the question of what is important to achieve for standardization: Is it the actual physical conditions, instructions, and procedures or, alternatively, the testing conditions that ensure adequate understanding of what is expected from the examinee and arrangement of environmental variables to allow subjects to work efficiently? Williams (1965) wrote: "The same words do not necessarily mean the same thing to different people and it is the meaning of the instructions that should be the same for all people rather than the wording" (p. xvii). The same rule could be applied to other test-taking variables. Examiners should strive to achieve standardized conditions in this broader sense.

Variation of test-administration procedures may be necessary in working with brain-injured subjects in order to meet this broader definition of standard conditions. Instructions may need to be repeated or amplified to ensure adequate understanding. Some subjects will need to be reminded periodically of what exactly they are to do, even within tests or subtests. The development and maintenance of necessary rapport may also entail more support, encouragement, or reassurance than is discussed in the standardization procedures. At times it may be appropriate or even necessary to acknowledge particular difficulties and to discuss them at the time they evidence themselves. Acknowledging subsequent better performances can also be desirable as a supportive and encouraging reinforcement of ongoing active participation in the testing process. These clinical interventions are designed to help develop and maintain an adequate examiner–patient test-taking relationship and would not appear to violate the intent of most standard procedures.

On the other hand, "testing the limits" during a process-oriented, qualitative assessment of particular behaviors will at times violate even broadly defined standardization, yet be essential to obtain certain clinically useful information. For example, on memory testing some patients report very little on story-recall measures. This may reflect a number of things: impaired memory encoding and storage, memory retrieval problems, concern over making possible errors, amotivation, or resistance to the examiner or to testing. To determine the cause for such apparent memory difficulties, the examiner could follow a sequence of encouragement, memory cues, and then multiple-choice responses to test the limits of a patient's abilities. If patients are able to perform significantly better with only encouragement, amotivation or fear of making errors would be suggested as the cause of the initial poor performance. Accepting and scoring these responses likely would fit within broadly defined standardization. Providing cues or multiple-choice responses would violate standardization; yet if recall improved would suggest that the difficulties were secondary to memory-retrieval problems rather than encoding and storage. In addition, cuing of immediate recall would invalidate standardization for delayed recall later. Such procedural variations and testing of the limits, although potentially clinically advantageous, adversely affect the applicability of established test norms collected under standardized administration.

In some circumstances, testing the limits can be completed after the standardized administration is completed. The WAIS–R as a Neuropsychological Test Instrument (Kaplan, Fein, Morris, & Delis, 1991) provides examples of this process. At times it is possible to answer questions regarding reasons for failures by administering other similar measures that help fractionate cognitive processes into component parts. These latter approaches preserve standardization and the use of the normative data.

Unclear Aspects of Standardization Procedures.   The Wechsler intelligence scales are some of the most carefully standardized instruments available. However, even here certain aspects of administration are not described in detail, and variations can result in substantial differences in performance for certain types of brain-injured patients. For example, on the Block Design subtest, there is a footnote in the WAIS-R manual (Wechsler, 1981) regarding placement of the examiner-made model for Design 1, but no instructions for placement of the booklet and blocks on subsequent items. Some examiners place the booklet on the table near the subject, with the blocks positioned to its right. Thus, neither the design booklet nor the blocks are situated at subjects' midline. For subjects with neglect, this creates a very different task than a midline placement of the design booklet and the blocks. The latter approach is preferable.

Many individuals with brain injury require substantially longer to process information than normal. Even nonaphasic patients may fail to fully process and comprehend long, complicated sentences if they are spoken at a normal conversational rate. This will adversely affect understanding of many test instructions as well as potentially hamper performance on a variety of test measures. For example, the WAIS-R Arithmetic subtest contains many long and complicated questions. No instructions are provided as to how to present these orally to subjects. However, processing and comprehension can be improved substantially if the questions are read somewhat more slowly, but even more importantly, if pauses are placed following clauses. The following question is an example similar to Item 8. When read with pauses (as indicated), many subjects who would otherwise get the item wrong instead will be able to correctly answer the question: "If you buy six (pause) 3-cent stamps (pause) and give the clerk 50 cents (pause), how much change should you get back?" This helps isolate calculation ability, by decreasing the language comprehension and attentional demands of the task.

Instructions for the WAIS-R Digit Span subtest indicate that the presentation rate should be 1 per second and the pitch of the presenter's voice should drop on the last digit of each trial. However, other administration factors that can influence performance are not addressed. For example, the monotone of the trial-to-trial presentation can be broken up with variations in voice volume, by side comments, or by asking "ready?" before each trial. These variations will tend to help subjects who have problems with sustained attention, whose immediate memory span is normal when fully alert.

Tests other than the WAIS-R are even more unclear regarding aspects of administration. Presentation rate and pauses can certainly influence performance on story-recall measures such as the Wechsler Memory Scale-Revised (WMS-R; Wechsler, 1987) Logical Memory subtest. However, the WMS-R manual provides no standardized presentation format other than that the stories should be "read" and is silent on the permissibility or advisability of varying rate or pauses. A final example is seen in the wide variability among examiners on when, what, and how much help to provide during testing. Test manuals are often not clear on these issues.

De-emphasis of Aspects of Standardization.   Standardized administration and scoring assumes that standard procedures were learned by examiners at some point in time. This may or may not have been the case. However, with the phenomenon of *Examiner Drift*, even after having learned standard procedures, examiners slowly and unwittingly modify aspects of administration and scoring as time goes by. This phenomenon tends to be ignored in clinical practice. In addition, clinicians sometimes make personal decisions about procedural issues out of convenience or individual preference. Unfortunately, the effects that such changes have on test performance are generally unknown but at the very least call into question the applicability of the standardization sample as a comparison group.

In working with psychology interns, I have noticed that many fail to use a stopwatch during administration of various WAIS-R subtests (e.g., Arithmetic or Picture Completion), despite the manual's instructions to do so. Many brain-injured patients have significantly delayed responses. However, without a stopwatch examiners cannot be certain whether a subject's response came within the time allowed. Although the untimed response data are certainly clinically important in knowing about basic neuropsychological abilities, only the carefully timed performance can be scored and compared to the norms.

Another area where standard administration is commonly ignored is on the Visual Reproduction subtest of the WMS-R (Wechsler, 1987). The manual clearly instructs the examiner to fold in half the sheet on which the client is to draw. This exposes a 5.5- by 8.5-inch page, roughly comparable in shape to the stimulus cards. This procedure prevents clients from seeing their drawings after they have completed them. These procedures standardize exposure duration and result in similar environmental cues in both stimulus presentation and production aspects of the task. However, many examiners "miss" these instructions in the manual and expose one side of the nonfolded 8½ by 11-inch sheet for the first two figures, and the other side for the second two figures. Do these two different methods of administration affect test performance? We really do not know, but they certainly could.

Variations in "Standard" Administration Procedures. In working with and talking to colleagues trained in various neuropsychology laboratories across the country, it is clear that there are a multitude of administration variations in standard practice. For example, on the Finger-Tapping Test, does the examiner alternate hands between trials or attain 5 (3, or some other number) dominant hand trials before proceeding to the nondominant hand? Reitan's (1979) instructions are to obtain 5 trials within a 5-point range with the dominant hand, before proceeding to the nondominant hand. How much time is structured into rest breaks between tapping trials, if breaks are employed? Does one use only the finger-tapper devices available from Reitan, or tappers available from other sources? (The tappers available from Dr. Reitan have been modified themselves over the years.) On other tasks, how much and how quickly does the examiner provide help when patients have difficulty (e.g., on the Category Test, Wisconsin Card Sorting Test, or Trail Making Test)? Do examiners follow Reitan's instructions (1979) of working through the first 3 to 5 circles on the Trail Making Test with the patient, both on the sample and on the actual test? Exactly how does an examiner deal with errors during testing on Trail Making or other tests? (In a multicenter cooperative study a few years ago, initially no two centers administered the Trail Making Test the same way.) Manuals themselves vary in administration instructions from one established neuropsychology laboratory to another.

Such variability in accepted practice suggests that procedural variations result in little or no difference in test performance. The data to support or refute this conclusion do not exist. Even if studies did demonstrate a lack of effect for test administration variation in nonbrain-damaged individuals, it does not logically follow that the same would hold true for any or all brain-injured populations. One mistake to avoid in researching this question would be to treat all groups or types of brain-injured patients the same. Patients with purely attentional problems are likely to be affected in one manner by procedural changes, those with aphasia in another, whereas others might respond similarly to nonimpaired individuals.

Administration Recommendations. The administration variations observed in clinical practice raise the issues of the clarity of instructions in test manuals and of how rigidly examiners follow and should follow such instructions. On the one hand, carefully following the test manual is essential in standardized testing to assure applicability of test norms. On the other hand, if the purpose of administering a test is to assess a particular aspect of brain–behavior relationships, it would be critical to make sure that the subject completely understood the task to be done and assure that other behaviors (e.g., motivation, arousal, impaired comprehension, etc.) did not interfere with the brain behavior of interest. In these latter cases, variations in instructions, level of help provided, and mode of patient response may be necessary to answer the clinical question of interest. Although it may be difficult to find out why test publishers have certain instructions or require the establishment of specific conditions for taking a test, obtaining this information would help the examiner determine when it is appropriate to amplify or modify aspects of procedural standardization and still be able to compare the results with the test's normative data.

The discussion at the beginning of this chapter about the difference between assessment and testing can serve as a general guide to test administration procedures and variations. The needs of the overall assessment are what are important, because testing is only a tool in the assessment process. Within that framework, some more specific principles can help guide the clinician when procedural questions arise:

Principle 1. Follow standardized procedures as outlined in the test manual as carefully as possible. However, some subjects have limitations that prevent them from following the specific conditions as outlined in test manuals. In that case, Principle 2 applies.

Principle 2. The testing conditions necessary to have each individual examinee meet the standardized testing conditions is what is important, rather than the actual instructional wording or procedures. Thus, at times the examiner should amplify or repeat instructions to make sure that examinees understand exactly what they are to do. The use of pauses or slowed rate of instructional presentation can be used to achieve adequate comprehension of instructional set. At other times alternative response modalities need to be provided (such as pointing), if examinees cannot engage in the standard response (e.g., spoken response). An example of this is on the WAIS-R Picture Completion subtest where any method of indicating the missing element is acceptable (it does not have to be verbally stated).

Principle 3. Minimize environmental factors extraneous to the brain–behavior relationship under study so that they do not interfere with an examinee's performance. If the clinician is not attempting to evaluate attentional resources, minimize distractions such as extraneous noises or clutter within the testing environment.

Principle 4. Make sure the examinee is alert and aroused sufficiently to engage in the brain behavior under study. Of course, the exception to this rule would be if arousal is the behavior under study. An adequate level of arousal can be optimized by judicious use of rest breaks or varying environmental factors such as type of tasks or examiner voice volume and inflection.

Principle 5. Present all perceptual and visuospatial tasks at examinees' midline. Although this does not compensate for neglect or field cuts, it allows for a consistent presentation orientation across patients and conditions. If, as the examiner, you suspect that a presentation off midline might enhance or impair performance, complete that after the standard administration as part of testing the limits.

Principle 6. On all timed tasks, carefully time each response with a stopwatch and record the time of the examinee's answer. The performance can then be scored both in the standardized timed fashion and alternatively in an untimed "testing the limits" fashion. Both sets of information can be useful data for interpretation.

Principle 7. Provide only enough help and encouragement to maintain the examinee's behavioral performance in the task under investigation. If patients begin to respond randomly, they are not engaged in the task and no information can be gleaned about their ability or disability in that area. Sufficient help must be provided to make sure they are attempting to perform the task, without providing more help than necessary and inadvertently and artificially enhancing their performance.

Principle 8. Periodically review the test manuals to minimize "examiner drift."

Principle 9. Remember neuropsychological evaluations are an assessment process, not just testing. In that process the assessment is directed by clinical questions. If there are conflicts between what must be done for the assessment versus the requirements of test administration, assessment needs should take precedence.

Additional Administration Concerns

Various Published Norms Collected with Different Administration Procedures.   A search of the literature reveals that different published norms for the same clinical test do not follow the same administration procedures. Given the variability in "standard administration practice" for common neuropsychological tests, this finding should not be surprising. Again, a prime example is the Finger-Tapping Test where some norms were collected following Reitan's (1979) instructions of five dominant-hand trials within five taps of each other, before proceeding to the nondominant hand. Other published norms follow somewhat different procedures (e.g., Spreen & Gaddes, 1969). There is some indication that these procedural variations do affect performance (Leckliter, Forster, Klonoff, & Knights, 1992). Given this variability, it is important for clinicians to be familiar with the norms they use in terms of how they were collected and their applicability to administration variations or unique patient populations.

Use and/or Calibration of Test Instruments.   Recently, I was called to consult on a case in which some preliminary neuropsychological testing had already been completed. The Finger-Tapping Test had been administered, but the performance was quite slow bilaterally and dropped off precipitously after the third trial in each hand. There was no other evidence of brain dysfunction. I decided to readminister the test. Upon securing the finger-tapper that had been used, I discovered that it was miscalibrated. The angle of the tapping lever was about 10° rather than the normal approximately 25°. For the counter to click over to the next number at the 10° angle, the lever had to hit the wooden support platform. Readjusting the tapper and readministering the test with 30-second rest periods between Trials 1, 2, and 3 and between 4 and 5, and a 60-second rest after Trial 3, resulted in a perfectly normal performance.

Reitan (personal communication, July 15, 1983) in his workshops discussed how the Finger-Tapping Test is one of the most frequently incorrectly administered measures in the Halstead–Reitan Battery, with inadequate rest breaks being a major problem. Less discussed is the matter of instrument calibration. In fact, calibration of the angle of the tapping lever is not mentioned in the test manual (Reitan, 1979). Grip strength is another commonly used motor test. Reitan (1979) discussed the importance of calibrating the dynamometer to patients' hand size but provided little information as to how to do this other than providing a range ("3 [small hand] and 5 [large hand]"; p. 69) and suggesting adjustment so that it "feels comfortable for the individual subject" (p. 69). Thus, neuropsychometricians and doctoral-level clinicians may be completely unaware of or inattentive to instrument calibration during test administration, even for instruments they frequently use. As with other aspects of administration, the principle underlying calibration procedures is adaptability across patients so that the behavior of interest is relatively isolated from extraneous but potentially interfering factors.

Variations or Alterations of Common Tests. Commonly used neuropsychology tests themselves have been altered for various reasons. Examples of this are the alternative or shortened forms of the Category Test (Calsyn, O'Leary, & Chaney, 1980; DeFilippis & McCampbell, 1979; Gregory, Paul, & Morrison, 1979; Russell & Levy, 1987; Wetzel & Boll, 1987) or modifications of the Wisconsin Card Sorting Test (Axelrod, Henry, & Woodard, 1992; Berg, 1948; Heaton, 1981; Nelson, 1976; Teuber, Battersby, & Bender, 1951) that have been proposed. In many cases, new norms are not provided, but rather the user is given a formula to convert the shortened or alternative test results to adjusted scores thought to be comparable to the original test. The few studies of alternative-form comparability that have been done suggest that the effects of these various changes and the applicability of the original test norms are unknown, and that new problems with reliability and validity are introduced (Taylor, Goldman, Leavitt, & Kleinman, 1984; Vanderploeg & Logan, 1989). Specifically, shortened forms of the Category Test are likely to misclassify focal right-hemisphere-damaged persons as normal (Taylor et al., 1984).

Summary of Administration Issues

Variations in standard administration and problematic norms are broader issues with which the field of clinical neuropsychology will have to deal if it does not want to be open to psychometric criticism. However, on an individual assessment level, it is essential for the examiner to know that any variation in procedure may adversely affect a number of factors: (a) collection of accurate and/or standardized data; (b) availability of reliable and valid norms for "modified" tests; (c) comparability with norms generated using different administration procedures; (d) comparability with previous or subsequent readministrations; and (e) comparability with testing conducted at other centers. Certain principles can aid the clinician in determining when and why it may be desirable to vary instructions and procedures during individual assessments and how to do so to create minimal disruption of standardization (see earlier under "Administration Recommendations").

In summary, it should be the practice of neuropsychologists to attempt to stay within the broader definition of standardized procedures suggested previously. This involves two principles. One is to carefully follow test manual instructions whenever possible, but to supplement them by whatever variations in instructions and procedures are necessary to make sure the patient understands exactly what to do. The second principle is to make sure that the patient is capable, at some level, of engaging in the behavioral response requested. These two conditions are essential in order to evaluate the results in a way that allows the neuropsychologist to be able to answer the clinical question for which a particular test was selected. However, there are also times when patients' limitations prevent them from meeting even broadly defined standardized administrations conditions, yet a particular instrument is still judged by the neuropsychologist to have applicability for addressing specific clinical questions. In these situations, test instruments can be utilized in a non-standardized manner and evaluated qualitatively. The important overarching principle is to have the assessment directed by clinical questions, the answers to which will result in a meaningful and useful evaluation (i.e., assessment, as opposed to testing).

The Testing Session

In Muriel Lezak's (1983) text, *Neuropsychological Assessment*, chapter 5, entitled "The Neuropsychological Examination: Procedures," provides an excellent discussion of the clinical issues important during the data-collection phase of a neuropsychological evaluation. She addresses the special problems of brain-damaged persons and the nuances of working with them. Here we briefly review some of these issues, focusing on how the testing session can be managed to obtain the most reliable and valid assessment possible of individuals' brain-related behavioral capabilities.

Obtaining a Patient's Maximal Performance

Neuropsychological assessment differs somewhat from other types of psychological assessment in that a goal of testing typically is to obtain the patient's best possible performance (Heaton & Heaton, 1981). In order to evaluate whether or not brain dysfunction is responsible for an impaired performance, all other possible etiologies must be eliminated, controlled, or at least considered. Thus, it becomes the responsibility of the examiner to help the patient attain his or her maximal level of performance, keeping in mind issues of standardization. To do so requires cognizance of possible sources of interference with test performance, and modification of instructions or procedures when necessary. Failure to do so, or at least failure to note that other factors interfered with test performance, become sources of possible interpretation error. Two areas are discussed as essential in obtaining patients' maximal performance:

(a) the "assessment relationship" and (b) sensitivity to patients' individual differences.

The Examiner–Patient Relationship. Establishing an effective working relationship with the patient is crucial to a successful testing session. This is commonly referred to as *developing rapport.* There is little point to engaging in testing if patients refuse to actively participate. If after an explanation of the nature, purpose, and importance of the testing patients decline to cooperate, their decision should be respected. If the neuropsychologist proceeds with the evaluation under those conditions, the results will be of questionable validity and the behavioral capabilities of the patient will remain obscure.

Our expectation of patients to work hard and do their best can be conveyed to them directly and their on-task efforts reinforced. Throughout the evaluation every effort ought to be made to treat the patient with honesty, courtesy, and dignity, in the manner in which we would want to be treated if the roles were reversed. Under ideal conditions the assessment is a mutual endeavor in which both examiner and examinee are working cooperatively on the task of trying to better understand the behavior, cognitive strengths and problems, and coping abilities of the examinee.

If we expect patients to give an honest effort on the various tasks we ask of them, they are entitled to honesty from us during the examination process. Lezak (1983) offered several practical suggestions in this regard. Do not "invite" a patient to take a particular test as a way of introduction, if in fact you really are not offering the patient a choice. Do not use the first person plural when asking the patient to do something ("Now let's try a few drawings."). Such phrasing is patronizing, demonstrates a lack of respect for patients, and can only interfere with a good assessment relationship. Lezak (1983) also expressed a personal distaste for the use of expressions such as "I would like you to . . ." or "I want you to . . ." when presenting test instructions. In addition to a matter of taste, such expressions are likely to prove particularly problematic with patients who have issues with authority (e.g., patients with a diagnosis of Antisocial Personality Disorder) or patients who have just "had enough" with trying to meet the wishes of medical staff when they, the patients, are the ones who are feeling poorly. Such test-instruction phrasing is common in many standard test administration procedures (see, for example, the instructions of the Wechsler Memory Scale-Revised (Wechsler, 1987) or the Memory Assessment Scale (Williams, 1991)). Unfortunately, it is likely to arouse an internal response of "I could care less what you want," precipitate an antagonistic examination session, and result in either unconscious or conscious decrements in test performance. Substituting phrases such as "Listen carefully to this story and tell it back to me as best you can" or "This next task is to see how well you can . . ." is both clinically advantageous and a relatively easy modification.

Emphasizing the importance of the patient–examiner relationship, Lezak (1983) also wrote about the necessity of preparing the patient for the assessment. She delineated seven topics that should be covered if the examiner wants to be assured of full cooperation and best effort: (a) the purpose of the examination, (b) the nature of the examination, (c) how the results will be used, (d) the nature and extent of confidentiality, (e) if and when feedback will be provided about the results, (f) an explanation of the testing procedures and the role of the patient, and (g) how the patient feels about the testing. Some of these points are considered so important that they have been written into the latest American Psychological Association's Ethical Principles of Psychologists and Code of Conduct (American Psychological Association, 1992). Assessment within the context of a defined professional relationship and the structuring of that relationship are outlined in the ethics code. Structuring the professional relationship should include discussion of fees, anticipated length of contact(s), and informed consent regarding nature, course, and potential benefits or lack thereof. Feedback to the patient of the results also is addressed as a specific ethical point. Although clinicians may pay some attention to these issues, unfortunately all too often these points are not addressed fully and satisfactorily.

Sensitivity to Patient's Individual Differences.   Performance on neuropsychological tests can be affected by a multitude of variables, including many of the items discussed earlier in the context of the case history (see Table 1.2). Table 1.5 enumerates others. To obtain a patient's maximal performance, the examiner must be aware of individual-specific potential problems that may interfere with test performance.

Many demographic attributes fall within the realm of subject–moderator variables, characteristics that make a group of individuals different in performance in a predictable fashion from the population at large (Anastasi, 1988). Unfortunately, in brain-impaired persons, the effects of such moderator variables may be exaggerated, but in an unpredictable fashion. Age, gender, level of education, cultural background, socioeconomic status, motivation, and attention are those most frequently discussed in this context (see, e.g., Anastasi, 1988; Hynd & Semrud-Clikeman, 1990). Additional variables that are less predictable, yet areas of equal concern, are issues of motivation, secondary gain, and malingering. Medical conditions and problems can also adversely affect performance on a variety of neuropsychological test measures and be incorrectly interpreted as reflecting brain damage. It is essential to be aware of subject-

TABLE 1.5
Factors That Can Affect Test Performance

---

1. Demographic
   a. Age
   b. Gender
   c. Education
   d. Handedness
   e. Socioeconomic status
2. Situational
   a. Motivation
   b. Secondary gain
   c. Malingering
3. Sensory/perceptual
   a. Hearing loss
   b. Visual acuity
   c. Field cuts and/or neglect
   d. Peripheral neuropathies
4. Peripheral psychomotor functioning
   a. Arthritis
   b. Past injuries
   c. Carpel Tunnel Syndrome
5. Attention and distractibility
6. Sensitivity to fatigue
7. Frustration tolerance
8. Psychiatric/psychological/personality
   a. Depression
   b. Psychosis
   c. Antisocial/authority problems
   d. Somatization disorders
   e. Anxiety disorders
   f. Alcohol or substance abuse
9. Medical or health status
10. Brain injury
    a. Intrasubject variance
    b. Intragroup variance

---

specific factors that make an individual's performance noncomparable with the general normative database, to use adjusted norms if available, and to modify one's interpretation regardless. In this context of the data-collection phase of the evaluation, awareness of these variables is essential in making sure that information about them is collected and their adverse affect on test performance is noted, if and when it occurs.

Brain dysfunction itself can be a moderator variable potentially resulting in unreliable test results. This may seem like a strange statement, but the variability commonly seen within and/or across tasks, within and/or across testing sessions, or unique to certain environmental conditions is certainly a different behavior than that of the brain-unimpaired normative comparison group. Test performance may be different in the morning than the afternoon, or early in a session as opposed to later. Astute behavioral observations regarding fatigue, environmental distractions, internal distractions, or other factors allow the examiner to help the client compensate for such effects if possible, or at least note their adverse effects as they occur. This avoids later possible misinterpretation of the results.

Hearing and vision problems can adversely affect performance on numerous tests, with such impaired test performance revealing nothing about brain dysfunction. A careful examiner can easily adjust for many sensory problems by making sure that patients utilize their glasses and hearing aids or compensate by enunciating clearly and speaking louder and more slowly. Compensating for high-frequency hearing loss (a not uncommon problem in elderly males) can sometimes be accomplished by these same procedures.

Similarly, impaired attention and concentration (whether secondary to mood disorders or brain injury) frequently will impair performance on tests of memory, mental arithmetic, and reasoning and problem solving. The careful examiner can learn to modify some administration procedures to compensate for attentional problems, if the purpose for utilizing a particular test is for some reason other than the assessment of attentional resources. Compensation might be accomplished through encouragement, reassurance, careful use of breaks, specific instructions, and reticular activating system-arousing techniques (such as varying types of tasks, or even voice volume and rate to avoid attentional habituation).

The knowledgeable clinician will be cognizant of variables possibly confounding test performance, will help clients compensate for them if possible, and will note them for later interpretive descriptive richness. Failure to carefully assess and control for these factors increases assessment error.

Allowing Deficits to Emerge

It is also the examiner's responsibility to provide every opportunity for patients to demonstrate their deficits. This aspect of proper evaluation has received less discussion than has "maximizing performance" and yet is equally important and just as much a source of possible assessment error.

Appropriate selection of tests is an area where examiners may or may not provide an opportunity for patients to demonstrate their problems. If measures sensitive to patients' deficits are not utilized, behavioral impairments may never be seen. The more knowledgeable and experienced the neuropsychologist, the more likely potential problem areas will be recognized, and the more likely appropriate tests will be utilized (Walsh, 1992).

To a certain extent, the issue is how much patients' compensatory strategies for carrying out a behavior and examiners' stylistic testing approaches are capitalized on or interfere with assessment tasks. One concrete example of this is on drawings of a Greek cross. Most individuals begin their drawing of the cross at the top and proceed clockwise. Thus, individuals with right-hemisphere damage must complete their drawing and connect with their starting point by working in their impaired hemispatial field. A number of right-hemisphere-impaired patients begin their cross drawings at the top, work counterclockwise, and by following this approach produce adequate figures. By subsequently asking them to redraw the cross by starting at the top and proceeding clockwise, severely distorted crosses are drawn (see Fig. 1.1). Multiple clinical examples could be provided where a slight variation in usual procedures resulted in very significant clinical information being revealed; or, where the selection of certain test instruments was essential to help identify a particular problem.

Another area where deficits may be missed is frontal lobe dysfunction. Many of the problems associated with frontal dysfunction manifest themselves best in unstructured and novel situations. However, neuropsychological testing tends to be very structured and rapidly becomes less than novel. Therefore, the clinical interview, the "assessment relationship" itself, the break periods from "formal assessment," and information from significant others become essential in the evaluation of aspects of frontal lobe functioning (e.g., response inhibition, behavioral self monitoring and self-correcting, maintenance of appropriate interpersonal behaviors, appreciation and appropriate expression of humor and wit, ability to form an "abstract attitude," and cognitive and behavioral flexibility). The examiner must not only create an environment where such deficits may freely emerge but also must be trained to correctly recognize and record them when they do. Furthermore, on tests relatively sensitive to such problems (e.g., Halstead Category Test, Wisconsin Card Sorting Test, Trail Making Test Part B, visuospatial mazes), a well-structured and supportive examiner may provide external cues and structure too readily in anticipation of problems or errors. In so doing, the opportunity for the patient to engage in perseverative, concrete, or "stimulus-bound" behaviors is thwarted.

Structuring the Testing Session

Issues important to structuring the testing session include introducing the testing, pacing and the use of breaks, ordering of the tests administered, and using single versus multiple sessions.

Introducing the Testing. Normally, the clinical interview, as discussed earlier, will precede formal testing. During the interview the ex-

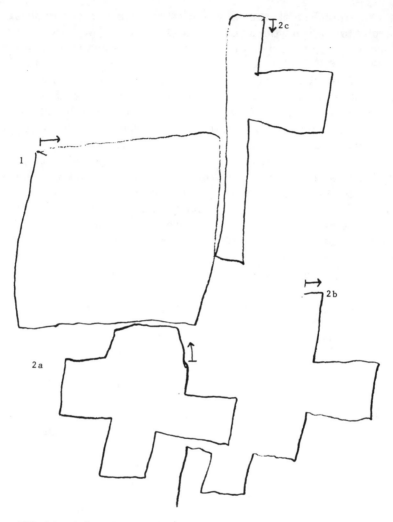

FIG. 1.1.   Aphasia Screening Test drawings of a 70-year-old male 5 weeks
after suffering a right frontal-parietal stroke. The square was drawn adequately from copy first followed by three attempts to copy a Greek cross
(2a, 2b, 2c). After the patient's initial cross drawing (2a) he was asked to
draw it again moving his pencil in a clockwise rather than counterclockwise direction.

aminer will typically introduce the examinee to the nature and purpose
of the evaluation. This should also include information regarding the
length of time the evaluation is likely to take, if and when breaks will
occur, and how meals will be handled, if the evaluation will span a meal-
time. Patients should be informed that the actual tests will be of varying
levels of difficulty, that no one is expected to do well on everything, but

that they should attempt to do their best on all measures to make the evaluation as useful as possible.

Because clinical interviews frequently move from more open-ended questions to structured questioning and history gathering, the subsequent move into actual testing can be accomplished smoothly. By starting with simpler measures such as orientation questions or brief attentional measures (e.g., Mental Control from the WMS-R or Digit Span), the examinee may not even note a shift from the direct questions of the case history. Performance on these simple measures will help the examiner evaluate to what extent basic attentional and motivational resources are likely to impact more difficult measures. Also, the examiner can develop a sense of how easily the patient understands and follows instructions, and how quickly he or she works.

Pacing and the Use of Breaks.   Examiners should be thoroughly familiar with the various tests so they can work smoothly and easily with patients, observe any unusual behaviors, and quickly record responses and observations. The pacing of testing should be dictated by the patient's ability and comfort level rather than by the examiner's preference; that is, the pacing should never interfere with a patient's ability to give his or her best performance. It should proceed quickly enough so that patients do not have idle time, but slowly enough so that they do not feel harried. Examiners' "fiddling" with test material or excessive time between tasks will lengthen the overall evaluation time and increase the likelihood that patient fatigue will become a confounding factor.

Brief breaks from testing should be given when patient fatigue appears to be adversely affecting performance. It is usually a good idea to take a 5- to 10-minute rest break about every 90 minutes whether or not the patient appears to need it. This will help maintain alertness. Patients tend to be appreciative of examiner's consideration of their emotional states and needs, but excessive attentiveness can be experienced as patronizing, can interfere with rapport, and can disrupt the assessment. A guiding principle is to pace the examination and use breaks to help patients do their best.

Ordering of the Tests.   There are several approaches to test administration ordering. One approach is to select and use tests to answer an ongoing series of clinical questions. The initial question would be whether the patient can engage in formal testing. As noted earlier, beginning with a few easier tasks will help answer that question. Subsequent clinical questions might concern the patient's competence in various cognitive-ability domains. Thus, a sequence of tests might move systematically through

the cognitive domains of interest: attention, basic sensory–perceptual abilities, psychomotor capability, working memory capacity, language competence, visuospatial competence, learning and memory abilities, and
executive abilities. Once having established ability to participate reliably
in testing, some neuropsychologists will utilize sensitive or more difficult
screening measures within the various domains and only attempt to "flesh
out" abilities within a domain if performance on the sensitive measure(s)
appears impaired.

Neuropsychologists utilizing a consistent set of tests should vary the
difficulty level so that patients can have a success experience after doing
poorly on some measure. Also, although it may be tempting to save the
most difficult measures for the end of the evaluation, this would result
in the patient having to take them when they are most fatigued. In addition, they may leave the evaluation with a feeling of failure or inade-
quacy.

Single Versus Multiple Testing Sessions.   Many neuropsychologists and patients prefer to complete the evaluation in one session and
schedule a follow-up session for feedback. As long as patients are able
to sustain their attention, motivation, and energy level to complete the
evaluation in one session, this approach is quite effective. However, many
of the more impaired patients cannot tolerate more than 30 to 90 minutes
of evaluation at a stretch. For these patients testing must be broken into
several sessions. Also, with forensic evaluations where motivation or
malingering may be an issue, the use of multiple sessions can be quite
revealing. Significant discrepancies in performance between sessions (and
within sessions), particularly if the pattern of difficulties does not fit any
known neurological condition, certainly raise the possibility of factors
other than brain impairment as accounting for the test findings. Patients
who are malingering are likely to have difficulty maintaining a consistently poor level of performance across repeated sessions.

Scoring and Clerical Errors

Scoring or clerical errors are very common. Greene (1980), for example,
reported that approximately 30% of hand-scored MMPI protocols have
some errors. On the MMPI, scoring is simply counting the number of items
affirmed on each scale and transferring that total onto a profile sheet.
Scoring on the WAIS-R and various neuropsychological test measures is
much more complicated and at times involves subjective judgments.

One example of a neuropsychological scoring error was provided by
a psychology intern several years ago. This intern indicated that the gero-
psychologist with whom she was working carefully determined age-

adjusted WAIS-R scaled scores on his elderly patients. However, he then proceeded to sum these age-adjusted scaled scores and look up those summary scores in the age-appropriate IQ tables to determine IQ scores. Thus, he was effectively adjusting twice for the patient's age. He had apparently been following that practice for several years. Whether this was a case of "examiner drift" or of having learned incorrect scoring procedures initially is uncertain, but this clinician was a doctoral-level psychologist who was specializing in geropsychology.

Little research exists regarding scoring problems with general neuropsychological tests; however, there is some research with the WAIS-R. Ryan, Prifitera, and Powers (1983) compared the scoring of 19 doctoral-level psychologists and 20 psychology graduate students on two WAIS-R protocols. Both experienced examiners and novices made many scoring errors. Generally, errors resulted in higher IQ scores than should have been obtained, but this was not always the case. Verbal IQ scores varied as much as 18 points among examiners and Performance IQs up to 17 points. Experienced clinicians did no better than the graduate students and considerably worse on Performance scales (10- to 17-point ranges for PhDs versus 4-point ranges for graduate students). Common error types included incorrectly scoring individual items, adding raw scores across subtests, and converting scaled scores to IQ scores. Other common WAIS-R scoring errors include failure to give credit for initial unadministered items on subtests such as Information and Arithmetic (this is also a common error on the Wide Range Achievement Test—Revised [WRAT-R]), incorrectly looking up scores from tables, or in converting scaled scores to percentage scores for the actual test report. Timed tests can also be problematic unless time limits are strictly followed.

One legitimate area for potential scoring disagreement comes in scoring various Vocabulary, Similarities, or Comprehension items on the WAIS-R or other Wechsler intelligence measures. Although scoring guidelines and sample responses are provided in the manual, patients not uncommonly provide answers that are not covered in the examples. The manual encourages clinicians to clarify ambiguous responses with questions such as, "Tell me a little more" or "Explain what you mean." It also indicates that if multiple acceptable responses are provided clinicians should score the best response. However, if multiple responses are provided and some of them would be 0-point responses, the examiner should ask, "Which one is it?" Despite these helpful suggestions, some subjects will give questionable responses, and the clinician must make a judgment about what value to assign.

Although there are times when minor scoring or clerical errors result in little difference in scores or in interpretation of test findings, a grave disservice may result when they do. Realizing how common scoring errors are, a rule of thumb would be to always cross-check test scores and certainly to cross-check scores that do not seem to fit with the clinical picture, past history, or with the rest of the test data. Neuropsychologists also should be knowledgeable of where errors are likely to occur and be particularly attentive in those areas.

SUMMARY

Neuropsychological assessment is a complex clinical activity. This chapter has addressed issues relevant to the data-collection phase of the assessment process. It was argued that the neuropsychological evaluation is a process that neither begins nor ends with testing. Instead, it begins before the patient is ever seen with an attempt to clarify and define the nature and purpose of each evaluation. The interview, case history, and behavioral observations were discussed as being as important in gathering information as formal neuropsychological testing. Methods and approaches to the interview process and case history development were reviewed.

Once a decision has been made to pursue formal testing, the neuropsychologist must carefully select which tests to utilize to evaluate the relevant cognitive domains of interest and identify possible areas of brain impairment. Important in test selection is the use of well-normed and validated measures of an appropriate level of difficulty for the patient under study. Issues in standardized testing were discussed at some length. It was suggested that what is important for standardized testing is the creation of the conditions that were present for the standardization sample, rather than an inflexible application of the standardized testing conditions. Some administration principles were offered to help guide the clinician in this area. Issues related to structuring the testing session were reviewed. Important in this regard is helping patients attain their maximal performance, although still allowing opportunities for them to demonstrate their problems and deficits. It was suggested that the pace of the session, the use of breaks, and the order of test administration should all be dictated by the patient's ability and comfort level, rather than by the examiner's preference. Finally, it was seen that problems related to the actual scoring of test results are quite common and can substantially impact possible interpretation of the evaluation findings.

Subsequent chapters cover the interpretation and application phases of the evaluation process. However, a necessary prerequisite for these stages of the evaluation is some kind of determination of a comparison standard for the individual being evaluated. Estimating premorbid level of functioning is therefore covered in the next chapter.

REFERENCES

American Psychological Association. (1992). Ethical principles of psychologists and code of conduct. *American Psychologist, 47*, 1597–1611.

Anastasi, A. (1988). *Psychological testing* (6th ed.). New York: Macmillan.

Axelrod, B. N., Henry, R. R., & Woodard, J. L. (1992). Analysis of an abbreviated form of the Wisconsin Card Sorting Test. *The Clinical Neuropsychologist, 6*, 27–31.

Berg, E. A. (1948). A simple objective test for measuring flexibility in thinking. *Journal of General Psychology, 39*, 15–22.

Butler, M., Retzlaff, P., & Vanderploeg, R. (1991). Neuropsychological test usage. *Professional Psychology: Research and Practice, 22*, 510–512.

Calsyn, D. A., O'Leary, M. R., & Chaney, E. F. (1980). Shortening the Category Test. *Journal of Consulting and Clinical Psychology, 48*, 788–789.

DeFilippis, N. A., & McCampbell, E. (1979). *The Booklet Category Test*. Odessa, FL: Psychological Assessment Resources.

Denburg, S. D., Carotte, R. M., & Denburg, J. A. (1987). Cognitive impairment in systemic lupus erythematosus: A neuropsychological study of individual and group deficits. *Journal of Clinical and Experimental Neuropsychology, 9*, 323–339.

Dunn, L. M., & Dunn, L. M. (1981). *Peabody Picture Vocabulary Test-Revised manual*. Circle Pines, MN: American Guidance Service.

Golden, C. J., Osmon, D. C., Moses, J. A., Jr., & Berg, R. A. (1981). *Interpretation of the Halstead–Reitan Neuropsychological Test Battery: A casebook approach*. New York: Grune & Stratton.

Greene, R. L. (1980). *The MMPI: An interpretive manual*. New York: Grune & Stratton.

Greenwald, A. G., Pratkanis, A. R., Leippe, M. R., & Baumgardner, M. H. (1986). Under what conditions does theory obstruct research progress? *Psychological Review, 93*, 216–229.

Gregory, R. J., Paul, J. J., & Morrison, M. W. (1979). A short form of the Category Test for adults. *Journal of Clinical Psychology, 35*, 795–798.

Hampton, J. R., Harrison, M. J. G., Mitchell, J. R. A., Pritchard, J. S., & Seymour, C. (1975). Relative contributions of history taking, physical examination, and laboratory investigation to diagnosis and management of medical outpatients. *British Medical Journal, 2*, 486–489.

Heaton, R. K. (1981). *A manual for the Wisconsin Card Sorting Test*. Odessa, FL: Psychological Assessment Resources.

Heaton, S. R., & Heaton, R. K. (1981). Testing the impaired patient. In S. B. Filskov & T. J. Boll (Eds.), *Handbook of clinical neuropsychology* (pp. 526–544). New York: Wiley.

Hynd, G. W., & Semrud-Clikeman, M. (1990). Neuropsychological assessment. In A. S. Kaufman (Ed.), *Assessing adolescent and adult intelligence* (pp. 638–695). Boston: Allyn & Bacon.

Jarvis, P. E., & Barth, J. T. (1984). *Halstead–Reitan Test Battery: An interpretive guide*. Odessa, FL: Psychological Assessment Resources.

Kaplan, E., Fein, D., Morris, R., & Delis, D. C. (1991). *WAIS-R as a neuropsychological instrument*. San Antonio, TX: The Psychological Corporation.

Leckliter, I. N., Forster, A. A., Klonoff, H., & Knights, R. M. (1992). A review of reference group data from normal children for the Halstead–Reitan Neuropsychological Test Battery for older children. *The Clinical Neuropsychologist, 6*, 201–229.

Lezak, M. D. (1983). *Neuropsychological assessment* (2nd ed.). New York: Oxford University Press.

Luria, A. R. (1980). *Higher cortical functions in man* (2nd ed., B. Haigh, Trans.). New York: Basic Books.

Maloney, M. P., & Ward, M. P. (1976). *Psychological assessment: A conceptual approach.* New York: Oxford University Press.

Matarazzo, J. D. (1990). Psychological assessment versus psychological testing. *American Psychologist, 45,* 999–1017.

Melendez, F. (1978). *Revised manual for the adult neuropsychological questionnaire.* Odessa, FL: Psychological Assessment Resources.

Milner, B. (1962). Laterality effects in audition. In V. B. Mountcastle (Ed.), *Interhemispheric relations and cerebral dominance* (pp. 177–195). Baltimore: Johns Hopkins University Press.

Nelson, H. E. (1976). A modified card sorting test sensitive to frontal lobe defects. *Cortex, 12,* 313–324.

Phay, A., Gainer, C., & Goldstein, G. (1986). Clinical interviewing of the patient and history in neuropsychological assessment. In T. Incagnoli, G. Goldstein, & C. J. Golden (Eds.), *Clinical application of neuropsychological test batteries* (pp. 45–73). New York: Plenum Press.

Reitan, R. M. (1979). *Manual for administration of neuropsychological test batteries for adults and children.* Tucson, AZ: Reitan Neuropsychology Laboratories.

Reitan, R. M., & Wolfson, D. (1989). The Seashore Rhythm Test and brain functions. *The Clinical Neuropsychologist, 3,* 70–78.

Russell, E. W., & Levy, M. (1987). Revision of the Halstead Category Test. *Journal of Consulting and Clinical Psychology, 55,* 898–901.

Ryan, J. J., Prifitera, A., & Powers, L. (1983). Scoring reliability on the WAIS-R. *Journal of Consulting and Clinical Psychology, 51,* 149–150.

Sattler, J. M. (1988). *Assessment of children* (3rd ed.). San Diego: Jerome M. Sattler.

Schinka, J. A. (1983). *Neuropsychological Status Examination manual.* Odessa, FL: Psychological Assessment Resources.

Sherer, M., Parson, O. A., Nixon, S. J., & Adams, R. L. (1991). Clinical validity of the Speech–Sounds Perception Test and the Seashore Rhythm Test. *Journal of Clinical and Experimental Neuropsychology, 13,* 741–751.

Skenazy, J., & Bigler, E. (1984). Neuropsychological findings in diabetes mellitus. *Journal of Clinical Psychology, 40,* 246–258.

Spreen, O., & Gaddes, W. H. (1969). Developmental norms for 15 neuropsychological tests age 6 to 15. *Cortex, 5,* 170–191.

Tarter, R. E., Van Thiel, D. H., & Edwards, K. (1988). *Medical neuropsychology: The impact of disease on behavior.* New York: Plenum Press.

Taylor, J. M., Goldman, H., Leavitt, J., & Kleinman, K. M. (1984). Limitations of the brief form of the Halstead Category Test. *Journal of Clinical Neuropsychology, 6,* 341–344.

Teuber, H.-L., Battersby, W. S., & Bender, M. B. (1951). Performance of complex visual tasks after cerebral lesions. *Journal of Nervous and Mental Disease, 114,* 413–429.

Vanderploeg, R. D., Goldman, H., & Kleinman, K. M. (1987). Relationship between systolic and diastolic blood pressure and cognitive functioning in hypertensive subjects: An extension of previous findings. *Archives of Clinical Neuropsychology, 2,* 101–109.

Vanderploeg, R. D., & Logan, S. G. (1989). Comparison of the Halstead Category Test and the Revised Category Test: Comment on Russell and Levy. *Journal of Consulting and Clinical Psychology, 57,* 315–316.

Walsh, K. (1992). Some gnomes worth knowing. *The Clinical Neuropsychologist, 6,* 119–133.

Wechsler, D. (1981). *WAIS-R manual.* New York: Psychological Corporation.

Wechsler, D. (1987). *Wechsler Memory Scale - Revised manual.* San Antonio: Psychological Corporation.

Wetzel, L., & Boll, T. J. (1987). *Short category test, booklet format*. Los Angeles: Western Psychological Services.

Williams, J. M. (1987). *Cognitive behavior rating scales manual: Research edition*. Odessa, FL: Psychological Assessment Resources.

Williams, J. M. (1991). *Memory assessment scales professional manual*. Odessa, FL: Psychological Assessment Resources.

Williams, M. (1965). *Brain damage and the mind*. Baltimore: Penguin Books.

CHAPTER TWO

Estimating Premorbid Level of Functioning

Rodney D. Vanderploeg
James A. Haley Veterans' Hospital
Tampa, Florida
and
University of South Florida

Test scores, in and of themselves, are meaningless. In analyzing neuropsychological assessment data, what is important are not test scores but rather the interpretation of those scores. Messick (1989) stated: "The validated interpretation gives meaning to the measure in the particular instance, and evidence on the generality of the interpretation over time and across . . . settings shows how stable or circumscribed that meaning is likely to be" (p.15). However, without some comparison standard, an interpretation cannot be generated; scores are simply numbers.

One comparison standard is other individuals who share important attributes with the test taker. The normative data provided by test publishers are examples of this type of comparison standard (population norms). Unfortunately, the quality of norms varies widely across various neuropsychology tests, with many norms based on relatively small samples that are not representative of the general population. Problems with norms are discussed further in chapters 6 and 7. Assuming adequate sampling quality, normative data allow clinicians to examine how their patients perform relative to the normative population. If the clinical question of interest is whether or not a particular patient is impaired in a manner suggestive of brain damage, then knowing that the patient performed worse than 95% of the normative sample (particularly if the sample was similar in age, gender, education, etc.) certainly suggests that some degree of impairment may be present. However, by definition 5% of the normative sample performed at a similarly low level or worse. Clinicians

43

cannot know, without additional information, whether or not their patient originally fell within this lower 5%, or whether some degree of performance decrement over premorbid levels is present. Alternatively, a patient's innate abilities may have been at the 90th percentile, whereas current test performances range from the 35th to 50th percentile. In this case using the population average as a basis for comparison would suggest no difficulties, when in fact a drop of about 1.5 standard deviations has occurred. Thus, a second important comparison standard is the individual's historical level of ability (self-standard). This is true for two important determinations: (a) assessing potential deficits or impairments, and (b) evaluating change across time. Clinical situations where the assessment of change is important include evaluations of worsening conditions (e.g., dementias) and evaluating recovery following a brain insult.

For most cognitive brain-related abilities, an innate level of ability must somehow be estimated and subsequently be used as the individual-specific comparison standard. This is referred to as an estimate of premorbid level of functioning. In deficit determination, exceptions to the need for individual-specific comparison standards are *pathognomonic signs*. Some brain behaviors have population-wide (at least for developmentally similar groups) normative-comparison standards (Lezak, 1983). Examples of such behaviors in adults include the ability to copy a simple drawing, follow simple commands, speak fluently without paraphasias, demonstrate the use of common tools (e.g., a hammer or key), perform simple mathematical calculations, and discriminate right from left. Impairment in such behaviors is a sign of brain dysfunction, the nature of the impaired behavior being pathognomonic of dysfunction in specific brain regions. Unfortunately, for most cognitive abilities original levels of functioning must be estimated.

Various methods have been proposed for making premorbid estimates, all of which have limitations. Relying on one or more methods without knowing or considering the inherent problems on a case-by-case basis is a sure way to make assessment errors. This chapter reviews methods of premorbid estimation and problems intrinsic to each. However, first the variability across various cognitive abilities known to occur in non-brain-damaged individuals is reviewed.

INTRAINDIVIDUAL VARIABILITY
ACROSS COGNITIVE ABILITIES

Premorbid estimation rests on a number of assumptions (Lezak, 1983). One assumption is that there is a single performance level that best represents each person's intellectual abilities. A related assumption is that marked discrepancies in performance on measures of different abilities are evidence of impairment. Evidence supporting these assumptions comes from several sources. Since the 1920s, Spearman was struck by the positive relationships that emerged among many different tests of complex mental functioning. He posited the concept of a general intelligence factor, g, which represents this association between all measures of intellectual functioning (Spearman, 1927). In factor-analytic studies of intellectual measures, the unrotated first principal factor is commonly used as an estimate of g (Kaufman, 1990). Supporting the concept of g is the finding that all subtests of the Wechsler Adult Intelligence Scale—Revised (WAIS-R; Wechsler, 1981) have at least moderate factor loadings (ranging from 0.59 for Digit Symbol to 0.86 for Vocabulary) on an initial principal factor (Parker, 1983).

Almost from its formulation, researchers have attempted to subdivide g into multiple factors of intellectual ability, which replace rather than coexist with g (e.g., Thurstone, 1938). Multiple factor theories carry no assumption that level of performance across the various factors should be similar. Thurstone (1938) administered a battery of 54 divergent tests to 240 students and factor analyzed the results. No general intellectual factor emerged, and eventually seven factors were described as best characterizing the data: number, word fluency, verbal meaning, memory, reasoning, space, and perceptual speed. These factors bear a striking resemblance to some ability domains assessed in current clinical neuropsychological test batteries. More recently, Gardner (1983, 1987) postulated a theory of multiple intelligences that was developed out of neurologic/biologic and multicultural evidence and was rooted in a developmental analysis. Gardner proposed at least seven independent intelligences: linguistic, logical–mathematical, spatial, musical, bodily–kinesthetic, interpersonal, and intrapersonal. There is no assumption of, and in fact considerable evidence against, a consistent level of ability across these intelligences.

Even within intellectual domains substantial variability may exist. Utilizing the standardization data of the WAIS-R, Matarazzo, Daniel, Prifitera, and Herman (1988) illustrated that over 18% of the standardization sample had at least two subtests that differed by three or more standard deviations (scatter ranges of 9 scale scores or more). This percentage increased to almost 33% in individuals with Full Scale IQ scores of 120 or greater. Table 2.1 shows the pattern of subtest scatter at different levels of intellectual ability for the WAIS-R standardization sample. As expected, with decreased overall range (i.e., lower Full Scale IQ scores), the range of subtest scatter decreases. However, even in a population with Full Scale IQ scores of less than 80, 30% have subtest scatter ranges of 2 standard deviations or greater. Similarly, high levels of subtest scatter exist for the Wechsler Intelligence Scale for Children-Revised (Kaufman, 1976a), the

TABLE 2.1
Percentage of Cases at or Above Each Level of Scatter in the
WAIS-R Standardization Sample, by Full Scale IQ

Scatter (Range)	Full Scale IQ					
	– 79	80–89	90–109	110–119	120 +	All
17	0.0%	0.0%	0.0%	0.0%	0.0%	0.0%
16	0.0	0.0	0.2	0.0	0.0	0.1
15	0.0	0.0	0.5	0.3	0.0	0.3
14	0.0	0.0	0.8	0.3	0.0	0.4
13	0.0	0.0	1.5	1.0	1.1	1.0
12	0.0	0.3	2.4	2.6	4.5	2.1
11	0.6	1.0	4.1	6.1	9.0	4.1
10	0.6	3.3	7.8	13.5	20.3	8.6
9	3.0	8.9	18.6	25.3	32.8	18.1
8	7.3	19.5	34.1	40.1	49.7	31.9
7	17.6	31.8	53.1	57.7	67.2	48.7
6	29.7	56.6	73.9	77.6	87.0	69.1
5	60.6	79.1	89.7	91.3	93.8	86.1
4	84.8	93.4	98.3	98.7	99.4	96.5
3	98.2	99.3	99.7	100.0	100.0	99.6
2	100.0	99.7	100.0	100.0	100.0	99.9
1	100.0	100.0	100.0	100.0	100.0	100.0
0	100.0	100.0	100.0	100.0	100.0	100.0
N	165	302	924	312	177	1,880
Mean Scatter	5.02	5.93	6.84	7.14	7.65	6.66
Standard Deviation	1.57	1.78	2.02	2.07	2.08	2.08
Median Scatter	5	6	7	7	7	6

Note: Data from Matarazzo, Daniel, Prifitera, and Herman (1988, Table 4). Data and table from the Wechsler Adult Intelligence Scale-Revised. Copyright © 1988, 1981, 1955 by The Psychological Corporation. Reprinted by permission. All rights reserved.
Scatter measured by the range of scaled scores across the 11 subtests.

McCarthy Scales of Children's Abilities (Kaufman, 1976b), the Wechsler Preschool and Primary Scale of Intelligence (Reynolds & Gutkin, 1981), and the Kaufman Assessment Battery for Children (Chatman, Reynolds, & Willson, 1984).

Subtest scatter ranges could be due to several possibilities. For example, a single outlier with all other subtests clustered together could result in the scatter ranges reported previously. Alternatively, scatter could be normally distributed across all 11 subtests within each person. The latter possibility is more intuitively logical. The subtest intercorrelation matrices reported in the WAIS-R manual support the second possibility. For some age groups the intercorrelation matrix contains as many as 6 values of 0.30 or less (9% or less shared variance). The lowest correlation is only 0.19 (less than 4% common variance).

McLean, Kaufman, and Reynolds (1989) examined the number of

WAIS-R subtests that differed by 3 or more points from a person's mean scaled score. In individuals with Full Scale IQ scores of 120 or greater, as many as 6 of the 11 subtests met this criteria in 10% of the sample. An average of 4 subtests met this criteria in over 10% of the entire standardization sample. Table 2.2 presents data for the number of deviant subtests (3 points or more) from a person's mean subtest scaled score for the entire standardization sample and across different levels of intelligence. Notice that WAIS-R subtest scatter is quite common in a non-brain-injured population. Fluctuation across other measures of brain–behavior functions is more poorly documented but is likely to be as or more variable. One study did report that the larger the number of neuropsychological measures the greater the range of obtained scores (Mortensen, Gade, & Reinisch, 1991).

Less scatter may exist within narrow cognitive ability domains. For example, within individuals the level of performance within measures of a specific ability (e.g., visual discrimination, spatial analysis, constructional tasks, verbal productive fluency, or word knowledge) may be limited, even though across these specific cognitive domains the level of performance could vary dramatically. Unfortunately, the information to evaluate this question does not currently exist. Data does exist to show that verbal scatter in a person's WAIS-R profile is essentially independent of the amount of performance scatter within individuals (Matarazzo et al., 1988). However, both verbal and performance scales are broad-band rather than narrow-band measures.

These data undermine both of the assumptions just listed that are inherent in premorbid estimation methods. Regarding the assumption of single-performance level best representing a person's cognitive abilities, the literature shows that because of intrinsic variability general premorbid functioning estimates will be an inaccurate performance standard for some of the specific intellectual and neuropsychological measures. Unfortunately which and how many of the current test measures should not be expected to conform with the premorbid estimated level of functioning cannot be estimated.

There are numerous reports in the neuropsychological literature suggesting that subtest scatter is associated with brain damage (Black, 1974; Doehring, Reitan, & Klove, 1961; Simpson & Vega, 1971). However, in regard to the second assumption (i.e., that marked discrepancies in performance suggest brain injury), we have seen that all performance variability cannot be assumed to suggest impairment. However, it may be that specific patterns of cognitive strengths and weakness can be identified that typically are associated with specific neurologic conditions, and which rarely or never are found in non-brain-impaired individuals. In these cases, the performance variability fits a specific pattern that is diag-

TABLE 2.2

Number of Significantly Deviating WAIS-R Subtest Scores (± 3 Points) from a Persons's Own Mean Required for Abnormality at Several Frequencies of Occurrence in the Normal Population, by Full Scale IQ

Frequency of Occurrence	Full Scale IQ																		Total Sample		
	79			80–89			90–109			110–119			120 +								
	V	P	FS	V	P	FS	V	P	FS	V	P	FS	V	P	FS	V	P	FS	V	P	FS
<10%	2	3	4	2	3	4	3	4	4	3	4	5	3	4	6	3	4	4
<05%	3	4	5	3	4	5	4	4	5	4	4	6	4	4	7	4	4	5
<02%	4	4	6	4	4	6	4	5	6	5	5	7	5	5	7	4	5	6
<01%	5	5	7	5	5	7	5	5	7	5	5	8	5	5	8	5	5	7
Sample Size	165			301			930			305			179			1880		

Note: Values in this table have been smoothed. (Data and table are from McLean, J.E., Kaufman, A.S., Reynolds, C.R. (1989). Base rates for WAIS-R subtest scatter as a guide for clinical and neuropsychological assessment. *Journal of Clinical Psychology, 45,* 919–926. Reprinted by permission of the copyright holder, Clinical Psychology Publishing Company, Inc., Brandon, VT 05733.)

nostic. The Fuld profile on the WAIS/WAIS-R has been an attempt to define one such pattern, in this case associated with cholinergic dysfunction and/or Alzheimer's disease (Fuld, 1984). The Fuld profile is computed using *age-corrected* scaled scores and is as follows: $A > B > C \leq D$ and $A > D$ (A = (Information + Vocabulary) / 2; B = (Similarities + Digit Span) / 2; C = (Digit Symbol + Block Design) / 2; D = (Object Assembly). The Fuld profile is present in about 40% to 55% of Alzheimer's patients (Brinkman & Braun, 1984; Filley, Kobayashi, & Heaton, 1987; Fuld, 1984), whereas present in only about 6% of the WAIS-R standardization sample (Satz et al., 1990) and found with low frequency in other patient populations (e.g., see Heinrichs & Celinski, 1987; Ryan & Paolo, 1989; Snow, Altman, Ridgley, & Rowed, 1988). However, this specific pattern of WAIS-R performance scatter must also be interpreted with caution. Not all studies have been supportive of its sensitivity or specificity (Gfeller & Rankin, 1991). In addition, it is absent in 45% to 60% of Alzheimer's patients and increases in frequency in neurologically normal individuals of advanced age and education (e.g., present in 13% to 15% of 65- to 74-year-old individuals with greater than 12 years of education; Satz et al., 1990).

Despite the variability present within a large proportion of neurologically normal individuals, the clinical need is still critical for an individual-specific comparison standard (or set of standards) to help evaluate and interpret current test performance.

PREMORBID ESTIMATION METHODS

For the purpose of this discussion, proposed premorbid estimation methods are divided into four basic types: (a) estimates based on historical data, (b) estimates based on aspects of current ability, (c) the "best performance method," and (d) estimates based on demographic information. Following this review of methods, recommendations are offered for the practicing clinical neuropsychologist.

Premorbid Estimates Based on Historical Data

Prior Evaluation Data

The ideal situation in clinical neuropsychological practice would be to have available for comparative purposes the results of a standardized multidimensional intelligence test (e.g., WISC-R, WISC-III, WAIS-R) completed prior to the onset of the suspected neurological disorder or behavior change. Although such intelligence test results are rarely available, in the United States results of some standardized aptitude testing frequently can be obtained. Nationally standardized assessment is completed within the educational system at a variety of points in time. At the elementary school level, the Cognitive Abilities Test (CAT) is commonly used. At secondary or high school level, the School and College Abilities Tests (SCAT) are popular. As part of the collegiate or postcollegiate application process, standardized testing is also required (e.g., college—Scholastic Aptitude Test [SAT] or American College Testing Program [ACT]; graduate school—Graduate Record Exam [GRE], medical school—Medical College Admission Test [MCAT]). Finally, military entrance exams (ASVAB) may be another source of information regarding premorbid cognitive functioning. Unfortunately, access to this information is frequently not readily available, although with some effort on the part of the neuropsychologist and the client and/or the client's family, it can be obtained.

It is important to recognize that the reference group for each of these standardized tests becomes progressively stratified. Standardized tests completed during elementary and secondary school (not including college admission tests) likely reflect the population at large (similar to the normative reference group for Wechsler's intelligence scales). However, fewer and fewer individuals take the more advanced measures, and those that do have increasingly higher levels of ability. For example, obtaining an overall score at the 50th percentile on the GRE is likely to be roughly equivalent to a percentile score of 85 on aptitude tests completed in high school (e.g., on the SAT), and the person's WAIS-R Full Scale IQ would likely be in the neighborhood of 115.

Another issue is that, the more component parts that standardized aptitude tests contain, the better the clinician will be able to estimate the degree of innate cognitive ability scatter across different domains. Multifactorial measures with verbal, mathematical/quantitative, logical/analytic, or other scores will permit individualized performance standards for specific cognitive abilities.

Past Levels of Achievement

If such standardized testing is not available, other aspects of a patient's history can provide estimates of premorbid level(s) of functioning. Educational and occupational attainment have relatively high correlations with intelligence (correlation with WAIS-R Full Scale IQ = 0.53 and 0.36, respectively; Barona, Reynolds, & Chastain, 1984). In addition, level of attainment in each can provide additional useful data in estimating premorbid ability levels. For example, school grades are modestly correlated with IQ. However, caution must be exercised because psychosocial and environmental factors can have a dramatic impact on academic performance. Also, assignment of grades can differ substantially across school levels, geographic regions, and eras. Clarifying the type of class and how an individual performed relative to his or her classroom peers regardless of actual grades obtained (e.g., upper 10%, upper third, middle third, or bottom third) allows for some control of grading differences between schools and eras.

History-based methods rely upon the examiner to carefully assess the history in sufficient depth to make judgments about the patient's premorbid functioning level. From these data clinicians, based on their experience, knowledge base, and clinical intuition, can form a "best guess" regarding level of premorbid functioning. For example, if the patient had completed high school as an average student (B and C grades), subsequently worked in blue-collar jobs, and never rose above the rank of a basic foreman, the examiner might hypothesize that the patient likely fell within the middle of the average range of intelligence (IQ range of 95 to 105). Average college graduates with lower level, small business management positions or careers in sales might be hypothesized to have a somewhat higher intelligence (IQ range of 110 to 115). Estimation accuracy can be enhanced by combining history of personal achievement with demographic data (e.g., mean intelligence associated with various levels of education or vocational attainment).

It is easy to see that the validity of history-based clinician estimates relies entirely upon the skill of the examiner, who in turn is forced to rely on basic assumptions about cognitive-ability levels. These assumptions may or may not be correct in general and, even if generally correct, may not apply to the specific case at hand. Assumptions likely include cognitive-ability levels associated with different levels of education, types of jobs, and responsibilities within those jobs.

Further Considerations

Given the mixed success of the history-based clinician estimation approach, it always would be prudent to carefully check the history for data from previous evaluations or standardized tests taken in school, the military, or on the job. In older patients this information may not exist, and even if it does it may not be available. Even if findings from prior testing are available, questions arise as to their reliability and validity in documenting premorbid functioning: Did the patient extend his or her best effort on prior testing? If the prior test data is from group testing (e.g., SAT), many factors can affect the scores: Did patients take preparatory courses to improve their performance? Did they cheat? Were they ill at the time they took the test? How anxious were they and did that affect their performance? Often the answers to these and other similar questions cannot be ascertained. Thus, even "hard data" from nationally standardized tests can result in inaccurate information regarding innate or premorbid cognitive-functioning levels. However, if results from multiple, previously administrated measures are available and level of performance was consistent across them, the clinician can have a fair sense of confidence in their validity in representing premorbid functioning. The ability of measures to adequately represent intraindividual scatter across cognitive abilities will depend upon the multidimensionality of each instrument.

Premorbid Estimates Based on Measures of Present Ability

Traditional "Hold" Measure(s) Approaches

Approaches based on "hold" measures rely upon the assessment of present abilities that are considered to be relatively resistant to neurological impairment. For example, certain WAIS subtests have been reported to be relatively resistant to the effects of aging and/or brain impairment (Wechsler, 1958). These "hold" subtests (Vocabulary, Information, Picture Completion, and Object Assembly) have therefore been used by some clinicians as the "best estimate" of premorbid functioning abilities, if they are discrepantly higher than other cognitive-ability measures. Another approach is that of simply using the performance on WAIS/WAIS-R Vocabulary (Yates, 1956), or the average of Vocabulary and Picture Completion, or the highest of these two, if one is substantially lower (McFie, 1975) as the best estimate of premorbid functioning.

The problems with such "hold" methods are obvious. Many types of brain damage significantly impact "hold" measures. Left-hemisphere damage, with or without aphasia, will certainly impact verbal "hold" measures (Swiercinsky & Warnock, 1977). In fact, brain impairment can adversely affect performance on all the Wechsler subtests (Russell, 1972). Additionally, depending upon each person's premorbid pattern of intellectual strengths and weaknesses, and the nature and location of his or her subsequent brain impairment, any WAIS/WAIS-R subtest may be highest postimpairment. Alternatively, all subtests may be lowered postimpairment, such that even the highest would result in an inaccurately low premorbid estimate. There is no way of being certain regarding which, if any, of these factors come into play on a case-by-case basis. Guiding the clinician's judgment about these possibilities could be knowledge about the area of brain damage/dysfunction from CT or MRI scans, EEGs, or SPECT or PET scans. Knowing the region(s) of brain injury could assist the clinician in judging whether or not a particular "hold" measure is likely to be useful for the patient in question (see McFie, 1969). Furthermore, these premorbid estimate methods are based on the assumption (as are all methods of estimating premorbid functioning) that premorbidly a person had relatively similar levels of function across all areas of brain-behavior abilities. As already discussed, the available evidence is against this assumption. Thus, it is not surprising that researchers have concluded that these "hold" approaches are simplistic, inaccurate, and not supported by the literature (Klesges & Troster, 1987; Klesges, Wilkening, & Golden, 1981; Larrabee, Largen, & Levin, 1985).

Current Reading Level Approaches

In an alternative present-ability approach to premorbid estimation, Nelson and colleagues (Nelson & McKenna, 1975; Nelson & O'Connell, 1978) noted that scores on a reading test "held" better than performance on a vocabulary measure following brain damage and subsequently developed the National Adult Reading Test (NART; Nelson, 1982). The NART is composed of 50 "irregular" words that cannot be pronounced through the use of common phonetic rules (e.g., yacht or naive). The use of "irregular" words capitalizes on patients' premorbid familiarity with the words and is a more reliable indicator of premorbid ability than the reading of "regular" words (Hart, Smith, & Swash, 1986; Nelson & O'Connell, 1978). Standardized on 120 normal British subjects, WAIS IQ prediction equations were developed, for which the standard errors of estimate were 7.6, 9.4, and 7.6 IQ points for VIQ, PIQ, and FSIQ, respectively. The NART has subsequently been cross validated and its psychometric properties evaluated and found acceptable (Crawford, Parker, Stewart, Besson, & DeLacey, 1989). Crawford et al. (1989) then combined the original and cross-validation samples and reported refined WAIS IQ regression equations.

A series of studies have reported NART performance to be relatively resistant to cortical atrophy (Nelson & O'Connell, 1978), dementia of the Alzheimer's type (DAT; Nebes, Martin, & Horn, 1984; O'Carroll, Baikie, & Whittick, 1987; O'Carroll & Gilleard, 1986), a variety of other organic conditions (alcoholic dementia, multiinfarct dementia, and closed head injury; Crawford, Besson, & Parker, 1988), depression (Crawford, Besson, Parker, Sutherland, & Keen, 1987), and schizophrenia, at least in outpatients (Crawford et al., 1992). However, results have not all been positive. Several studies have reported discrepancies between demented and control subjects on NART-predicted IQ scores (Hart et al., 1986; Stebbins, Wilson, Gilley, Bernard, & Fox, 1990), particularly in moderately to severely demented subjects (Stebbins, Wilson, et al., 1990). Even in those with only mild dementia, the NART appears to underestimate IQ in patients who have accompanying language deficits (Stebbins, Gilley, Wilson, Bernard, & Fox, 1990).

Recently, Crawford and colleagues (Crawford, Stewart, Parker, Besson, & Cochrane, 1989) have combined performance on the NART with various demographic measures reasoning that (a) unique variance to the two sets of measures might better relate to intellectual ability and thus together account for more IQ score variance, and (b) demographic variables may mediate the relationship between NART and IQ. Demographic variables included in the study were age, gender, education, and occupation (called "social class" in their study). With the exception of education, each demographic variable added significantly in stepwise regression equations for WAIS FSIQ, VIQ, and PIQ. Education was not included in final regression equations, which may be a problem. Cross validation and construct validity studies have also been performed (Crawford, Nelson, Blackmore, Cochrane, & Allan, 1990; Crawford, Cochrane, Besson, Parker, & Stewart, 1990). These combined NART/Demographic regression equations account for significantly more variance than either set of variables independently (combined = 73% FSIQ variance; NART alone = 66%; demographic alone = 50%), and the standard errors of measurement for these equations are slightly lower than those from the NART alone.

Schwartz and Saffran (1987) developed a revision of the NART, which they call the AMNART (American version of the NART). They replaced 23 words from the British NART that were unfamiliar to American readers and standardized it on 109 normal adults ages 40 to 89. WAIS regression equations utilizing AMNART error scores and level of education were developed (Schwartz & Saffran, 1987). A later validation study using discrepancies between predicted WAIS VIQ scores based on the AMNART and a prorated WAIS VIQ based on current performance on Information, Similarities, and Vocabulary scores showed acceptable sensitivity (.83) and specificity (.81) in distinguishing between demented and nondemented subjects (Grober, Sliwinski, Schwartz, & Saffran, 1989). Scores on the AMNART and years of education have subsequently been used to generate a WAIS-R VIQ regression equation, which utility was then evaluated in dementia determination (Grober & Sliwinski, 1991). AMNART/education-predicted premorbid WAIS-R VIQ scores did not differ between demented and nondemented subjects, whereas prorated WAIS-R VIQ scores did. In addition, AMNART-estimated premorbid IQ appeared to be relatively unaffected by the presence of a mild language disturbance (Grober & Sliwinski, 1991). The addition of the demographic variable of education may account for the AMNART/education WAIS-R VIQ regression equation being less sensitive to mild language impairment than is the NART (Stebbins, Gilley et al., 1990).

Blair and Spreen (1989) developed a third version of the NART (NART-R). They expanded and revised the NART word list for North American pronunciations (61 total items) and standardized it on a mixed Canadian and U.S. sample (N = 66). WAIS-R IQ prediction equations were developed. Although demographic variables were included in this study, they did not account for a significant amount of the variance beyond the use of NART-R error scores alone and were not included in the final prediction equations (failing to cross validate Crawford and his colleagues work on the increased effectiveness of the combined NART-demographic equations). Standard errors of estimate were 6.56, 10.67, and 7.73 for WAIS-R VIQ, PIQ, and FSIQ, respectively, roughly comparable to the original NART.

Further Considerations

Support for more traditional "hold" measures such as various subtests from the WAIS-R (Information, Vocabulary, Picture Completion, and Object Assembly) is unimpressive due to these subtests being adversely affected by various types of brain injury. However, research is more encouraging regarding the use of reading of irregular words as a predictor of premorbid intellectual ability. In its various forms the NART has shown promise for premorbid intelligence estimation of WAIS/WAIS-R VIQ and FSIQ. It is a less effective predictor of PIQ. Although the NART may do an adequate job of estimating premorbid levels of language-based abilities, it is not reasonable to assume that it should predict performance on nonverbal measures. Consistent with this is the finding that the NART accounts for approximately twice the WAIS Verbal IQ variance (60%) compared to Performance IQ variance (32%; Nelson, 1982). The discrepancy for the NART-R is even greater, 69% of WAIS-R VIQ variance but only 16% for PIQ (Blair & Spreen, 1989).

Including demographic variables in NART IQ predictor regression equations significantly increases the amount of WAIS IQ score variance explained. However, this has not been the case for the NART-R. The AMNART regression equation for WAIS-R VIQ includes only the demographic variable of education. In future studies with larger samples, it may be that including additional demographic variables with the AMNART or NART-R will increase their predictive power and accuracy. The inclusion of demographic variables in AMNART or NART-R IQ regression equations should make them more resistant to the effects of neurological impairment. However, all "hold" approaches to premorbid estimation will invariably be affected by some types of brain damage. In the case of the NART, a dominant hemisphere injury resulting in even a mild alexia will negate its utility.

At this time WAIS-R regression equations (at least VIQ) are available for the NART-R and the AMNART, and only these measures are appropriate for use with patients in North America. The NART would be the instrument of choice in Britain.

Best Performance Premorbid Estimate Method

Lezak (1983) proposed "the best performance method." She suggested that the highest level of cognitive ability that a client has demonstrated in the past or currently exhibits should be the performance standard against which all others are compared. This method utilizes current test scores, behavioral observations, reports from family or friends, previous test scores, prior academic or vocational achievement, and/or other historical information, with the highest performance serving as the best estimate of premorbid cognitive status. Therefore it is a combination of the history and current performance methods discussed earlier, except for its reliance upon the best level of performance.

The best performance method will invariably predict a higher level of premorbid functioning than other methods, and more often than not it will estimate too high a level of premorbid functioning. It is easy to see why this would be true for non-brain-impaired subjects given the performance scatter identified in the WAIS-R standardization sample. As an example, this method would suggest that the highest WAIS-R subtest score and the mean score across all 11 subtests should be about the same. This is obviously rarely the case. However, given that in neurologically impaired subjects all areas of cognitive ability may be somewhat impaired from premorbid levels (Russell, 1972), it could be that the remaining highest performance would best represent premorbid ability level. This was investigated in a study by Mortensen et al. (1991). The results indicated that the best performance method leads to a gross overestimation of functioning (15 to 30 IQ points) for both neurologically normal subjects and patients with diffuse cerebral atrophy.

Premorbid Estimates Based on Demographic Variables

Demographic variables are known to be associated with level of intelligence (Fogel, 1964; Ladd, 1964; Matarazzo, 1972) and are unaffected by the onset of a brain injury. Therefore, utilizing the demographic characteristics of individual patients has been proposed as a method for estimating premorbid functioning.

Clinician-Based Demographic Tabular Approach

Reynolds, Chastain, Kaufman, and McLean (1987) provided information regarding the relationship between demographic variables (gender, race, geographic region, residence [urban or rural], education, and occupation) and WAIS-R IQ scores in the standardization sample (see Table 2.3). Differences due to gender, geographic region, and urban–rural residence are small in magnitude (ranging from 1 to 3 IQ points) and not

TABLE 2.3
Means and Standard Deviations on Verbal, Performance, and Full Scale IQs
for the WAIS-R Standardization Sample, by Demographic Variable

Variable	N	VIQ	(SD)	PIQ	(SD)	FSIQ	(SD)
Gender							
Male	940	100.9	(15.1)	100.5	(15.2)	100.9	(15.3)
Female	940	98.7	(14.7)	99.1	(15.1)	98.7	(14.9)
Race							
White	1664	101.2	(14.5)	101.3	(14.7)	101.4	(14.7)
Black	192	87.9	(13.1)	87.3	(13.7)	86.9	(13.0)
Others	24	94.2	(13.1)	96.5	(13.8)	94.0	(12.9)
Region							
Northeast	464	101.7	(14.8)	101.4	(14.9)	101.6	(15.0)
North Central	497	98.6	(14.3)	100.0	(14.4)	99.0	(14.2)
South	576	98.6	(15.7)	97.1	(16.1)	98.0	(16.3)
West	343	101.0	(14.3)	101.9	(14.2)	101.5	(14.3)
Residence							
Urban	1421	100.4	(15.0)	100.0	(15.2)	100.3	(15.2)
Rural	459	98.0	(14.4)	99.2	(15.1)	98.4	(14.8)
Education (Years)							
1 (0–7 years)	133	82.2	(13.6)	84.5	(15.0)	82.5	(14.3)
2 (8 years)	158	90.2	(11.0)	93.0	(14.4)	90.8	(12.0)
3 (9–11 years)	472	96.1	(13.8)	97.7	(14.9)	96.4	(14.2)
4 (12 years [H.S. grad.])	652	100.1	(12.1)	100.2	(13.5)	100.0	(12.5)
5 (13–15 years)	251	107.7	(10.9)	105.4	(12.0)	107.3	(11.1)
6 (16+ years [College grad.])	214	115.7	(11.6)	111.0	(12.9)	115.2	(12.2)
Occupation							
1 Professional & Technical	206	111.3	(12.8)	108.2	(13.8)	111.0	(13.4)
2 Managerial, Clerical, Sales	409	104.3	(12.3)	103.3	(13.1)	104.1	(12.6)
3 Skilled Workers	213	98.4	(11.9)	101.2	(13.6)	99.5	(12.6)
4 Semiskilled Workers	404	92.7	(13.6)	94.5	(15.3)	93.1	(14.2)
5 Unskilled Workers	68	88.9	(15.3)	90.8	(15.4)	89.1	(15.2)
6 Not in Labor Force	580	99.2	(15.5)	98.5	(15.3)	98.9	(15.6)

Note: Values have been rounded off to one decimal point. Reprinted from *Journal of School Psychology, 25*, Reynolds, Chastain, Kaufman, & McLean, Demographic characteristics and IQ among adults: Analysis of the WAIS-R standardization sample as a function of the stratification variables, 323–342, Copyright (1987), with permission from Pergamon Press Ltd, Headington Hill Hall, Oxford OX3 0BW, UK.

clinically significant. On the other hand, the effects of education, race, and occupation are substantial.

Education accounts for the most variance in WAIS-R performance: 31%, 17%, and 28% of VIQ, PIQ, and FSIQ variance, respectively (Barona et al., 1984). Race accounts for 8%, 8%, and 9% and occupation for 14%, 9%, and 13% of VIQ, PIQ, and FSIQ variance, respectively (Barona et al., 1984). However, occupation is highly correlated with education, and the absence of 31% of the standardization sample from the work force makes the occupational data less useful. Utilizing all demographic variables collectively in a multiple regression analysis accounts for only 7% to 8% more variance than education alone (Barona et al., 1984). Education is clearly the best single predictor of intelligence.

Table 2.3 could be utilized by neuropsychologists to gain a preliminary general level of expected performance for individual patients. Take, for example, John Smith, a mythical 44-year-old southern Caucasian male with a high school education who went on to develop and manage his own urban small equipment and power tool rental business. Based on his 12th-grade level of education, one might expect a baseline FSIQ of 100, add 4 points to that for his occupational attainment, and an additional 3 to 7 points based on his gender, race, and urban residence, and subtract 2 points for his southern regional location. The estimated level of FSIQ would be 105 to 109. Problems with this approach are not only the subjectivity involved but the fact that various demographic variables are correlated with each other and consequently cannot be utilized independently.

Regression Formula-Based Demographic Approaches

Demographically based regression equations eliminate the subjectivity inherent in the clinical tabular approach just described and adjust for the intercorrelations among the demographic variables. Based on the standardization samples, such regression equations have been developed for both the WAIS (Wilson, Rosenbaum, Brown, Rourke, & Whitman, 1978) and the WAIS-R (Barona et al., 1984). Table 2.4 presents these regression equations and their standard errors of estimate. Using these equations our mythical Mr. Smith's WAIS FSIQ would be estimated as 111.38, whereas his WAIS-R FSIQ would be 105.05. The 6.33 point difference between WAIS and WAIS-R predicted scores is close to the expected 8-point difference (Wechsler, 1981). In this example tabular and regression equation approaches result in similar estimated scores.

Cross-validation studies of the WAIS (Wilson et al., 1978) and WAIS-R (Barona et al., 1984) regression formulas have been mixed. At the group level, these regression equations do an adequate job of predicting mean

TABLE 2.4
Demographically Based Regression Formulas
for Estimating Wechsler IQ Scores

Estimated IQ Score	Formula
WAIS VIQ =	0.18 (age) − 2.02 (sex) − 8.99 (race) + 3.09 (educ.) + 0.97 (occup.) + 70.80
	SEE = 10.2; R^2 = .53
WAIS PIQ =	0.14 (age) − 0.66 (sex) − 12.91 (race) + 2.44 (educ.) + 0.91 (occup.) + 81.55
	SEE = 11.4; R^2 = .42
WAIS FSIQ =	0.17 (age) − 1.53 (sex) − 11.33 (race) + 2.97 (educ.) + 1.01 (occup.) + 74.05
	SEE = 10.2; R^2 = .54
Sex:	Male = 1, Female = 2
Race:	White = 1, Nonwhite = 2
Occupation:	For Wechsler's (1955, p. 7) 13 occupational categories scored: 5, 1, 7, 7, 6, 3, 3, 5, 0, 1, 4, 10, 0, respectively
WAIS-R VIQ =	54.23 + 0.49 (age) + 1.92 (sex) + 4.24 (race) + 5.25 (educ.) + 1.89 (occup.) + 1.24 (U-R resid.)
	SEE = 11.79; R^2 = .38
WAIS-R PIQ =	61.58 + 0.31 (age) + 1.09 (sex) + 4.95 (race) + 3.75 (educ.) + 1.54 (occup.) + 0.82 (region)
	SEE = 13.23; R^2 = .24
WAIS-R FSIQ =	54.96 + 0.47 (age) + 1.76 (sex) + 4.71 (race) + 5.02 (educ.) + 1.89 (occup.) + 0.59 (region)
	SEE = 12.14; R^2 = .36
Sex:	Female = 1, Male = 2
Race:	Black = 1, Other ethnicity = 2, White = 3
Educ:	0–7 years = 1, 8 = 2, 9–11 = 3, 12 = 4, 13–15 = 5, 16+ = 6
Age:	16–17 years = 1, 18–19 = 2, 20–24 = 3, 25–34 = 4, 35–44 = 5, 45–54 = 6, 55–64 = 7, 65–69 = 8, 70–74 = 9
Region:	Southern = 1, North Central = 2, Western = 3, Northeastern = 4
Residence:	Rural = 1, Urban = 2
Occupation:	Farm Laborers, Farm Foremen, & Laborers (unskilled) = 1
	Operatives, Service Workers, Farmers, & Farm Managers (semiskilled) = 2
	Not in Labor Force = 3
	Craftsmen & Foremen (skilled workers) = 4
	Managers, Officials, Proprietors, Clerical, & Sales Workers = 5
	Professional & Technical = 6

Note: SEE = Standard Error of Estimate. Formulas and Standard Errors of Estimate (*SEE*) from Wilson, Rosenbaum, Brown, Rourke, & Whitman (1978) for the WAIS and Barona, Reynolds, & Chastain (1984) for the WAIS-R.

IQ scores. However, at the individual level these equations predict IQ scores outside the actual IQ range of subjects more than half the time. As might be expected, they do best at predicting performance when actual ability falls within the Average range, whereas tending to underestimate high IQ scores and overestimate low IQ scores. The possible range of FSIQ scores for the WAIS formula ranges from about 55 to 150; however, the FSIQ range for the WAIS-R formula is much more restricted, 69 to 120.

Studies of the WAIS regression formulas using patients referred for evaluation who were judged to be either recovered head trauma cases (Bolter, Gouvier, Veneklasen, & Long, 1982; Gouvier, Bolter, Veneklasen, & Long, 1983) or pseudoneurologic (Klesges, Fisher, Vasey, & Pheley, 1985) have been disappointing. These studies reported either low correlations between obtained WAIS IQ scores and predicted scores, or marginal levels of correct classification (defined as correct if within one standard error of measurement). Summarizing across these studies, Klesges and Troster (1987) concluded that the classification power of these WAIS regression formulas was "rarely beyond chance levels" (p. 6). However, as Crawford (1989) pointed out, these studies are methodologically flawed. In particular, the utilization of clinical samples in these cross-validation attempts is problematic. At least at some point in time, subjects were seen as clinically impaired, and whether or not they had fully recovered at the time of the study is certainly debatable. In clinical samples, correlations between predicted and obtained scores should be lower than in nonclinical populations, and predicted scores would be expected to exceed obtained scores. Both were the case in these studies.

Two general approaches have been utilized to examine the predictive accuracy of WAIS/WAIS-R regression equations. One approach is to determine what proportion of predicted scores fall within one standard error of estimate (*SEE*) of the actual scores of subjects (Bolter et al., 1982; Eppinger, Craig, Adams, & Parsons, 1987; Gouvier et al., 1983). Because *SEE*s are standard deviations, predicted scores should fall outside ± one *SEE* of the actual scores only 32% of the time, regardless of the IQ level of the score. A second approach is to investigate what proportion of the predicted scores falls within the same IQ range (e.g., Borderline, Low Average, Average, High Average) as the actual scores (Sweet, Moberg, & Tovian, 1990). The second approach is clinically more meaningful but is also a more stringent criterion. Standard errors of estimate are about 10 IQ points for the WAIS and 12 points for the WAIS-R regression equations, thus allowing a possible acceptable range of 20 to 24 points. (These are huge "acceptable ranges" and may be too large to be clinically useful.) On the other hand, outside of the Average range, which does have a spread of 20 IQ points, IQ ranges consist of a spread of only 10 points.

Goldstein, Gary, and Levin (1986) investigated the accuracy of the WAIS regression equations for estimating premorbid intelligence in 69 neurologically normal adults. They reported that linear relationships did exist between predicted and actual IQ scores for all three scales, Verbal, Performance, and Full Scale. In addition, statistical analysis did not find a significant difference between predicted and actual IQ scores. However, the slopes of their three regression lines were significantly different than 1.0, indicating that some predicted scores were overestimates and others underestimates of the actual values. By examining their scatter plots of the data, it is possible to analyze the percentage of predicted scores that fell within one *SEE* or within the same IQ range as actual scores. The results of these analyses are disappointing. The Wilson et al.'s (1978) regression formulas correctly classified subjects within the obtained WAIS IQ range less than half the time: 48%, 46%, and 49% for VIQ, PIQ, and FSIQ, respectively. As would be expected, the percentages of predicted scores within one *SEE* of actual scores were higher: 66%, 66%, and 64% for VIQ, PIQ, and FSIQ, respectively.

A more recent study using 77 neurologically normal psychiatric subjects evaluated with the WAIS-R obtained similar results (Sweet et al., 1990). Eight IQ points were subtracted from the WAIS regression-predicted scores to correct for the use of the WAIS-R rather than the WAIS (see Karzmark, Heaton, Grant, & Matthews, 1985). The percentages of corrected WAIS-predicted IQ scores that fell within the same IQ range as the obtained WAIS-R scores were only 32%, 40%, and 40% for VIQ, PIQ, and FSIQ, respectively. The WAIS-R regression equations (Barona et al., 1984) were similarly ineffective in correctly classifying subjects within the obtained WAIS-R IQ range: 35%, 40%, and 39% for VIQ, PIQ, and FSIQ, respectively. In addition, the WAIS-R formulas never predicted scores outside of Low Average, Average, or High Average ranges, although both uncorrected and corrected WAIS formulas did. This is not surprising in that the possible predictive range of the WAIS-R formulas is only 69 to 120 (Barona et al., 1984). Sweet et al. (1990) concluded that "neither formula does better than a judgment of intellectual classification formed on base rates alone" (p. 43).

There have been two additional studies that reported more favorable results, one regarding the WAIS regression equations (Karzmark et al., 1985), the other for the WAIS-R (Eppinger et al., 1987). However, some of the findings in both studies were statistical anomalies; therefore, the results should be viewed with caution. Karzmark et al. (1985) reported a high 70% predictive accuracy (predicted IQ score within a generous ± 10 points of actual score) for the WAIS FSIQ regression equation in a sample of subjects with no history of neurological risk factors. In addition, they reported finding "a progressive shift from underestimation of

FSIQ at the lower levels of predicted FSIQ to overestimation at the higher levels" (p. 416). They also found predictive accuracy to be worse for scores within the Average range (67%) than for above-average scores (72% to 77%). These findings run counter to what is expected with regression analyses. Regression analyses by their very nature will regress extreme scores toward the mean, not away from the mean as was reported. In fact, as would be expected, the predicted FSIQ mean of the sample (110.9) was regressed from the actual group mean (112.8) toward the population mean of 100. In addition, with regression analyses predictive accuracy should be best within the Average range, not in the High Average to Very Superior range as found.

Eppinger et al. (1987) reported similarly high levels of predictive accuracy for the WAIS-R regression equations in a neurologically normal sample: 75%, 71%, and 69% for VIQ, PIQ, and FSIQ, respectively. In this case accuracy was defined as predicted IQ scores within one *SEE* of actual scores (± 12 to 13 IQ points). What makes the results of this study anomalous was that the regression equations accounted for more variance in this cross-validation sample than in the original Barona et al. (1984) study. Cross-validation studies almost always result in a drop in the amount of variance accounted for by the original formulas, not an increase. Thus, the sample in this study may be nonrepresentative of the population, and the favorable findings may not be generalizable.

In conclusion, by base rates always predicting an Average level of premorbid functioning would result in a correct IQ range prediction 50% of the time. The challenge is to correctly predict premorbid functioning outside of the Average range. Regression equations have not been particularly useful in this regard, as repeated studies have found (WAIS: Bolter et al., 1982; Goldstein et al., 1986; Gouvier et al., 1983; Klesges et al., 1985; WAIS and WAIS-R: Sweet et al., 1990). Although these WAIS/WAIS-R regression formulas appear to be generally reliable for groups of patients (Eppinger et al., 1987; Goldstein et al., 1986; Karzmark et al., 1985), there is no assurance that they will be accurate for individual cases. Unfortunately, it is the individual case, not the group, that faces the practicing clinical neuropsychologist. In the clinical situation, regression formulas at best provide a general range as to expected level of functioning, but they cannot be relied upon for an accurate individual-specific comparison standard.

Further Considerations

There are two primary differences between clinician-based and regression formula-based demographic premorbid estimation methods. First, clinicians rather than actuarial formulas make the estimate. The clinician-based estimation method is likely to be inherently inconsistent and influenced by subjective factors and consequently suffer from lower inter-clinician reliability simply because it is less standardized. On the other hand, the second difference, which is positive, is that clinicians can take aspects of history and interview behavior into account that equations cannot. This allows for "fine tuning" of estimation based on individual achievement and relative standing within stratified comparison groups. For example, a high school-educated individual with a 4.0 or straight A grade-point average (GPA) is likely to have higher levels of innate or premorbid functioning than a high school graduate with a 1.3 or D + GPA. Demographic-based regression equations would predict the same IQ scores in both cases.

PREMORBID ESTIMATION RECOMMENDATIONS

Estimation based on standardized test data from a multidimensional intelligence or academic aptitude test administered prior to any suspected neurological impairment is clearly the most empirically justified approach to premorbid estimation. However, even here the actual test data should be examined carefully for correct administration and scoring if at all possible. In addition, performance on such test data should be compared to all other available indicators of premorbid level of functioning to help assess its reliability. However, these data are rarely available. Failing the availability of preinjury standardized testing, current performance on the NART, AMNART, and/or NART-R can account for more variance in WAIS/WAIS-R VIQ than any other available premorbid estimation method (60% to 69%). However, dominant hemisphere dysfunction, particularly if a language disturbance results, undermines the utility of the NART. The various forms of the NART are not as effective in accounting for variance in PIQ (16% to 32%). Demographically based regression equations are currently the best predictors of PIQ, accounting for 24% or 42% of WAIS-R or WAIS PIQ variance, respectively (Barona et al., 1984; Wilson et al., 1978). Based on this information, the following algorithm to the estimation of premorbid level(s) of functioning is offered:

1. Determine if performance on previously administered standardized testing can be obtained. These scores are likely to provide the most reliable and valid premorbid estimations.

2. Calculate the WAIS or WAIS-R demographically based regression equation-estimated IQ scores (from Table 2.4). WAIS regression equations can be used if a correction is made by subtracting 7 points for VIQ and 8 points for PIQ and FSIQ from the regression-predicted scores (Karzmark

et al., 1985; Wechsler, 1981). Use of the WAIS equations allows a broad-er range of possible predicted IQ scores, accounts for more actual IQ vari-ance, and has smaller standard errors of estimate.

3. Estimate a verbal premorbid level of intelligence from a variety of current performance "hold measures," the NART-R or AMNART, as well as WAIS-R Vocabulary and Information age-adjusted subtest scaled scores. (The NART is inappropriate for American patients but would be the in-strument of choice for British subjects.) Examine these estimates for con-sistency and attempt to account for any inconsistent findings.

Estimate a nonverbal premorbid level of intelligence from current per-formance measures such as WAIS-R Picture Completion or Object Assem-bly age-adjusted subtest scores.

Examine all current performance measures (across the entire neuro-psychological test battery) for evidence of functioning at a higher level than was provided by the traditional "hold" measures. Compare all data for consistency within ability domains (e.g., verbal or nonverbal).

4. Compare estimates derived from Steps 2 and 3 (preceding) for con-cordance. Establish "windows of performance" within which the in-dividual was estimated to have functioned (verbal and nonverbal). The boundaries of these "windows of performance" can be set at 1 to 1.5 standard errors of estimate above and below the predicted scores (ap-proximately ± 10 IQ points), depending on how conservative an esti-mate range is desired.

5. Evaluate academic information for level of performance relative to peers. Consult Table 2.3 to determine "expected" level of functioning based on educational data. In addition, historical data should be examined for possible discrepancies in premorbid functioning between verbal and nonverbal abilities by comparing classroom performance in verbally oriented classes (e.g., history, literature, grammar, political science, science, etc.) with more visuospatial- or psychomotor-oriented classes (e.g., drafting, homemaking, shop, typing, etc.). Ask about innate levels of athletic ability (psychomotor speed, strength, and coordination) rela-tive to peers, whether or not they participated in organized sports. Com-pare this estimated innate athletic ability to innate verbally oriented classroom ability to determine if premorbid discrepancies in performance levels likely existed. Finally, evaluate innate levels of organization and problem-solving abilities by asking about skills in structuring and organiz-ing term papers or class projects, relative to performance on other aspects of academics.

6. Examine the occupational history and determine the highest level of occupation achieved. Ask about the patient's performance in that po-sition relative to peers in similar positions. Consult Table 2.3 to deter-mine "expected" level of functioning based on that occupational data.

7. Adjust the estimated "windows of performance" from Step 4 (up or down, as well as narrowing the window if possible) by the historically based data regarding academic and occupational performance from Steps 5 and 6.

8. Utilize these estimated "windows of performance" as the individual-specific comparison standard for performance on current intellectual and neuropsychological measures.

REFERENCES

Barona, A., Reynolds, C. R., & Chastain, R. (1984). A demographically based index of premorbid intelligence for the WAIS-R. *Journal of Consulting and Clinical Psychology, 52,* 885–887.

Black, F. W. (1974). Cognitive effects of unilateral brain lesions secondary to penetrating missile wounds. *Perceptual and Motor Skills, 38,* 387–391.

Blair, J. R., & Spreen, O. (1989). Predicting premorbid IQ: A revision of the National Adult Reading Test. *The Clinical Neuropsychologist, 3,* 129–136.

Bolter, J., Gouvier, W., Veneklasen, J., & Long, C. (1982). Using demographic information to predict IQ: A test of clinical validity with head trauma patients. *Clinical Neuropsychology, 4,* 171–174.

Brinkman, S. D., & Braun, P. (1984). Classification of dementia patients by a WAIS profile related to central cholinergic deficiencies. *Journal of Clinical Neuropsychology, 6,* 393–400.

Chatman, S. P., Reynolds, C. R., & Willson, V. L. (1984). Multiple indexes of test scatter on the Kaufman Assessment Battery for Children. *Journal of Learning Disabilities, 17,* 523–532.

Crawford, J. R. (1989). Estimation of premorbid intelligence: A review of recent developments. In J. R. Crawford & D. M. Parker (Eds.), *Developments in clinical and experimental neuropsychology* (pp. 55–74). New York: Plenum Press.

Crawford, J. R., Besson, J. A. O., Bremner, M., Ebmeier, K. P., Cochrane, R. H. B., & Kirkwood, K. (1992). Estimation of premorbid intelligence in schizophrenia. *British Journal of Psychiatry, 161,* 69–74.

Crawford, J. R., Besson, J. A. O., & Parker, D. M. (1988). Estimation of premorbid intelligence in organic conditions. *British Journal of Psychiatry, 153,* 178–181.

Crawford, J. R., Besson, J. A. O., Parker, D. M., Sutherland, K. M., & Keen, P. L. (1987). Estimation of premorbid intellectual status in depression. *British Journal of Clinical Psychology, 26,* 313–314.

Crawford, J. R., Cochrane, R. H. B., Besson, J. A. O., Parker, D. M., & Stewart, L. E. (1990). Premorbid IQ estimates obtained by combining the NART and demographic variables: Construct validity. *Personality and Individual Differences, 11,* 209–210.

Crawford, J. R., Nelson, H. E., Blackmore, L., Cochrane, R. H. B., & Allan, K. M. (1990). Estimating premorbid intelligence by combining the NART and demographic variables: An examination of the NART standardization sample and supplementary equations. *Personality and Individual Differences, 11,* 1153–1157.

Crawford, J. R., Parker, D. M., Stewart, L. E., Besson, J. A. O., & DeLacey, G. (1989). Prediction of WAIS IQ with the National Adult Reading Test: Cross-validation and extension. *British Journal of Clinical Psychology, 28,* 267–273.

Crawford, J. R., Stewart, L. E., Parker, D. M., Besson, J. A. O., & Cochrane, R. H. B. (1989). Estimation of premorbid intelligence: Combining psychometric and demographic approaches improves predictive accuracy. *Personality and Individual Differences, 10,* 793–796.

Doehring, D. G., Reitan, R. M., & Klove, H. (1961). Changes in patterns of intelligence test performance associated with homonymous visual field defects. *Journal of Nervous and Mental Disease, 132,* 227–233.

Eppinger, M. G., Craig, P. L., Adams, R. L., & Parsons, O. A. (1987). The WAIS-R index for estimating premorbid intelligence: Cross-validation and clinical utility. *Journal of Consulting and Clinical Psychology, 55,* 86–90.

Filley, C. M., Kobayashi, J., & Heaton, R. K. (1987). Wechsler Intelligence Scale profiles, the cholinergic system, and Alzheimer's disease. *Journal of Clinical and Experimental Neuropsychology, 9,* 180–186.

Fogel, M. (1964). The intelligence quotient as an index of brain damage. *American Journal of Orthopsychiatry, 34,* 555–562.

Fuld, P. A. (1984). Test profile of cholinergic dysfunction and of Alzheimer-type dementia. *Journal of Clinical Neuropsychology, 6,* 380–392.

Gardner, H. (1983). *Frames of mind: The theory of multiple intelligences.* New York: Basic Books.

Gardner, H. (1987). The assessment of intelligences: A neuropsychological perspective. In M. J. Meier, A. L. Benton, & L. Diller (Eds.), *Neuropsychological rehabilitation* (pp. 59–70). New York: Guilford Press.

Gfeller, J. D., & Rankin, E. J. (1991). The WAIS-R profile as a cognitive marker of Alzheimer's disease: A misguided venture? *Journal of Clinical and Experimental Neuropsychology, 13,* 629–636.

Goldstein, F. C., Gary, H. E., Jr., & Levin, H. S. (1986). Assessment of the accuracy of regression equations proposed for estimating premorbid intellectual functioning on the Wechsler Adult Intelligence Scale. *Journal of Clinical and Experimental Neuropsychology, 8,* 405–412.

Gouvier, W., Bolter, J., Veneklasen, J., & Long, C. (1983). Premorbid verbal and performance IQ from demographic data: Further findings with head trauma patients. *Clinical Neuropsychology, 5,* 119–121.

Grober, E., & Sliwinski, M. (1991). Development and validation of a model for estimating premorbid verbal intelligence in the elderly. *Journal of Clinical and Experimental Neuropsychology, 13,* 933–949.

Grober, E., Sliwinski, M., Schwartz, M., & Saffran, E. (1989). *The American version of the NART for predicting premorbid intelligence.* Unpublished manuscript.

Hart, S., Smith, C. M., & Swash, M. (1986). Assessing intellectual deterioration. *British Journal of Clinical Psychology, 25,* 119–124.

Heinrichs, R. W., & Celinski, M. J. (1987). Frequency of occurrence of a WAIS dementia profile in male head trauma patients. *Journal of Clinical and Experimental Neuropsychology, 9,* 187–190.

Karzmark, P., Heaton, R. K., Grant, I., & Matthews, C. G. (1985). Use of demographic variables to predict Full Scale IQ: A replication and extension. *Journal of Clinical and Experimental Neuropsychology, 7,* 412–420.

Kaufman, A. S. (1976a). A new approach to the interpretation of test scatter on the WISC-R. *Journal of Learning Disabilities, 9,* 160–168.

Kaufman, A. S. (1976b). Do normal children have flat ability profiles? *Psychology in the Schools, 13,* 284–285.

Kaufman, A. S. (1990). *Assessing adolescent and adult intelligence.* Boston: Allyn & Bacon.

Klesges, R. C., Fisher, L., Vasey, M., & Pheley, A. (1985). Predicting adult premorbid functioning levels: Another look. *International Journal of Clinical Neuropsychology, 7,* 1–3.

Klesges, R. C., & Troster, A. I. (1987). A review of premorbid indices of intellectual and neuropsychological functioning: What have we learned in the past five years? *The International Journal of Clinical Neuropsychology, 9,* 1–11.

Klesges, R. C., Wilkening, G. N., & Golden, C. J. (1981). Premorbid indices of intelligence: A review. *Clinical Neuropsychology, 3*, 32–39.

Ladd, C. (1964). WAIS performance of brain damaged and neurotic patients. *Journal of Clinical Psychology, 20*, 114–117.

Larrabee, G. J., Largen, J. W., & Levin, H. S. (1985). Sensitivity of age-decline resistant ("hold") WAIS subtests to Alzheimer's disease. *Journal of Clinical and Experimental Neuropsychology, 7*, 497–504.

Lezak, M. D. (1983). *Neuropsychological assessment* (2nd ed.). New York: Oxford University Press.

Matarazzo, J. D. (1972). *Wechsler's measurement and appraisal of adult intelligence* (5th ed., enlarged). New York: Oxford University Press.

Matarazzo, J. D., Daniel, M. H., Prifitera, A., & Herman, D. O. (1988). Inter-subtest scatter in the WAIS-R standardization sample. *Journal of Clinical Psychology, 44*, 940–950.

McFie, J. (1969). The diagnostic significance of disorders of higher nervous activity. Syndromes related to frontal, temporal, parietal, and occipital lesions. In P. J. Vinken & G. W. Bruyn (Eds.), *Handbook of clinical neurology: Vol. 4* (pp. 1–12). New York: Wiley.

McFie, J. (1975). *Assessment of organic intellectual impairment.* New York: Academic Press.

McLean, J. E., Kaufman, A. S., & Reynolds, C. R. (1989). Base rates for WAIS-R subtest scatter as a guide for clinical and neuropsychological assessment. *Journal of Clinical Psychology, 45*, 919–926.

Messick, S. (1989). Validity. In R. L. Linn (Ed.), *Educational measurement* (3rd ed., pp. 13–103). New York: Macmillan.

Mortensen, E. L., Gade, A., & Reinisch, J. M. (1991). A critical note on Lezak's "best performance method" in clinical neuropsychology. *Journal of Clinical and Experimental Neuropsychology, 13*, 361–371.

Nebes, R. D., Martin, D. C., & Horn, L. C. (1984). Sparing of semantic memory in Alzheimer's disease. *Journal of Abnormal Psychology, 93*, 321–330.

Nelson, H. E. (1982). *National Adult Reading Test (NART): Test manual.* Windsor: NFER-Nelson.

Nelson, H. E., & McKenna, P. (1975). The use of current reading ability in the assessment of dementia. *British Journal of Social and Clinical Psychology, 14*, 259–267.

Nelson, H. E., & O'Connell, A. (1978). Dementia: The estimation of premorbid intelligence levels using the new adult reading test. *Cortex, 14*, 234–244.

O'Carroll, R. E., Baikie, E. M., & Whittick, J. E. (1987). Does the National Adult Reading Test hold in dementia? *British Journal of Clinical Psychology, 26*, 315–316.

O'Carroll, R. E., & Gilleard, C. J. (1986). Estimation of premorbid intelligence in dementia. *British Journal of Clinical Psychology, 25*, 157–158.

Parker, K. C. H. (1983). Factor analysis of the WAIS-R at nine age levels between 16 and 74 years. *Journal of Consulting and Clinical Psychology, 51*, 302–308.

Reynolds, C. R., Chastain, R. L., Kaufman, A. S., & McLean, J. E. (1987). Demographic characteristics and IQ among adults: Analysis of the WAIS-R standardization sample as a function of the stratification variables. *Journal of School Psychology, 25*, 323–342.

Reynolds, C. R., & Gutkin, T. B. (1981). Test scatter on the WPPSI: Normative analyses of the WPPSI. *Journal of Learning Disability, 14*, 460–464.

Russell, E. (1972). WAIS factor analysis with brain damaged subjects using criterion measures. *Journal of Consulting and Clinical Psychology, 39*, 133–139.

Ryan, J. J., & Paolo, A. M. (1989). Frequency of occurrence of a WAIS dementia pattern in schizophrenia and bipolar affective disorder. *The Clinical Neuropsychologist, 3*, 45–48.

Satz, P., Hynd, G.W., D'Elia, L., Daniel, M. H., Van Gorp, W., & Connor, R. (1990). A WAIS-R marker for accelerated aging and dementia, Alzheimer's type?: Base rates of the Fuld formula in the WAIS-R standardization sample. *Journal of Clinical and Experimental Neuropsychology, 12*, 759–765.

Schwartz, M., & Saffran, E. (1987). *The American-Nart: Replication and extension of the British findings on the persistence of word pronunciation skills in patients with dementia.* Unpublished manuscript, Philadelphia.

Simpson, C. D., & Vega, A. (1971). Unilateral brain damage and patterns of age-corrected WAIS subtest scores. *Journal of Clinical Psychology, 27*, 204–208.

Snow, W. G., Altman, I. M., Ridgley, B. A., & Rowed, D. (1988, January). *Fuld's WAIS profile in normal pressure hydrocephalus.* Paper presented at the annual meeting of the International Neuropsychological Society, New Orleans.

Spearman, C. (1927). *The abilities of man.* London: Macmillan.

Stebbins, G. T., Gilley, D. W., Wilson, R. S., Bernard, B. A., & Fox, J. H. (1990). Effects of language disturbances on premorbid estimates of IQ in mild dementia. *The Clinical Neuropsychologist, 4*, 64–68.

Stebbins, G. T., Wilson, R. S., Gilley, D. W., Bernard, B. A., & Fox, J. H. (1990). Use of the National Adult Reading Test to estimate premorbid IQ in dementia. *The Clinical Neuropsychologist, 4*, 18–24.

Sweet, J. J., Moberg, P. J., & Tovian, S. M. (1990). Evaluation of Wechsler Adult Intelligence Scale-Revised premorbid IQ formulas in clinical populations. *Psychological Assessment, 2*, 41–44.

Swiercinsky, D. P., & Warnock, J. K. (1977). Comparison of the neuropsychological key and discriminant analysis approaches in predicting cerebral damage and localization. *Journal of Consulting and Clinical Psychology, 45*, 808–814.

Thurstone, L. L. (1938). Primary mental abilities. *Psychometric Monographs*, (1).

Wechsler, D. (1955). *Manual for the Wechsler Adult Intelligence Scale (WAIS).* New York: The Psychological Corporation.

Wechsler, D. (1958). *The measurement and appraisal of adult intelligence* (4th ed.). Baltimore: Williams & Wilkins.

Wechsler, D. (1981). *Manual for the Wechsler Adult Intelligence Scale—Revised (WAIS-R).* New York: The Psychological Corporation.

Wilson, R. S., Rosenbaum, G., Brown, G., Rourke, D., & Whitman, D. (1978). An index of premorbid intelligence. *Journal of Consulting and Clinical Psychology, 46*, 1554–1555.

Yates, A. (1956). The use of vocabulary in the measurement of intelligence deterioration: A review. *Journal of Mental Science, 102*, 409–440.

CHAPTER THREE

Principles of Neuropsychological Interpretation

Cynthia R. Cimino
University of South Florida

Interpretation of neuropsychological data is the process by which significance and meaning are derived from the information obtained during the evaluation process. In this regard, what comes to mind most readily is the interpretation of test scores obtained during assessment. Test scores in and of themselves have little meaning in isolation. However, when compared to some normative standard, test scores provide much information regarding how the individual performs relative to similarly aged peers, the extent to which that score deviates from the "norm" or average score, and the degree to which that score is likely to reflect spared or impaired abilities.

Although interpretation of test scores is a significant element of the assessment process, it is only one aspect of neuropsychological interpretation. In fact, it is not the case that interpretation occurs only after neuropsychological testing is complete. Neuropsychological interpretation represents a multistage process. This process begins with analysis of the information obtained from records, interview, and behavioral observations and continues on through the selection of test instruments, quantitative and qualitative assessment of performance, and comparisons across as well as within cognitive domains. In essence, neuropsychological interpretation is involved in the assessment enterprise from start to finish.

A very important aspect of the interpretation process involves the integration of information and data from multiple sources including history, behavioral observations, interview, and test results. Neuropsychological interpretation involves continual checks as these additional sources of information are obtained. These data sources, whether they be test scores, elements of the history, information obtained through interview of the patient or significant other, or observations of the patient's test or extra-test behaviors, are continually evaluated with respect to each other. They are reviewed and re-reviewed to adequately integrate these various sources of information, with the end result of this integration being the identification of recognizable and consistent patterns of performance. Interpretation involves much more than assigning meaning to test scores. It is the process by which all sources of information about the patient are evaluated and then integrated to form the most coherent clinical picture of that particular individual.

In approaching this topic, it is worth emphasizing the position presented by Walsh (1992) in his address to the First INS-ASSBI Pacific Rim Conference in which he states that "clinical neuropsychology is not about test data and the application of statistical rules alone but about a much underused process called thinking" (p. 132). In keeping with this spirit, this chapter is organized around several domains that are intended to influence how one "thinks" about various aspects of neuropsychological interpretation; it does not provide a cookbook or step-by-step approach to neuropsychological interpretation. These domains may serve as guides in helping to develop the kinds of thought processes that are of prime importance in neuropsychological interpretation and also may serve as a useful means of helping to avoid common errors of interpretation that arise in evaluation of neuropsychological data. These seven domains are identified in Table 3.1.

IMPORTANCE OF A CONCEPTUAL MODEL
OF BRAIN–BEHAVIOR RELATIONSHIPS

The first of these areas is a conceptual model of brain-behavior relationships. In neuropsychological assessment, this represents one of the most basic and fundamental aspects of the interpretive process yet it is all too

TABLE 3.1
Conceptualization and Interpretation

1. Importance of a Conceptual Model of Brain–Behavior Relationships
2. Influence of Subject Specific Variables
3. Determining When a Difference is a True and Meaningful Difference
4. Effects of the Interaction of Different Cognitive Domains
5. Consistency/Inconsistency Across and Within Cognitive Domains
6. Distinguishing Neurologic, Psychiatric, and Test-Taking Conditions that May Overlap
7. Avoiding Erroneous Assumptions and Inferences

often overlooked. The extent to which interpretation of data can progress in a systematic, organized, and veridical fashion is dependent on an overarching conceptual model of brain-behavior relationships. This approach provides the necessary foundation for making neuropsychological sense out of the data and is one of the key elements in minimizing or avoiding errors in interpretation. Lezak (1983) has identified four domains of knowledge essential in neuropsychological assessment (see Table 3.2). These domains form the building blocks for developing a conceptual model of brain-behavior relationships. More importantly, a conceptual model of brain-behavior relationships is built upon a working knowledge of the manner and extent to which these different domains *interact*.

Building Blocks of a Conceptual Model

Neuroanatomy

Knowledge of functional neuroanatomy is a key building block in the development of a conceptual model of brain–behavior relationships. The significance of neuroanatomy in the interpretation process is recognized to varying degrees by different schools of thought. It is often the knowledge domain that presents the greatest hurdle to students and practitioners of neuropsychology. At first glance, it is often unclear to many how neuroanatomy can have direct and significant relevance to neuropsychological assessment. However, as one continues to observe the performance of patients with varying etiologies and accumulates a repertoire of experience, it becomes apparent that this source of knowledge is key to stretching the limits of thinking about cases and the capacity to work through interpretive dilemmas that present confusing or conflicting information.

Research in neuroanatomy and neuropsychology have revealed much about the organization and behavioral significance of cortical and subcortical regions. Group as well as single-case studies in lesioned patients have provided much information about associations between anatomical structures and psychological processes. Nevertheless, the brain is not composed of discrete and isolated anatomic loci, each associated with a particular function or psychological process. Rather, the brain represents a complex and integrated network composed of many functional ana-

TABLE 3.2
Foundations of a Conceptual Model of Brain–Behavior Relationships

1. Neuroanatomy
2. Neuropathologic Conditions and Their Sequelae
3. Clinical Psychology and Psychopathology
4. Psychometric Properties and Principles

tomic systems (Luria, 1980). Within this framework, one must consider not only the presumed psychological functions associated with a particular region but also the afferent and efferent connections of that region. Geschwind's seminal paper in 1965 highlighted this emphasis on a functional systems approach. Furthermore, he suggested that deficits also may arise as a result of white matter damage resulting in disconnection of two separate anatomic regions.

An example of the extent to which a functional systems approach can influence conceptualization in neuropsychology is evident in recent work in the visual system in humans and other animals. Several investigators have identified distinct behaviors associated with two functional visual systems: one termed the superior visual route coursing from occipital lobe through parietal regions and one an inferior visual route traversing from occipital regions through temporal zones (Levin, Warach, & Farah, 1985; Mishkin, Ungerleider, & Macko, 1983; Ungerleider & Mishkin, 1982). Evidence has accumulated to suggest that damage to the superior route is likely to involve spatial aspects of visual processing. Investigators have referred to it as the "where" system. In contrast, damage to the inferior route is likely to involve aspects of object processing in the visual domain, a system investigators have referred to as the "what" system. Armed with this knowledge, one is in a better position to anticipate the kinds of processing deficits with which a patient is likely to present. Similarly, such knowledge helps to organize thinking about several seemingly distinct and varied disorders of higher order visual processing. Using this organizing framework, it is apparent that visual-processing disorders that involve some aspects of spatial processing such as optic ataxia, simultanagnosia, or other visuospatial disorders are more likely to be present when damage to the superior route is involved. On the other hand, disorders that involve object processing in the visual domain such as prosopagnosia, object agnosia, and some alexias are more likely to involve damage to the inferior route described before.

Neuropathologic Conditions and Their Sequelae

Knowledge of neuropathologic conditions and their sequelae is a fundamental base of knowledge that has particular relevance to interpretation in neuropsychological assessment. Disorders of the central nervous system may have very diverse effects on behavior and test performance; yet specific patterns of performance have been identified for different conditions. In addition, acute and/or progressive disorders will present with both focal deficits related to particular anatomic areas of dysfunction, as well as diffuse effects due to edema, disturbed biochemical homeostasis, or disruptions of vascular perfusion. For example, stroke may result in diffuse effects such as general slowing in motor and cognitive responses as well as specific effects associated with the region of damage or its associated connections (Lezak, 1983). In head-injured populations, effects of impact may influence the integrity of tissue not only at the site of impact but also in regions well beyond that of the presumed site of impact (Levin, Benton, & Grossman, 1982). Several sources are now available that provide specific case examples of various disorders highlighting distinctive features and patterns of performance (Orsini, Van Gorp, & Boone, 1988; Walsh, 1991). A working knowledge of anatomical systems and pathological processes involved in various disorders is one key element to predicting and identifying patterns of behavioral dysfunction. Similarly, knowing potential patterns of test performance associated with various disorders allows one to recognize inconsistencies as they arise.

Clinical Psychology and Psychopathology

Knowledge of clinical psychology and psychopathology is a fundamental aspect in development of a conceptual model of brain–behavior relationships. By its very nature, neuropsychology represents a multidisciplinary approach and a need to draw from various domains of knowledge. A firm base in understanding the symptoms, course, and treatment of various psychiatric disorders and the extent to which such disorders may influence test performance is important. On the other side of the coin, various neurological disorders may present with psychiatric symptoms such as alterations in mood, affect, and other psychological features that may influence performance. Severe anxiety and/or depression may influence performance on some tasks but not on others. Neuropsychological measures that emphasize aspects of attention and memory are most likely to be affected relative to tasks where these components are kept to a minimum. An awareness and knowledge of such factors that can influence task performance and the types of neuropsychological measures most susceptible to such factors can be very useful tools in neuropsychological interpretation.

Psychometric Properties and Principles

Lastly, a foundation in the domain of test theory and psychometric principles is at the very heart of test interpretation. At a concrete level, this entails appropriate usage of normative data. Several neuropsychological tests have associated with them different administration procedures; the examiner must be careful to select the appropriate set of norms based on the procedure used in testing. In a similar vein, the composition of the normative group should be comparable to the patient. This has become a very relevant issue as the segment of the population in the upper decades has continued and will continue to steadily increase, whereas available norms may not contain the growing segment of 70-, 80-, and even 90-year-old adults referred for evaluation. Age effects vary considerably across different neuropsychological tests, and it is not reasonable to assume that norms derived from a sample of 60-year-olds are applicable to 70- or 80-year-olds. A working knowledge of psychometric properties including the reliability and validity of various neuropsychological tests is also important. This information has become more readily available in several books (Benton, Hamsher, Varney, & Spreen, 1983; Franzen, 1989; Lezak, 1983; Spreen & Strauss, 1991) and journal articles published within the area of neuropsychology.

The difficulty level of neuropsychological measures is also a consideration when interpreting test performance. In testing patients where only mild difficulties in a particular cognitive domain are anticipated, a range of performance in the standardization sample is desirable. Depending on the patient's estimated level of ability, one test may result in normal performance only because the difficulty level of the task was too easy. For example, naming performance on the Western Aphasia Battery (Kertesz, 1982) may not reveal deficits in naming ability, whereas performance on a more difficult measure with greater variability in the performance of the normative sample such as the Boston Naming Test (Kaplan, Goodglass, & Weintraub, 1978) may well be able to detect such mild deficits. If evaluation of naming ability was restricted to data from the Western Aphasia Battery, one might erroneously conclude that naming abilities were intact when, in fact, mild naming deficits are present.

Developing a conceptual model of brain–behavior relationships involves the capacity to integrate information from several knowledge domains. Such integration is not achieved over a short time span, and it is something that certainly requires a significant degree of persistence and effort. As new findings are revealed and information is acquired, this model will grow and change with the experiences of the individual. With the development of training guidelines for neuropsychology recommended by the INS-Division 40 Task Force on Education, Accreditation, and Credentialing (1987), it is apparent that the importance of a conceptual model of brain–behavior relationships in neuropsychology has become more widely recognized. Neuropsychology represents a unique domain within psychology that calls upon a truly multidisciplinary approach to the process of assessment.

Utility of a Conceptual Model

A more fundamental question that arises when considering a conceptual model of brain–behavior relationships is: "In what practical way is having a conceptual knowledge of brain–behavior relationships important?";

that is, in concrete terms, how can it serve as a useful guide to neuropsychological interpretation? Some of these issues have already been addressed to some extent by the material presented earlier, but this is an issue that warrants additional attention. Table 3.3 identifies six potential ways in which such knowledge can facilitate the interpretive process and help avoid errors in interpretation. Each of these are considered in turn.

Expectations of Performance

Having a conceptual model of brain–behavior relationships allows the examiner to set some reasonable expectation of the level of performance. It sets a window of expectation within which one can continually compare history, test performance, and other observations. For example, in head-injured populations knowledge of the relationships between length of coma, post-traumatic amnesia, and other variables allows one to set some reasonable expectation of performance based on prior research in the area and allows a determination of the extent to which the patient's observed performance matches the expected level of performance (Levin et al., 1982). If emergency medical records indicate that the patient suffered no loss of consciousness and no discernible evidence of post-traumatic amnesia, yet memory performance is falling 3 standard deviations below the mean, this represents a very discrepant picture from what is known about such relationships and should alert the examiner to consider other potential causes for such test performance.

Anticipate Deficits

A conceptual model provides the examiner with the capacity to anticipate deficits associated with various neurobehavioral disorders or known anatomic lesions. At the very start, it allows the examiner to anticipate deficits and generate hypotheses about potential test performance. For some clinicians, it may serve as a means of guiding the assessment and selection of test instruments. If there is some information available on the patient's history, presentation, and presumed diagnosis, one can develop predictions of specific test performance that can be tested in the

TABLE 3.3
Utility of a Conceptual Model of Brain–Behavior Relationships

1. Sets Some Reasonable Expectation of Performance
2. Anticipate Deficits Associated with Neurobehavioral Disorder
3. Recognition of Performance that Is Inconsistent with a Neurobehavioral Disorder
4. Recognition of Neighborhood Signs
5. Recognition of Low Base-Rate Conditions
6. Aids Qualitative Interpretations of Test Performance

evaluation process and interpreted. This is perhaps one of the most useful aspects for individuals who are in the beginning stages of conducting neuropsychological assessment. When approaching the assessment, it is always useful to have a frame of reference from which to proceed. Knowing which functions are likely to be involved and in need of more thorough evaluation and coming to the evaluation prepared with such knowledge is an excellent point of departure.

Recognition of Inconsistent Performance

In addition to anticipating potential deficits, a conceptual model of brain–behavior relationships aids the examiner in recognizing performance that is inconsistent with a neurobehavioral disorder. If one is well acquainted with the prototypic features associated with a particular disorder, then one is in a very good position to recognize when aspects of performance are inconsistent with that disorder. For example, knowledge that Alzheimer's disease affects predominantly association and not primary motor and sensory cortices until more advanced stages of the disease might lead the examiner to question a presumed diagnosis of primary degenerative dementia of the Alzheimer's type in a patient who demonstrates asymmetries in performance on motor tasks. Involvement of primary motor systems is not a typical feature in the early stages of Alzheimer's disease (Cummings & Benson, 1992), and it is the examiner's task to determine the extent to which this finding of asymmetric performance on motor tasks makes sense in the overall clinical context. It is possible that such deficits could represent merely the results of an old peripheral injury. In contrast, these deficits may, in fact, represent the residua of motor deficits following some cerebral insult. In either case, it behooves the examiner to recognize findings that may be inconsistent with a presumed diagnosis and to attempt to integrate these findings into a more coherent conceptualization of the patient.

Recognition of Neighborhood Signs

Weintraub and Mesulam (1985) suggested that recognition of neighborhood signs may be a useful means of localizing a lesion within a particular anatomic network. Recognition of neighborhood signs, however, is dependent upon a working knowledge of brain–behavior relationships. The example they provide assesses the utility of neighborhood signs in the neglect syndrome. Disorders like neglect can be caused by damage in many different cortical and subcortical regions, and these interconnected regions together form an anatomic network of attention (Heilman, Watson, & Valenstein, 1985; Mesulam, 1985). At the outset, knowledge of such a functional system would alert the examiner to the potential for occurrence of inattention to stimuli on one side of space. In addition, consideration of the occurrence of neighborhood signs such as a visual field loss or motor signs would help localize the lesion within this system. If the lesion is cortically based, presence of visual field loss would likely place the extent of the lesion more posterior, whereas the presence of motor signs would place the lesion more anterior. Recognition of neighborhood signs would, in effect, allow the examiner to make inferences about where in this functional system damage is likely to have occurred. Furthermore, it may help one hypothesize what additional cognitive processes associated with this system or interacting systems are likely to be impaired.

Recognition of Low Base-Rate Conditions

Knowledge of brain–behavior relationships may allow consideration of a low base-rate diagnosis in a patient when a higher base-rate diagnosis has been proposed. Often in inpatient or even outpatient settings, the examiner is provided with some diagnostic information on the patient in the form of medical history, neurological exam, or even prior neuropsychological testing. Although it is helpful to use this information as a working hypothesis when approaching the assessment and interpretation of neuropsychological data, it is important that the examiner not remain completely wedded to the presumed diagnosis at the exclusion of paying close attention to what the neuropsychological data are revealing. The following case illustrates this point.

A 56-year-old woman presented with profound memory disturbance and mild-to-moderate "frontal" or executive/self-regulatory difficulties. Nevertheless, she was average to above average in all other domains of function including attention, language, visuoconstructional, visuospatial, and visuoperceptual abilities. Although she did not meet formal criteria, the working hypothesis was that this patient was perhaps in the very early stages of a primary degenerative dementia. It is not unusual for such patients to present initially and for some extended period of time with predominantly memory deficits. However, it is also possible that other low probability events could account for her problems. Based on her test findings and knowledge that some memory structures such as the dorsal medial nucleus of the thalamus (Butters & Stuss, 1989; Squire, 1987) have significant projections to the frontal lobe (Alexander & Fuster, 1973) allowed us to entertain the possibility of an alternate although low base-rate condition. The patient demonstrated a profound memory disturbance within the context of only mild executive/self-regulatory difficulties. Given this pattern of performance, it was likely that her performance was most consistent with an amnestic syndrome presenting with executive/

self-regulatory deficits. Damage to medial thalamic nuclei such as the dorsal medial nucleus of the thalamus can result in a profound amnestic disturbance as well as executive/self-regulatory difficulties due to strong projections from this nucleus to prefrontal cortex (Butters & Stuss, 1989; Graff-Radford, Damasio, Yamada, Eslinger, & Damasio, 1985; Speedie & Heilman, 1982, 1983; Squire & Moore, 1979). The patient was given an MRI and bilateral medial thalamic lesions were found. No motor or sensory symptoms were demonstrated because of the location of the lesion, so there were no apparent tip-offs that this was a vascular event. In addition, there was no report from family members to give a historical account of whether memory changes were evident in an acute fashion or were progressive over time. Given this woman's age and general clinical presentation, a likely or high base-rate disorder would have been a progressive degenerative dementia. Nevertheless, the patient did not present with any semblance of language disorder (not even mild naming problems) or visuoconstructional deficits that are more typical in an Alzheimer's picture. In this case, the inferential process was guided by the data and not by the likely probability of a diagnosis that had been previously considered.

This case is useful in illustrating how knowledge of neuroanatomy can have some very significant and powerful practical implications. In this particular case, it allowed for the recognition of neuropsychological data that were not necessarily inconsistent with the initial presumed diagnosis but not the most consistent. In addition, it widened the range of possibilities that could be entertained to account for the pattern of test findings. Lastly, the conceptualization of the case had some very practical implications for the patient and her family. The progressive course of a patient with a presumed degenerative dementia compared to that of a patient with medial thalamic lesions where the deficits may potentially improve and then stabilize had very different implications for the patient and her family's lives. In this regard, the courses of the two disorders would have significantly different impacts on the patient and her family and would have resulted in very different kinds of interventions.

Aids Qualitative Interpretations of Neuropsychological Data

Lastly, a conceptual knowledge of brain-behavior relationships assists qualitative interpretations of test performance. Edith Kaplan (1983, 1989) has been the pioneer in qualitative aspects of neuropsychological test interpretation. She has emphasized that knowledge of brain-behavior relationships is an essential component of anticipating deficits, making inferences about the nature of a patient's approach to a task, and analyzing error types. That a patient fails a particular item or task is no more important than *how* that patient fails the item or task. Neuropsychological interpretation should consider not only the quantitative aspects of the patient's performance but also the qualitative aspects of the patient's performance. Different approaches to neuropsychological assessment have traditionally been classified along the continuum of quantitative versus qualitative approaches. Today, it is fair to say that those who engage in neuropsychological assessment with any regularity are likely to consider, at least at some level, both aspects of task performance. A strong conceptual knowledge of brain-behavior relationships is a key element in the richness, complexity, and accuracy of qualitative interpretations. Qualitative analysis of test performance also may help to discern the extent to which motivation and effort are evident in the patient's performance. So at the most fundamental level, such an analysis helps to make determinations about the validity of neuropsychological data.

At a more complex level, process analysis involves close attention to the manner in which the patient attempts and/or completes test items. For example, does the patient's approach to drawing a figure or cancelling lines proceed in a typical left-to-right fashion, or does the patient proceed with most tasks in a less typical right-to-left fashion? Similarly, Kaplan and others (Goodglass & Kaplan, 1979; Kaplan, 1989; Milberg, Hebben, & Kaplan, 1986) have delineated some aspects of performance on the Block Design subtest that may be useful in discerning the potential anatomic basis of qualitative differences in performance. For example, these authors emphasized the relative importance of whether the overall configuration of the design is preserved in the patient's block construction. They indicated that a violation of the two-by-two or three-by-three configuration on items is more likely to occur following right-hemisphere damage, whereas an error of internal detail with a relative preservation of the overall configuration of the item is more likely to be observed following left-hemisphere damage. These and other types of qualitative observations of performance may serve as useful means of identifying common strategies used across various tasks, identifying involvement of anatomic systems, and as a means of identifying potential strengths and weaknesses that can be used to guide rehabilitative and/or compensatory strategies.

INFLUENCE OF SUBJECT-SPECIFIC VARIABLES

When interpreting neuropsychological data, it is important to consider some subject-specific variables that may influence performance. A listing of some of the more common subject factors that are likely to influence performance are depicted in Table 3.4. These can, for heuristic

TABLE 3.4
Influence of Subject-Specific Factors

Demographic/Historic Factors
- Age
- Sex
- Handedness
- Education (LD)
- Occupation
- Socioeconomic Status
- Premorbid Cognitive/Intellectual Abilities
- Native Language/Culture
- Medical History

State Factors
- Poor attention
- Fatigue
- Poor motivation
- Secondary gain
- Malingering

Psychiatric/Psychological/Personality Factors
- Depression
- Anxiety
- Psychosis
- Alcohol/Drug Abuse
- Antisocial Disorder
- Somatization Disorder

purposes, be divided into demographic/historic factors, state factors, and psychiatric/psychological/personality factors.

Demographic/Historic Factors

Age, gender, and education are factors particularly relevant to procedures that use standard cutoff scores such as some of the Halstead–Reitan Battery tests. Although the use of an absolute standard cutoff score is still a common practice in clinical neuropsychology, the validity of this approach is questionable. Various abilities and associated neuropsychological measures are influenced to greater and lesser degrees by the effects of age (Heaton, Grant, & Matthews, 1986; Leckliter & Matarazzo, 1989). Using a single cutoff score that does not take into account the marked changes in performance associated with age can result in significant errors of interpretation. Recently, several authors have provided new normative data that adjusts for the influence of subject-specific variables such as age, education, and/or gender on such tasks (Heaton, Grant, & Matthews, 1991; Russell & Starkey, 1993).

The influence of age on test performance underscores the importance of using age-corrected scaled scores on the Wechsler Adult Intelligence Scale-Revised (WAIS-R; Wechsler, 1981) when making subtest comparisons. This point is often overlooked when making statements about the pattern of performance across various subtests and the possible interpretive implications for other neuropsychological data. When making comparisons of this type, age-corrected scaled scores must be used. For example, significant age effects are readily apparent on subtests such as Digit Symbol. If regular scaled scores are used, these scaled scores are derived from the 25- to 34-year-old reference group. If the patient is 60 years old, then the patient's regular scaled score would represent his or her performance relative to that of 25- to 34-year-olds. Using this as the comparative standard, one might erroneously interpret the patient's performance as impaired. For purposes of assessment, the most appropriate comparison is that of similarly aged peers. In this case, the examiner must calculate the patient's age-corrected scaled score that utilizes the appropriate comparison to individuals aged 55 to 64 years of age.

Handedness is another factor to consider in neuropsychological interpretation. The most common method of determining handedness is to ask the patient their preferred hand for writing. However, on further inquiry it is often the case, particularly with left-handed individuals and often with some right-handed individuals, that there are some activities for which they have a contralateral preference. Additional questioning of hand preferences or the use of a formal handedness inventory may be useful in more clearly defining the nature and extent of hand preference (Annett, 1967; Briggs & Nebes, 1975). One obvious domain that this factor will influence is interpretation of data from motor tasks. The typical right-hand superiority on tasks such as tapping and grip strength will be reversed for those left-hand-dominant individuals. Another domain for which handedness can influence the interpretation of neuropsychological data is that of language processing. Whereas the majority of left handers are left-hemisphere dominant for language, this is not the case for a subgroup of these individuals (Branch, Milner, & Rasmussen, 1964). Attention to this fact may help clarify results that do not conform to the typical pattern of test findings.

Factors such as educational level and the presence or absence of a learning disability are important to consider. Several neuropsychological measures are highly correlated with education. Whereas many neuropsychological measures provide normative comparisons for different age ranges, the availability of normative data for various educational levels often is lacking. The examiner should be acquainted with new sources of normative data as they become available and pay close attention to those tasks that may be particularly sensitive to education effects. Information from the interview about educational history, potential difficulty with subject material, or presence of a learning disability can be invaluable in accounting for neuropsychological performance. Also, this information can be an important component in avoiding potential errors of interpretation by avoiding the erroneous assumption that the behavior was initially within normal limits.

Various occupations can result in uneven performance across tasks that may be accounted for by a special, developed ability. A more difficult determination may involve the interpretation of average or even low-average abilities in an individual of superior talent in a particular domain. This may present one of the most difficult interpretive scenarios but again must be approached in a systematic fashion by considering information from history, interview, test results, and observation. Socioeconomic status in combination with many of the factors listed in Table 3.4 such as education and occupation may be useful in providing estimates of premorbid abilities that are critical to the interpretive process. This is discussed in greater detail in chapter 2.

Lezak (1988) suggested that aggregate measures of behavior such as IQ scores fail to provide the specific type of information necessary to characterize the neuropsychological status of a patient. She emphasized that summary scores, such as the IQ, may provide misleading summaries of disparate abilities that do not fully capture the various spared and impaired abilities of the patient. This is a valid criticism of the use of IQ scores in general in the practice of neuropsychology. However, global estimates of the cognitive/intellectual ability of an individual may have some utility in comparing premorbid to current performance, particularly when those levels fall at the extremes. For example, an individual whose premorbid Full Scale IQ score was estimated to be 85 is predicted to perform quite differently on neuropsychological measures than an individual whose Full Scale IQ score was estimated to be 145. We can use this information to construct a window within which performance on neuropsychological measures is likely to fall. We know that many individuals whose estimated intelligence falls well below average usually perform well below average or in impaired ranges on neuropsychological measures (Lezak, 1983). Again, having information about global estimates of cognitive ability can be useful in some instances, especially when those estimates tend to fall at the extreme ends of the continuum.

Factors such as native language and culture may alert the examiner to the need to consider alternative interpretations of neuropsychological data. The patient's fluency in English, relative ease of communication, and years of experience within a culture are important factors that should be taken into account. Obviously, native language and culture should be considered at the outset during interview and administration of neuro-psychological measures. However, these factors become an important part of the interpretation of the data as well. Native language and culture may significantly influence performance on measures that place significant demands on language processing or familiarity with items specific to a culture.

A careful consideration of medical history is of prime importance in the process of interpreting neuropsychological data. A variety of systemic diseases can have significant and even profound effects on neuropsychological functioning and must be carefully considered in the interpretive process. In addition, certain systemic disorders such as heart disease are strongly associated with cerebral vascular disease and may result in cognitive impairment (Barclay, Weiss, Mattis, Bond, & Blass, 1988; Todnem & Vik-Mo, 1986). Other medical disorders such as poorly controlled diabetes, endocrine disorders, metabolic disorders, and liver or kidney disease are just a few of the diseases that can result in diffuse effects on cerebral function (Tarter, Van Thiel, & Edwards, 1988). A careful consideration of medical history may help to make better sense out of asymmetric performance on motor tasks that is due to peripheral damage to the limb itself rather than erroneously attributing it to central involvement.

Lastly, medication effects cannot be overlooked and must be carefully considered. Many prescription medications can have adverse effects on neuropsychological function. These effects are often most noticeable on tasks that require sustained attention and concentration and on measures of memory function. Medication containing anticholinergic agents may have significant effects in these domains (Drachman & Leavitt, 1974). One population that is particularly sensitive to these effects are the elderly, making diagnostic determinations in this group more difficult. Consideration of the types of medication and the potential influence on cognitive function is important to keep in mind when interpreting neuropsychological data.

State Factors

Of all subject-specific factors, state factors are perhaps some of the most important factors in determining whether the information obtained is valid and interpretable. Unless it is clear that a patient is able and/or willing to maintain some acceptable level of motivation and effort, the information garnered from neuropsychological evaluation may be questionable at best. Performance that is characterized by lack of motivation and effort may render neuropsychological data uninterpretable; nevertheless, these observations in and of themselves may provide valuable information about the qualitative aspects of the patient's perform-ance. These factors may be of particular importance when dealing with issues of potential feigned performance, secondary gain, or malingering.

State factors such as excessive fatigue and poor attention may signifi-cantly influence performance on neuropsychological measures. Unlike those mentioned previously, fatigue and attentional influences may not necessarily render neuropsychological data invalid or uninterpretable, but such factors will decidedly influence the interpretation of performance on neuropsychological measures. Assuming that the patient is demon-strating adequate motivation and effort, performance that is impaired due to marked attentional deficits or undue fatigue may be valid to the ex-tent that such performance represents the functional level at which that patient is capable of performing. The nature of these influences on neu-ropsychological interpretation is addressed to a greater extent in subse-quent sections.

Psychiatric/Psychological/Personality Factors

Psychiatric, psychological, and personality factors are important domains to consider in interpreting neuropsychological data. Personality and other psychiatric disturbance may present with alterations in many of the state factors noted earlier such as attention, concentration, motivation, and effort that can significantly influence performance. In fact, many of these symptoms are listed as criterion for diagnosis in various disorders with-in the *Diagnostic and Statistical Manual of Mental Disorders* (3rd ed., rev.) (*DSMIII-R*; American Psychiatric Association, 1987). Psychotic dis-turbance may manifest itself in deficits in attention, concentration, bi-zarre thinking, and use of language. Similarly, anxiety and affective disorders may significantly influence domains of attention and memory and the pattern of performance within those domains must be carefully assessed to derive an accurate interpretation. The problem of affective disturbance in the elderly presents a particular problem for interpreta-tion of neuropsychological data. These and other issues are addressed in greater detail in the section that deals with distinguishing neurologic, psychiatric, and test-taking conditions that may overlap.

DETERMINING WHEN A DIFFERENCE IS A TRUE AND MEANINGFUL DIFFERENCE

In determining when test scores reflect a true and meaningful difference, three types of determinations can be made. These include single score, multiple score, and change in performance determinations. Single-score determinations ask the question, "Is a single score significantly different from normal?'' Multiple-score determinations ask the question, ''Are two scores significantly different from each other?'' Change in performance determinations ask the question, ''Has the score on a particular neuropsychological measure changed over time?''

Single-Score Determinations

When asking the question whether a single score on a neuropsychological measure differs from ''normal,'' it must be determined whether normal represents average performance as defined by population-specific norms or whether normal represents what is expected performance for any given individual. For individuals of extremely high premorbid abilities, average performance as defined by population-specific norms may not be what is expected performance for that individual. Performance that is within the low average or even average range may represent performance within ''normal'' limits for most individuals, yet, for someone of extremely high premorbid abilities, that may not represent normal performance and certainly not what is expected performance. Such cases require special consideration when interpreting test scores.

It is usually the case, however, that for most individuals single-score determinations can be made with respect to average performance as defined by population-specific norms. Nevertheless, some judgment may be required in determining when a particular score falls outside the normal range. Although normative data may be provided, on some neuropsychological measures there is not a clear, explicit indication of how far from the average of the normative sample a score must be to be considered a significant deviation from the norm and reflect a neuropsychological impairment. As a general rule of thumb, a score that falls 2 standard deviations from the average for the appropriate comparison group very likely reflects an impaired score on that test (assuming premorbid performance was within normal limits). However, scores that fall between 1 and 2 standard deviations below the average, and, in particular, those that fall between 1½ and 2 standard deviations below the average (borderline range), may require more careful consideration in interpretation. Foremost among these considerations is the estimated premorbid level of the patient.

Another approach to single-score determinations is the use of standard cutoff scores. Cutoff scores compare an individual's performance against some previously determined cutoff for that test usually without regard to factors such as age or education. In contrast, population-specific norms provide norms for different age and sometimes education groups using a standard deviation criterion for impairment. In one study of tests using standard cutoff scores, the percentage of test scores for normal subjects falling into the impaired range was 15% to 80% for different tests of the Halstead–Reitan Battery (Bornstein, 1986). These findings underscore the importance of utilizing either correction factors or population-specific norms that take into account age and education.

The influence of factors such as age and education on neuropsychological measures is becoming more widely recognized, and the use of population-specific norms or adjustments for such factors is highly recommended. Population-specific norms are an improvement over standard cutoff scores. Nevertheless, it is still the case that many neuropsychological measures have norms available for different age groups yet do not account for other important variables such as education or gender.

Multiple-Score Determinations

When making multiple-score determinations there is the problem of a lack of a common metric across tasks. Lezak (1983) has suggested the use of standard score conversions. The application of z or T score conversions may be beneficial in determining the extent to which a patient's scores on distinct measures deviate from the average performance level. Although this may be one of the best available solutions to this dilemma, the amount of intertest differences may vary secondary to difficulty level of test instruments rather than neuropsychological competence. In addition, samples from which normative data are derived differ in their composition. With the preceding caveats in mind, converting multiple scores to a common metric allows for an examination of which scores fall into the normal range and which fall outside of the normal range of function. In this way, the examiner is able to discern a pattern of spared and impaired functions. This type of profile analysis is a common approach to the interpretation of neuropsychological data.

Another approach (Kaufman, 1990) to determining differences between scores is reflected in procedures used with the Wechsler Adult Intelligence Scale-Revised (WAIS-R; Wechsler, 1981). In this approach, test scores may be significantly different from each other in two distinct ways. The difference between two scores may be significant at a statistical level; that is, the difference between scores may be a true and reliable difference rather than representing merely a difference in fluctuations in error of measurement on the two tests. Secondly, the difference between scores may be significant or meaningful to the extent that such a difference occurs relatively infrequently in the population. The first represents determination of a significant statistical difference between the two scores, and the second represents determination of a meaningful difference between the two scores (a difference that occurs infrequently in the population). Obviously, for two scores to be meaningfully different they must also be significantly different from each other at a statistical level.

Some information on these differences is available for measures of Verbal IQ (VIQ) and Performance IQ (PIQ) differences on the WAIS-R and can be used for illustrative purposes. A difference of 12 points between VIQ and PIQ is considered to be statistically significant; yet, this difference occurs in approximately 28% of the normal population, a relatively frequent occurrence (Matarazzo & Herman, 1985). Therefore, whereas this difference may represent a statistically significant difference, it may not represent a clinically significant difference.

Furthermore, VIQ–PIQ differences vary considerably with respect to overall level of IQ, and this must be carefully considered when interpreting such differences (Matarazzo & Herman, 1985). As IQ increases one is more likely to find a larger VIQ–PIQ difference. For example, a difference of 12 points between VIQ and PIQ occurs in approximately 9.1% of individuals with IQs of 79 or below. Yet, this same difference of 12 points between VIQ and PIQ occurs for nearly 37.9% of individuals with IQs of 120 and above. This finding underscores the relative importance of considering level of IQ when making interpretations of VIQ–PIQ differences. Kaufman (1990) has constructed useful tables from Matarazzo and Herman (1985) that can aid in this process.

Unfortunately, comparable data for the majority of neuropsychological measures is not available. The Wechsler Memory Scale-Revised (WMS-R; Wechsler, 1987) does provide information on the amount necessary for a difference between various memory indices to be considered statistically significant. However, there is no information on the extent to which such differences are observed in the normative sample.

Change in Score Determinations

When assessing recovery, the question becomes when is a change a true change from the original score obtained on a particular measure; that is, when does a change represent practice effects versus true recovery. Most neuropsychological measures do not contain estimates of anticipated gains in scores associated with practice effects making such inferences difficult. In addition, some measures are more prone to the effects of practice than others. There is some information available on the influence of practice effects on the WAIS-R that can be of potential usefulness. Kaufman (1990) has constructed a helpful table from data of Matarazzo and Herman (1984) that provides information on degree of unusualness associated with particular gains and losses in VIQ, PIQ, and Full Scale IQ (FSIQ). In this regard, it is noteworthy that practice effects and subsequent gains in PIQ are substantially larger than gains in VIQ. A gain of 15 points in FSIQ was a relatively infrequent occurrence observed in only 5% of subjects. In this particular circumstance, the examiner is better able to conclude that such a gain is likely to represent a change from initial testing or recovery. In this same sample, a gain of 12 points in VIQ was observed in only 5% of subjects. However, a gain of 23 points in PIQ was needed to correspond to the same infrequent occurrence of 5% in this same sample of subjects. These findings emphasize the relative importance of taking into account different influences of practice in changes on VIQ and PIQ measures. These data may be of use when determining whether gains on these various scales represent meaningful gains in intellectual functioning over time.

In addition to potential gains in function, in certain cases it may be important to determine when the patient's performance represents a worsening in function. As a general rule of thumb, losses in IQ points at a second test administration are infrequent. Based on Matarazzo and Herman's data, a loss of 5 points on VIQ, PIQ, or FSIQ at second test administration was a relatively unusual occurrence demonstrated in only 5% of their sample. When losses in these measures are observed on second test administration, this should alert the examiner to the possibility of worsening of function. Kaufman (1990) provided tables based on Matarazzo and Herman's data that list the observed frequency of losses in the various IQ measures from initial test to retest.

Unfortunately, specific information on anticipated gains on repeat administrations of neuropsychological measures is lacking. Such data would provide valuable information in determining the extent to which significant improvement or deterioration is present. This may have important implications in treatment settings for determining whether recovery has taken place. In addition, this information is likely to have implications in forensic determinations.

EFFECTS OF THE INTERACTION
OF DIFFERENT COGNITIVE DOMAINS

The law of parsimony and Occam's razor are as apt for inferences about clinical neuropsychological data as they are for inferences about research data. Therefore, it is important to try to identify the most elementary disturbance that can account for failure on a complex task. When reviewing neuropsychological data, it is important to keep in mind that deficits across tasks that appear to be quite different in nature could possibly be attributed to a single underlying difficulty. In evaluating performance on any task, it is important to consider the extent to which performance on that task represents the influence of other cognitive domains. Most neuropsychological measures cannot be considered "pure" measures in the sense that only a single ability is measured. When interpreting performance on a particular neuropsychological test, it is important to keep in mind the component features of that task and the abilities necessary to complete it. On a typical task of naming ability, a patient is shown a picture of an object and asked to name it. What are some of the abilities required in completion of this task? At the most fundamental level, the patient must have an adequate degree of arousal and attention to comply with the task demands. The patient must be able to comprehend task instructions. The patient also will need to be able to adequately perceive the stimulus material, so primary visual processing must be intact. At a more complex level of visuoperceptual processing, the patient must be able to recognize the specific object. In addition, the patient must be capable of searching and retrieving the correct name for the item from their lexicon. Lastly, the patient must be able to adequately output the response in the form of a verbal utterance. Based on this example, it can be seen that when interpreting the results of neuropsychological measures the examiner must remain ever vigilant to the complex nature of tests. There are at least three important points to keep in mind when determining whether the basis for impaired performance on a task is due to the interaction of different cognitive domains. These points are identified in Table 3.5.

Diffuse Versus Specific Effects

General cognitive slowing is an example of one diffuse effect of a brain injury that can influence task performance. Response slowing often accompanies brain damage, and its effects on test performance must be evaluated separately from the actual loss of information-processing abilities in any specific cognitive domain. Lezak (1983) emphasized the importance of determining whether the patient fails an item because the patient is unable to provide the correct response or able to provide the correct response but only beyond the specified time limits. On the WAIS-R Block Design subtest, for example, both types of responses would constitute a failure on the standard administration of the subtest. Nevertheless, the types of inferences that one can make about the patient's visuoconstructional abilities may be markedly different. Several authors

TABLE 3.5
Effects of the Interaction of Different Cognitive Domains

1. Diffuse versus Specific Effects
2. Influence of Lower Order Abilities on Higher Order Abilities
3. Primary versus Secondary Effects

have suggested that when using the WAIS-R a timed as well as an untimed PIQ should be derived in an attempt to separate the effects of a specific deficit on performance and the effects of general slowing on performance. The inferences that can be derived from performance of a patient who is unable to achieve even a partially correct solution given ample time and the performance of a patient who is capable of producing correct reproductions on the Block Design subtest but only beyond the time limit specified are quite different. In the first case, we might infer that the patient's visuoconstructional abilities as assessed by Block Design are disrupted due to the patient's inability to approximate the correct response even when imposed time limits are minimized. In the second case, we might infer that the patient's visuoconstructional abilities as assessed by the Block Design subtest appear to be available to the patient but likely influenced by significant slowing of responses. More recently, Kaplan, Fein, Morris, and Delis (1991) have devised a modified version of the WAIS-R called the WAIS-R as a Neuropsychological Instrument (WAIS-R NI). The manual and accompanying materials allow for modifications in test procedures similar to the example just given. They also suggest other modifications that create opportunities for observing aspects of task performance not available with standard administration.

Lower Order Versus Higher Order Deficits

The ability to perform higher order, complex cognitive tasks is based on the integrity of more basic functions. At the very least, the patient must possess an adequate level of arousal to sustain their performance on any given task. Fluctuating levels of arousal and/or marked waxing and waning of attention when the patient is performing a complex cognitive task, such as constructing a copy of the Rey–Osterrieth Figure (Osterrieth, 1944; Rey, 1941), would make it erroneous to infer that a patient's poor performance reflects a marked visuoconstructional disorder. In this case, it is the inadequate levels of arousal and attention that have incapacitated the patient's performance. Interpreting performance on higher order tasks in patients with significant difficulties in arousal and attention must proceed with caution. In patients with extreme difficulties, interpretation is particularly problematic. In these cases, poor performance on higher order tasks may not be interpretable in terms of the usual interpretation for such tasks. For example, on a task of simple arithmetic word problems, patients may fail not because of deficits in arithmetic abilities but because they are unable to adequately attend to the items and retain them in memory long enough to complete the task. Although it is correct to conclude that performance on the arithmetic task was impaired, this performance should not be interpreted in terms of poor arithmetic abilities but in terms of the influence of a lower order ability such as attention that has resulted in poor performance on a higher order task, the arithmetic task.

Several tasks of writing ability involve the presentation of a standard picture to the patient. The patient's task is to write what he or she sees going on in the picture. In administering such tasks, the primary interest is in obtaining writing samples from the patient under standard conditions. However, if patients have a basic defect in visual scanning and produce an impoverished output or an incomplete description because they are unable to appreciate or incorporate various aspects of the picture into a complete whole, performance could be erroneously interpreted as impoverished written language, when, in fact, performance was due to difficulties in adequately scanning the picture at the outset. In a similar vein, difficulties associated with hemispatial neglect in which patients may fail to orient, report, or respond to stimuli contralateral to their lesion could potentially influence performance on a seemingly disparate higher order ability such as receptive vocabulary. Some tasks that assess receptive vocabulary such as the Peabody Picture Vocabulary Test-Revised (PPVT-R; Dunn & Dunn, 1981) utilize a pictorial multiple-choice format in which the patient must point to the item that correctly portrays a word presented to them. A patient with left-sided neglect following a right-hemisphere lesion may fail to orient to response alternatives presented on the left side of space (Heilman et al., 1985). In assessing the patient's responses on such tasks, the examiner should remain vigilant to where in space a patient's errors tended to occur. Similarly, more recent investigations have identified that patients sustaining bilateral damage to parietal regions are likely to demonstrate neglect and inattention for lower parts of space, whereas patients with bilateral temporal lesions may show the opposite pattern, neglect of upper parts of space (Rapcsak, Cimino, & Heilman, 1988; Shelton, Bowers, & Heilman, 1990). Therefore, allocation of attention in space may play a role in patients' patterns of performance on the PPVT-R or other measures.

Primary Versus Secondary Effects

In attempting to discern the basis for impaired performance on any task, a useful starting point is to determine whether deficits are in the ability or abilities that are assumed to underlie that task or are due to other deficits not assumed to be primary determinants of task performance; that is, a distinction is made between deficits that are primary in nature and deficits that are secondary in nature. A primary deficit in visuoconstructional abilities refers to the fact that failure on such tasks is most likely accounted for by true deficits in visuoconstructional ability that cannot be accounted for by difficulties in any other cognitive domain. A secondary deficit would reflect the situation where poor performance on a task such as visuoconstructional ability is secondarily influenced by a deficit in some other domain of function (either higher order or lower order). In one of the examples given before, we might indicate that poor performance on visuoconstructional tasks was secondarily influenced by marked deficits in arousal and attention.

The Hooper Visual Organizational Test (Hooper, 1958) is a complex test of visuoperceptual and visuosynthetic processing that requires the patient to recognize pictures of objects that have been cut up and rearranged. The purpose of administering this task is to assess abilities of visuoperceptual and visuosynthetic abilities. However, if a patient is unable to produce the name of the object, this failure may be due to significant anomia and not to problems in visuoperceptual/visuosynthetic ability per se. Many items on the Hooper are relatively high-frequency items that minimize, to some extent, the influence of naming difficulties. However, it is still the case that naming deficits can influence performance on this task, particularly when those deficits are pronounced. To investigate this possibility, the examiner should consider the patient's performance on more formal measures of naming ability or examine other data for naming failures. In this case, one would infer that performance on this visuoperceptual/visuosynthetic task was secondarily influenced by naming difficulties, and that it did not present evidence of a primary disturbance in visuoperceptual/visuosynthetic abilities unless there was evidence to suggest otherwise.

On measures of memory function, it is essential to determine whether deficits in other processing domains can fully account for performance on various memory measures. For example, memory assessment usually includes the evaluation of both verbal and nonverbal memory functions. The Wechsler Memory Scale-Revised (WMS-R; Wechsler, 1987) is one such measure. Two subtests, Logical Memory and Visual Reproduction, require the immediate recall of short stories and line drawings, respectively. Subjects are again asked to reproduce these same items following a 30-minute delay. If a patient presents with significant language difficulties, it may be difficult to interpret performance on verbal memory measures apart from language disturbance. Similarly, for patients with significant visuoperceptual difficulties, it may be difficult to infer performance on nonverbal aspects of memory independently of the visuoperceptual deficits. Obviously, the magnitude of the deficits in language or visuoperceptual abilities is an important factor to consider.

One aspect of task performance that can be of some benefit in interpreting these findings is to examine how performance in the immediate recall condition compares to performance in the delayed recall condition. Patients may have difficulty encoding the information as reflected by poor performance in the immediate memory condition but retain nearly all of that information over time as reflected by performance in the delayed recall condition. If so, the primary deficit is likely in perception, secondarily resulting in impaired memory performance. It is difficult to argue for the existence of material-specific memory deficit in this situation where specific verbal- or visuoperceptual-processing deficits appear to set a limit in terms of the amount of information that initially enters the system at immediate recall, although very little loss of this same information over time is observed. A second possibility is that performance in the delayed recall condition is significantly worse than performance in the immediate recall condition. The latter scenario does demonstrate loss of information over time. In this case, the examiner may be better able to interpret performance in terms of material-specific memory failure. These types of determinations require a significant degree of thought on the part of the examiner.

EVALUATING THE CONSISTENCY OF NEUROPSYCHOLOGICAL DATA

The extent to which neuropsychological data are consistent is at the very heart of the integrative aspects of neuropsychological interpretation. In evaluating consistency of neuropsychological data, one must consider the extent to which test data are consistent both within a cognitive domain as well as across various cognitive domains. This evaluation of consistency involves not only determinations of whether the neuropsychological test data are consistent but also the extent to which test data are consistent with other neuropsychological data such as history and behavioral observations of test and extratest behavior. In determining the consistency of neuropsychological data, at least six different aspects should be considered. These are listed in Table 3.6.

TABLE 3.6
Evaluating the Consistency of Neuropsychological Data

1. Comparisons Across Multiple Measures within a Cognitive Domain
2. Determining Whether Deficits are Primary or Secondary in Nature
3. Comparison of Level and Pattern of Performance with Expectations
4. Consistency of Test Behavior and Extratest Behavior
5. Easier Tasks Performed at Poorer Levels than More Difficult Tasks
6. Poorer than Chance Performance

Comparisons across Multiple Measures
within a Cognitive Domain

Examining the consistency of performance within a cognitive domain is one aspect of integrating results during the interpretation of overall neuropsychological performance. In this regard, several authors have suggested the need for administration of multiple measures within a cognitive domain to better assess the consistency of performance (Larrabee, 1990; Weintraub & Mesulam, 1985). This redundancy of information is an excellent means of evaluating the extent to which the patient's performance is consistent across tests assumed to be measuring the same function. To the extent that results are consistent within a cognitive domain, the examiner is in a stronger position to interpret the results as reflecting spared or impaired function; that is, if all tasks within the language domain are intact, the examiner is better able to infer that such results reflect spared language abilities. Similarly, if all tests of memory are impaired, the examiner is again better able to infer that these results are consistent with the interpretation of impaired memory function.

However, more often than not, the examiner is in the position of interpreting neuropsychological data within a cognitive domain that do not, at least on the surface, appear consistent. In such cases, the examiner must carefully consider task demands that are inherent in the neuropsychological measures. The issues already discussed related to interactions between cognitive domains are essential in determining whether or not findings are internally consistent.

For example, within the memory domain a patient may be within normal limits on measures of verbal memory function but impaired on nonverbal memory measures. In this case, we would expect that performance should be consistent across various verbal memory measures assuming that these tasks do not differ on some significant dimension that could otherwise account for the difference in performance. Similarly, we would expect that performance should be consistent across various nonverbal memory measures, again assuming that these tasks do not differ on some significant dimension that could otherwise account for the difference in performance. As another example, the patient may show poor performance on tasks utilizing free recall and yet perform much better on recognition memory measures, a pattern found in Huntington's disease patients (Butters, Wolfe, Martone, Granholm, & Cermak, 1985). Whereas these results represent seemingly discrepant findings within the memory domain, they may well be consistent within the context of certain neurobehavioral disorders and their clinical presentation.

In a similar vein, the examiner must reconsider the assumption that various measures within a cognitive domain are tapping the same function.

Consideration of the mode of input (visual, auditory, verbal, nonverbal, etc.) as well as the mode of output (verbal response, pointing response, graphomotor response, etc.) help make sense out of seemingly discrepant findings. Although tasks may be grouped together under various domains, they often differ greatly with respect to task requirements and even specific aspects of the domain in question. For example, whereas language function may be considered to be a single domain of function, within that domain are disparate abilities including fluency, comprehension, naming, repetition, reading, writing, spelling, and so on that may be spared or impaired to greater or lesser degrees. In examining data for consistency it is important to consider all aspects of task requirements and processing demands. Analysis of consistency within a domain is an important step in deriving accurate and veridical interpretations of neuropsychological data. This is particularly important in forensic neuropsychology and in cases in which malingering or feigned performance is suspected.

Determining Whether Deficits are Primary or Secondary in Nature

Determining whether deficits are primary or secondary in nature may be involved in evaluating the consistency of neuropsychological data. If within a particular cognitive domain results do not appear consistent, the examiner may question whether deficits observed in performance on a particular task are primary or secondary in nature. In addressing this issue, it may be helpful to make comparisons across various cognitive domains to determine whether evidence to support the secondary influence on a particular task is present. Let us suppose that a patient is able to perform higher order visual processing tasks that require the subject to actually reproduce the item such as in the copy phases of the Benton Visual Retention Test (Benton, 1974) or the Rey-Osterrieth Complex Figure (Osterrieth, 1944; Rey, 1941). Let us also assume that the patient is able to perform well on visuoperceptual and visuospatial tasks in which he or she must recognize the correct response by pointing to the correct response alternative such as in the Benton Facial Recognition Task (Benton & Van Allen, 1968) and the Benton Line Orientation Task (Benton, Hannay, & Varney, 1975). However, this same patient performs poorly on the Hooper Visual Organization Test (Hooper, 1958) and Gollin Figures (Gollin, 1960), in which the patient must indicate the correct response by naming the item. In this case, we may suspect that poor performance on these latter tasks may be secondarily influenced by poor naming abilities. To assess this possible interpretation, we must look at data across cognitive domains. More specifically, we would look to performance in the language domain particularly on tasks of naming ability to ascertain whether naming deficits are also present on these tasks. Looking both within a cognitive domain and across cognitive domains can be very helpful in resolving apparent inconsistencies in neuropsychological data to arrive at more parsimonious and veridical interpretations of performance.

Similarly, consideration of the influence of fatigue on task performance may be necessary when interpreting the consistency of results and the extent to which deficits are of a primary or secondary nature. If the neuropsychological evaluation is especially long, undue fatigue may interfere with the patient's ability to complete the task at hand. If optimal conditions for assessment are desirable, this may not yield the patient's maximal performance. On the other hand, it may be the case that specific deficits emerge only when the system is stressed as with fatigue, and such information could potentially be very useful in terms of its impact on the patient's daily functioning. Alternatively, the influence of fatigue could represent nonspecific effects on task performance. To disentangle potential specific effects of fatigue on a particular cognitive domain versus nonspecific effects of fatigue on performance in general, we would need to look at the pattern of performance across the testing session and across various cognitive domains. If fatigue effects were general and nonspecific, we would expect to find poorer performance as the testing session progressed on tasks administered most recently, irrespective of the cognitive domain. In contrast, if fatigue was influential in eliciting specific effects in a particular cognitive domain, again we would expect these deficits to arise toward the end of the testing session, but only on those tasks within that particular cognitive domain.

Comparison of Level and Pattern of Performance with Expectations

Consistency between a patient's level and pattern of performance, as assessed by neuropsychological measures, and examiner expectations of the level and pattern of performance of the patient is an important aspect of the interpretation process. Expectations may relate to the level of performance relative to some estimate of premorbid abilities. Similarly, expectations may relate to the pattern of performance known to be associated with various neurobehavioral, psychiatric, or other medical disorders. Comparing obtained data with expected premorbid functioning is essential to the determination of impairment, whereas comparison with specific medical disorders helps delineate the etiological condition. A caveat to this aspect of the interpretation process is to remain vigilant to the tendency to disregard data that is inconsistent with expectations, that is, the tendency toward confirmatory bias.

The extent to which an examiner can generate expectations of test performance and anticipate the potential level and pattern of performance is highly dependent upon the knowledge base and experience of the examiner. In addition, the extent to which the examiner can formulate useful expectations for any particular patient is determined by the information available at the time of the assessment in the form of background information, prior testing, medical history, and current clinical presentation. Knowledge of patterns of deficits associated with various neurobehavioral disorders is also essential. In cases where there is the potential for litigation or secondary gain such as compensation, the extent to which the level and pattern of performance are consistent with expectations becomes potentially even more important to the interpretive endeavor.

Consistency of Test Behavior and Extratest Behavior

Evaluating the consistency of test behaviors with extratest behaviors represents an important level of analysis. If there is a question about patients' ability to maintain adequate attention and sustained concentration on the task at hand during assessment, this may be evident in observations of patients' extratest behavior as well. For example, patients may fail to attend to the examiner appropriately, show significant delays in their responses to questions, or lose their train of thought in conversation. Similarly, if memory difficulties are present, patients are likely to manifest these deficits in extratest behaviors by being unable to recall the name of the examiner or prior physicians, repeating the same statements or questions without being aware of doing so, demonstrating difficulty in following the thread of interview by forgetting the question, and so on. Severe impairment on memory measures, yet accurate recall in vivid detail of the events of that morning's test session, events that occurred at home during the past week, and otherwise good recall of information without the benefit of cuing is a highly discrepant pattern. Attempts to resolve such discrepancies are an essential aspect of neuropsychological interpretation.

Easier Tasks Performed at Poorer Levels than More Difficult Tasks

Observing whether easier tasks are performed at poorer levels than more difficult tasks is also an important element in assessing the consistency of neuropsychological data. Performance of higher order or more difficult tasks is predicated on the integrity of lower order or more basic abilities. Thus, performance on easier tasks should be equal to or better than performance on more difficult tasks. We would not expect performance on more difficult tasks to exceed that of impaired performance on easier tasks. For example, on the Trail Making Test (Reitan & Wolfson, 1985) typically a patient would not be expected to perform poorer on Trails A than Trails B. Normal performance on Trails B is predicated on the ability to successfully complete Trails A. Trails A consists of 25 circles, numbered from 1 to 25, distributed randomly on a sheet of paper. Patients are required to sequentially connect circles with a pencil. Trails B is similar except that the circles are numbered from 1 to 13 and lettered from A to L. Again, patients are required to connect the circles, proceeding in an ascending sequence, but now alternating between numbers and letters. In addition to similar visual-scanning requirements, Trails B requires mental flexibility and the ability to integrate number and alphabetic sequences. Normal performance on Trails B in the context of impaired performance on Trails A represents an unusual performance, inconsistent with typical patterns of performance on these measures.

Similarly, on the Stroop task (Stroop, 1935) we would not expect performance on the noninterference condition (reading of simple color words [blue, green, red] or naming the color of ink patches) to be in the impaired range, whereas performance on the interference condition (e.g., saying the color of the green ink in which "color word" RED was printed) fell within the normal range. This pattern of performance does not make sense in terms of what is known about cognitive requirements in these two conditions. Similarly, on memory measures we would not expect that recognition memory performance would be significantly worse than performance in a free recall condition. A recognition memory task is typically easier than free recall, and most individuals' performance improves somewhat under test conditions utilizing recognition. The opposite pattern of performance in which recognition memory is significantly worse than free recall should raise questions about the consistency of the patient's performance.

Poorer than Chance Performance

Observations of poorer than chance performance are of greatest concern in cases where the validity of neuropsychological data is in question. In fact, examination of chance versus worse than chance performance has been suggested as a method for assessing symptom exaggeration (i.e., Symptom Validity testing; Binder & Pankratz, 1987; Hiscock & Hiscock, 1989). For example, Symptom Validity testing of memory is based on the assumption that, if impairment is actually present on a task in which the patient must make a yes–no decision, the patient with true memory difficulties should perform no worse than chance. In this case, the patient would be expected to provide the correct response on about 50% of trials. However, performance that is significantly below chance would be a rare phenomenon in such patients and when present would suggest some knowledge of the distinction between correct and incorrect responses.

In addition to observing inconsistencies across neuropsychological data, the use of Symptom Validity testing may prove to be of benefit in cases where feigned performance is suspected. It must be emphasized that distinguishing between conditions in which a patient deliberately or consciously attempts to feign performance and conditions in which nonconscious feigning are present may be very difficult determinations to make. Although conscious versus nonconscious etiologies for worse than chance performance have very different implications in terms of treatment planning, compensation, and legal proceedings, both represent findings inconsistent with an organic-based memory disorder. However, it also may be the case that deliberate attempts to alter performance may co-exist with real neuropsychological deficits. In such cases accurate estimates of a patient's performance may be difficult if not impossible to establish.

DISTINGUISHING NEUROLOGIC, PSYCHIATRIC, AND TEST-TAKING CONDITIONS THAT MAY OVERLAP

As part of the conceptualization and interpretation of neuropsychological data, the examiner is often in the position of attempting to distinguish between several different conditions that might account for the patient's overall presentation. For example, hallucinations, delusions, paranoia, and other psychotic features can be observed in neurologic and psychiatric disorders. Delusions following neurologic insult are most likely to occur following focal right-hemisphere damage superimposed on diffuse atrophy (Levine & Grek, 1984). One content-specific delusional belief termed Capgras syndrome is the delusional belief that well-known individuals, such as family members, have identical doubles or imposters. This phenomenon can be observed following focal neurologic damage but to the novice may appear to be more consistent with a psychiatric disturbance such as schizophrenia than a neurologic disorder (Malloy, Cimino, & Westlake, 1992). Various neurologic disorders also overlap in clinical presentation and neuropsychological test performance patterns. The case described earlier of a patient with an amnestic disorder and accompanying mild executive problems following bilateral thalamic infarcts had initially been thought to have Alzheimer's disease. These are just two examples of the many types of overlapping conditions of which the examiner must remain aware in distinguishing among neurologic, psychiatric, and test-taking conditions.

In evaluating neuropsychological test data, the examiner must keep in mind that a particular performance may be arrived at in many different ways and for a variety of reasons. That a patient's performance on a neuropsychological measure falls in the impaired range does not necessarily mean that such a performance reflects "brain impairment." Interpretation of poor performance will examine the extent to which poor performance may be attributable to some degree of neurologic involvement versus psychiatric, personality factors, or test-taking conditions such as conscious or nonconscious feigned performance. Distinguishing among these various disorders requires close scrutiny of all available data through a systematic and careful consideration of factors identified in Table 3.7.

History

In attempting to discern various conditions that might account for neuropsychological data, consideration of history is often crucial. In cases where there is some evidence of psychiatric disturbance together with poor performance on some neuropsychological measures, the history may clarify the interpretation of performance. A case involving history of prior psychiatric disturbance including hospitalizations or treatments may be interpreted somewhat differently than a case in which presentation of psychiatric symptoms is of new and recent onset. Similarly, the distinction between dementia and pseudodementia may be aided by history, although this remains one of the most difficult differentiations to make. In cases where there is no formal psychiatric history available, some indication from the interview of recurring bouts of depression might suggest a long-standing problem in this domain. In cases where depression occurs in the context of poor performance on neuropsychological measures, consideration of whether the onset of cognitive difficulties was slow and insidious, as in the case of most progressive degenerative dementias, or relatively abrupt and coincident with a worsening of depressive symptomatology may be useful information in attempting to discern these two conditions (Caine, 1986; Lezak, 1983). Similarly, interviews with family and significant others may provide useful information on behavior patterns including preoccupation with bodily concerns, dependent traits,

TABLE 3.7
Distinguishing Neurologic, Psychiatric and Test Taking

1. History
2. Test-Taking Behavior
3. Extratest Behavior
4. Knowledge of Cognitive Changes Associated with Different Disorders

poor relationships with others, or a tendency to withdraw that may suggest that such traits represent either relatively enduring patterns of behavior or manifestations of undiagnosed psychiatric disturbance.

Many disorders are known to have some genetic component, and family medical history may be useful in differential diagnosis. Family history may be an important variable to consider when disorders are entertained such as Alzheimer's disease, Huntington's disease, schizophrenia, affective disorder, and many others. In addition, in cases where conscious feigned performance is suspected, a history of multiple litigations or antisocial behavior may raise the question of potential secondary gain as accounting for performance on neuropsychological measures.

Test-Taking Behavior

Consideration of the test-taking behavior of the individual may be of benefit in distinguishing between etiological conditions or when feigned performance is suspected. In working on items does the patient appear to be exerting adequate effort and motivation? Lack of concern for repeated failures on tasks in the context of good awareness of such performance may lead one to question the occurrence of feigned performance. The patient's tendency to consistently hesitate before responding may also alert the examiner to attempts to modify output prior to responding. In cases where depression is suspected, the examiner should be alert to self-deprecating statements and excessive self-monitoring of performance. A tendency to give up easily or become increasingly frustrated with failures may be consistent with test-taking behaviors observed in depression. Some authors (Post, 1975; Wells, 1979) have identified the occurrence of "I don't know" responses as a potential indicator in performance of depressed patients relative to dementia patients; however, this does not appear to be supported empirically (O'Boyle & Amadeo, 1989; Young, Manley, & Alexopoulos, 1985). Nevertheless, depressed patients are observed to have more conservative response criteria relative to patients with dementia (Corwin, Paselow, Feenan, Rotosen, & Fieve, 1990).

Extratest Behaviors

In addition to careful observation of test-taking behaviors, a consideration of extratest behaviors may prove to be of benefit. Incidental observations of behavior provide useful information about a patient's consistency of performance between cognitive abilities as assessed by neuropsychological assessment and cognitive abilities as demonstrated by the individual's behavior in the environment. Recently, a patient was tested who performed beyond 2 standard deviations below that of similarly aged peers on nearly all memory measures presented to her. Nevertheless, during a break in testing she was able to wind her way through the many halls of a medical clinic to find a smoking area and subsequently return at the designated time to the testing room without any apparent difficulty. In addition, she was able to execute these behaviors despite the fact that this was her first visit to the clinic. In patients with severe memory difficulties, such good recall of locations in space in an unfamiliar environment would be difficult without additional cues and reminders. This observation together with other information about the pattern of her test performance raised questions about the validity of her performance on neuropsychological measures.

Knowledge of Cognitive Changes Associated with Different Disorders

Lastly, knowledge of cognitive changes associated with different disorders is perhaps the most important domain that can assist the examiner in differentiating neurologic, psychiatric, and test-taking conditions that may overlap. Knowledge of various patterns of performance associated with different neurologic and psychiatric disorders allows the examiner to recognize patterns of performance that are most consistent with a disorder as well as to recognize aspects of performance that may be inconsistent with a disorder. For example, in differentiating dementia and depression several aspects of performance may help in distinguishing the relative contribution of depression to performance on neuropsychological measures. Pseudodementia or the dementia associated with depression is likely to share many features in common with subcortical dementias (King & Caine, 1990). The presence of cortical signs such as apraxia and aphasia are not likely to be observed in depression but are very likely to be present in a cortical dementia. Similarly, the memory disturbance associated with depression may result in characteristically different patterns of performance than the memory disturbance associated with dementia. In depression, memory disturbance is often secondary to attention and concentration difficulties inherent in the disorder. This results in poor initial registration of information but relatively little loss of this same information over time. Assessing the rate of forgetting of information by comparing immediate recall to subsequent delayed recall is one potentially useful aspect of memory performance in helping to differentiate depression from dementia (Hart, Kwentus, Taylor, & Harkins, 1987). Memory performance of depressed patients is also characterized by poor performance on tasks that require significant effort. Weingartner (1986) reported that, when attempts are made to increase the inherent organization and structure of information presented at learning, depressed patients' performances improve. This may be reflected in impaired free recall of material in the context of relatively preserved recognition memory that represents a less effortful test condition (Kaszniak, Poon, & Riege, 1986). Some qualitative features of performance suggest that depressed patients may show poorer recall of neutral or positive material relative to material with a negative theme, so called mood-congruent effects (Blaney, 1986; Singer & Salovey, 1988). Self-report measures suggest that depressed patients tend to underestimate their memory performance, whereas demented patients are more likely to overestimate the capabilities of their memory performance (O'Boyle, Amadeo, & Self, 1990; O'Hara, Hinrichs, Kohout, Wallace, & Lemke, 1986). In differentiating such cases, the relative importance of serial testing of both cognitive abilities and affect/mood changes are perhaps one of the most useful means of distinguishing between these two disorders. However, it must be kept in mind that dementia and depression are not mutually exclusive. Many patients may present with depression in the early phase of dementia and following them over time with serial testing may be the only successful means of determining whether a true dementia is present.

AVOIDING ERRONEOUS ASSUMPTIONS AND INFERENCES

In the process of interpreting neuropsychological data, we often make certain assumptions about the individual's test performance. If these assumptions go unchecked, interpretation of the data may not represent an accurate reflection of the patient's neuropsychological status. Similarly, interpretation of test data can proceed from certain inferences about test performance that may be neither logical nor accurate. Table 3.8 lists several of these erroneous assumptions and inferences that may occur in the context of interpretation. When interpreting neuropsychological data, it is important to question whether the assumptions made about a patient's performance are in fact met. Similarly, it may be useful to consider whether the interpretation of a patient's neuropsychological data involves inferences that may threaten the validity of that interpretation.

TABLE 3.8
Avoiding Erroneous Assumptions and Inferences

1. Performance was normal in the past
2. Face Validity as True Validity
3. Impaired Performance on Test X Necessarily Implies Damage to Region Y
4. Overinterpretation and Underinterpretation of Neuropsychological Data

Performance was Normal in the Past

A common assumption in the interpretation of neuropsychological data
is that the patient's performance was normal in the past. Whereas this
may be the case in the majority of patients evaluated, this assumption
should never go unchecked. Assuming that performance was normal in
the past, when in fact performance has always been significantly below
the average range, may lead to the erroneous interpretation that this
represents a change in performance from baseline. One common situation in which this assumption may be violated is in the presence of a learning disability. Poor performance in domains such as reading, spelling, or
arithmetic may be erroneously interpreted as reflecting a change from
baseline performance if these difficulties have been long-standing in nature. A more thorough investigation of history and consideration of this
information when interpreting neuropsychological data would avoid this
error.

Similarly, performance on motor tasks that strongly suggests an abnormal pattern of asymmetric performance should be considered within
the context of this assumption. Such patterns of performance may alert
us to the potential of unilateral brain impairment. However, factors other
than central nervous system involvement may result in asymmetries on
motor tasks. A history of peripheral nerve damage could account for such
a pattern of performance. A careful consideration of history or direct inquiry of the patient would avoid an error in interpretation. In a case where
performance for both hands falls within normal limits but an unusually
large split is observed, it may be tempting to assume that this pattern
represents a change from baseline performance. This assumption,
however, might be incorrect in an athlete with overdeveloped abilities
in one limb. Again, in this case attention to aspects of the patient's history or direct questioning may help to make better sense out of seemingly
abnormal performance.

Face Validity as True Validity

A common error of interpretation involves the mistaken assumption that
face validity of a neuropsychological measure is in fact a true type of validity. According to Anastasi (1988), validity of a test is defined as "the
degree to which the test actually measures what it purports to measure"
(p. 28). This can be established through a variety of different methods
such as determining the extent to which the test predicts performance
on some criterion measure, correlations with other tests known to measure a particular ability, use of factor analysis, and a variety of other means.

In contrast, face validity refers to what the test appears to be measuring; that is, does the test look like or appear to be a test of memory, arithmetic abilities, visuoconstructional abilities, or naming abilities? In fact, face validity is not a true validity in the psychometric sense of the word. As examiners, we must not be persuaded to believe that because a test looks like it is measuring a certain cognitive ability or because the name of the test or its instruction manual refers to one particular cognitive ability that this particular test measures *only* that ability. Similarly, as Walsh (1992) indicated, we must not "be seduced into taking poor performance on a test to mean that the function said by the test makers to be measured by the test has been affected" (p. 127). It may be the case that an impaired score on that test can be achieved for a variety of reasons. Again, by maintaining an awareness of the complexity of neuropsychological measures and the many component processes involved in the completion of that measure, the examiner is in a better position to avoid this erroneous assumption.

Impaired Performance on Test X Necessarily Implies Damage to Region Y

It is often the case that in the process of interpreting neuropsychological data errors of inference arise that lead to incorrect interpretations of the patient's performance. One common error of inference is that, if damage to a specific brain region is associated with poor performance on a particular task, poor performance on that test implies dysfunction of that region in all subjects (Miller, 1983). To illustrate the effects of such an inference, Weintraub and Mesulam (1985) provided the example of memory deficits associated with left- and right-temporal lobe damage. They suggested that because several studies have shown that patients with left-temporal damage are likely to develop a material-specific verbal memory deficit, clinicians have a tendency to infer that the presence of a verbal memory deficit always implies the presence of left-temporal lobe lesions. This inference is incorrect. We now know that left- or right-sided lesions to subcortical structures such as the dorsal medial nucleus of the thalamus may also result in material-specific verbal and nonverbal memory deficits, respectively (Speedie & Heilman, 1982, 1983). Larrabee (1990) provided another example of this erroneous inference in diagnostic decisions regarding the presence or absence of "brain damage." In this instance the examiner may erroneously assume that, because brain-impaired patients fail on neuropsychological measures, any patient who fails on a neuropsychological measure must have brain impairment. This type of mistaken inference can lead to gross misinterpretations of neuropsychological data that neglect consideration of the fact that patients may fail on neuropsychological measures for many reasons other than brain impairment.

Overinterpretation and Underinterpretation of Neuropsychological Data

Errors of overinterpretation and errors of underinterpretation are based on two misleading and erroneous inferences. Errors of overinterpretation may be due to the mistaken inference that an impaired score equals brain impairment. This inference is very similar to that described earlier in which the examiner infers that because brain-impaired patients fail on neuropsychological measures then any patient who fails a neuropsychological measure must have brain impairment. Errors of underinterpretation reflect an erroneous inference that is the converse of that aforementioned; that is, no impaired score is equal to no brain impairment. Walsh (1992) noted, "We should bear in mind Teuber's dictum 'absence of evidence is not evidence of absence.' " Cases in which neurological impairment exists in the context of normal performance on neuropsychological measures are some of the most difficult diagnostic determinations in neuropsychology. In general, there are two scenarios in which this may be the case. The first involves cases in which the individual possesses superior premorbid abilities or talents. The second involves cases of isolated frontal lobe pathology.

In cases of superior premorbid abilities or talents, an average level of performance in a particular cognitive domain may represent a significant decline in performance from that individual's premorbid status. However, detection of such a decline may be difficult using standard neuropsychological measures. A careful consideration of premorbid estimates of ability would be very helpful in determining the extent to which the current level of performance matches that of expected performance. Use of recent normative data that includes individuals of higher educational levels or intellectual levels as part of the normative sample also would be of benefit. Some recently developed neuropsychological screening measures such as the Assessment of Cognitive Skills (ACS) have been geared toward detection of age-inappropriate cognitive changes in individuals with a presumed high premorbid level of ability as well as in individuals with premorbid abilities estimated to be in the average range (Cimino, Behner, Cattarin, & Tantleff, 1991; Weintraub et al., 1991). Availability of measures with higher ceilings on performance and appropriate normative comparisons may help to address this difficult diagnostic determination.

Cases in which isolated frontal lobe pathology is present may present as significant diagnostic dilemmas. Several authors (Lezak, 1983; Walsh, 1987, 1991) commented on the relative insensitivity of intellectual measures in capturing the variety of adaptive behavior deficits observed in frontal lobe pathology. A patient may evidence gross deficits in everyday instances of judgment, planning, and decision making that render that patient virtually incapable of functioning effectively or independently in their environment. Nevertheless, that patient may score average or even well above average on measures of intellectual functioning such as the WAIS-R (Wechsler, 1981). An even more striking example of the insensitivity of standard clinical measures to the disruptive effects of frontal pathology is the case EVR reported by Eslinger and Damasio (1985), who underwent bilateral ablation of ventromedial frontal cortices for the treatment of meningioma. In addition to scoring in the superior range on measures of intellectual ability, this patient demonstrated no deficits in memory, language, visuoperceptual, or visuospatial abilities. Of even greater significance is the fact that this patient performed normally on tasks assumed to measure so-called "frontal" or executive/self-regulatory abilities. EVR's performance on the Wisconsin Card Sorting Test, the Category Test, verbal fluency, cognitive estimations (Shallice & Evans, 1978), and judgments of recency and frequency (Milner & Petrides, 1984) were all within normal limits. Nevertheless, this patient exhibited marked adaptive behavior deficits that made it impossible for him to maintain employment and function effectively in his environment due to marked difficulties in planning, decision making, and social behavior.

This case underscores the potential insensitivity of neuropsychological measures in assessing adaptive behaviors that determine the extent to which a patient is able to function competently and independently in their environment. This case also underscores the relative importance of considering *all* available data in the interpretation of a patient's performance. Test scores represent only one, albeit important, element in the conceptualization and interpretation of neuropsychological data. Integration of information from the patient's history, data from interview of the patient, family, or significant others, observations of the patient's test and extratest behaviors, as well as consideration of test performance is necessary to allow for consistent and veridical interpretations of the patient's current neuropsychological status.

SUMMARY

This chapter highlights various fundamental principles involved in neuropsychological interpretation. The chapter is not intended to provide a step-by-step or cookbook approach to interpretation. Rather, this chapter is meant to serve as a guide in developing the kinds of thought processes necessary in careful consideration and interpretation of neuropsychological data. Neuropsychological interpretation is viewed as a multistaged process that involves integration of data from multiple sources only one of which is test scores. The examiner must consider all available data in the form of history, interview, behavioral observations, and test scores. Furthermore, these sources of information must be checked against each other for evidence of consistencies as well as for potential inconsistencies in arriving at veridical interpretations of the patient's current neuropsychological status and likely etiological conditions.

An invaluable tool in approaching the interpretation process is that of a conceptual model of brain-behavior relationships. A conceptual model of brain–behavior relationships involves a working knowledge of how neuroanatomy, neuropathologic conditions and their sequelae, clinical psychology/psychopathology, and psychometric properties and principles interact. From this foundation, the examiner is better able to anticipate potential patterns of behavior as well as recognize consistencies and inconsistencies when they arise, recognize unusual presentations of neurobehavioral disorders, and provide accurate and rich accounts of the qualitative aspects of the patient's performance. Attention to subject-specific variables that may influence neuropsychological data is also discussed with special consideration of how these factors may influence interpretation. Similarly, the importance of recognizing that neuropsychological measures represent complex and often multifactorial tasks and that such tasks may be failed for a variety of reasons is emphasized. This notion is of prime importance in recognizing that cognitive domains may interact, and that poor performance on a task may represent either true primary deficits in a particular cognitive domain or secondary effects produced by deficits in a seemingly unrelated cognitive domain. Evaluation of consistencies as well as inconsistencies in neuropsychological data are important aspects in the interpretation process. This evaluation together with knowledge of the patterns of performance in various neurobehavioral and/or psychiatric disorders are important elements in distinguishing among neurologic, psychiatric, and test-taking conditions that may overlap. Lastly, some common erroneous assumptions and inferences of interpretation were considered.

REFERENCES

Alexander, G. E., & Fuster, J. M. (1973). Effects of cooling prefrontal cortex on cell firing in the nucleus medialis dorsalis. *Brain Research, 61*, 93–105.

American Psychiatric Association. (1987). *Diagnostic and Statistical Manual of Mental Disorders (3rd ed., rev.). DSMIII-R.* Washington, DC: American Psychiatric Association.

Anastasi, A. (1988). *Psychological testing* (6th ed.). New York: Macmillan.

Annett, M. (1967). The binomial distribution of right, mixed and left handedness. *Quarterly Journal of Experimental Psychology, 61*, 303–321.

Barclay, L. L., Weiss, E. M., Mattis, S., Bond, O., & Blass, J. P. (1988). Unrecognized cognitive impairment in cardiac rehabilitation patients. *Journal of the American Geriatrics Society, 36*, 22–28.

Benton, A. L. (1974). *Visual Retention Test.* New York: Psychological Corporation.

Benton, A. L., Hamsher, K. deS., Varney, N. R., & Spreen, O. (1983). *Contributions to neuropsychological assessment.* New York: Oxford University Press.

Benton, A. L., Hannay, H. J., & Varney, N. (1975). Visual perception of line direction in patients with unilateral brain disease. *Neurology, 25*, 907–910.

Benton, A. L., & Van Allen, M. (1968). Impairment in facial recognition in patients with cerebral disease. *Cortex, 4*, 344–358.

Binder, L. M., & Pankratz, L. (1987). Neuropsychological evidence of a factitious memory complaint. *Journal of Clinical and Experimental Neuropsychology, 9*, 167–171.

Blaney, P. H. (1986). Affect and memory: A review. *Psychological Bulletin, 99*, 229–246.

Bornstein, R. A. (1986). Classification rates obtained with "standard" cut-off scores on selected neuropsychological measures. *Journal of Clinical and Experimental Neuropsychology, 8*, 413–420.

Briggs, G. G., & Nebes, R. D. (1975). Patterns of hand preference in a student population. *Cortex, 11*, 230–238.

Butters, N., & Stuss, D. (1989). Diencephalic amnesia. In F. Boller & J. Grafman (Eds.), *Handbook of neuropsychology* (Vol. 3, pp. 107–148). Amsterdam: Elsevier.

Butters, N., Wolfe, J., Martone, M., Granholm, E., & Cermak, L. S. (1985). Memory disorders associated with Huntington's disease: Verbal recall, verbal recognition and procedural memory. *Neuropsychologia, 6*, 729–744.

Caine, E. D. (1986). The neuropsychology of depression: The pseudodementia syndrome. In I. Grant & K. M. Adams (Eds.), *Neuropsychological assessment of neuropsychiatric disorders* (pp. 221–243). New York: Oxford University Press.

Cimino, C. R., Behner, G., Cattarin, J., & Tantleff, S. (1991). Concurrent validity of the Assessment of Cognitive Skills (ACS). *Journal of Clinical and Experimental Neuropsychology, 13*, 106.

Corwin, J., Peselow, E. D., Feenan, K., Rotrosen, J., & Fieve, R. (1990). Disorders of decision in affective disease: An effect of B-adrenergic dysfunction? *Biological Psychiatry, 27*, 813–833.

Cummings, J. J., & Benson, D. F. (1992). *Dementia: A clinical approach* (2nd ed.). Boston: Butterworth-Heinemann.

Drachman, D. A., & Leavitt, J. (1974). Human memory and the cholinergic system. *Archives of Neurology, 30*, 113–121.

Dunn, L. M., & Dunn, L. M. (1981). *Peabody Picture Vocabulary Test-Revised, Manual.* Circle Pine, MN: American Guidance Service.

Eslinger, P. J., & Damasio, A. R. (1985). Severe disturbance of higher cognition after frontal lobe ablation: Patient EVR. *Neurology, 35*, 1731–1741.

Franzen, M. D. (1989). *Reliability and validity in neuropsychological assessment.* New York: Plenum Press.

Geschwind, N. (1965). Disconnexion syndromes in animals and man. *Brain, 88*, 237–294, 585–644.

Gollin, E. S. (1960). Developmental studies of visual recognition of incomplete objects. *Perceptual and Motor Skills, 11*, 289–298.

Goodglass, H., & Kaplan, E. (1979). Assessment of cognitive deficit in the brain-injured patient. In M. S. Gazzaniga (Ed.), *Handbook of behavioral neurobiology* (Vol. 2, pp. 2–33). New York: Plenum Press.

110   CIMINO

Graff-Radford, N., Damasio, H., Yamada, T., Eslinger, P. J., & Damasio, A. R. (1985). Non-haemorrhagic thalamic infarction. *Brain, 108*, 485–516.

Hart, R. P., Kwentus, J. A., Taylor, J. R., & Harkins, S. W. (1987). Rate of forgetting in dementia and depression. *Journal of Consulting and Clinical Psychology, 55*, 101–105.

Heaton, R. K., Grant, I., & Matthews, C. G. (1986). Differences in neuropsychological test performance associated with age, education, and sex. In I. Grant & K. M. Adams (Eds.), *Neuropsychological assessment of neuropsychiatric disorders* (pp. 100–120). New York: Oxford University Press.

Heaton, R. K., Grant, I., & Matthews, C. G. (1991). *Comprehensive norms for an expanded Halstead–Reitan battery: Demographic corrections, research findings, and clinical applications.* Odessa, FL: Psychological Assessment Resources.

Heilman, K. M., Watson, R. T., & Valenstein, E. (1985). Neglect and related disorders. In K. M. Heilman & E. Valenstein (Eds.), *Clinical neuropsychology* (2nd ed., pp. 243–293). New York: Oxford University Press.

Hiscock, M., & Hiscock, C. K. (1989). Refining the forced-choice method for the detection of malingering. *Journal of Clinical and Experimental Neuropsychology, 11*, 967–974.

Hooper, H. E. (1958). *The Hooper Visual Organization Test Manual.* Los Angeles: Western Psychological Services.

INS-Division 40 Task Force on Education, Accreditation and Credentialing. (1987). Guidelines for doctoral training programs in clinical neuropsychology. *The Clinical Neuropsychologist, 1*, 29–34.

Kaplan, E. (1983). Process and achievement revisited. In S. Wapner & B. Kaplan (Eds.), *Toward a holistic developmental psychology* (pp. 143–156). Hillsdale, NJ: Lawrence Erlbaum Associates.

Kaplan, E. (1989). A process approach to neuropsychological assessment. In T. Boll & B. K. Bryant (Eds.), *Clinical neuropsychology and brain function: Research, measurement, and practice* (pp. 127–167). Washington, DC: American Psychological Association.

Kaplan, E., Fein, D., Morris, R., & Delis, D. C. (1991). *WAIS-R as a neuropsychological instrument.* San Antonio, TX: The Psychological Corporation.

Kaplan, E., Goodglass, H., & Weintraub, S. (1978). *The Boston Naming Test.* Philadelphia: Lea & Febiger.

Kaszniak, A. W., Poon, L. W., & Riege, W. (1986). Assessing memory deficits: An information-processing approach. In L. W. Poon (Ed.), *Handbook of clinical memory assessment in older adults* (pp. 168–188). Washington, DC: American Psychological Association.

Kaufman, A. S. (1990). *Assessing adolescent and adult intelligence.* Boston: Allyn & Bacon.

Kertesz, A. (1982). *The Western Aphasia Battery Test Manual.* New York: Grune & Stratton.

King, D. A., & Caine, E. D. (1990). Depression. In J. L. Cummings (Ed.), *Subcortical dementia* (pp. 218–230). New York: Oxford University Press.

Larrabee, G. J. (1990). Cautions in the use of neuropsychological evaluation in legal settings. *Neuropsychology, 4*, 239–247.

Leckliter, I. N., & Matarazzo, J. D. (1989). The influence of age, education, IQ, gender and alcohol abuse on Halstead–Reitan Neuropsychological Test Battery performance. *Journal of Clinical Psychology, 45*, 484–511.

Levin, H. S., Benton, A. L., & Grossman, R. G. (1982). *Neurobehavioral consequences of closed head injury.* New York: Oxford University Press.

Levine, D., Warach, J., & Farah, M. (1985). Two visual systems in mental imagery: Dissociations of "what" and "where" in imagery disorders due to bilateral posterior cerebral lesions. *Neurology, 35*, 1010–1018.

Levine, D. N., & Grek, A. (1984). The anatomical basis of delusions after right cerebral infarction. *Neurology, 34*, 577–582.

Lezak, M. D. (1983). *Neuropsychological assessment* (2nd ed.). New York: Oxford University Press.

Lezak, M. D. (1988). IQ: RIP. *Journal of Clinical and Experimental Neuropsychology, 10*, 351–361.

Luria, A. R. (1980). *Higher cortical functions in man* (2nd ed.). New York: Basic Books.

Malloy, P., Cimino, C., & Westlake, R. (1992). Differential diagnosis of primary and secondary Capgras delusions. *Neuropsychiatry, Neuropsychology and Behavioral Neurology, 5*, 83–96.

Matarazzo, J. D., & Herman, D. O. (1984). Base rate data for the WAIS-R: Test–retest stability and VIQ–PIQ differences. *Journal of Clinical Neuropsychology, 6*, 351–366.

Matarazzo, J. D., & Herman, D. O. (1985). Clinical uses of the WAIS-R: Base rates of differences between VIQ and PIQ in the WAIS-R standardization sample. In B. B. Wolman (Ed.), *Handbook of intelligence* (pp. 899–932). New York: Wiley.

Mesulam, M. M. (1985). A cortical network for directed attention and unilateral neglect. *Annals of Neurology, 10*, 309–325.

Milberg, W. P., Hebben, N., & Kaplan, E. (1986). The Boston process approach to neuropsychological assessment. In I. Grant & K. M. Adams (Eds.), *Neuropsychological assessment of neuropsychiatric disorders* (pp. 65–86). New York: Oxford University Press.

Miller, E. (1983). A note on the interpretation of data derived from neuropsychological tests. *Cortex, 19*, 131–132.

Milner, B., & Petrides, M. (1984). Behavioral effects of frontal-lobe lesions in man. *Trends in Neurosciences, 7*, 403–407.

Mishkin, M., Ungerleider, L., & Macko, K. (1983, October). Object vision and spatial vision: Two cortical pathways. *Trends in Neuroscience*, 414–417.

O'Boyle, M., & Amadeo, M. (1989). Don't know responses in elderly demented and depressed patients. *Journal of Geriatric Psychiatry and Neurology, 2*, 83–86.

O'Boyle, M., Amadeo, M., & Self, D. (1990). Cognitive complaints in elderly depressed and pseudodemented patients. *Psychology and Aging, 5*, 467–468.

O'Hara, M. W., Hinrichs, J. V., Kohout, F. J., Wallace, R. B., & Lemke, J. H. (1986). Memory complaint and memory performance in the depressed elderly. *Psychology and Aging, 1*, 208–214.

Orsini, D. L., Van Gorp, W. G., & Boone, K. B. (1988). *The neuropsychology casebook*. New York: Springer-Verlag.

Osterrieth, P. A. (1944). Le test de copie d'une figure complexe. *Archives de Psychologie, 30*, 206–356.

Post, F. (1975). Dementia, depression and pseudodementia. In D. F. Benson & D. Blumer (Eds.), *Psychiatric aspects of neurologic disease* (pp. 99–120). New York: Grune & Stratton.

Rapcsak, S. Z., Cimino, C. R., & Heilman, K. M. (1988). Altitudinal neglect. *Neurology, 38*, 277–281.

Reitan, R. M., & Wolfson, D. (1985). *The Halstead–Reitan Neuropsychological Test Battery*. Tucson: Neuropsychology Press.

Rey, A. (1941). L'examen psychologique dans les cas d'encephalopathie traumatique. *Archives de Psychologie, 28*, 286–340.

Russell, E. W., & Starkey, R. I. (1993). *Halstead Russell Neuropsychological Evaluation System (HRNES)* [Manual and Computer program]. Los Angeles: Western Psychological Services.

Shallice, T., & Evans, M. E. (1978). The involvement of the frontal lobes in cognitive estimation. *Cortex, 14*, 294–303.

Shelton, P. A., Bowers, D., & Heilman, K. M. (1990). Peripersonal and vertical neglect. *Brain, 113*, 191–205.

Singer, J., & Salovey, P. (1988). Mood and memory: Evaluating the network theory of affect. *Clinical Psychology Review, 8*, 211–251.

Speedie, L., & Heilman, K. M. (1982). Amnestic disturbance following infarction of the left dorsomedial nucleus of the thalamus. *Neuropsychologia, 20,* 597–604.

Speedie, L., & Heilman, K. M. (1983). Anterograde memory deficits for visuospatial material after infarction of the right thalamus. *Archives of Neurology, 40,* 183–186.

Spreen, O., & Strauss, E. (1991). *A compendium of neuropsychological tests: Administration, norms, and commentary.* New York: Oxford University Press.

Squire, L. R. (1987). *Memory and brain.* New York: Oxford University Press.

Squire, L. R., & Moore, R. Y. (1979). Dorsal thalamic lesions in a noted case of chronic memory dysfunction. *Annals of Neurology, 6,* 503–506.

Stroop, J. R. (1935). Studies of interference in serial verbal reactions. *Journal of Experimental Psychology, 18,* 643–662.

Tarter, R. E., Van Thiel, D. H., & Edwards, K. (1988). *Medical neuropsychology: The impact of disease on behavior.* New York: Plenum Press.

Todnem, K., & Vik-Mo, H. (1986). Cerebral ischemic attacks as complication of heart disease: The value of echocardiography. *Acta Neurologica Scandinavica, 74,* 323–327.

Ungerleider, L. G., & Mishkin, M. (1982). Two cortical visual systems. In D. J. Ingle, M. H. Goodale, & R. J. W. Mansfield (Eds.), *The analysis of visual behavior* (pp. 549–585). Cambridge: MIT Press.

Walsh, K. W. (1987). *Neuropsychology: A clinical approach.* Melbourne: Churchill Livingstone.

Walsh, K. W. (1991). *Understanding brain damage* (2nd ed.). Melbourne: Churchill Livingstone.

Walsh, K. W. (1992). Some gnomes worth knowing. *The Clinical Neuropsychologist, 6,* 119–133.

Wechsler, D. (1981). *Wechsler Adult Intelligence Scale-Revised.* New York: Psychological Corporation.

Wechsler, D. (1987). *Wechsler Memory Scale-Revised.* San Antonio: Psychological Corporation.

Weingartner, H. (1986). Automatic and effort-demanding cognitive processes in depression. In L. Poon (Ed.), *Handbook of clinical memory assessment in older adults* (pp. 218–227). Washington, DC: American Psychological Association.

Weintraub, S., & Mesulam, M. M. (1985). Mental state assessment of young and elderly adults in behavioral neurology. In M. M. Mesulam (Ed.), *Principles of behavioral neurology* (pp. 71–122). Philadelphia: F. A. Davis.

Weintraub, S., Powell, D. H., Caflin, R., Funkenstein, H. H., Kaplan, E. F., Whitla, D. K., Horgan, P. A., Porte, H. S., Ware, J., Whipple, B. S., & Bernstein, F. B. (1991). The "assessment of cognitive skills" (ACS): Mental status screening. *Journal of Clinical and Experimental Neuropsychology, 13,* 106.

Wells, C. E. (1979). Pseudodementia. *American Journal of Psychiatry, 136,* 895–900.

Young, R. C., Manley, M. W., & Alexopoulos, G. S. (1985). "I don't know" responses in elderly depressives and in dementia. *Journal of the American Geriatrics Society, 33,* 253–257.

CHAPTER FOUR

Application of Neuropsychological Assessment Results

Bruce Crosson
University of Florida

The ultimate reason for conducting a neuropsychological assessment is that test results provide useful information to a consumer. For any single evaluation, the consumer may be one or more of the following: the patient, the patient's family, a referring physician, rehabilitation team members, mental health professionals, other health care professionals, attorneys or judges, school or academic personnel, and others. The purpose of a neuropsychological evaluation varies widely from case to case but might fit under one or more of three general categories: diagnostic, rehabilitative, and forensic. The practical importance of findings depends on both the consumer and on the reasons for conducting the evaluation. The clinical neuropsychologist must take these factors into account in communicating test results.

The utility of an assessment also depends on the characteristics of instruments employed in the testing endeavor. Each test instrument has strengths and weaknesses relative to the referral question and the context in which the assessment is to be applied. To evaluate such strengths and weaknesses, it is necessary for the examiner to be intimately familiar with the technical properties of the tests he or she administers (e.g., reliability, validity, test norms). These concerns are addressed in professional guidelines for test administration and application (American Psychological Association: Ethical Principles of Psychologists, Principle 8, 1987; Standards for Educational and Psychological Tests, 1974).

The purpose of this chapter is to discuss the process of applying neuropsychological findings to various referral questions and contexts. The first section addresses general properties of neuropsychological tests relevant to applications; limitations are specifically addressed. The following three sections address issues in different referral contexts: diagnostic, rehabilitative, and forensic. Finally, issues in delivering evaluation feedback to patients and family members are discussed. In each section, case examples are given to illustrate important points for application. The reader should keep in mind that the practice of neuropsychology is complex in any context, and the contexts in which neuropsychology might be practiced are numerous and diverse. For these reasons, it would be impossible to cover all the issues concerning neuropsychological assessment in a single chapter. Rather, this chapter raises common issues that can by example demonstrate how various problems might be addressed.

PROPERTIES OF NEUROPSYCHOLOGICAL TESTS

Test Properties Affecting Applications

Neuropsychological assessment has sprung from two traditions that have a bearing on our ability to apply test findings to various questions: the tradition of the psychological laboratory and the tradition of psychometrics. In keeping with these influences, neuropsychological measures often attempt to isolate a particular ability or skill from other abilities or skills. For example, we consider it desirable that a test of visual-perceptual ability not be strongly related to measures of language abilities, and that a measure of language ability not be strongly related to visual-spatial abilities. It is further desirable that tests tap universal abilities, not specific skills acquired through an occupation or pastime. For example, the WAIS-R (Wechsler, 1981) purports to measure more universal intellectual abilities applicable to a broad range of activities, not specific skills such as repairing washing machines or teaching accounting. Although the skills and aptitudes that we do measure have some bearing on the ability to perform such occupational activities, the inferences we can make about a person's ability to perform them are much less direct because we do not measure the activities directly.

Another characteristic of most neuropsychological tests is that we attempt to obtain an optimal performance from the patient (Lezak, 1983). Distractions are kept to a minimum, and efforts are made to be certain that instructions are understood. Further, tasks are performed at the initiation of the evaluator not the patient, and the patient provides very little in the way of either initiative or his or her own structure (Lezak, 1983). When interpreting results, the neuropsychologist must keep in mind that environments outside the neuropsychology laboratory may be less than optimal in terms of distractions, degree of structure, the amount of independent initiation required, and other dimensions. Yet, these are the environments in which patients must live and function. Distractions cannot always be avoided, and degree of structure is not always optimal.

Changes in personality functioning may be essential diagnostic clues and may determine success or failure in rehabilitation endeavors such as return to work. Yet, neuropsychological tests typically do not measure some types of personality change (Lezak, 1978). Frontal lobe functions are particularly important for many facets of personality (see Damasio, 1985). For example, the orbital frontal lobes are involved in control of impulses and emotions. Mesial frontal structures, including the anterior cingulate area, are involved in initiation and motivation. The dorsolateral frontal lobes are involved in planning and organization. Patients showing multiple personality changes after frontal injury can do well on extended neuropsychological batteries (e.g., Eslinger & Damasio, 1985). The crux of this matter is the structure of neuropsychological evaluation that minimizes the need for initiation, independent organization, and impulse control. Thus, neuropsychological test procedures are not designed to optimize detection of personality changes related to frontal dysfunction.

Prigatano (1986) and Crosson (1987) noted the need to differentiate between sources of personality dysfunction after head-injury or frontolimbic damage. Potential sources of such dysfunction include neurological injury, emotional reaction to deficits and circumstances caused by neurological injury, premorbid personality problems or disorders, or some combination of these factors. Proper diagnosis of causative factors can have a profound impact on treatment of these problems. Traditional personality testing may give some hints of dysfunction, but it quite often fails to distinguish between the possible causes. For example, Alfano, Neilson, Paniak, and Finlayson (1992) have alluded to such problems in interpretation of the Minnesota Multiphasic Personality Inventory (MMPI).

Reliability and, in particular, validity considerations also will affect test interpretation and, therefore, application of assessment results. Although many neuropsychological tests are designed to measure a specific construct, most of our instruments are multidimensionally complex. To perform any test, patients must be able to apprehend information through the sensory modalities, perceive and analyze such information, and produce an output. Even a test as simple as Finger Oscillation, which is designed to measure motor output, requires the patient to understand a set of instructions relative to the apparatus involved. Misunderstanding of task demands can lead to altered performance even on this test.

Often times, assumptions are made regarding the construct that certain tests measure that are erroneous or only partially correct. Such errors may be proliferated uncritically in the literature by relying more on clinical lore than on hard data to describe what tests measure. Not infrequently, the construct itself has been accepted without adequate examination. One of the best examples of this type of error is the uncritical interpretation of Digit Span from the WAIS-R as a test of attention. This interpretation has been made for nearly 50 years (e.g., Kitzinger & Blumberg, 1951; Rapaport, Gill, & Schafer, 1945) and is seldom challenged. As Posner and Rafal (1986) and Sohlberg and Mateer (1989) noted, however, a unidimensional construct of attention is inadequate to account for varying clinical phenomena. Posner and Rafal break attention down into three components: arousal, vigilance, and selective attention. Sohlberg and Mateer break attention down into five components: focused attention, sustained attention, selective attention, alternating attention, and divided attention. As noted in the case example that follows, aspects of attention can be quite impaired even when Digit Span scores seem to indicate that attention is a strength of performance. In addition to the modest attentional demands of Digit Span, it is obvious that this test requires an ability to decode the auditory information at least at some level, an ability to repeat, and an ability to hold information in short-term memory until it is repeated. Numerous examples can be found where construct validity of tests is misunderstood.

In summary, inherent properties of neuropsychological tests affect our ability to derive adequate cognitive and behavioral diagnoses. Inadequate specification of cognitive and behavioral strengths and deficits in turn can hamper our ability to arrive at adequate diagnoses, to make valid rehabilitation recommendations, and/or to advise members of the legal profession regarding the functional limitations of a brain-injured person. The left side of Table 4.1 summarizes the properties of neuropsychological tests mentioned earlier that raise issues in applications. A case example illustrates a few of these points.

Case 1 was a woman in her early 20s who was involved in a motor vehicle accident. She had 15 years of education. Acute magnetic resonance (MR) scans demonstrated bilateral contusions in the frontotemporal region, greater on the right side; an intracerebral hemorrhage in the left globus pallidus and posterior limb of the internal capsule; and white matter shearing bilaterally in the centrum semiovale. Significant deficits on neuropsychological testing included: bilaterally slowed finger oscillation, several uncorrected errors on the Stroop Test, impairment on all trials of the Tactual Performance Test, and a lowered Performance IQ. Of interest is that among the Verbal Subtests of the WAIS-R (Fig. 4.1), the patient scored considerably higher on Digit Span than on other Verbal subtests (i.e., by at least one standard deviation). Assessing this patient's

TABLE 4.1
Neuropsychological Test Properties

Properties of Neuropsychological Tests Affecting Application	Application Principles for Neuropsychological Tests That Address Inherent Limitations in Instruments
1. Attempts to isolate test scores from everyday skills limit the ability of tests to predict everyday skills.	1-4. Always conduct an in-depth interview during evaluation. A portion of this interview should be dedicated to addressing problems not typically covered by the neuropsychological tests employed.
2. Creation of a test environment that promotes optimal performance fails to take into account that everyday tasks are performed in a suboptimal environment.	
3. Structured examination sessions may mask deficits in initiation, organization and planning, or impulse control problems (i.e., frontal lobe deficits).	1-4. Make detailed behavioral observations during evaluation, and, where possible, use them to address problems that test scores do not reveal.
4. Tests scores may not be helpful in determining the source of personality disturbances seen in some types of injury.	
5. Neuropsychological tests may be designed to measure a particular construct, but most tests require multiple cognitive skills for completion.	5. Be aware of the complexity of neuropsychological tests and the multiple reasons for poor performance on tests.
6. Constructs used to define some test findings may be inadequately conceptualized and/or outdated.	6. Do not uncritically accept the collective clinical wisdom regarding the constructs that tests measure. Search for patterns among tests that will reveal the nature of an impairment.

strengths was an important part of her rehabilitative neuropsychological evaluation, and, as noted before, this Digit Span score might traditionally be interpreted as a strength in the patient's attention.

Yet, her participation in various rehabilitation tasks demonstrated that she had significant problems in attention. In fact, this facet of her performance was clearly identified in a functional evaluation done at the same time as the neuropsychological evaluation. One example of her attentional problems was noted on her job trial during rehabilitation. She had to photocopy articles, and she would copy only half of several pages in various articles. Ordinarily, she would not realize that she had made this mistake. It was necessary for her therapist to intervene to help her master this problem.

A problem of further interest became evident by interviewing the patient and by observing her in rehabilitation. The patient was prone to experiencing strong emotional reactions (positive and negative) that were appropriate in type but out of proportion in intensity to the circumstances in which she experienced them. This problem with emotional disinhibi-

WAIS-R

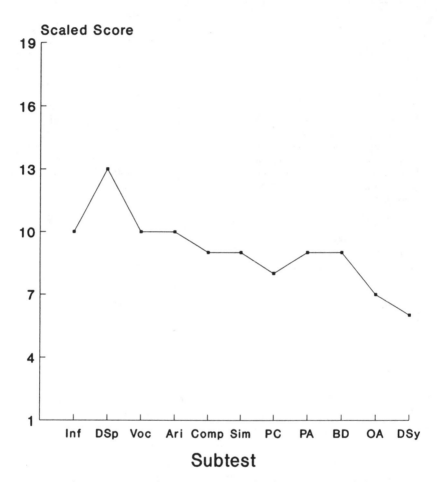

FIG. 4.1.   WAIS-R profile for *Case 1*. Note that the Digit Span scaled score
is at least one standard deviation higher than any other subtest.

tion was not evident in structured neuropsychological evaluation, where
she was not likely to experience the strong emotional reactions. Her therapists determined that her attention was particularly vulnerable to disruption at times when she was experiencing an emotional reaction. Thus,
her emotional responses also required some attention during rehabilitation.

This case illustrates at least a couple of attributes of neuropsychological tests that must be taken into account in using the evaluation to plan
treatment. First, if the traditional interpretation of WAIS-R Digit Span had

been used, she would have been judged to have a strength in attentional capacity when, in fact, she had a deficit in this area. Second, her problem with emotions was not evident in the optimized neuropsychological testing environment, nor would the specifics of this problem have been evident on standard personality assessment instruments. The following are a few principles in the application of neuropsychological tests that can help to avoid such problems.

Principles for Application

The right side of Table 4.1 briefly summarizes some principles for the application of neuropsychological tests that are useful in addressing the limitations listed on the left side of the table. The most basic and important principle is to conduct an in-depth interview during any neuropsychological evaluation. Such an interview should cover several important topics: The patient's functioning in everyday activities should be described by the patient, and preferrably by an objective relative. Performance in the face of distraction or in other suboptimal circumstances should be explored. The patient's ability to organize and plan should be addressed in interview. Personality deficits such as impulse-control problems or difficulties should be noted. In all these areas, changes from premorbid status should be noted. One should not assume that a problem identified during interview is the result of a neurological injury or illness unless it can be established that the problem arose or was exacerbated concomitantly with the injury or disease.

Some deficits not measured by or not defined by testing can be revealed by careful observation during neuropsychological evaluation. Examples of inappropriate behavior may be seen in patient interactions with the examiner, such as asking inappropriately personal questions or making rude or abrasive remarks. If behaviors like these are frequent, the examiner may attempt a brief intervention. The results of such interventions can provide useful information regarding a patient's ability to respond to cuing and structure. Not infrequently, patients will spontaneously help an examiner manipulate test materials or put them away. Although the absence of such behavior has no diagnostic value, its presence is unusual in patients with adynamic motivational disorders. As a third example, a patient's awareness of deficits can be probed during evaluation. Questioning patients about performance difficulties to see if they recognize impaired performance may test their ability to recognize deficits. There are numerous other ways in which observation can provide useful information.

Mistakes in interpretation and application can be avoided if examiners keep in mind the complexity of neuropsychological instruments. As noted before, even in relatively simple tests like Digit Span from the WAIS-R, there are multiple ways of obtaining good or impaired scores. There are at least three ways of addressing the multidimensional nature of test instruments during neuropsychological evaluation: (a) observing the process by which a patient completes or fails a task, (b) supplementing standard administration formats with alternative presentation formats to explore various hypotheses, and (c) analyzing findings between multiple tests to uncover consistencies between them.

Edith Kaplan has been a leader in developing the process approach to neuropsychological assessment, and this approach is epitimized by the WAIS-R as a Neuropsychological Instrument (Kaplan, Fein, Morris, & Delis, 1991). Kaplan has used the preceding three principles to help determine the underlying cause for impaired scores on WAIS-R subtests. For example, the process by which a patient completes Block Design is recorded. Errors in the right side of designs or errors in the internal details of designs may indicate dominant hemisphere dysfunction. Errors in the left side of designs or violating the square configuration of the design may indicate nondominant hemisphere dysfunction. As another example, if a patient shows a poor performance on the Information subtest, a multiple-choice format can be administered to determine if retrieval deficits play a role in the poor performance.

Consistently poor performance on multiple tests that share an underlying skill can be used to decipher which of the various skills required by a single test contributes to impaired performance. For example, poor performance on Digit Span, the Seashore Rhythm Test, and the Speech Sounds Perception Test could be due to an inability to sustain attention (i.e., a vigilance deficit), although other alternatives might be considered.

A fourth application principle for tests states that the usual way of interpreting a test should not be accepted without examining potential alternative explanations. Searching for patterns among test scores may be helpful in providing alternative explanations for a test score. For example, the Picture Completion subtest of the WAIS-R has typically been interpreted as a measure of attention to visual detail. However, given a standard administration, most patients are inclined to attempt to name the missing part. Thus, patients with language deficits may score poorly on Picture Completion, not because they have difficulty finding and recognizing the missing parts, but because they have difficulty finding the word (i.e., naming) to express the concept. Similarly, a patient may misname objects represented in line drawings, not because he or she has an anomia but because of a problem visually recognizing the picture. Semantic cues have been built into the Boston Naming Test (Kaplan, Goodglass, & Weintraub, 1983) to help tease apart visual recognition from naming errors. In short, mistakes in test interpretation will lead to misapplication of results. The reader may wish to peruse chapter 3 of this volume for greater detail.

In summary, the properties of neuropsychological instruments, the assessment environment, limitations regarding validity, and interpretive problems all have a bearing on application of assessment results to various referral questions and contexts. Although some problems can be overcome by developing better tests, the inherent limitations of our measurements must also be accepted. Problems in application of findings can be minimized by careful interviewing to uncover aspects of behavior that testing may not tap, by making careful behavioral observations for the same reason, and by attending to the complexity of individual tests and the patterns between tests. Given this background, we are now prepared to examine how the context of an evaluation affects the application of test results. Three clinical contexts are examined: diagnostic, rehabilitative, and forensic.

DIAGNOSTIC CONTEXT

Importance of Neuropsychological Findings for Diagnosis

It was once common in some locales for neuropsychological interpretations to play a major role in neurological diagnostic workups. Neuropsychological test results were not only used to attempt to localize a brain dysfunction but even to speculate about the underlying neuropathology. The advent of sophisticated computerized imaging techniques that could be applied to the visualization of structural changes in the brain has greatly reduced the need for neuropsychological evaluations as purely diagnostic instruments. However, a number of important diagnostic applications of neuropsychological assessment continue to be important.

The following are some instances in which neuropsychological evaluation can be useful in making a diagnostic decision: (a) In cases where dementia is suspected and medical colleagues have ruled out toxic, metabolic, structural, and infectious causes of cognitive complaints, it may be important to document the nature and degree of cognitive deficit. Such documentation may be particularly important in the early stages of a dementing process when symptoms are subtle. Neuropsychologists may be called on to distinguish between symptoms likely to be caused by progressive degenerative processes versus affective disturbances or other psychiatric problems. (b) Frequently, neuropsychologists are called on to assist in diagnosis of psychiatric symptoms. Known or suspected brain disease, injury, or dysfunction can produce symptoms similar to those of psychiatric syndromes such as schizophrenia, mania, depression, or other disorders. Patterns of performance on neuropsychological tests may be useful in distinguishing between these psychiatric syndromes and the impact of brain injury, stroke, toxic and metabolic disturbances, degenerative disorders, and other brain dysfunctions. (c) Persons occasionally experience seemingly minor events that could have implications for neurological functioning, such as a "minor" head injury or brief exposure to toxic matter. Animal models for "minor" head injury (e.g., Povlishock & Coburn, 1989) suggest that microscopic injury to white matter can occur without grosser structural changes that might be detected by computerized tomography and magnetic resonance scans. This type of damage may account for some of the behavioral changes seen after "minor" head injury (e.g., see Gentilini, Nichelli, & Schoenhuber, 1989; Gronwall, 1989; Rimel, Giordani, Barth, Boll, & Jane, 1981). In these types of cases, the neuropsychologist may be called on to determine if the "minor" injury or brief toxic exposure has caused cognitive sequelae. (d) Neuropsychological patterns may be useful in conjunction with other medical diagnostic techniques in determining seizure foci. In this diagnostic process, neuropsychological findings will be compared to findings from noninvasive and/or invasive EEG findings, ictal behaviors, neurological examination, structural brain imaging (magnetic resonance or computed tomography), and functional brain imaging (positron emission tomography or single photon emission computed tomography).

In cases such as these, neuropsychological findings influence both the ultimate diagnosis and the treatment decisions, either by diagnostic implications or by suggesting behavioral management strategies. Thus, diagnostic accuracy is of paramount importance. In the case of a progressive dementia, the family and the patient may want to know a prognosis to assist in making personal, business, or career decisions and to anticipate future needs. On the other hand, prematurely applying a diagnosis of dementia could have a devastating impact on a patient's self-esteem as well as causing disruption in personal and vocational activities. When dementia can be diagnosed, neuropsychological findings may have legal implications regarding competency and guardianship. In the case of psychiatric diagnoses, medication choices and behavioral management can be in part based on information and diagnostic impressions derived from the neuropsychological evaluation. In the case of minor head injury, patients may not understand why their abilities have changed in some areas and how to deal with those changes. A good neuropsychological evaluation can clarify what abilities have changed and suggest methods for dealing with changes. Often, there are also forensic implications for minor head injury. In the case of seizure-surgery candidates, neuropsychological findings, as well as other diagnostic data, play a role in determining the appropriateness of surgery and the probable focus of dysfunction. Thus, in each case where neuropsychological assessment plays a role in diagnosis, the implications for accuracy are profound.

Potential Problems in Diagnostic Application of Neuropsychological Assessment Results

In many cases where assessment goals are diagnostic, the neuropsychologist is dependent on the pattern of test scores in order to diagnose a dysfunction. For example, the relative performance on verbal versus visual-spatial measures can sometimes be used to lateralize dysfunction to the left or right hemisphere. This information might be useful in lateralizing an epileptogenic focus or establishing other types of dysfunction. However, keep in mind that a particular patient might have significant variations in abilities that are unrelated to the diagnostic question. Sometimes, for example, participation in a given occupation might lead to better development of verbal or visual spatial skills. A certain amount of individual variability between test scores should be expected. The critical question in examining a particular patient's pattern of scores is whether one is dealing with a normal degree of variation in abilities or a neuropsychologically meaningful deviation. Vanderploeg discusses issues relevant to premorbid functioning in chapter 2 of this volume.

Other premorbid variables may exist that have a direct impact on the interpretation of cognitive test results. For example, Haas, Cope, and Hall (1987) found a surprisingly high percentage of poor premorbid academic performance in their head-injured sample, suggesting that persons with learning disabilities are probably more susceptible to head injury. The cognitive effects of learning disability can be mistaken for those of head injury if a history of premorbid learning disability is not discovered during evaluation. The high incidence of alcohol involvement in traumatic injuries also suggests a greater incidence of alcoholism in head-injury samples (Alberts & Binder, 1991). It is known that chronic alcoholism causes memory changes that are related to underlying changes in the brain even for patients not experiencing amnesic syndromes (see Butters, 1985). Thus, the effects of chronic alcoholism might be mistaken for the effects of head injury or other neurological problems if such a history is not uncovered. Patterns of cultural and language differences can be confused with neurologically mediated cognitive changes as well (Sohlberg & Mateer, 1989). These premorbid variables will have different diagnostic and prognostic implications. They may not merit treatment intervention at all, but when they do treatment will be different than it would for a bonafide neurological event.

Similarly, the proximal event leading to a neuropsychological referral may not be the only possible reason for cognitive changes. If the neuropsychologist does not obtain a good history of cognitive functioning and probe for other possible causes of cognitive dysfunction, she or he may be misled by the pattern of test scores. For example, an older patient may have been experiencing some decline in functioning prior to a minor head injury that prompted referral. Their spouse may have taken over financial responsibilities several months prior to the injury because the patient was functioning inadequately. Such a circumstance might raise questions about dementia in addition to potential changes related to the head injury.

Another frequent diagnostic problem is differentiating psychiatric or psychological disturbances from brain dysfunction. Commonly, this is a difficult task because psychiatric disorders can show some of the same symptoms as acquired brain disorders. For example, patients with schizophrenia can show deficits on tasks thought to measure frontal lobe functioning (e.g., Weinberger, Berman, & Zec, 1986), on right- as compared to left-hemispatial attention (e.g., Posner, Early, Reiman, Pardo, & Dhawan, 1988), on naming tasks (e.g., Barr, Bilder, Goldberg, Kaplan, & Mukherjee, 1989), on speed of processing verbal versus nonverbal information (e.g., Posner et al., 1988), on maintenance of spoken discourse themes (e.g., Hoffman, Stopek, & Andreasen, 1986), on verbal memory span (e.g., Grove & Andreasen, 1985), and other functions. In fact, chronic schizophrenics are the psychiatric patients who may be regularly classified as having brain damage on the basis of neuropsychological findings (Heaton & Crowley, 1981). Further, some might argue that dilated ventricles, which can be found particularly in male schizophrenics (see Andreasen et al., 1990), or structural abnormalities in the limbic system and basal ganglia (e.g., Bogerts, Meertz, & Schönfeldt-Bausch, 1985) mean that schizophrenics have brain dysfunctions. Whereas this latter statement has a great deal of validity, the question remains as to whether neuropsychological tests can be helpful in discriminating schizophrenic patients from patients with other types of brain dysfunction. Proper diagnosis can have treatment implications.

Although other psychiatric patients are less commonly diagnosed as brain injured on neuropsychological tests, psychiatric syndromes other than schizophrenia can produce impaired performance on neuropsychological tests. As an example, patients with depression can have slowed mentation, poor concentration, and memory deficits. Indeed, this pattern of deficits has led some to draw parallels between depressed patients and patients with subcortical dementias (see King & Caine, 1990). Frontal and subcortical dysfunctions can produce symptoms of depression or mania (Robinson, Kubos, Starr, Rao, & Price, 1984; Starkstein, Robinson,

Berthier, Parikh, & Price, 1988; Starkstein, Robinson, & Price, 1987). If not carefully examined, patients with psychogenic amnesia can be mistaken for patients with brain damage. Chapter 3 by Cimino can be consulted for further information regarding distinguishing psychiatric disorder from brain dysfunction.

As noted earlier, neuropsychological tests may not be designed to capture certain aspects of personality functioning that might be relevant to diagnosis. Similarly, these instruments do not tap other aspects of psychological functioning that are particularly important in distinguishing brain dysfunction from psychiatric syndromes. Evidence regarding social and occupational functioning can be important in diagnosing schizophrenia, affective disorders, and certain personality disorders. Sleep disturbance, appetite disturbance, or fluctuations in weight, dysphoria, euphoria, suicidal ideation, poor judgment, rapid changes in mood, changes in sexual functioning, and other areas may be relevant to the diagnosis of affective disorder. Evidence of repression or denial can be relevant to diagnosis of dissociative disorders. Yet, most of these items are not tested by neuropsychological instruments.

In many of the aspects of neurological dysfunction and psychiatric disorder not covered by neuropsychological tests, it will be necessary to gather information through interview. In doing so, examiners should remember that patients with neurological and psychiatric dysfunction may not be aware of many of their dysfunctions. *Anosognosia* is a term coined by Babinski in 1914 for unawareness of deficits (Bauer & Rubens, 1985). After right-hemisphere injury (e.g., the more acute phase of right-hemisphere stroke), dramatic examples of anosognosia can be seen in patients who may be unaware of a hemiplegia or a hemianopia. However, problems in awareness of deficits also occur after frontal injury (Stuss, 1991). The implication concerning interview is that patients with awareness deficits may not be able to give an accurate account of their problems and changes related to brain injury. Patients with neurological dysfunction also may experience psychological denial to avoid the unpleasant implications of their deficits. Such denial also keeps the patient from providing accurate information about deficits during evaluation.

For these reasons, it is usually good practice to interview an independent source who is close enough to the patient to give an accurate picture of the patient's difficulties. Most often such a person is a relative, but the neuropsychologist must be aware that some relatives may have difficulties or motivations that limit their ability to give an accurate account of the patient's behavior. For example, after a head injury or stroke, or given a progressive dementia, family members as well as patients may use psychological denial to avoid the intensely unpleasant emotions that recognition of the patient's deficits causes. In these cases, the neuropsychologist will have to be prepared to assess the accuracy of the relative's report.

Not infrequently, neuropsychological results do not clearly answer a referral question or answer the question incompletely. For example, deficits in attention and memory may be seen in a patient for whom the diagnostic issue is differentiating depression from dementia. Depression may be present, but deficits are of a severity or pattern that could indicate other processes in addition to depression. Or, perhaps the level or pattern of results could be accounted for by the depression, but the history is suggestive of dementia. As another example, a patient with a mild head injury is demonstrating attentional and memory deficits at a level consistent with a mild head injury, but the patient is also experiencing symptoms of post-traumatic stress disorder, and the anxiety associated with this disorder may affect attention and memory. One mistake that can be made in similar instances is attempting to reach premature closure on a diagnosis.

In some cases, disorders will evolve over time. Dementias such as Alzheimer's disease, Pick's disease, or Binswanger's disease usually show a temporal progression. Severe head injuries may demonstrate improvement months after the injury. Progress may be made over varying intervals in other types of brain damage as well. In the case of differential diagnosis of dementia, families, patients, and referring physicians may make important decisions about careers, finances, legal matters, and social relationships based upon the diagnostic label. Considerable damage can be done if the label is applied when there are ambiguities about the diagnosis. Testing across multiple occasions may be needed to achieve an accurate diagnosis. In instances of head injury or other types of brain damage, significant improvement from tests done soon after injury may occur. Significant problems may ensue if attempts are made to predict long-term outcome too soon after injury. Again, important decisions can be made regarding the patient on the basis of inadequate predictions. The issue of improving performance after brain injury or disease is discussed further during the next major section of this chapter.

In summary, pitfalls in the application of neuropsychological findings to diagnostic questions can limit their utility in this endeavor. The cost of making an error in diagnosis frequently can be quite high, especially when the diagnosis is the basis for making critical personal, financial, career, or treatment decisions. For this reason, it is crucial that clinical neuropsychologists be aware of potential problems that might affect the rendering of accurate diagnostic information. Some of these potential problems were mentioned earlier and are summarized on the left side of Table 4.2. However, this list is by no means comprehensive. The reader has probably already realized that different diagnostic circumstances may

TABLE 4.2
Application Issues in the Diagnostic Context

Potential Pitfalls in Diagnostic Applications of Neuropsychological Assessments	Principles for Application of Neuropsychological Assessments in Diagnostic Contexts
1. Premorbid patterns of strength and weakness can be mistaken for neuropsychologically meaningful information.	1. Gather as much information as possible about premorbid cognitive strengths and weaknesses.
2. Proximal events prompting referral for neuropsychological assessment may not be the only cause of cognitive dysfunction.	2. Ascertain from history any other potential causes of cognitive dysfunction.
3. Premorbid conditions with specific patterns of cognitive functioning can be mistaken as the product of neurological injury or disease.	3. Inquire about premorbid educational, cultural, legal, and substance abuse history.
4. Psychiatric illnesses cause cognitive dysfunction that may be misinterpreted as representing other types of neuropsychological dysfunction.	4. Be aware of patterns of cognitive dysfunction caused by psychiatric illnesses.
5. In addition to not tapping important personality functions, neuropsychological tests do not measure aspects of social and occupational functioning that might be relevant to discriminating psychiatric disorders from other types of brain dysfunction.	5. Obtain a good history of social and occupational functioning.
6. Decreased self-awareness makes patients unable to convey accurate information regarding their deficits during interview.	6. Where possible, check for awareness of changes during interview, and interview relatives when available.
7. Motivations of relatives may limit their ability to give accurate information regarding patients' deficits during interview.	7. When interviewing relatives, assess motivations that might obscure information regarding patient's deficits.
8. Neuropsychological results may leave ambiguities with respect to some diagnostic questions.	8. Do not attempt to reach premature closure when data present ambiguities regarding diagnostic questions.
9. A single battery of neuropsychological tests may not capture elements of progression that are relevant to certain diagnoses.	9. In cases where progression of deficits would be expected for a given diagnosis, but the diagnosis cannot be unambiguously made, recommend re-evaluation at an appropriate interval.

raise their own unique set of issues. Practitioners must be continually alert for such dilemmas and develop methods for dealing with them.

Case 2 was a young woman in her early 20s. She was in our country studying English in preparation for enrolling in training relevant to her career. She was hit by an automobile while riding her bicycle. She may have been briefly unconscious at the scene of the accident. In the emergency room, she was alert but confused. CT scan of the brain was unremarkable; she was admitted to the neurosurgery unit for observation. After 3 days, the patient could not remember her name, and she was eventually identified by an acquaintance.

The neuropsychologist was consulted at this time. The patient's limited ability to communicate in English precluded a longer neuropsychological battery. The patient was given the Digit Span, Picture Completion, and Block Design subtests from the WAIS-R. She was also given the Galveston Orientation and Amnesia Test (GOAT: Levin, Benton, & Grossman, 1981), and the stories and figures from the Wechsler Memory Scale-Revised (WMS-R; Wechsler, 1987). The Digit Span scaled score of 8 was slightly below average, and the Picture Completion scaled score of 10 was average. Given the language component to both of these subtests (Picture Completion has a naming requirement), they may have underestimated functioning. The Block Design subtest was performed quite well, yielding a perfect performance with a scaled score of 19! Because others had told her, the patient was able to remember her name and her home country, but she was unable to remember any other personal information such as address and birthdate on the GOAT. On the other hand, she was able to name the hospital and was oriented to the various elements of time. Her somewhat limited recall of WMS-R stories may have been related to language phenomena, but it is important to note that she lost no information from immediate (14 of 50 ideas) to delayed (14 of 50 ideas) recall. Further, the patient remembered 38 of 41 details of the WMS-R designs on immediate recall and lost minimal information (36 of 41) at delayed recall. Both of these visual memory scores were at the 86th percentile.

The diagnostic issue was to determine whether the patient was in a state of post-traumatic amnesia or had other, possibly psychological, reasons for her amnesia. Remember that significant traumatic brain injury may exist even in the presence of a normal CT scan (Jennett & Teasdale, 1981). However, there were several reasons to implicate psychological causation. First and probably most important, the patient's retention of information (especially visual) across a delay suggests she was not in a state of post-traumatic amnesia. Patients in post-traumatic amnesia have a rapid rate of forgetting (Levin, High, & Eisenberg, 1988) that causes them to lose most information over even very short intervals (Levin et al., 1981). Second, the normal sequence in recovery of orientation is person, place, and time (Levin, 1989). Although other orders of recovery occur, it is extremely unusual for a patient emerging from post-traumatic amnesia to be oriented to place and time and yet to be disoriented to most aspects of person. Third, Performance subtests of the WAIS-R are likely to be most sensitive to brain dysfunction, especially during the early phases (Mandleberg & Brooks, 1975; Uzzell, Zimmerman, Dolinskas, & Obrist, 1979), and this patient performed quite well on Block Design.

Given these facts, a diagnosis of generalized psychogenic amnesia was suggested, and psychotherapy was initiated. Over the course of the next few days, the patient recovered her personal past. She discussed with her therapist a personal traumatic circumstance that she had discussed with no one previously. Other personal and family stressors that may have been contributory were also uncovered. The patient resumed her normal level of functioning. It is likely that the patient would have eventually recovered her personal history even if a correct diagnosis had not been made. Nonetheless, the therapy initiated with the proper diagnosis did offer her the opportunity to integrate elements of her past into her functioning, making her less vulnerable to future difficulties in functioning. Thus, this case illustrates the importance of knowing detailed information about relevant neuropsychological diagnoses and the alternative psychiatric diagnoses that might be applied to a case.

Principles for Application

Principles for the application of neuropsychological assessments to diagnostic contexts are summarized on the right side of Table 4.2. The principles are indexed by number to the problem on the left side of the table for which they provide a solution. The first is to gather as much information as possible about premorbid strengths and weaknesses. In chapter 2 of this volume, Vanderploeg discusses estimating premorbid levels of functioning, and such information is invaluable when trying to ascertain if a patient's functioning has deteriorated from premorbid levels. However, premorbid patterns of functioning may also be critical in making diagnostic statements. When a patient has attended college, a person's college major may give some insight into premorbid abilities. High school and college grades, achievement test scores, and college entrance scores may also be indicators of premorbid achievement. Favorite subjects and subjects that patients have found difficult may be valuable pieces of information. Occupation may give information about what skills a patient has had to develop and level of occupational attainment may be useful in estimating premorbid levels of functioning. Hobbies and interests may be similarly useful. Once some general expectations regarding premorbid abilities have been developed, the neuropsychologist must decide whether test patterns reflect this premorbid functioning or the diagnostic entity in question.

A second recommendation is to gather as complete a history of potential causes of cognitive changes as possible. As already noted, obvious recent events prompting referrals are not always the cause of a particular pattern of scores. Other possible causes of cognitive complaints must be ruled out. During interview, the patient's history should be examined for any possible decline in cognitive functioning that may not be obvious from the referral question and recent complaints. A psychiatric history should be taken. Possible past neurological events such as head injury, meningitis, vascular events, or other entities that may affect cognitive performance should be ruled out. History of drug or alcohol abuse, excessive use of caffeine or other substances that may affect behavior or cognitive performance must be ascertained. As noted before, learning disability, attention-deficit disorder, and language and cultural differences may all cause patterns of performance that can be mistaken for signs of brain injury by the unwary examiner.

When neuropsychologists are called on to differentiate the effects of known or suspected brain dysfunction from psychiatric disorder, they must know both the cognitive effects of the brain dysfunction and the cognitive effects of the psychiatric disturbance in question. As noted, psychiatric disorders such as schizophrenia, affective disorder, or dissociative disorders have symptoms that can mimic neuropsychological dysfunction. Works discussing the impact of psychiatric disorder on neuropsychological functioning (e.g., Heaton & Crowley, 1981) can be consulted and monitored for new developments, especially by practitioners who frequently must differentiate the cognitive effects of psychiatric from neurologic disorders. Similarly, the literature concerning various neuropsychological manifestations of brain dysfunctions should be consulted as well. Even very experienced neuropsychologists find it necessary to consult the literature when diagnostic entities they rarely see become an issue for a particular case.

Regarding the differentiation of brain dysfunction and psychiatric disorder, social and occupational functioning often can provide useful diagnostic information. Indeed, in disorders such as schizophrenia, deterioration of social and occupational functioning are among their diagnostic criteria (American Psychiatric Association, 1987: Diagnostic and Statistical Manual of Mental Disorders, 3rd ed. rev.). For this reason, a good social and occupational history should be obtained. The neuropsychologist should keep in mind questions such as: Has the patient been able to maintain stable relationships at different points in her or his life? If not, why not? Has the patient ever been arrested or had other significant trouble with the law? Has the patient been able to maintain a stable employment history? What is the longest period the patient has worked in a single job? What are the factors that may have influenced job changes? These are just a few of the questions that should be routinely investigated during interview.

As noted earlier, the information a patient gives regarding cognitive complaints can be affected either by unawareness or by denial of deficits. One must be aware of such possibilities during the interview process. Occasionally, it is possible to check for unawareness or denial by simple questioning. For example, patients can be asked what significant others say about their functioning. Patients may be aware of a difference in their own and others' opinions even though they are unaware of deficits. If the neuropsychologist suspects certain deficits based on referral or other information, she or he can probe for recognition of such deficits as an indicator of awareness. Alertness for indications of defensiveness may help in detecting denial.

Of course, relatives should be interviewed when possible. If one suspects that a relative may not be honest in the presence of the patient, the relative should be interviewed separately. Discrepancies between the relative's and the patient's report can confirm suspicions of unawareness or denial on the patient's part. Nonetheless, neuropsychologists must be alert for motivations on the part of the relative being interviewed that will obscure information about the patient's functioning. Frequently, relatives may be motivated to believe the patient is functioning better than she or he actually may be, but relatives may be motivated to make patients look worse than they are as well. Relatives can be questioned regarding how easy it has been for them to accept changes in the patient's functioning or about what their greatest fears might be. Answers to these and similar questions can help determine if the relative might be denying the nature or severity of deficits. Indications of anxiety when talking about certain subjects or unwillingness to entertain the possibility of change may be among the numerous indicators that relatives may be overestimating functioning. It should be obvious from this discussion that neuropsychologists must be more than technically competent in the administration, scoring, and interpretation of tests; there are numerous diagnostic circumstances when a premium is placed on excellence in clinical interviewing.

As noted earlier, significant damage to patients' lives can occur if the neuropsychological practitioner attempts to reach diagnostic closure in the face of significant ambiguity. Such diagnostic errors can lead to poor decisions regarding career, financial, and other matters. In the face of unresolvable ambiguity, it is best to state the diagnostic dilemma(s) as clearly as possible, highlighting the diagnostic possibilities and the data supporting each possibility. Frequently, the consumer of the diagnostic neuropsychological evaluation is a physician or health care team who has other sources of diagnostic information available. If such persons understand the nature of ambiguities clearly, they may be able (a) to resolve the ambiguity on the basis of other available information, (b) to plan the best strategy for gathering further data to resolve diagnostic questions, or (c) to plot the best course of treatment given the circumstances. Thus, presenting a clear discussion of the possibilities may facilitate diagnosis and treatment, whereas attempts to reach premature closure can cost valuable time and resources when treatment efforts and plans are misdirected.

In cases where a progressive disorder is suspected, such as in Alzheimer's disease, diagnostic ambiguities may be resolved with reevaluation after some period of time. Thus, when the diagnosis is in doubt and progressive disorder is suspected, reevaluation after a specified period of time should be recommended. It is worth noting in this regard that broad-spectrum cognitive and intellectual functions in Alzheimer's disease may remain stable for some period of time (possibly several months) after memory decline has begun (Haxby, Raffaele, Gillette, Schapiro, & Rapoport, 1992). Thus, a single reevaluation may be inadequate for tracking the course of intellectual decline, and multiple reevaluations may be needed before nonmemory disturbances involving language, praxis, and gnosis may be detected and provide strong evidence of an Alzheimer's disease diagnosis.

In summary, it is possible to mistake one diagnostic entity for another on the basis of neuropsychological results. Such mistakes can be minimized if the neuropsychologist uses as many sources of information as are available to derive a diagnostic opinion. Important data include premorbid cognitive, social, and occupational history. In a discussion of patients' deficits during interview, an attempt should be made to estimate awareness of deficits, and a collateral source of information to the patient should be interviewed when possible. Finally, the practitioner should avoid drawing premature conclusions when data do not justify closure and recommend retesting after a specified time when it is likely to add clarity to the diagnostic picture.

REHABILITATION CONTEXT

Importance of Neuropsychological Findings for Rehabilitation

During the 1980s, clinical neuropsychologists became increasingly involved in the rehabilitation of neurologically impaired patients. This was particularly evident in the rapid proliferation of head-trauma rehabilitation programs. There is only one justification for a clinical neuropsychological evaluation with rehabilitation patients: It must somehow contribute to improving the patient's ability to cope with his or her ultimate community environment. Such a contribution can be made by (a) defining cognitive dysfunctions that are a target for rehabilitation efforts,

133

(b) measuring progress during rehabilitation and recovery so that goals can be revised if necessary, (c) helping to define realistic goals for community re-entry, and (d) defining non-neuropsychological emotional problems that may interfere with rehabilitation.

Potential Problems in Rehabilitation Applications of Neuropsychological Assessment Results

Although the ultimate goals of rehabilitation are functional in nature (i.e., the aims are to increase a person's ability to function in the community), neuropsychological evaluations are conducted with tests that are artificial and microcosmic. The reasons for this type of test structure were discussed earlier and relate to the needs to break cognitive deficits into their simplist components and to establish normative samples that are biased as little as possible by occupations and interests, putting all examinees on "equal footing." These purposes create a paradox in that neuropsychological tests measure various components of cognitive functioning but are isolated from the various functional contexts in which patients must eventually perform on a day-to-day basis. This isolation from functional contexts means that our tests are at best indirect indicators of a person's ability to perform any particular functional activity and at worst misleading in some circumstances. The experienced examiner will recognize the limitations of various neuropsychological instruments in interpreting and integrating results. This discrepancy between the abilities that tests measure and the functional activities patients must routinely perform is central to many of the problems addressed next.

With respect to functional activities, referral sources, rehabilitation team members, family members, and patients may want to know, "Is the patient capable of living alone?" "Can the patient drive?" "Is she or he capable of managing her or his financial affairs?" "Is the patient capable of working? If so, in what capacity?" "How can the family deal with irritability or irrational anger?" "What remedies are there for memory dysfunction?" "What can be done about sporadic, seemingly capricious, lapses in memory?" Answers to such questions affect rehabilitation planning, the patient's quality of life, and the ability to exercise rights and privileges that most of us take for granted. Yet, factors other than those we typically measure during evaluation may affect the answers. For example, personality dysfunction has already been mentioned. Or, a person's ability to rely on a premorbid knowledge base for some particular job can on occasion assist in overcoming considerable cognitive deficit.

Some of the problems that are relevant to applications in the rehabilitation setting have been discussed in previous sections. To gain an accurate assessment of a patient's various cognitive abilities, neuropsychological testing is conducted in an optimal environment. In particular, examiners go to great lengths to minimize distractions. Yet, patients' daily environments are not free from distractions. Thus, the ability of a patient to function in a less than optimal environment is not typically assessed to any great extent.

Concerns of reliability and particularly validity affect the usefulness of a test in a rehabilitation. If the construct validity of an instrument is in doubt, it is likely to be of little value in understanding how cognitive functions have broken down. If the predictive validity has not been established, the prognostic value of a test is questionable. If a test cannot help to understand how cognition has faltered or what outcomes are likely, it is of no use in rehabilitation.

It is worth mentioning again that neuropsychological tests, for the most part, are not designed to measure personality changes that occur after some forms of brain damage. These changes may have a devastating impact on a patient's ability to function on the job and in the family (Lezak, 1978) and frequently are the most salient reason for rehabilitation and re-entry failures. Personality change is particularly common after traumatic brain injury, affecting 60% or more of severely injured patients even when minimal cognitive and motor deficits are present (Jennett, Snoek, Bond, & Brooks, 1981). The propensity for frontotemporal damage in this type of injury (Jennett & Teasdale, 1981) accounts for much of the personality change. Sohlberg and Mateer (1989) and Lezak (1986) noted the importance and the difficulty of measuring this type of change. Types of personality change that may occur include: irritability, other emotional lability, impulse-control problems (disinhibition), decreased initiation and motivation, lack of empathy, loss of ability to take a self-critical attitude, and inability to profit from feedback.

However, emotional changes are caused not only by actual neurological damage, but patients also have reactions to their injuries. Depression, denial, and anger are common in patients who are struggling to incorporate significant loss of function into their self-concepts. It is important to distinguish such psychological reactions from neurologically induced personality changes because the treatment implications are different. For persons struggling with self-concept issues, assistance in integrating changes can be offered. Frequently, individual or group psychotherapy can significantly facilitate emotional adjustment (Prigatano, 1986). On the other hand, education and compensation for neurologically induced personality change can be recommended (e.g., Crosson, 1987). Examiners should further realize that not all problems relating to personality may be traceable to neurological substrates or emotional reactions to injury. Patients may carry significant premorbid personality or psychiatric disturbances into the rehabilitation setting. There are indications in the literature that the incidence of pre-existing personality or psychiatric dysfunction may be greater in a head-injury population than in the general population (Alberts & Binder, 1991; Levin et al., 1981).

Another problem mentioned briefly before is the change in functioning over time. It is particularly likely that the acute effects of brain damage will be mitigated across time. Thus, long-term rehabilitation planning cannot be based upon neuropsychological assessments conducted relatively soon after the damage occurred. Attempting to make precise long-term prognostic statements on the basis of acute neuropsychological data frequently can mislead patients, family, and referral sources. Further, when recovery exceeds or fails to meet predictions, patients and family members lose trust in medical, psychological, and rehabilitation professionals. Lezak (1986) has estimated that most patients have reached a neuropsychological "plateau" by 2 or 3 years postonset. However, it is the experience of this author that significant changes in cognitive functioning may occur at least as long as 5 years post onset in some head-injured patients if test–retest intervals are long enough. The dilemma for rehabilitation neuropsychologists and their patients is that long-term planning cannot be delayed for years waiting for evidence of plateau.

Lezak (1986) noted another error committed by some examiners. Some clinicians make the mistake of having observation serve test instruments, as opposed to having testing serve the purpose of observation. When too much emphasis is placed on test scores and actuarial approaches, valuable information is lost. Nowhere is this more true than in attempts to evaluate awareness. It has been noted that patients who have an intellectual awareness of their deficits may still be unable to recognize "on line" when a deficit is impacting performance (Barco, Crosson, Bolesta, Werts, & Stout, 1991; Crosson et al., 1989). This is termed *emergent awareness*, and this form of awareness is critical to the adequate performance. It can only be assessed during neuropsychological evaluations if the examiner looks beyond test scores and makes a concerted effort to evaluate awareness.

The next step after assessing awareness is to estimate a patient's ability to compensate for deficits. As rehabilitation progresses into its more chronic phase, compensation for lasting deficits becomes increasingly important. The ability to compensate is intimately tied to awareness, because patients who are unaware of how a deficit is impacting them will not think to compensate (Barco et al., 1991; Crosson et al., 1989). The neuropsychologist can use the evaluation as an observational tool to estimate a patient's ability to compensate for deficits. Even so, a complete understanding of how a patient is able to compensate can only be accomplished through extended, intensive rehabilitation.

Issues relevant to the application of neuropsychological tests to rehabilitation are summarized on the left side of Table 4.3. When evalua-

TABLE 4.3
Application Issues in the Rehabilitation Context

Potential Pitfalls in Rehabilitation Applications of Neuropsychological Assessment	Principles for the Application of Neuropsychological Assessments in Rehabilitation Contexts
1. Neuropsychological tests generally do not measure the functional activities that are the ultimate target of rehabilitation treatments.	1a. Inquire regarding problems with functional activities during interview and assess contradictions between this information and test results.
	1b. Be conservative in making predictions about functional activities based on neuropsychological evaluations.
	1c. Refer patients for functional evaluations of activities in question.
2. Test results obtained in an optimal environment must be used to predict performance in less than optimal environments.	2. Inquire regarding environmental factors (e.g., distractions, lack of structure, etc.) that may impact functional performance.
3. To facilitate rehabilitation treatment, neuropsychologists must distinguish between emotional reactions to injury, neurologically induced emotional changes, and premorbid personality patterns.	3a. Inquire about premorbid and postinjury emotional and personality difficulties and their context during interview.
	3b. Continue to assess emotional reactions as rehabilitation progresses.
4. Changes in neuropsychological functioning during rehabilitation may make results of previous neuropsychological evaluations obsolete.	4a. During the initial phases of rehabilitation, keep assessments short, deficit specific, and frequent.
	4b. During the more chronic phases of rehabilitation, recommend repeat evaluations if significant changes are likely to occur.
5. Test scores alone will not allow the examiner to assess a patient's ability to be aware of and compensate for deficits.	5. Build into assessments methods for assessing awareness of deficits and ability to compensate for deficits.

tions are conducted to assist in maximizing daily functions in the community, the neuropsychologist must focus on the practical implications of deficits. In this context, a high premium is placed on construct and predictive validity. Yet, as Lezak (1986) noted, we cannot be satisfied with test scores alone; we must use tests as an observational tool and understand the limitations of our instruments. Indeed, a good neuropsychological evaluation should only be considered a point of departure for rehabilitative treatment planning. Assessment must be an integral part of each treatment session. The results of each treatment task provide new data, which will lead to successive revisions of the original treatment plan as more facets of a patient's cognitive strengths and weaknesses are discovered and the patient improves during rehabilitation. Applications to rehabilitation can be quite complex. The following three case examples illustrate how premorbid learning, awareness deficits, and emotional reactions played a part in rehabilitation. In each case, some type of continuing assessment was an important facet of treatment.

Case 3 was a male in his 40s who was involved in a motor vehicle accident. He taught advanced mathematics as a career. His MR scan demonstrated massive left-temporal lobe damage, involving most of the mesial and inferior temporal lobe. Consistent with this damage, the patient demonstrated decreased performance (0 percentile) on the Visual Naming subtest of the Multilingual Aphasia Examination (MAE; Benton & Hamsher, 1989). Auditory–verbal comprehension (MAE Token Test = 82nd percentile), repetition (MAE Sentence Repetition = 43rd percentile), and word list generation (MAE Controlled Oral Word Association = 74th percentile) were all within normal limits. Although his narrative language included circumlocutions and a few word-finding errors, he generally could be understood at 4 months post injury. His narrative language was somewhat less impaired than naming performance would lead one to believe. As measured by the California Verbal Learning Test (CVLT; Delis, Kramer, Kaplan, & Ober, 1987), verbal memory was severely impaired: Total learning trials performance, all delayed recall trials, and discriminability for the recognition trial were all 3 to 4 standard deviations below the normative mean. Intrusion errors were a common element of performance. Left-hemisphere dysfunction was also manifested in a lower Verbal than Performance IQ on the WAIS-R (VIQ = 102, PIQ = 111), but above-average scores on Vocabulary (scaled score = 12) and Comprehension (scaled score = 11) indicate that language output was less impaired than visual naming.

The patient's neurosurgeon felt that he would make a good adjustment to his injury even without intensive rehabilitation. The patient refused language therapy and likewise was not interested in more intensive rehabilitation. He planned to return to teaching shortly after his injury. He taught one course with which he was quite familiar, and he prepared a more complex course for the following semester. Because of concerns regarding his possible success, a follow-up schedule was arranged. During these visits, the patient revealed he was successful in his classroom teaching. There was independent confirmation. He occasionally asked for the help of his colleagues in preparing certain aspects of his courses. He also continued other public speaking activities, but he found it more difficult to write about mathematical concepts.

Thus, in spite of language and verbal memory deficits, the patient made a successful re-entry into teaching. Even though we recognized his spoken language to be better than his naming score would indicate, we had been pessimistic regarding his ability to succeed. Our prognosis failed to take into account at least two factors: (a) The patient's extensive knowledge about mathematics was largely intact and not tapped by our testing; (b) the patient's previous teaching experience was extraordinarily useful in providing him with structure and a set of procedures within which he was able to function. In other words, we did not weigh heavily enough in our prognosis how his knowledge of mathematics and teaching experience would be useful during his re-entry.

Case 4 was a male in his 30s. At 17 years post closed head injury, his MR scan showed diffuse atrophic enlargement of the lateral ventricles as well as the upper third ventricle. There was also thinning of the corpus callosum just anterior to the splenium, a defect in the midbrain tegmentum, and areas of increased signal intensity in the periventricular white matter and in the centrum semiovale.

His WAIS-R profile demonstrated a significant Verbal–Performance discrepancy (VIQ = 116, PIQ = 98) on the WAIS-R, with the Verbal IQ in the high-average range. The patient had severe verbal memory problems as measured by the CVLT (learning trials total and delayed recall trials all 4 standard deviations below normative mean, with recognition trial discriminablility somewhat better) and the Wechsler Memory Scale (Wechsler, 1945) paragraphs. Other problem areas on neuropsychological evaluation included left-hand impairment on the Tactual Performance Test, impaired localization on the Tactual Performance Test, and mildly slowed Finger Tapping with the left hand.

On the surface, the patient looked like an excellent candidate for rehabilitation with excellent verbal skills. However, during rehabilitation, the team discovered that he could not recognize problems when they were happening. The type of awareness for which this patient had a deficit has been termed *emergent awareness* (Crosson et al., 1989). The major means for assessing emergent awareness are through clinical observation (Barco et al., 1991). Relevant to this observation regarding his awareness was the fact that he had failed four professional programs before seeking help. Each time, he was able to perform adequately in the classroom, and it was the practical application experiences that he could not pass. On a job trial as a physical therapy aide, the patient was observed to leave out parts of treatment regimes or to confuse patients when writing unofficial notes. (Of course, he was supervised closely enough that these mistakes did not jeopardize patient care.) The patient was unable to realize that he was making these mistakes, and he had to rely on feedback from his supervisor. Attempts to remediate and compensate for this emergent-awareness deficit met with only minimal success. Thus, the emergent-awareness deficit had to be considered a permanent deficit. The implication was that he would require close supervision so that someone could catch and inform him of his errors.

For this case, neuropsychological tests did not tap his ability to recognize problem situations when they occurred. This problem was critical for understanding the patient's difficulties in work environments. The best predictor of this deficit on neuropsychological assessment may have been the indicators of right-hemisphere deficit, but the correlation between these indicators and the functional problem is far from a one-to-one correspondence.

Case 5 was a male in his 20s who received a head injury in a fall during an industrial accident. He had a partial right-temporal lobectomy to relieve intracranial pressure and remove contused tissue. Acute CT scan also had indicated edema in the left-parietal, temporal, and occipital lobes.

Although the patient did not show classical symptoms of aphasia or a recognizable aphasic syndrome, language testing revealed significant deficits: MAE Visual Naming = 2nd percentile; MAE Sentence Repetition = 0 percentile; MAE Token Test < 1st percentile; MAE Controlled Oral Word Association < 1st percentile. His verbal memory as measured by the CVLT was impaired (learning trial total and delayed recall trials 4 to 5 standard deviations below normative mean, with discriminability on recognition trial 2 standard deviations below mean). Verbal memory problems were related, at least to some degree, to his language impairments. His Verbal IQ (79) was in the borderline range of functioning, and his Performance IQ (87) was in the low-normal range of functioning. Other impaired performances were seen on the Seashore Rhythm Test, Part B of the Trail Making Test, and the Porteus Maze Test (Porteus, 1959). The patient also had a right homonymous hemianopsia.

During the course of his rehabilitation, it was discovered that the patient was having difficulty controlling his anger, and he was even becoming physically aggressive with his wife. At the same time, it was determined that the patient was depressed. The depression was related to his situation. Although the patient had significant language, verbal intellectual, and verbal memory deficits on testing, it had been determined in therapy that he was able to understand and respond to verbally presented concepts in several instances. Therefore, it was decided to handle the problems in individual as well as group psychotherapy. As his depression lessened with therapy, so did his problems with anger control.

It was important to distinguish anger problems that are related directly to brain injury from those that are related to a reaction to the injury and from those that involve personality structure. Those that are related to the patient's emotional reaction to injury may be amenable to psychotherapy. For those related to neurological injury, it may be best to assume in the chronic phase of recovery that they may be present indefinitely and work on management strategies. Characterological anger problems are sometimes the hardest to treat successfully in brain-injury rehabilitation programs.

Principles for Application

These cases are examples of how neuropsychological test results failed to provide a complete understanding of patient functioning relevant to rehabilitation. In Case 3, isolation of neuropsychological instruments from functional contexts provided information that led to an underestimation of the patient's abilities. In Case 4, the neuropsychological test data suggested that problems in awareness might have been present, but there was no way of confirming this hypothesis on the basis of test scores alone. In Case 5, it was necessary to distinguish the source of the patient's anger as well as to understand his functional communication abilities to arrive at an appropriate treatment strategy. In each instance, information other than that from neuropsychological tests was necessary to implement plans that would maximize the patient's functioning. Thus, the diagnostic process and the outcomes in these cases suggest that optimal practice of neuropsychology in a rehabilitation does not end with the completion of an initial evaluation. Optimal practice in a rehabilitation setting involves integration of the neuropsychologist into the treatment team, following the patient over time, and understanding how various causes of emotional difficulties may impact treatment and day-to-day living. As rehabilitation progresses, as the patient becomes more aware of deficits and reacts emotionally, as recovery takes place, as the patient acquires or reacquires skills through rehabilitation, and as limitations become better defined with data gathered during treatment, the neuropsychologist can provide valuable guidance in altering treatment plans and outcome expectations.

Keeping the rehabilitation process in mind, some recommendations can make the formal testing and assessment process more effective. The suggestions for rehabilitative applications on the right-hand side of Table 4.3 have been indexed by number to the problems listed on the left-hand side of this table. The first suggestion is to inquire of patients and family members about difficulties in functional activities. For many outpatients, such inquiries will be quite extensive. They should involve what activities the patient performs on a regular basis, any difficulties with such activities, activities the patient has tried to perform but cannot, and the reasons the patient cannot perform those activities. Any difficulties arising in the day-to-day family life can also be useful information.

Because patients do not generally perform functional activities in as ideal an environment as the neuropsychology lab, examiners should inquire regarding environmental factors that impact performance of these activities. For example, what happens when the patient is distracted from an activity? What happens if the patient is not given structure? Does the patient initiate activities on his or her own? Can the patient remember when requested to perform various activities? What compensations have been tried, and which ones have been useful?

Once a picture of functional activities and problems has been established, the examiner can compare this picture to test results. Providing relatives and patients have given a relatively accurate picture of daily functioning (see previous section for problems assessing accuracy of report), any contradictions between what the patient can or cannot do and what might be predicted from test results can provide useful information. In instances where such contradictions exist, the examiner should look for what assets or deficits might have been missed. Do examination results lead to gross underestimation or overestimation of the patient's abilities? And, what are the implications of this information for rehabilitation?

Because test results frequently do not correspond with functional abilities in a highly accurate fashion, neuropsychologists should be somewhat conservative in making prognostic statements for rehabilitation. There is a delicate balance between preventing patients from doing an activity of which they might be capable and allowing patients to participate in an activity at which they probably will fail. Other factors including the patient's level of awareness, his or her ability to ultimately compensate for deficits, his or her motivation to participate in the activity, or the level of support for the activity in the environment may affect treatment-planning decisions. In some instances where awareness is low and patients insist on performing an activity in which the probability of failure is high, it is better to orchestrate a functional trial and use the results to attempt to change course.

When neuropsychological results and functional reports are in conflict, or when the bearing of neuropsychological findings on functional capacities is not clear, a functional evaluation of the specific activity should be recommended. In many rehabilitation programs today, such functional evaluations are a routine part of rehabilitation. Even the independent neuropsychological practitioner performing an evaluation for rehabilitative reasons may find occasion to make referrals for functional evaluations. For example, driving evaluations can be found in many large rehabilitation centers. Such evaluations may use simulators or even actual driving trials to generate recommendations about a patient's driving status.

Neuropsychologists in a rehabilitation setting should be certain to make adequate inquiry regarding premorbid and postinjury emotional difficulties and changes. Based on knowledge of psychopathology, emotional changes due to neurological injury, and familiarity with reactions to injury, some estimation of the source of emotional problems can be made. Often times when trying to differentiate between neurological and reactive causes for emotional difficulties, the circumstances that trigger emotional reactions will give a clue. For example, if a patient tends to have an emotional reaction when he or she is confronted by a task he or she cannot do, when relatives have to do tasks the patient once did, or when reminded of the discrepancies between premorbid and postinjury abilities, it is likely that the patient is experiencing a reaction to the deficits created by the injury, at least in part. On the other hand, if a patient is more irritable with numerous minor stressors without respect to what such stressors represent to him or her, then the patient may have a neurologically induced change in emotions.

As rehabilitation progresses, the neuropsychologist should continue to assess emotional factors. Sometimes, additional information will clarify a diagnosis. In other instances, as patients become more aware of their deficits, and particularly the functional implications, anger and/or denial will become more evident. In either instance, changes in treatment plans may be justified. In the case of emotional reactions, patients with severe brain injury frequently have substantial insights into their psychological dilemmas and can benefit from psychotherapy (e.g., see Prigatano, 1986).

The likelihood that a patient will make substantial changes can also impact the neuropsychological evaluation. In the early parts of rehabilitation, soon after injury or stroke, patients will be likely to change rapidly. An evaluation conducted today may not present an accurate picture of the patient's abilities in as little as a week. Sohlberg and Mateer (1989) recommended keeping evaluations short, deficit specific, and frequent during this period. Longer, more traditional neuropsychological evaluations may be performed later when they are likely to be useful over several weeks of rehabilitation.

However, even in the more chronic phases of rehabilitation, it may be necessary to repeat more extensive evaluations if the patient is expected to show significant improvement. Improvement may be anticipated as a result of rehabilitation or as a result of continued recovery. In such cases, treatment or community re-entry plans may be altered if changes seem to so justify. Thus, neuropsychological tests can quantify underlying cognitive changes. Of course, evaluation results would have to be collated with information about changes in functional activities to increase predictive accuracy.

Finally, in addition to interviewing patients and family to make an estimate of awareness of deficits (see previous section), the neuropsychologist can build into evaluations ways of qualitatively assessing awareness of deficits. This information is particularly useful in rehabilitation because knowledge of awareness deficits can significantly impact rehabilitation. Barco et al. (1991) discussed assessment and treatment of awareness deficits during rehabilitation. The earlier awareness deficits are described, the earlier treatment can begin. To assess awareness, examiners can ask patients how well they think they did on various tasks. Observations of attempts to compensate for deficits during evaluation are also informative because such attempts indicate not only some awareness of a problem but also the capacity to compensate.

In summary, the rehabilitation process can be greatly enhanced if the neuropsychologist keeps in mind the likely discrepancies between test performance and functional abilities. Such discrepancies necessitate not only gathering information about functional activities during interview but also recommendations for functional evaluations. Although emotional factors and awareness will be assessed in the process of rehabilitation, initial neuropsychological evaluations can make a contribution to identifying and specifying such problems early in the rehabilitation process.

FORENSIC CONTEXT

Importance of Neuropsychological Findings for Forensic Questions

There are numerous ways in which a neuropsychologist might become involved in the legal system. Suspected or established brain damage or dysfunction may have a bearing on any number of legal questions. With respect to the criminal arena, competency to stand trial, sanity at the time of an offense, and mitigating circumstances relevant to sentencing are among the most common issues. With respect to civil proceedings, a neuropsychologist may be called on to establish the existence of impairment relative to brain damage or dysfunction in personal injury, workers compensation, or medical malpractice cases. Neuropsychological functioning might be relevant to cases involving guardianship for person or property as well.

Melton, Petrila, Poythress, and Slobogin (1987) discussed the uneasy alliance between psychology and the legal profession, and they present some of the reasons why this is the case. In fact, the professional worlds of psychologists and attorneys are frequently quite different regarding basic assumptions. In the legal context, free will is usually presumed as a basic tenet, whereas the science of psychology usually holds human behavior to be determined by any number of influences. Attorneys and psychologists also may differ on what is considered a fact. For the former, a fact, once established, is more or less an all-or-nothing matter, whereas for the latter it is a matter of probabilities with varying degrees of ambiguity. The method of arriving at facts is also different. Attorneys will tend to sharpen conflict as a means of examining disputed issues, but psychologists will tend to look for some convergence of data. Further, psychologists are taught to minimize, prevent, or resolve conflict to promote positive interactions. Thus, the assumptions made and methods used by psychologists are often in conflict with the assumptions made by and needs of attorneys.

The complexities for a neuropsychologist functioning within the legal system are so vast that it would be difficult to cover them comprehensively in any thing short of an entire volume. Rather, this chapter highlights some of the general issues that a neuropsychologist just beginning forensic activity might wish to consider. For greater detail in forensic psychology and forensic neuropsychology, the reader is referred to some of the volumes dedicated solely to this issue (e.g., Blau, 1984; Doerr & Carlin, 1991; Melton et al., 1987).

Potential Problems in Forensic Applications of Neuropsychological Assessment Results

One of the first problems to be addressed is the pressure in forensic evaluations to derive a definitive opinion regarding the issue in question. As an attorney begins to build his or her case, it will become obvious that the neuropsychological evaluation could best support the case if a certain outcome were obtained. In criminal cases, the stakes may be quite high. For example, a client's life might hinge on the outcome of an evaluation in a first-degree murder case. Likewise, large sums of money may be at stake in personal injury cases. Subtle, and unfortunately sometimes not so subtle, pressures may be put on the clinician to produce a certain outcome from the evaluation or a certain type of testimony (e.g., see Wedding, 1991). Further, and even more likely, the neuropsychologist may be pressured by the legal needs to give more definitive answers to questions than data justify. For example, the effects of minor head injury are frequently difficult to distinguish from depression or other emotional reactions, and the disposition of the case may hinge on making such a distinction.

A related question is the limits of a neuropsychologist's competence from a legal perspective. The question of competence can be relevant to both the admissibility of a neuropsychologist's testimony and to the way a neuropsychologist presents him or herself and his or her data to the court. Regarding the issue of admissibility, most jurisdictions in the United States have found neuropsychologists' testimony admissible regarding the presence or absence of brain damage (Richardson & Adams, 1992). However, in some jurisdictions, a neuropsychologist's testimony regarding causal linkage to a particular event, such as a head injury, has been ruled inadmissible. There are not many rulings regarding the admissibility of neuropsychological testimony with respect to prognosis, but Richardson and Adams (1992) suggested that admissibility of testimony regarding prognosis should be expected to parallel admissibility of testimony regarding causal linkage.

Regarding the way neuropsychologists present themselves and their data, they are often asked to answer questions that may relate to the medical status of the patient. For example, it is not unheard of for a neuropsychologist to be asked questions related to neuropathology or neuroanatomy. The nature and range of testimony that a neuropsychologist should give, irrespective of its admissibility, can become an ethical issue. The ability of neuropsychological tests to predict a given functional outcome is as much at issue here as it is in the rehabilitation arena (see preceding discussion). Faust (1991), for example, has suggested that neuropsychologists generally should not testify in forensic cases in part because the validity for neuropsychological tests to make such predictions has not been established.

Issues of diagnostic accuracy in clinical neuropsychology are a matter of some dispute, especially regarding their usefulness in legal proceedings (e.g., see Faust, 1991; Wedding, 1991; cf. Barth, Ryan, & Hawk, 1991; Richardson & Adams, 1992). Although I advocate caution in applying clinical neuropsychological findings to forensic as well as rehabilitation and diagnostic cases, it should be noted that some of the reasoning suggesting a lack of diagnostic accuracy is based on studies where clinicians were attempting to make actuarial predictions in the absence of data normally available in most clinical contexts, including forensic evaluations. Although it was once popular to perform "blind" interpretations in clinical neuropsychology, no well-trained clinician today will attempt to make diagnostic statements in the absence of face-to-face contact with the patient, including a diagnostic interview. Whereas some authors justifiably criticize neuropsychological tests for a lack of functional validity, many of the studies they cite regarding the validity of clinical judgments fail to assess clinical judgment the way it is practiced on a day-to-day basis (see Barth et al., 1991).

Nonetheless, one problematic area for the practice of forensic neuropsychology is the issue of malingering (Faust, 1991). Lezak (1983) described some methods designed to detect malingering. The Rey 15 Item Test is one popular method that requires patients to remember 15 items across a short delay. In fact, the items are highly related and routinely grouped into obvious sets, reducing the memory demand. Symptom-validity testing (Binder & Pankratz, 1987; Pankratz, 1979; Pankratz, Fausti, & Peed, 1975) has also gained some popularity. Using this procedure, 100 trials of some two-alternative forced-choice procedure relevant to presenting complaints are presented. By chance alone, the patient should obtain a score of 50% correct; with a large number of trials, significant deviation below this level is taken as suggestive of malingering. Although this strategy appears promising, a recent study by White (1992) demonstrated that informed malingerers (college students) score considerably above the 50% correct level on a symptom-validity task for memory, although they score below actual amnesics and head-injured patients. Preliminary analyses indicate that average response time may be the most promising indicator of conscious efforts to manipulate the data (White, 1992). White's data are relatively consistent with similar data from Bickart, Meyer, and Connell (1991). Another means for detecting malingering is internal inconsistencies among interview and test data. However, the bottom line regarding malingering at this time is that it may be difficult to detect in some instances.

Another issue facing neuropsychologists in forensic cases is the adversarial nature of the legal process. Clinicians who are unfamiliar with the process will most certainly find it a foreign method of seeking "truth." Blau (1984) noted that psychologists should be aware that opinions will be subjected to scrutiny regarding the minutest of details by opposing attorneys. In an adversarial system of justice, the job of the latter is to put the expert opinions you offer to the test. For this reason, opposing attorneys are likely to retain their own psychologists or neuropsychologists to examine test reports and depositions for errors, flawed reasoning, or other ways in which the opinions may lack credibility. Thus, neuropsychologists can expect to have their opinions attacked, sometimes in a fairly sophisticated manner.

Finally, attorneys may find neuropsychological procedures and opinions as foreign as psychologists find legal procedures (Melton et al., 1987; Richardson & Adams, 1992). Not only may attorneys be unfamiliar with the strengths of neuropsychological tests, but it probably should be assumed that jurors will know little about these instruments and their utility. If they do not deal with psychologists often, attorneys may be unfamiliar with rulings that impact on the admissibility of evidence in certain jurisdictions. In addition to having little information about tests, some attorneys also will not know how to identify a qualified neuropsychologist. Poor work done by unqualified professionals will ultimately hurt the credibility and effectiveness of the profession in general.

A few very basic issues concerning forensic neuropsychology have been discussed previously and outlined in Table 4.4. The practical limitations of our instruments often will limit our ability to answer all the questions an attorney might pose. In the adversarial atmosphere of legal proceedings, some pressure may build to answer questions that might not be capable of being answered. However, the neuropsychologist should note that most attorneys are relatively uninformed about neuropsychological techniques and instruments, further making communication difficult.

TABLE 4.4
Application Issues in the Forensic Context

Potential Pitfalls in Forensic Applications of Neuropsychological Assessments	Principles for Application of Neuropsychological Assessments in Forensic Contexts
1. Neuropsychologists may be placed under indirect or direct pressure to have their data support a particular point of view.	1a. Limit one's role to acting as the attorney's or the court's consultant regarding various aspects of a case related to neuropsychological issues.
	1b. Advise attorneys about the strengths and weaknesses of their case on the basis of the neuropsychological data.
2. Neuropsychologists may be pressured to answer questions for which the data do not justify a clear answer.	2. Clarify ambiguities but do not try to remove them if the data do not so justify.
3. Neuropsychologists' testimony regarding causation of brain dysfunction has been ruled inadmissible in some jurisdictions.	3. Know rulings in the jurisdiction appropriate to the case regarding neuropsychological testimony.
4. During testimony, neuropsychologists may be asked to testify about matters outside their realm of expertise.	4. Do not testify about matters outside a neuropsychologist's realm of expertise.
5. Validity for predicting specific functional outcomes may be limited.	5a. Know the limitations of test instruments relevant to the purpose for which they are being used.
	5b. Recommend gathering functional data if necessary.
6. In some instances, the ability of neuropsychological instruments to detect malingering may be limited.	6a. Employ tests for malingering where appropriate.
	6b. Do not overstate the validity of neuropsychological procedures in detecting malingering.
7. The adversarial nature of legal proceedings may be foreign to neuropsychologists.	7a. Prepare testimony as if your colleagues were going to scrutinize it.
	7b. Understand and accept attorneys' adversarial role in legal proceedings.
8. Attorneys may be unfamiliar with neuropsychological issues relevant to some cases.	8a. Educate attorneys about relevant neuropsychological issues.
	8b. Educate attorneys regarding who is qualified to testify as a neuropsychological expert.

Case 6 was a 71-year-old male who was tested 2 months after a motor vehicle accident. Although the referral came directly from his neurologist, the patient had retained an attorney with whom the clinicians were in contact. The patient was a front-seat occupant in an automobile struck from behind; the force of the impact threw the glasses he was wearing into the rear of the car. He claimed to remember the impact of the accident, and he remembered events soon after the accident with no signifi-

cant gaps in memory otherwise. Thus, the periods of unconsciousness and/or posttraumatic amnesia were minimal if any. Because of headaches and dizziness subsequent to the accident, the patient had an MR scan 3 weeks after the accident, which demonstrated a left parietal subacute subdural hematoma with minimal impingement on the left occipital horn. Complaints at the time of testing included short-term memory problems, difficulty concentrating, and dizziness and nausea when he tilted his head and looked upward. Headaches had decreased since the accident, however.

The patient had a 12th-grade education, was right handed, and had a stable blue-collar job history. Medical history included disability retirement in his 50s after ulcer surgery. He had prostate and intestinal surgeries 2 years before the evaluation. He was under treatment for cardiac problems. The patient's wife noted that he had some memory problems prior to the accident.

WAIS-R results showed a significant Verbal–Performance discrepancy in favor of Performance IQ (VIQ = 100, PIQ = 120). Although some difference in this direction might be expected given his background, the magnitude was on the high side. On WMS-R stories, the patient's recall was below expectations at immediate recall (28th percentile), but delayed-recall performance was more in line with expectations based on Verbal IQ performance (52nd percentile). His recall of the Complex Figure followed the same pattern (immediate recall = 37th percentile; delayed recall = 75th percentile). However, almost every aspect of performance on the California Verbal Learning Test was significantly below expectations for his age (total learning trials and delayed free-recall trials 2 standard deviations below normative mean, with some improvement on cued recall), suggesting he was having difficulty with rote verbal memory. There was an extraordinary number of intrusions in the CVLT performance as well.

Although most of his language scores were within normal limits (MAE Sentence Repetition = 43rd percentile; MAE Token Test = 82nd percentile; MAE Controlled Oral Word Association = 80th percentile; no errors on Reading Sentences and Paragraphs from Boston Diagnostic Aphasia Examination: Goodglass & Kaplan, 1983), his Visual Naming was below expectations (18th percentile). The source of grammatical and punctuation errors in his writing sample was unclear. Visuospatial performances were within the normal range. Motor performance was within normal limits. Although some executive and frontal functions were within normal limits, he was unable to achieve any sorts in 64 cards of the Wisconsin Card Sorting Test.

Thus, the patient had evidence for a subtle language disturbance. He did poorly with rote verbal learning. He had difficulty with problem solving, which was below expectations for his age (Spreen & Strauss, 1991), especially given his IQ. Although these findings could be consistent with a head injury and subsequent left-parietal subdural hematoma, there were at least a couple of problems that had an impact on the usefulness of such a statement from a legal as well as a diagnostic standpoint. First, the patient's wife had given a history of memory problems before the accident, and a progressive or other process unrelated to the accident was a possibility. Second, there was a probability of some improvement given the short time between the accident and testing. For these reasons, a reevaluation was recommended and performed 9 months later. Unfortunately, the patient's performance appeared to improve in some areas (e.g., Visual Naming) and decline in other areas (e.g., Performance IQ and delayed recall for WMS-R paragraphs and geometric designs). One might have expected some improvement if the head injury and subdural hematoma had been the cause of impairments. On the other hand, one might have expected decline if progressive dementia had been the cause of the original performance deficits. Thus, neither pattern was supported. Neuropsychological assessment, therefore, was not able to clarify the issue of causality, even after repeated assessment. These findings were carefully and clearly stated given the legal implications.

Principles for Application

On the right side of Table 4.4, some general principles for applying neuropsychological assessments to the forensic context are outlined. These principles are indexed by number to the problem on the left side of the table for which the principle provides a solution. Foremost among these applications is getting a proper conceptualization of the job a neuropsychologist must perform in forensic settings. The job is not to tell the attorney what will best strengthen his or her case if the data do not justify it. If the opposing attorney has competent experts, this will ultimately weaken the case. In the forensic setting, the neuropsychologist frequently can conceptualize her or his role as a consultative one to the attorney and the court. On the basis of the best interpretation of the data, the neuropsychologist can advise the attorney regarding the meaning of the data and its potential impact on the case. If the interpretation substantially weakens the case, the attorney should know why this is so. Of course, this is a collaborative effort, and hopefully the attorney will be willing to discuss the case he or she is building with the psychologist. In general, the "hired gun" philosophy of testifying is to be avoided. When data are distorted to fit the "needs" of a case, everyone ultimately loses because the system will be hindered in reaching a reasonable approximation of the facts. If ambiguities exist in the data and a definitive conclusion cannot be reached, explain the nature of the ambiguities clearly.

The neuropsychologist who does not testify frequently may find it difficult to keep up with the changing precedents regarding neuropsychological expert testimony in the appropriate jurisdiction. In such instances, the neuropsychologist might consider asking the attorney with whom he or she is working for the relevant rulings. If the attorney seems unaware that such precedents might exist, then the neuropsychologist can inform him or her that such rulings do exist in some jurisdictions. The neuropsychologist who makes a significant part of his or her livelihood by testifying frequently should make an attempt to keep up on rulings in relevant jurisdictions that may affect neuropsychological testimony. If an attorney is unaware of the relevant rulings, he or she can be informed of them.

Another principle is: Do not testify about matters outside a neuropsychologist's area of expertise. On the surface, this seems relatively straightforward. However, results obtained by other professionals may play a prominent role in reaching a neuropsychological opinion. One state supreme court ruled that a doctor might testify regarding the results obtained by another professional if such results were customarily used by the medical profession in arriving at opinions (Rothke, 1992). It is unclear when and where such a ruling might apply to psychologists, but when in doubt neuropsychologists can consult the attorney with whom they are working.

As noted before, some (e.g., Faust, 1991) suggested that limited evidence regarding the validity of neuropsychological tests in predicting functional outcomes is one factor that should preclude neuropsychologists from acting as expert witnesses. Although I wholeheartedly agree with comments regarding the limitations of test data for predicting specific functional outcomes, the position that neuropsychologists should not act as expert witnesses seems extreme. Most neuropsychological instruments have been developed to measure cognitive status, not functional ability, although there are a few notable exceptions (e.g., Rivermead Behavioural Memory Test: Wilson, Cockburn, & Baddeley, 1991). The validity of many neuropsychological tests for detecting cognitive dysfunction related to brain injury or disease is actually quite good and useful forensically (Barth et al., 1991). Further, in combination with a good history regarding functional activities, neuropsychological tests may indeed be helpful in distinguishing the reasons for functional difficulties in a way that may have functional prognostic significance. This may be true especially for neuropsychologists who have developed some expertise in rehabilitation and are in a position to understand the relationship between their test scores and eventual outcomes. Nonetheless, it is incumbent on the neuropsychologist to acknowledge the limitations of the test scores in predicting functional outcomes. The neuropsychologist should be familiar with limitations of the tests used for particular applications. Specific functional evaluations can be recommended when relevant and available. But, it is up to the trier of facts (i.e., the court) to determine the weight given to neuropsychological evidence (Richardson & Adams, 1992).

Richardson and Adams (1992) recommended that the best approach to causation is to use a "historically structured fact-based approach" (p. 306). Such an approach might emphasize functioning before the injury and after the injury, the reports and tests reviewed, the results of tests given by the neuropsychologist, and facts established through other sources. In some jurisdictions, Richardson and Adams recommended avoiding a "medical" or physiological approach to establishing causation. These matters should be discussed with the attorney with whom the neuropsychologist is working prior to testimony.

Regarding malingering, the neuropsychologist can consider employing tests designed to detect malingering when indicated. However, the ability of these tests to detect malingering should not be overstated. Additionally, interview, test, and history data can be examined for internal inconsistencies that might indicate a conscious effort to manipulate test outcomes. Specific interview tactics may be designed to assess whether the patient will exaggerate complaints. For example, the examiner might question a patient about the presence of specific improbable symptoms to ascertain if the patient tends to overendorse pathology.

Given that an opposing attorney might hire his or her own neuropsychologist to examine test data and statements for veracity, testimony should be prepared as if one's colleagues were going to examine it. Such preparation will lessen the likelihood that it will be discredited.

Regarding the legal process, whether it is criminal or civil, the neuropsychologist must realize it is adversarial in nature. As such, it is a substantially different method of attempting to establish facts than are our methods of inquiry. The validity of the diagnostic opinion will usually not be taken as a given. Questioning of the validity of an opinion should not be taken personally but should be assumed as a part of the procedure.

In the process of preparing a case, attorneys will be better consumers of neuropsychological information if they are well informed about the nature and limitations of the data. Further, several authors (e.g., Richardson & Adams, 1992; Rothke, 1992; Satz, 1988) suggested that neuropsychologists educate attorneys regarding who is qualified as an expert in neuropsychology. It has been suggested that APA Division 40 guidelines (INS-Division 40 Task Force on Education, Accreditation, and Credentialing, 1987) be used as criteria.

In summary, neuropsychological data can be helpful to courts and attorneys in making legal decisions. If neuropsychological information is to be useful, however, it must be presented in a relatively objective manner by a qualified professional. Although it is not perfect, our data may be among the best available in answering certain types of questions. When appropriate, it is necessary that limitations of neuropsychological findings be clearly stated. In rendering opinions, the experienced neuropsychologist remains mindful of limitations, including ability to detect malingering.

GIVING FEEDBACK TO PATIENTS AND FAMILIES

Importance of Providing Feedback

To maximize the usefulness of a neuropsychological evaluation to the patient, it is often desirable to give him or her feedback about performance. Feedback can be used to provide information about cognitive strengths and weaknesses and to enact interventions that will facilitate performance of various functional activities. Indeed, feedback is considered such an integral aspect of psychological evaluation that it has been mandated by the recently revised American Psychological Association ethical standards (American Psychological Association, 1992, Principle 2.09). However, this process should not be undertaken lightly by the clinician. It is the part of a neuropsychological evaluation that may take the most skill and experience.

The difficulty predicting a specific functional outcome from neuropsychological test scores is among the most important limitations. As already mentioned, errors in prognostic statements can have a devastating impact on patients and families, not only in terms of practical decisions but also in terms of patients' self-esteem. A particular patient's level of acceptance may determine how much information about deficits he or she is able to process. Although it is desirable that patients be maximally aware of their deficits, too large of a single dose of awareness may cause anxiety, resentment, or anger, and paradoxically increase denial.

Generally, brain-behavior relationships are quite complex and not easily understood by lay persons. In addition, behavioral neuroscientists use terminology that is unfamiliar to lay persons or differs from common usage. For example, when neuropsychologists speak of short-term memory, they often are referring to the type of memory in which information is held in temporary storage and lasts less than a minute. When lay persons speak of short-term memory, most frequently they are referring to recent as opposed to remote memory. Thus, when giving feedback about testing, neuropsychologists cannot assume basic knowledge necessary to understand test results nor can they assume lay persons understand the professional jargon they use for a shorthand among themselves on a daily basis. Many patients and their family members will be somewhat intimidated by psychologists or other health care professionals. If so, they may not ask questions about data they do not understand. Because questions from patients and family members give the neuropsychologist feedback regarding what patients do and do not understand, the lack of such interactive feedback makes it difficult to know what concepts are understood. It almost does not need to be said that neuropsychological information is of no use to patients and families if they do not understand it.

Another potential problem in giving feedback is that neuropsychological assessments are usually deficit oriented. It is by discovering and analyzing deficit patterns that neuropsychologists make diagnostic statements and determine what cognitive problems might underlie specific functional deficits. It is a mistake, however, to focus exclusively or even primarily on deficits when delivering feedback (or when planning rehabilitative treatment). Focusing primarily on deficits may make patients feel devastated, significantly injuring self-esteem and making them more vulnerable to depression. Or, it can have the effect of activating denial to protect an understandably fragile self-esteem. In formal rehabilitation efforts or in struggling to make an adjustment to brain dysfunction, some level of self-esteem, as well as some degree of self-awareness, is helpful in accepting changes in functioning and their implications. Therefore, the neuropsychologist must be aware of the potential impact of feedback regarding deficits and consider strengths as well.

A final consideration in giving feedback about assessment results is the other professionals who are working with the patient. At times it is proper for the neuropsychologist to give feedback, whereas at other times it may be better for other health care professionals to give feedback about test results. For example, when neuropsychological assessment is done for diagnostic reasons, it may be only one source of information used to make a diagnosis. A referring neurologist or psychiatrist may be using CT or MR scans, various lab tests, response to medications, consultations from other professionals, his or her own medical examinations and histories, as well as other sources of information to assist in making a diagnosis. In such instances, it is important that giving neuropsychological feedback not interfere with the patient care provided by the referring professional or provide premature diagnostic closure. The potential impact of conflicting information must be considered when deciding whether or not to give feedback and when to give it.

Problems arising in giving neuropsychological feedback to patients are summarized on the left side of Table 4.5. The primary challenge of feedback is to make assessment results meaningful and useful to patients. The

TABLE 4.5
Application Issues in Feedback to Patients and Families

Potential Pitfalls in Giving Patients and Families Feedback about Neuropsychological Assessments	Principles for Giving Feedback about Neuropsychological Assessments to Patients and Family Members
1. Limitations in predicting functional abilities from neuropsychological data may decrease the usefulness of the information for patients and family members.	1. Conduct feedback sessions in an interactive, collaborative fashion in which the functional importance of findings can be further explored with patients and family members.
2. Patients' and family members' level of acceptance of the consequences of neurological impairment may limit their ability to accept feedback.	2. Try to estimate a patient's level of emotional acceptance and look for signs that the patient may be having trouble with acceptance during feedback.
3. Patients and family members may have a limited knowledge base to aid in the understanding of neuropsychological data.	3a. Check frequently with the patient and family members to make certain they are understanding the various concepts being presented.
	3b. Check frequently with the patient and family members to ascertain that they have the basic knowledge to comprehend assessment results.
	3c. When basic knowledge is not present, educate the patient and family.
4. A deficit-oriented approach to feedback can have a negative emotional impact on patients and family members.	4. Present balanced feedback, focusing on cognitive strengths as well as deficits.
5. It may not always be appropriate for the neuropsychologist to give extensive feedback to the patient, particularly if the assessment is being used by another health care professional as a part of a more extended diagnostic process.	5. Communicate with referral sources to ascertain the appropriateness of giving feedback to patients.

obstacles to doing so include (a) limitations in predicting functional abilities from neuropsychological tests, (b) the ability of patients and family to accept feedback, (c) limited basic knowledge of patients and family, and (d) a temptation on the part of the neuropsychologist to focus primarily on deficits. The neuropsychologist should also consider the appropriateness of and timing for giving direct feedback in individual cases.

Case 7 was a woman in her 20s. She was involved in a motor vehicle accident approximately 2½ years before testing and was self-referred because of increased academic difficulties. She was not unconscious after the accident by her own recollection. However, she was confused periodically for about a day, and posttraumatic headaches led her to seek medical attention one day after the accident. A CT scan at that time was unremarkable. Previously an excellent student, she had begun to have academic difficulties after the accident. She attributed the academic difficulties to memory problems. By the time she was seen the "memory" difficulties were better, but she reported she was not back to premorbid levels and was still having some academic difficulty. In particular, she stated that she had to read material twice before she could remember it, a change from premorbid functioning.

The patient had above-average intellectual functioning (Verbal IQ = 105, Performance IQ = 117). Memory testing was also above average for both verbal memory (California Verbal Learning Test) and visual memory (Rey–Osterreith Complex Figure). Because minor head injury frequently causes attentional problems, tests with attentional components were given (Paced Auditory Serial Addition Test, Stroop Neuropsychological Screening Test, Auditory Consonant Trigrams). Performance on all these tests were within normal limits. On the other hand, the patient had a significantly below-normal score on the Boston Naming Test (4 standard deviations below normative mean). Her Spelling score on the Wide Range Achievement Test-Revised (Jastak & Wilkinson, 1984) was below average (25th percentile). When this issue was discussed with the patient's mother after the test score was obtained, she indicated that the patient had been an excellent speller before the accident but had lost this ability. The patient also admitted that spelling had been a problem since the accident when this score was brought to her attention. Although the patient scored within normal limits on literal (72nd percentile) and inferential (64th percentile) reading comprehension, her ability to read quickly (24th percentile) was more problematic (Stanford Diagnostic Reading Test: Karlsen, Madden, & Gardner, 1974).

Taking all these facets into consideration, it was determined that the patient had a subtle language difficulty. Actually, she was already using a spell check program on her computer when she wrote papers for school. After consulting with a speech/language pathologist, it was decided that the patient's language difficulty was not severe enough to justify treatment, although there was agreement on the diagnosis. During feedback, the word-finding difficulties were verified; she experienced them on an occasional basis. Some effort was made to differentiate for the patient between memory difficulty, which she thought she had, and the subtle language deficits she demonstrated. Some of the "memory" problems she described were probably related to word-retrieval difficulty. It was emphasized that memory might actually be considered a strength. Additional recommendations were made, such as that she try to explain the concept or use an alternative word when she had word-finding difficulty. One of the main issues concerned course load, and it was recommended that she take a reduced course load. Finally, it was suggested that the patient could seek special services at school. The office of student services at her school often worked with students and professors to minimize learning problems.

Prior to testing in this case, the neuropsychologist suspected that the patient would have attention and memory problems, which can occur after minor head injury. When language problems were found instead, further interviewing was done during assessment and feedback to confirm spelling and word-finding problems. Reading problems were consistent with self-report during interview. Because the patient had not recognized the difference between language problems and memory deficit, this difference was explained, and the strength in her memory performance was noted. Recommendations were made on the basis of test findings. This case example illustrates how the feedback session can be used as part of ongoing assessment. The neuropsychologist may need to seek further information after reviewing test findings, either during the evaluation or during the feedback session. It also demonstrates how the patient's understanding of a problem may need to be corrected or modified to facilitate optimum adjustment to deficits.

Principles for Application

Principles for giving feedback to patients and family members are presented on the right side of Table 4.5. Principles are indexed by number to the problems on the left side of Table 4.5 for which they provide a solution. First, many of the functional limitations of neuropsychological tests can be overcome by conducting feedback sessions in an interactive and collaborative fashion, encouraging the participation of patients and family members. The feedback session should not simply be considered a vehicle for imparting knowledge to the patient and his or her family. It should also be considered an opportunity for gathering further information that will help the neuropsychologist understand the patient and will help the patient and family understand the difficulties present and the strengths that can be used to increase functional capabilities. For example, when discussing a memory problem, the neuropsychologist may ask several questions to ascertain under what circumstances the patient might have noticed the memory problem (if it had not already been covered in interview). The neuropsychologist should also check frequently to make certain the patient and family are understanding the feedback and initiate further elaboration as warranted.

Because the patient's or the family's level of emotional acceptance may affect how well they can integrate feedback, the neuropsychologist should attempt to estimate the level of acceptance. This may be done by noting what the patient does when he or she is having significant difficulty with tasks during evaluation and by noting how they react to questions about deficits during interview. Probes may also be made during the initial part of the feedback session. The patient can ask how they felt they did during testing, or it can be noted that some problems were found and ask if it surprises the patient or family member. The neuropsychologist can also watch the patient and family for reactions to specific feedback that may indicate difficulty accepting the feedback. At such points in the feedback session, differences between the neuropsychologist and the patient and family generally should be clarified. The process of clarification potentially can add information about the nature of deficits from a functional standpoint. It may be that differences of opinion can be resolved through clarification. But, even if differences cannot be resolved, it is often best if the differences can be clearly stated. In working through this process, it should be remembered that the patient and family are entitled to an opinion, and that opinion may be different than that of the neuropsychologist. Reaching total correspondence of opinion among patient, family, and neuropsychologist is not necessarily the goal of every feedback session. Patients and family may be able to understand the importance of feedback at a later time when its relevance is more immediate or when they are more ready to accept it. Efforts to obtain agreement regarding feedback when patients and family are not ready to accept it may lessen the possibility that they can use the information when circumstances change.

Not infrequently, patients and family will not have some basic piece of information that would help them to understand some deficit or strength clearly. For example, a problem with word finding might not be well differentiated from other types of memory problems by patients. In such instances, the differences between word-finding problems and the ability to acquire new information may have to be emphasized, as in the preceding case example. As another example of misunderstanding a deficit, a patient might understand a hemianopia as a difficulty seeing out of one eye. The neuropsychologist should be frequently checking for such misunderstandings during feedback sessions. Patients and family members should be educated regarding such basic facts as necessary and appropriate.

On a different issue, the difficulty that giving deficit-oriented feedback presents can be addressed by giving more balanced feedback that emphasizes both strengths and deficits. Oftentimes, emphasizing strengths as well as weaknesses will allow a patient to leave a feedback session feeling that his or her self-concept is more intact. Because the probability of denial being invoked is related to the degree of perceived threat to self-esteem, emphasizing strengths will reduce the probability of eliciting denial. If some modicum of hope can be fostered by taking strengths into account, the patient also may be more ready to participate in rehabilitation. Finally, it should be noted that presenting both strengths and weakness gives a more accurate picture of the patient's functioning than focusing entirely on deficits.

Lastly, it may not always be obvious when a neuropsychologist should give extensive feedback regarding testing and when this should be avoided or delayed. Such a decision may depend partly on the preferences of the referral source, but other factors should be taken into account as well. In some instances, it might be desirable to delay feedback until a more definitive diagnosis is reached. For example, the nature of feedback might change if a patient has a degenerative process versus some more stable or improving condition. Such dilemmas can be most easily resolved by communicating with the referral source and jointly making a decision about giving feedback. In instances where the neuropsychologist works frequently with a single referral source in certain types of cases, it is possible that routine procedures regarding feedback can be developed.

In summary, feedback is most useful to patients and family if it is presented in an interactive and collaborative environment where the functional implications of the data can be further explored. The neuropsychologist can also check to make certain that patients and family understand feedback and have the basic knowledge necessary to understand it. Education and clarification may be necessary. Another principle of feedback is to present strengths as well as weaknesses. Finally, the neuropsychologist will need to check with referral sources about the appropriateness of extensive neuropsychological feedback.

CONCLUSIONS

The potential problems in applications of neuropsychological assessment are numerous. This chapter has attempted to present a few, but there are numerous issues that have been not been addressed. A more complete enumeration and classification of applications problems would take an entire volume; so the current chapter should be considered only a sampling.

The potential issues in any particular assessment will depend upon a variety of factors. Among the most important are the referral source to whom assessment findings are addressed and the referral question. This chapter has attempted to show how different contexts for evaluations might lead to modification of clinical practice. In so doing, evaluations were divided into diagnostic, rehabilitative, and forensic. However, knowing the general type of evaluation is usually not enough. For example, questions may differ between inpatient and outpatient rehabilitation programs; stroke rehabilitation versus head-injury rehabilitation programs will generate varying types of questions. With each different question come different potential problems. Further, even rehabilitation programs treating identical patient populations may differ significantly if they are structured differently. For example, in some outpatient rehabilitation programs the neuropsychologist may have responsibility for conducting cognitive rehabilitation, and in others the neuropsychologist may play only a consultative role for this endeavor. Each potential role raises different demands on assessment, and clinical practice will vary to some degree with the different demands.

One factor that is common to all assessment contexts is the important functional aspects of behavior that neuropsychological tests may not measure. Although attempts are being made to develop more ecologically valid measures, it seems unlikely that neuropsychologists will ever opt for completely functional batteries. The attempt to specify how cognition breaks down is an important endeavor and cannot be determined in the relatively brief behavioral sample of an evaluation if complex functional tasks are used. Perhaps what we must learn is that many specific breakdowns in cognition do not imply a corresponding functional deficit on a one-to-one basis. Yet, understanding the breakdown in cognition may have important functional implications once the cognitive evaluation and a functional evaluation are collated. Even then, functional implications may not be entirely understood until treatment is well under way. If this is the case, then neuropsychologists may always have to be aware of the functional limitations of their instruments. We can seek other sources of functional information, including patient's and family members' observations, functional evaluations conducted by other professionals, and, frequently most importantly, observations of patients performing various functional activities during treatment.

Unfortunately, no "cookbook" approach to applications issues in neuropsychological assessment will ever be successful. Ultimately, each individual clinician will have to assess the environment in which he or she practices, the needs of his or her referral sources, and the needs of his or her patients and families. From this assessment, potential applications issues can be determined, and means for addressing the problems can be developed. As a clinician's day-to-day practice evolves, new problems will be discovered, and ways of addressing them will be devised. In other words, the good clinician will be constantly alert for problems in the application of neuropsychological assessment results and ways of managing them.

REFERENCES

Alberts, M. S., & Binder, L. M. (1991). Premorbid psychosocial factors that influence cognitive rehabilitation following traumatic brain injury. In J. S. Kreutzer & P. H. Wehman (Eds.), *Cognitive rehabilitation for persons with traumatic brain injury* (pp. 95–103). Baltimore: Paul H. Brookes.

Alfano, D. P., Neilson, P. M., Paniak, C. E., & Finlayson, M. A. J. (1992). The MMPI and closed-head injury. *The Clinical Neuropsychologist, 6,* 134–142.

American Psychiatric Association. (1987). *Diagnostic and statistical manual of mental disorders* (3rd ed. rev.). Washington, DC: American Psychiatric Association.

American Psychological Association. (1974). *Standards for educational and psychological tests.* Washington, DC: American Psychological Association.

American Psychological Association. (1987). *Casebook on ethical principles of psychologists.* Washington, DC: American Psychological Association.

American Psychological Association. (1992). Ethical principles of psychologists and code of conduct. *American Psychologist, 47,* 1597–1611.

Andreasen, N. C., Ehrhardt, J. C., Swayze, V. W., Alliger, R. J., Yuh, W. T. C., Cohen, B., & Ziebell, S. (1990). Magnetic resonance imaging of the brain in schizophrenia: The pathophysiologic significance of structural abnormalities. *Archives of General Psychiatry, 47,* 35–44.

Barco, P. P., Crosson, B., Bolesta, M. M., Werts, D., & Stout, R. (1991). Training awareness and compensation in postacute head injury rehabilitation. In J. S. Kreutzer & P. H. Wehman (Eds.), *Cognitive rehabilitation for persons with traumatic brain injury* (pp. 129–146). Baltimore: Paul H. Brookes.

Barr, W. B., Bilder, R. M., Goldberg, E., Kaplan, E., & Mukherjee, S. (1989). The neuropsychology of schizophrenic speech. *Journal of Communication Disorders, 22,* 327–349.

Barth, J. T., Ryan, T. V., & Hawk, G. L. (1991). Forensic neuropsychology: A reply to the method skeptics. *Neuropsychology Review, 2,* 251–266.

Bauer, R. M., & Rubens, A. B. (1985). Agnosia. In K. M. Heilman & E. Valenstein (Eds.), *Clinical neuropsychology* (pp. 187–241). New York: Oxford University Press.

Benton, A. L., & Hamsher, K. deS. (1989). *Multilingual aphasia examination* (2nd ed.). Iowa City: AJA Associates.

Bickart, W. T., Meyer, R. G., & Connell, D. K. (1991). The symptom validity technique as a measure of feigned short-term memory deficit. *American Journal of Forensic Psychology, 9*(2), 3–11.

Binder, L. M., & Pankratz, L. (1987). Neuropsychological evidence of a factitious memory complaint. *Journal of Clinical and Experimental Neuropsychology, 9,* 167–171.

Blau, T. H. (1984). *The psychologist as expert witness.* New York: Wiley.

Bogerts, B., Meertz, E., & Schönfeldt-Bausch, R. (1985). Basal ganglia and limbic system pathology in schizophrenia: A morphometric study. *Archives of General Psychiatry, 42,* 784–791.

Butters, N. (1985). Alcoholic Korsakoff's syndrome: Some unresolved issues concerning etiology, neuropathology, and cognitive deficits. *Journal of Clinical and Experimental Neuropsychology, 7,* 181–210.

Crosson, B. (1987). Treatment of interpersonal deficits for head-trauma patients in inpatient rehabilitation settings. *The Clinical Neuropsychologist, 1,* 335–352.

Crosson, B., Barco, P. P., Velozo, C. A., Bolesta, M. M., Cooper, P. V., Werts, D., & Brobeck, T. C. (1989). Awareness and compensation in post-acute head injury rehabilitation. *Journal of Head Trauma Rehabilitation, 4*(3), 46–54.

Damasio, A. R. (1985). The frontal lobes. In K. M. Heilman & E. Valenstein (Eds.), *Clinical neuropsychology* (pp. 339–375). New York: Oxford University Press.

Delis, D. C., Kramer, J. H., Kaplan, E., & Ober, B. A. (1987). *California Verbal Learning Test*. San Antonio, TX: Psychological Corporation.

Doerr, H. O., & Carlin, A. S. (Eds.). (1991). *Forensic neuropsychology: Legal and scientific bases*. New York: Guilford Press.

Eslinger, P. J., & Damasio, A. R. (1985). Disturbance of higher cognition after bilateral frontal lobe ablation: Patient EVR. *Neurology, 35*, 1731–1741.

Faust, D. (1991). Forensic neuropsychology: The art of practicing a science that does not yet exist. *Neuropsychology Review, 2*, 205–231.

Gentilini, M., Nichelli, P., & Schoenhuber, R. (1989). Assessment of attention in mild head injury. In H. S. Levin, H. M. Eisenberg, & A. L. Benton (Eds.), *Mild head injury* (pp. 163–175). New York: Oxford University Press.

Goodglass, H., & Kaplan, E. (1983). *Boston Diagnostic Aphasia Examination*. Philadelphia: Lea & Febiger.

Gronwall, D. (1989). Cumulative and persisting effects of concussion on attention and cognition. In H. S. Levin, H. M. Eisenberg, & A. L. Benton (Eds.), *Mild head injury* (pp. 153–162). New York: Oxford University Press.

Grove, W. M., & Andreasen, N. C. (1985). Language and thinking in psychosis: Is there an input abnormality? *Archives of General Psychiatry, 42*, 26–32.

Haas, J. F., Cope, D. N., & Hall, K. (1987). Premorbid prevalence of poor academic performance in severe head injury. *Journal of Neurology, Neurosurgery, and Psychiatry, 50*, 52–56.

Haxby, J. V., Raffaele, K., Gillette, J., Schapiro, M. B., & Rapoport, S. I. (1992). Individual trajectories of cognitive decline in patients of the Alzheimer type. *Journal of Clinical and Experimental Neuropsychology, 14*, 575–592.

Heaton, R. K., & Crowley, T. J. (1981). Effects of psychiatric disorders and their somatic treatments on neuropsychological test results. In S. B. Filskov & T. J. Boll (Eds.), *Handbook of clinical neuropsychology* (pp. 481–525). New York. Wiley.

Hoffman, R. E., Stopek, S., & Andreasen, N. C. (1986). A comparative study of manic vs. schizophrenic speech disorganization. *Archives of General Psychiatry, 43*, 831–838.

INS-Division 40 Task Force on Education, Accreditation, and Credentialing. (1987). Guidelines for doctoral training programs in clinical neuropsychology. *The Clinical Neuropsychologist, 1*, 29–34.

Jastak, S., & Wilkinson, G. S. (1984). *Wide Range Achievement Test-Revised*. Wilmington, DE: Jastak Associates.

Jennett, B., Snoek, J., Bond, M. R., & Brooks, N. (1981). Disability after severe head injury: Observations on the use of the Glasgow Outcome Scale. *Journal of Neurology, Neurosurgery, and Psychiatry, 44*, 285–293.

Jennett, B., & Teasdale, G. (1981). *Management of head injury*. Philadelphia: F. A. Davis.

Kaplan, E., Fein, D., Morris, R., & Delis, D. C. (1991). *WAIS-R as a neuropsychological instrument*. San Antonio, TX: Psychological Corporation.

Kaplan, E., Goodglass, H., & Weintraub, S. (1983). *Boston Naming Test*. Philadelphia: Lea & Febiger.

Karlsen, B., Madden, R., & Gardner, E. F. (1974). *Stanford Diagnostic Reading Test*. New York: Harcourt Brace Jovanovich.

King, D. A., & Caine, E. D. (1990). Depression. In J. L. Cummings (Ed.), *Subcortical dementia* (pp. 218–230). New York: Oxford University Press.

Kitzinger, H., & Blumberg, E. (1951). Supplemental guide for administering and scoring the Wechsler–Bellevue Intelligence Scale (Form 1). *Psychological Monographs, 65*, 1–20.

Levin, H. S. (1989). Memory deficit after closed-head injury. *Journal of Clinical and Experimental Neuropsychology, 12*, 129–153.

Levin, H. S., Benton, A. L., & Grossman, R. G. (1981). *Neurobehavioral consequences of closed head injury*. New York: Oxford University Press.

Levin, H. S., High, W. M., & Eisenberg, H. M. (1988). Learning and forgetting during post-traumatic amnesia in head injured patients. *Journal of Neurology, Neurosurgery, and Psychiatry, 51*, 14–20.

Lezak, M. D. (1978). Living with the characterologically altered brain injured patient. *Journal of Clinical Psychiatry, 39*, 592–598.

Lezak, M. D. (1983). *Neuropsychological assessment* (2nd ed.). New York: Oxford University Press.

Lezak, M. D. (1986). Assessment for rehabilitation planning. In M. J. Meier, A. L. Benton, & L. Diller (Eds.), *Neuropsychological rehabilitation* (pp. 41–58). New York: Guilford Press.

Mandleberg, I. A., & Brooks, D. N. (1975). Cognitive recovery after severe head injury: Serial testing on the Wechsler Adult Intelligence Scale. *Journal of Neurology, Neurosurgery, and Psychiatry, 38*, 1121–1126.

Melton, G. B., Petrila, J., Poythress, N. G., & Slobogin, C. (1987). *Psychological evaluations for the courts*. New York: Guilford Press.

Pankratz, L. (1979). Symptom validity testing and symptom retraining: Procedures for the assessment and treatment of functional sensory deficits. *Journal of Consulting and Clinical Psychology, 47*, 409–410.

Pankratz, L., Fausti, S. A., & Peed, S. (1975). A forced-choice technique to evaluate deafness in the hysterical or malingering patient. *Journal of Consulting and Clinical Psychology, 43*, 421–422.

Porteus, S. D. (1959). *The Maze Test and clinical psychology*. Palo Alto, CA: Pacific Books.

Posner, M. I., Early, T. S., Reiman, E. M., Pardo, P. J., & Dhawan, M. (1988). Asymmetries in hemispheric control of attention in schizophrenia. *Archives of General Psychiatry, 45*, 814–821.

Posner, M. I., & Rafal, R. D. (1986). Cognitive theories of attention and the rehabilitation of attentional deficits. In M. J. Meier, A. L. Benton, & L. Diller (Eds.), *Neuropsychological rehabilitation* (pp. 182–201). New York: Guilford Press.

Povlishock, J. T., & Coburn, T. H. (1989). Morphopathological change associated with mild head injury. In H. S. Levin, H. M. Eisenberg, & A. L. Benton (Eds.), *Mild head injury* (pp. 37–53). New York: Oxford University Press.

Prigatano, G. P. (1986). Psychotherapy after brain injury. In G. P. Prigatano (Ed.), *Neuropsychological rehabilitation after brain injury* (pp. 67–95). Baltimore: The Johns Hopkins University Press.

Rapaport, D., Gill, M., & Schafer, R. (1945). *Diagnostic psychological testing* (Vol. 1). Chicago: Year Book Publishers.

Richardson, R. E. L., & Adams, R. L. (1992). Neuropsychologists as expert witnesses: Issues of admissibility. *The Clinical Neuropsychologist, 6*, 295–308.

Rimel, R. W., Girodani, B., Barth, J. T., Boll, T. J., & Jane, J. A. (1981). Disability caused by minor head injury. *Neurosurgery, 9*, 221–228.

Robinson, R. G., Kubos, K. L., Starr, L. B., Rao, K., & Price, T. R. (1984). Mood disorders in stroke patients: Importance of location of lesion. *Brain, 107*, 81–93.

Rothke, S. (1992). Expert testimony by neuropsychologists: Addendum to Schwartz and Satz. *The Clinical Neuropsychologist, 6*, 85–91.

Satz, P. (1988). Neuropsychological testimony: Some emerging concerns. *The Clinical Neuropsychologist, 2*, 89–100.

Sohlberg, M. M., & Mateer, C. A. (1989). *Introduction to cognitive rehabilitation: Theory and practice*. New York: Guilford Press.

Spreen, O., & Strauss, E. (1991). *A compendium of neuropsychological tests: Administration, norms, and commentary*. New York: Oxford University Press.

Starkstein, S. E., Robinson, R. G., Berthier, M. L., Parikh, R. M., & Price, T. R. (1988). Differential mood changes following basal ganglia vs. thalamic lesions. *Archives of Neurology, 45*, 725–730.

Starkstein, S. E., Robinson, R. G., & Price, T. R. (1987). Comparison of cortical and subcortical lesions in the production of poststroke mood disorders. *Brain, 110*, 1045–1059.

Stuss, D. T. (1991). Self, awareness, and the frontal lobes: A neuropsychological perspective. In J. Strauss & G. R. Goethals (Eds.), *The self: An interdisciplinary approach* (pp. 255–278). New York: Springer-Verlag.

Uzzell, B. P., Zimmerman, R. A., Dolinskas, C. A., & Obrist, W. D. (1979). Lateralized psychological impairment associated with CT lesions in head injured patients. *Cortex, 15*, 391–401.

Wechsler, D. (1945). A standardized memory scale for clinical use. *The Journal of Psychology, 19*, 87–95.

Wechsler, D. (1981). *Wechsler Adult Intelligence Scale-Revised*. San Antonio, TX: Psychological Corporation.

Wechsler, D. (1987). *Wechsler Memory Scale-Revised*. San Antonio, TX: Psychological Corporation.

Wedding, D. (1991). Clinical judgment in forensic neuropsychology: A comment on the risks of claiming more than can be delivered. *Neuropsychology Review, 2*, 233–239.

Weinberger, D. R., Berman, K. F., & Zec, R. F. (1986). Physiological dysfunction of dorsolateral prefrontal cortex in schizophrenia: I. Regional cerbral blood flow (RCBF) evidence. *Archives of General Psychiatry, 43*, 114–125.

White, T. G. (1992). *The use of indirect tests in the evaluation of malingered or exaggerated memory performance*. Unpublished doctoral dissertation, University of Florida, Gainesville.

Wilson, B., Cockburn, J., & Baddeley, A. (1991). *Rivermead Behavioural Memory Test*. Suffolk, England: Thames Valley Test Company.

CHAPTER FIVE

Issues in Child Neuropsychological Assessment

Eileen B. Fennell
University of Florida

Neuropsychological assessment of children and young adolescents imposes certain unique demands on the examiner. Although the question of the impact of a lesion on brain behavior is a central theme in all neuropsychological assessments, the effects of differing types of brain lesions on developing brain systems pose a somewhat different challenge to those who assess children and adolescents. Knowledge about the primary or secondary effects of lesions must be applied in the context of brain systems whose functional relationships are still under development (Kolb, 1989). Furthermore, the child neuropsychologist must possess a clear understanding of the typical emergence of intellectual, memory, language, motor, and visuospatial skills to appreciate deviations from patterns of normal development. Finally, the child neuropsychologist must have an appreciation of the spectrum of behavioral symptoms and disorders that can be manifestations of childhood psychopathology or family discord (Walker & Roberts, 1992). Thus, the task of the examiner is to integrate knowledge about normal and pathological development to better describe and predict the impact of a brain lesion on developing brain.

This chapter presents an overview of relevant issues in assessing children and young adolescents. In the first section, general issues in child neuropsychological assessment are addressed. After that, a brief overview of types of child assessment and models of influence applied in child or adolescent cases is discussed. Following that overview, the next section presents a broad model of areas to be examined when this age group is assessed. The content of a clinical interview and the essential elements of a comprehensive examination and report are also described. Issues relating to psychometric measurement, test norms, and test revisions form the content of the next section. The chapter concludes with a discussion of current needs and future directions in child neuropsychological assessment.

GENERAL ISSUES IN ASSESSING CHILDREN

Historical Trends

In a recent review, Tramontana and Hooper (1988) characterized child neuropsychology as emerging through four historical stages. The first stage from the mid-1940s to the mid-1960s was dominated by the single-test approach in which single tests were used to diagnose brain damage or organicity. The major intent was to separate brain-damaged children from normal children according to differences in their scores on a particular test such as the Bender Visual Motor Gestalt Test (Koppitz, 1964), or by interpreting patterns of performance on an omnibus measure such as the Wechsler Intelligence Scale for Children (Wechsler, 1960). By the mid-1960s a second stage of development occurred in which fixed batteries of tests were administered to brain-damaged children (Ernhart, Graham, Eichman, Marshall, & Thurston, 1963). By the early 1970s, the earliest normative data on the Reitan battery for collections of children with head injuries and other types of brain impairments became available (Reitan & Davison, 1974). The third stage began in the late 1970s and early 1980s when child neuropsychologists began to emphasize the functional effects of various types of childhood disorders rather than attempting solely to arrive at a decision about the presence or absence of brain disorder (Rourke, 1982). The most recent, fourth stage, involves an emphasis on the ability of individual tests or test batteries to better relate the impact of a brain lesion to the demands of everyday functioning. The role of the neuropsychologist has begun to include both prescriptions for interventions at home or in school in order to accommodate the special needs of a child with a developmental disability as well as the development of specific remediation strategies. I would suggest that a fifth stage in child neuropsychology has begun to emerge. As a result of recent advances in medical care, large numbers of children are surviving previously fatal illnesses directly affecting the central nervous system (e.g., brain tumors) or illnesses whose successful treatment may compromise central nervous system functioning (e.g., childhood cancers). With the emergence of organ transplantation, child neuropsychologists are increasingly called on to understand the effects of such dramatic interventions on subsequent development, as well as to advise physicians, parents, and schools about the special needs of these children. Thus, to the empirical knowledge gained since the 1940s about common handicapping conditions (e.g., learning disabilities, attention-deficit disorders, autism, head trauma, cerebral palsy, and epilepsy), the child neuropsychologist must be familiar with new evidence about the impact of systemic illness and its treatment on survivors of acute and chronic medical disorders of childhood.

Issues in Child Neuropsychological Assessment

Since the 1980s, some excellent textbooks devoted to the field of child neuropsychology have been published (Hynd & Willis, 1988; Reynolds & Fletcher-Janzen, 1989; Rourke, Bakker, Fisk, & Strange, 1983; Rourke, Fisk, & Strange, 1986; Rutter, 1983; Spreen, Tupper, Risser, Tuokko, & Edgell, 1984; Tramontana & Hooper, 1988, 1992). These publications document the diversity of information now becoming available about the impact of acquired or congenital brain disorders on children's development. A common feature of all is the recognition of three key variables that affect the outcome of brain lesions in children: (a) type of lesion, (b) location of lesion, and (c) age at time of lesion.

Type of Lesion

Type of lesion refers to the underlying pathological processes that have primary effects on the central nervous system. Among these are: disorders of central nervous system development (e.g., spina bifida); tumors (e.g., gliomas); vascular lesions (e.g., malformations, infarcts); infections (e.g., meningitis); injury (e.g., closed head trauma); paroxysmal disorders (e.g., epilepsy); and hereditary disorders (e.g., Prader-Willi syndrome; Menkes, 1990). Also, there are a number of developmental disorders with a putative basis in primary central nervous system dysfunction including specific learning disabilities and attention-deficit hyperactivity. In addition, there are some systemic disorders that exert a secondary effect on the central nervous system. These include: cardiac disease (e.g., ventriculo–septal defects); hematological disorders (e.g., sickle cell anemia); chronic renal or liver disease; endocrine dysfunction (e.g., juvenile onset diabetes); and other multisystem pathologies (e.g., cystic fibrosis). Finally, treatment of systemic disease with irradiation, chemotherapy, or immune suppression can also affect the functions of the central nervous system (Berg & Linton, 1989; Tartar, Van Thiel, & Edwards, 1988).

In addition to differences in type of lesion according to its primary, secondary, or tertiary effects on the central nervous system, types of lesions may vary in what has been termed *velocity* of a lesion (Reitan & Davison, 1974). Lesions may be described as static versus progressive or acute versus chronic. *Static* means a lesion that typically is not evolving, whereas the term *progressive* implies that the lesion is continuing to evolve and its effects may progress. An example of a static lesion in children would be a small stroke in the thalamus suffered during the perinatal period that has resulted in mild spasticity. In contrast, there are a number of progressive lesions of childhood, including, for example, an enlarging brainstem astrocytoma (Menkes, 1990). Lesions can also be described in terms of their acuteness or chronicity. As suggested by these terms, acute lesions are typically of recent origin and frequently lead to both focal and generalized effects of the child's brain. Chronic lesions are more long-term, are frequently static, and may allow for some compensatory reorganization of brain systems. An example of such a case is the neuropsychological profile of a 16-year-old female who suffered a stroke involving the left-middle cerebral artery (Stringer & Fennell, 1987).

It is essential for the practicing child neuropsychologist to develop greater knowledge of the effects of type of lesion on brain functioning in children. This requires the examiner to remain current on the clinical neuropsychological literature about the behavioral effects of different types of primary or secondary lesions as it becomes available through professional psychological and medical journals and textbooks. Fundamental to an appreciation of the effects of different types of lesions is a current knowledge base about childhood neurological disorders and neurological or neurosurgical treatments (Fenichel, 1988; Fishman, 1987; Menkes, 1990).

Location of Lesion

Location of lesion is another important brain variable in child neuropsychological assessment. Increasingly, our appreciation of brain–behavior relationships has expanded from a focus on cortical and brainstem structures to the complexities of the subcortical regions and cerebellum (Crosson, 1992; Schmahmann, 1991; Tranel, 1992). Appreciation of the multiple numbers of interconnected pathways that project to and from the cerebellum and brainstem to cortical regions (Kolb & Whishaw, 1990) is essential. Although current medical technology such as CT, MRI, PET, or SPECT scans has permitted more precise localization of brain lesions, medical science still relies on the neuropsychologist to describe the dynamic impact of a lesion on behavior. It is also important to recognize that there may be both focal and more generalized effects of a brain lesion. For this reason, the child neuropsychologist should possess a working understanding of functional neuroanatomy beyond the historical focus on lobes of the brain (Reitan & Davison, 1974; Selz & Reitan, 1979a).

Unfortunately, much of what we understand about regional differences in brain functioning is derived from studies of adult lesion cases (Heilman & Valenstein, 1985). Nevertheless, an appreciation of differences in the organization of mature functional systems should be linked to knowledge about differences in normal cognitive development (Schneider & Pressley, 1990; Williams, 1983) and about differences in the rate of regional development of the child's brain (Kolb, 1989). For example, our understanding of the anatomical basis of memory processes such as encoding and retrieval has been linked to functional networks involving medial temporal, diencephalic, and orbitofrontal structures of the brain. These structures myelinate at different rates and at different ages (Yakolev & Lecours, 1967). It should not be surprising, therefore, that younger children may normally manifest problems in developing memory-encoding strategies (Kail, 1985) until these structures are more fully matured. The naive neuropsychologist who invokes a semantic encoding deficit in a 6-year-old child demonstrates a clear lack of information about the normal development of children's memory strategies (Schneider & Pressley, 1990).

Age at the Time of Lesion

The individual's age at the time of acquiring the lesion is a particularly important variable in child neuropsychology (Boll, 1983; Boll & Barth, 1981). Injury to the brain from the many types of lesions described earlier can occur prenatally, peri- or postnatally, during infancy, or throughout the course of early childhood into adolescence. Depending on when the lesion occurred, there may be different effects on the brain systems that are developing or have yet to develop (Hynd & Willis, 1988; Kolb, 1989; Spreen et al., 1984). There may be both an acute effect of the injury such as neuronal death as well as more long-term effects on the development of functional connections such as the growth of aberrant connections (Goldman, Rosvold, & Mishkin, 1970; Stringer & Fennell, 1987). Two closely related concepts are critical periods for development and plasticity. The concept of critical period refers to developmental stages when specific functional behaviors develop tied to anatomic maturation (Spreen et al., 1984). There are critical periods that have been identified in prenatal and postnatal development that are affected both by brain lesions or by the lack of stimulation (Kolb & Whishaw, 1990). From a developmental perspective, focal lesions in regions prior to their complete anatomic maturation may not result in behavioral deficits until later, when that anatomic substrate becomes critical to the attainment of some neuropsychological function. For example, the frontal lobes do not completely mature until late adolescence. A significant frontal injury at 4 years of age may result in no noticeable problems until age 18 when that adolescent fails to develop normal executive control abilities (e.g., behavioral self-control and appropriate inhibition of "unacceptable" urges and impulses) or cognitive abstraction and reasoning skills.

Plasticity is a related concept that is based on observation of the capacity of the brain to adapt to change. Earlier views (Kennard Principle; Schneider, 1979) held that it was better to have a brain lesion earlier than later in life, based on the apparent ability of the immature brain to develop functions after early lesions. However, more recent views recognize that, whereas function may be achieved, it may be compromised in some fashion (Goldman & Galkin, 1978). With prenatal and perinatal neurological disorders or insults, the child has never experienced the functioning of a normal brain. Such children grow up adapting as best they can to their limitations. In this regard, Reitan (1984) concluded that early brain lesions, regardless of lateralization, cause devastating effects on the child's potential for developing normal abilities, whereas damage later in childhood may result in more selective impairments because normal maturational processes have had an opportunity to further advance cognitive development.

The child neuropsychologist must have a clear view of the emergence of normal functional abilities with which to compare the behavior of a child who has suffered from some type of brain lesion (Gesell & Amatruda, 1974). Absence of this window through which to view behavior may lead to incorrect decisions regarding the presence or absence of behavioral effects of the brain lesion. Further, this implies that the child neuropsychologist must inevitably adapt a longitudinal-developmental approach to assessment. Fletcher and Taylor (1984) articulated one such approach that views child neuropsychology as requiring knowledge of the manifest behavioral pathology of the child, the biological–neurological substrate underlying the pathology, the limits that these factors impose on the developing behavioral competencies of the child, and the moderating effects of the family system or educational setting.

APPROACHES IN CHILD NEUROPSYCHOLOGY

As with adult neuropsychology (see chapters 7 and 8 in this volume), there are three main assessment approaches in child neuropsychology (Fennell & Bauer, 1989): the fixed battery approach, the flexible battery approach, and the individualized or patient-centered approach. These approaches are distinguished by the nature of the test battery employed by the examiner.

The *fixed battery approach* involves the administration of the same set of standardized tests to each child seen, regardless of diagnostic question. The battery may vary somewhat according to the age of the child, typically differentiating younger (5 to 8 years old) from older (9 to 15 years old) children. These batteries have generally been empirically derived and are based upon their ability to separate normal children from groups of children with brain dysfunction. The work of Reitan and his co-workers, resulting in the Reitan–Indiana Neuropsychological Test Battery for Children (ages 5 to 8 years) and the Halstead–Reitan Neuropsychological Test Battery for Children (ages 9 to 14 years) (Reitan & Davison, 1974; Reitan & Wolfson, 1992a, 1992b), and the more recent Nebraska Neuropsychological Children's Battery (Golden, 1989) are examples of this approach. The emphasis in most fixed batteries is on quantitative differentiation of patient groups from normal children. As a result, there is little emphasis on such qualitative indices as age-related changes in how a score is achieved. Some fixed batteries include rules for decision making (Selz & Reitan, 1979b). A major concern for the examiner who uses a fixed battery is the match between the sample of brain-injured children who were used in the validation or cross-validation studies and the child in the clinical evaluation to whom these interpretive rules will be applied.

The *flexible battery approach* typically utilizes a core battery of tests that are administered with additional tests that are selected to address specific referral questions (Rourke et al., 1986) or to clarify findings that emerge from the core battery. One such example would be the use of a screening battery followed by the use of a comprehensive language battery in the assessment of language deficits following closed injury (Ewings-Cobbs, Levin, Eisenberg, & Fletcher, 1987). This type of approach allows the examiner to follow both a nomothetic approach (core battery) and an ideographic approach (additional tests) to better describe a particular childhood syndrome. Often the additional tests are derived from clinical evaluations of selected groups of brain-impaired children but may also include more laboratory-based assessment techniques such as dichotic listening, use of computerized continuous performance tasks, or specialized tests of lateralized brain functions.

In the *patient-centered approach*, the examiner selects tests to be employed based on both the referral question and the child's performance on a given task. Unlike the two approaches just described, the emphasis in this examination is on the isolation of the specific neurological mechanism that underlies a particular behavioral disorder. Thus, this approach requires that the examiner have a very thorough understanding of the clinical presentation of a variety of specific brain disorders as well as an underlying model of brain functioning against which to match the clinical findings and infer the brain pathology (Fennell & Bauer, 1989; Tramontana & Hooper, 1988).

Regardless of approach to assessment, most child neuropsychologists assess children with a set of tests that tap many areas of brain functioning. Thus, typically, tests of intellectual functioning, memory, language, sensory, motor, and visuospatial functions are included in the examination. What differs is the emphasis placed by the examiner on the match or mismatch between examination results and the following: (a) the performance of normal children; (b) the performance of children with specific brain injuries (e.g., children with closed head injuries); (c) the performance of children with similar types and location of lesions (e.g., children with lesions of the cerebellar hemispheres); (d) the known behavioral effects of a lesion in a specific functional system; and (e) the changes in test performance that are a function of age at time of lesion and/or time since the lesion occurred. It is this comparison between the individual case and multiple comparison groups that is fundamental to the inferential process in child neuropsychology (Fennell & Bauer, 1989).

A MODEL FOR NEUROPSYCHOLOGICAL ASSESSMENT OF CHILDREN

Domains of Assessment

The neuropsychological examination of a child or young adolescent involves assessment of several broad domains of functioning. These can be defined as (a) the biological domain, (b) the social–interpersonal domain, and (c) the educational domain. Each domain should be examined from the framework of past history of development and current problems. Within the biological domain, the examiner seeks to obtain knowledge about prior development including past medical history, history of the specific complaint, prior medical diagnostic evaluations, and any family history factors that could affect the presenting problem. The child's performance on the neuropsychological examination constitutes the descriptive basis for current problems. Along with scores on the neuropsychological exam, parents of younger children may frequently complete general development inventories such as the Childhood Development Inventory (Ireton & Twang, 1992) and the Vineland Adaptive Behavior Scales (Sparrow, Balla, & Cicchetti, 1984). Similarly, the social–interpersonal domain involves exploration of the prior history of social or behavior problems manifested by the child, history of familial disorders or discord, and the family's response to the child's behavioral problem. With young children, parent-report measures of problem behaviors may be employed such as the Child Behavior Checklist (Achenbach & Edelbrock, 1983). Older children who can read may also complete several self-report measures assessing affective symptoms such as anxiety (Spielberger, 1973) or depression (Kovacs, 1992), as well as indices of self-esteem (Harter, 1983) or the MMPI-A (Butcher et al., 1992). Finally, because a major task of childhood is to succeed in school, the educational domain needs to be examined. A careful history of schooling beginning from any preschool experiences should be obtained from the parents. Information to be gathered includes not only academic but also behavioral problems that the child encountered. Prior achievement testing, school changes, placement in any special classes, and history of school adjustment should be carefully gathered during interview. Current placement and any problems in achievement or adjustment is also needed, including teacher reports of problem behaviors. When not available, the child may be given an individualized achievement test to assess for competencies in current grade placement such as the Woodcock–Johnson Psychoeducational Battery—Revised (Woodcock & Mather, 1989). Although many neuropsychologists prefer to use a briefer achievement-screening instrument such as the Wide Range Achievement Test—Revised (Jastak & Wilkinson, 1984), these briefer instruments may suboptimally assess reading competence and mathematics ability (Goldman, L'Engle-Stein, & Guerry, 1983).

The intent of the careful examination in each of these three domains is to be able to develop a clear understanding of developmental factors that could affect the current presentation of biological, social, or educational problems of the child. Against this background of developmental history, special behavioral problems that the child exhibits on the neuropsychological examination, in social or interpersonal relationships, or in educational settings may be evaluated. This evaluation requires that the child neuropsychologists possess knowledge regarding the developmental effects and outcomes of brain, social, or educational problems. For example, if a child suffered a closed head injury at age 6 years, the child neuropsychologist must be familiar with the early and late behavioral effects of closed head injury to ascertain whether the current problems of the child are a direct result of the injury (Fennell & Mickle, 1992). However, if this same child comes from a family in which there are two siblings and one parent with a history of learning disabilities, the decision-making process becomes more complicated and must include an understanding of the neuropsychology of learning disabilities. Further, if the child has manifested problems in hyperactivity or inattention but has been medicated for a seizure disorder, the examiner must appreciate the potential effects of epilepsy or anticonvulsant medication on test performance (Menkes, 1990). Finally, it is rarely the case that children (or adults) undergo a neuropsychological assessment prior to an adverse event.

However, if this same child had been given a McCarthy Scale of Children's Abilities (McCarthy, 1972) at age 4 years but is now administered the Wechsler Preschool and Primary Scale of Intelligence—Revised (Wechsler, 1989) in the context of a personal injury lawsuit, the child neuropsychologist must interpret differences in scores between tests that occurred prior to and subsequent to a brain injury. Appreciation of the comparability between tests requires that the child neuropsychologist remain cognizant of the psychometric characteristics of many childhood measures.

Elements of a Comprehensive Child Neuropsychological Examination

Table 5.1 presents the essential elements of a comprehensive neuropsychological examination. Prior to beginning the examination, the neuropsychologist should review all records of prior medical treatments or diagnostic procedures undertaken on the child. Often parents have an incomplete understanding of the meaning of these procedures or are unable to recall critical information related to the child's health status. When CT scans or EEGs have been conducted, these should be summarized in the report. The clinical interview is intended to develop a history of the child and the family from the three perspectives described earlier: the biological (medical and neurological), the social–interpersonal (psychological and emotional development), and the educational (experiences and competencies). The typical interview may last for an hour or longer depending on the purpose of the examination. Within the biological domain, the examiner should begin with the mother's pregnancy and delivery and proceed through each year of development to the present date. Early childhood milestones should be examined (language or motor milestones, toilet training, early peer experiences). It is often helpful to ask the parents to compare this child to other siblings with regard to milestones. As noted earlier, careful descriptions of preschool and school history should be obtained. If the child has sustained an acquired lesion (e.g., head trauma, infection), it is important to obtain a detailed description of behavioral changes early and later in time from the date of the acquired injury. Questions of early temperament and adjustment should precede any detailed description of current behavioral problems. This will minimize the inclination to attribute all behavioral problems to the injury or lesion in question. Again, it is helpful to obtain comparisons of this child with siblings. It is also helpful to gather information about parenting styles, including discipline methods or conflicts between the parents

TABLE 5.1
Essential Elements in a Child Neuropsychological Examination

1. Clinical Interview
   a. History
   b. Current Problems
2. Neuropsychological Tests
   a. Intelligence
   b. Memory
      1) Verbal
      2) Nonverbal
   c. Learning
      1) Verbal
      2) Nonverbal
   d. Language
      1) Expression
         Oral
         Written
         Fluency
      2) Comprehensive
   e. Motor
      1) Fine Motor Speed
      2) Manual Dexterity
      3) Gross Motor
   f. Visuospatial Functions
      1) Analysis
      2) Synthesis
      3) Construction
   g. Frontal Executive
      1) Attention
      2) Speed of Responding
      3) Response Inhibition
      4) Tracking
      5) Abstraction
3. Achievement
   a. History
   b. Current
4. Social Emotional Functioning
   a. Child Behavioral Problems
   b. Family Problems

over child-rearing practices. Finally, the interview should develop a detailed description of current problems experienced by the child at home, at school, and at play. Parental and sibling reactions to these problems should be explored. At the conclusion of the interview, the child neuropsychologist may wish to restate his or her understanding of the purpose of the examination as well as the questions to which the parents hope to obtain answers as a result of the examination.

The types of neuropsychological tests that can be given in the examination are outlined in the next section of Table 5.1. It is not the intent of this chapter to provide detailed descriptions of the measures to be used. Instead, the scope of the examination is presented. The typical examination covering these areas will last about 4 to 4.5 hours, depending on the age of the child and his or her difficulty with different task demands. If a child is to be followed with repeated examinations, tests should be selected within each area that have an adequate span across the ages. Some broad-band memory batteries and verbal learning tests normed specifically for children are now available, such as the Wide Range Assessment of Memory and Learning (WRAML; Sheslow & Adams, 1990). Knowledge about normal memory development and memory strategies in children is essential to meaningfully interpret scores from such batteries or tests (Kail, 1985; Schneider & Pressley, 1990). There are also tests of language competency in children now available, such as the Clinical Evaluation of Language Fundamentals—Revised (CELF-R; Semel, Wiig, & Secord, 1987). However, unless the examiner is very familiar with the different types of language and articulation disorders that children can manifest, these batteries should not be attempted by the examiner. Instead, when questions of language disorder emerge from the initial examination, the child should be referred to a speech pathologist for a comprehensive speech and language assessment. Examiners who wish to assess the broad domain of visuomotor or visuoperceptual functioning should be very familiar with the normal developmental course of these skills (Williams, 1983). Similarly, appreciation of the development of so-called "frontal lobe" behaviors is a prerequisite to interpreting the meaning of any abnormalities noted in test performance.

Once neuropsychological test scores have been obtained, the examiner may proceed through both a quantitative and qualitative analysis of the test findings. The intent here is to integrate the data into a meaningful picture of the child's functioning. Next, the examiner should begin to relate the current data to any developmental history factors. Following this, the examiner should compare the current picture and history with what is known about child neuropsychological disorders, including the presumptive brain systems or structures involved in the behavior pathology. Next, problems in academic achievement and school adjustment must be integrated, as well as any evidence of behavioral or psychiatric pathology. The examiner must attempt to determine whether these problems are directly related to brain pathology, have arisen in reaction to brain pathology, or are a consequence of the family's or child's inability to cope with the direct or indirect effects of the underlying brain disorder. Finally, the child neuropsychologist should write a report that covers both past and present problems, describes the nature of the child's neurobehavioral problems, relates these problems back to the history, and offers recommendations to help the child, the family, or the school adapt to these problems, and to enhance the child's ability to meet the demands in his or her environment to continue to develop and grow.

MEASUREMENT ISSUES
IN CHILD NEUROPSYCHOLOGICAL ASSESSMENT

Psychometric Issues

Recently, a number of widely used measures of children's intelligence have been updated and revised. These include the Stanford–Binet, the Wechsler Preschool and Primary Scale of Intelligence, and the Wechsler Intelligence Scale for Children (Stanford–Binet IV: Thorndike, Hagen, & Sattler, 1986; WPPSI-R: Wechsler, 1989; WISC-III: Wechsler, 1991). Paralleling changes in tests comparability observed when the Wechsler Adult Intelligence Scale was revised in 1981 (Wechsler, 1981), these test revisions have resulted in slightly lower scores compared to earlier versions of these tests. Also, new subtests have been added or old tests substantially revised (Sattler, 1988). The child neuropsychologist should be very familiar with changes in scores and content resulting from these revisions to avoid misinterpreting the meaning of declines in scores when the new forms are employed. Shortly, an upward extended revision of the Bayley Scales will also be available to those who work with younger aged children (Bayley, 1991).

Test Norms

A continuing problem in child neuropsychology is the need for better normed and standardized tests of cognitive functions such as memory, learning, and visuospatial skills. Despite the critical role that such functions play in describing brain development, there is still a relative lack of good measures of verbal and nonverbal memory and learning and of visuospatial analytic or synthetic skills available across the age span from 4 or 5 to 15 years. Often normative data, when available, is provided by grade level (e.g., Benton's Multilingual Aphasic Examination; Benton & Hamsher, 1989, up to the sixth grade only) or is provided for discontinuous age groups (e.g., Children's Auditory Verbal Learning Test; Talley, 1990) with no adjustment for intellectual level. A further problem relates to the conceptual basis of many available childhood tests. For example, children's measures that simply step down the number of items given to adults such as the Nebraska Neuropsychological Battery for

Children (Golden, 1989) or use an adult test model of mnemonic strategies (e.g., California Verbal Learning Test for Children: Delis, Kramer, Kaplan, & Ober, 1993) ignore the very real differences in cognitive strategies that occur along the course of development of a particular skill. Thus, the child neuropsychologist who utilizes such measures should be very familiar with the limitations of these tests in accounting for normal variations in development and in the types of clinical groups on which normative data was derived.

Normative Data in Special Populations

There continues to be a need for better normative data on the test performances of groups of children suffering from a variety of neurological and systemic disorders (Fennell & Bauer, 1989). Examination of recent texts in child neurology and neuropsychology suggests that, with the exception of such disorders as learning disabilities and attention deficit-hyperactivity disorder, most data available about the neuropsychological profiles of common childhood neurological and systemic disorders relates to intellectual functioning and school achievement (Hynd & Willis, 1988; Menkes, 1990). Recently, clinical neuropsychological data on children treated for the leukemias (Berg et al., 1983), diabetes (Ryan & Morrow, 1987), renal disease (Fennell, Fennell, Mings, & Morris, 1988), cardiac disease (Aram, Ekelman, Ben-Shachar, & Lewinsohn, 1985), and organ transplantation (Bailey, Wood, Razzouk, Arsdell, & Gundry, 1989) are becoming available. This parallels the growth of the clinical specialty of Pediatric Psychology (Routh, 1988) as a hospital-based practice area. Increasingly, child neuropsychologists work as part of a team of pediatric psychologists, physicians, nurses, and other health professionals providing diagnostic and treatment services to children and their families faced with the stresses associated with coping with the effects of chronic medical disorders (including neurological disorders) and their treatments. Neuropsychologists who work with these children must not only be familiar with the specific primary, secondary, or tertiary effects of these illnesses but also must be flexible in their clinical assessment. Modifications in testing procedures may be necessary to accommodate to the adverse effects of physical illness or its treatment including fatigue, medication side effects, disruption due to medical procedures, and the limitations of bedside testing. Lengthy testing procedures more typical of outpatient visits may not be possible. As a result, the neuropsychologist may find it necessary to develop a shorter and more focused testing procedure designed to answer more immediate questions related to patient status and management.

Table 5.2 presents an example of an abbreviated battery that can be completed in about 1.5 to 2 hours. At our university, such approaches have been utilized with pediatric patients undergoing bone marrow transplantation procedures, with patients initiating chemotherapy or irradiation for brain tumors, and with pediatric patients being followed for organ transplantation and AIDS. Selection of such a modified test battery should be guided by an awareness of the potential brain effects of the disease process or its treatment as well as the tests' ability to address specific neurobehavioral deficits that may affect treatment decisions (e.g., memory dysfunction) and neurobehavioral syndromes that may reflect adverse treatment effects (e.g., attentional disorder). In responding to these questions, the child neuropsychologist needs to communicate the limitations

TABLE 5.2

An Example of an Abbreviated Child
Neuropsychological Assessment Battery

Cognition
    Vocabulary (WISC-III)[1]
    Comprehension (WISC-III)[1]
    Block Design (WISC-III)[1]
    Object Assembly (WISC-III)[1]

Memory
    Digit Span (WISC-III)[1]
    Wide Range Assessment of Memory and Learning (WRAML)[2]
    Story Recall[2]
    Verbal Learning[2]

Motor
    Repetitive and Successive Finger Movements[3]

Constructional
    Beery VMI[4]

Frontal
    Symbol Search (WISC-III)[1]
    Mazes (WISC-III)[1]
    Trail Making Test[5]
    Go NoGo
    Verbal Fluency[6]

[1]Wechsler (1991)
[2]Sheslow & Adams (1990)
[3]Denckla (1973)
[4]Beery (1989)
[5]Reitan & Davison (1974)
[6]Benton & Hamsher (1989)

of the tests selected and the need for appropriate comprehensive follow-up when this is possible. As the healing child returns to school, it is imperative that a careful, comprehensive assessment be undertaken to allow better description of any potential residual dysfunctions that may impact on the child's ability to function in the classroom.

FUTURE DIRECTIONS IN CHILD NEUROPSYCHOLOGICAL ASSESSMENT

As noted earlier, the next few years should see the continued development of normative data among groups of children suffering from a variety of neurological or systemic disorders. A similar growth of knowledge about the neuropsychology of other childhood disorders is also needed and anticipated. Among these are continued studies of neurodevelopmental disorders such as autism, studies of childhood conduct disorders, psychiatric disorders including childhood schizophrenia and childhood affective disorders, and the neuropsychology of retardation. Much research is still needed in genetic disorders such as Angelmann's and Prader–Willi Syndrome. The recent intensive investigation of the neurobehavioral effects of pediatric AIDS is still beset with many methodological problems that affect our interpretation of treatment interventions (Fennell, in press). Ideally, future research will profit from the subtyping of different neurological and medical conditions similar to the approaches to subtyping of learning disabilities and attention-deficit disorders (Barkley, 1990; Satz & Morris, 1981) that has proved helpful in discerning differences between and among subgroups of children affected by these disorders. There is a continued need for longitudinal studies that will provide information on the long-term effects of brain lesion acquired at various ages or present from the earliest stages of brain development. Without such data, the ability of the child neuropsychologist to prescribe for the future needs of the affected child will remain limited. Finally, there is a clear need for research on the effectiveness of cognitive-remediation therapies currently available to children (Lyons, Moats, & Flynn, 1988). Linkages between child neuropsychological assessment and treatment planning largely remain empirically rather than theoretically driven (Rourke et al., 1986). Large-scale studies of cognitive-remediation treatments in children are, as yet, unavailable, and the limitations of our current assessment approaches need to be remedied. Fortunately, for the child neuropsychologist, these future needs pose a positive challenge for continued enhancement of our scientific knowledge base and our clinical assessment and intervention skills.

REFERENCES

Achenbach, T. M., & Edelbrock, C. (1983). *Manual for the Child Behavior Checklist*. Burlington, VT: University Associates in Psychiatry.

Aram, D. M., Ekelman, B. L., Ben-Shachar, G., & Lewinsohn, M. W. (1985). Intelligence and hypoxemia in children with congenital heart disease: Fact or artifact? *Journal of the American College of Cardiology, 6*, 889–893.

Bailey, L. L., Wood, M., Razzouk, A., Arsdell, G. V., & Gundry, S. (1989). Heart transplantation during the first 12 years of life. *Archives of Surgery, 124*, 1221–1226.

Barkley, R. A. (1990). *Attention deficit–hyperactivity disorder: A handbook for diagnosis and treatment*. New York: Guilford Press.

Bayley, N. (1991). *Manual for the administration of the standardization procedure items of the Bayley Scales of Infant Development—Revised*. Unpublished manuscript.

Beery, K. (1989). *Manual for the Developmental Test of Visual–Motor Integration*. Cleveland, OH: Modern Curriculum Press.

Benton, A. L., & Hamsher, K. deS. (1989). *Multilingual Aphasia Exam: Manual of instructions* (2nd ed.). Odessa, FL: Psychological Assessment Resources.

Berg, R. A., Ch'ien, L. T., Bowman, W. P., Ochs, J., Lancaster, W., Goff, J. R., & Anderson, H. R. (1983). The neuropsychological effects of acute lymphocytic leukemia and its treatment—A three year report: Intellectual functioning and academic achievement. *International Journal of Clinical Neuropsychology, 5*, 9–13.

Berg, R. A., & Linton, J. C. (1989). Neuropsychological sequelae of chronic medical disorders. In C. R. Reynolds & E. Fletcher-Janzen (Eds.), *Handbook of clinical child neuropsychology* (pp. 107–127). New York: Plenum Press.

Boll, T. M. (1983). Neuropsychological assessment of the child: Myths, current status and future progress. In C.E. Walker & M. C. Roberts (Eds.), *Handbook of clinical child psychology* (pp. 186–208). New York: Wiley.

Boll, T. M., & Barth, J. (1981). Neuropsychology of brain damage in children. In S. Filskov & T. J. Boll (Eds.), *Handbook of clinical neuropsychology* (Vol. I, pp. 418–452). New York: Wiley.

Butcher, J. N., Williams, C. L., Graham, J. R., Archer, R. P., Tollegen, A., Ben-Porath, Y. F., & Kaemmer, B. (1992). *MMPI-A (Minnesota Multiphasic Personality Inventory— Adolescent): Manual for administration, scoring, & interpretation*. Minneapolis: University of Minnesota Press.

Crosson, B. (1992). *Subcortical functions in language and memory*. New York: Guilford Press.

Delis, D. C., Kramer, J., Kaplan, E., & Ober, B. A. (1993). *California Verbal Learning Test for Children*. San Antonio, TX: The Psychological Corporation.

Denckla, M. B. (1973). Development in speed of repetitive and successive finger movements in normal children. *Developmental Medicine and Child Neurology, 16*, 729–741.

Ernhart, C. B., Graham, F. K., Eichman, P. L., Marshall, J. M., & Thurston, D. (1963). Brain injury in the preschool child: Some developmental considerations. II. Comparisons of brain-injured and normal children. *Psychological Monographs, 27*(No. 574), 17–33.

Ewings-Cobb, L., Levin, H. S., Eisenberg, H. M., & Fletcher, J. M. (1987). Language functions following closed head injury in children and adolescents. *Journal of Clinical and Experimental Neuropsychology, 2*, 575–592.

Fenichel, G. M. (1988). *Clinical pediatric neurology: A signs and symptoms approach*. Philadelphia: W. B. Saunders.

Fennell, E. B. (in press). Assessing neurobehavioral changes in HIV infants and children: A methodological approach. *Proceedings of the New York Academy of Sciences*. (Pediatric AIDS: Clinical, Pathological and Basic Science Perspectives.)

Fennell, E. B., & Bauer, R. M. (1989). Models of inference in evaluating brain–behavior relationships in children. In C. R. Reynolds & E. Fletcher-Janzen (Eds.), *Handbook of clinical child neuropsychology* (pp. 167–177). New York: Plenum Press.

Fennell, E. B., Fennell, R. S., Mings, E., & Morris, M. K. (1988). The effects of various modes of therapy for end-stage renal disease on cognitive performance in a pediatric population—A preliminary report. *The International Journal of Pediatric Nephrology, 7*, 107–112.

Fennell, E. B., & Mickle, J. P. (1992). Behavioral effects of head trauma in children and adolescents. In M. Tramontana & S. R. Hooper (Eds.), *Advances in child neuropsychology* (Vol. 1). New York: Springer-Verlag.

Fishman, M. A. (1987). *Pediatric neurology*. New York: Grune & Stratton.

Fletcher, J. M., & Taylor, H. G. (1984). Neuropsychological approaches to children: Towards a developmental neuropsychology. *Journal of Clinical Neuropsychology, 6*, 39–56.

Gesell, A. L., & Amatruda, C. S. (1974). *Developmental diagnosis: The evaluation and management of normal and abnormal neuropsychologic development in infancy and early childhood* (3rd ed.). Hagerstown, MD: Harper & Row.

Golden, C. J. (1989). The Nebraska Neuropsychological Children's Battery. In C. R. Reynolds & E. Fletcher-Janzen (Eds.), *Handbook of clinical child neuropsychology* (pp. 193–204). New York: Plenum Press.

Goldman, P. S., & Galkin, T. W. (1978). Prenatal removal of frontal association cortex in the fetal rhesus monkey: Anatomical and functional consequences in postnatal life. *Brain Research, 152*, 451–485.

Goldman, J. R., L'Engle-Stein, C., & Guerry, S. (1983). *Psychological methods of child assessment*. New York: Bruner Mazel.

Goldman, P. S., Rosvold, H. E., & Mishkin, M. (1970). Evidence for behavioral impairments following prefrontal lobectomy in the infant monkey. *Journal of Comparative and Physiological Psychology, 70*, 454–462.

Harter, S. (1983). *Supplementary description of the Self-Perception Profile for Children. Revision of Perceived Competence Scale for Children*. Unpublished manuscript, University of Denver.

Heilman, K. M., & Valenstein, E. (1985). *Clinical neuropsychology* (2nd ed.). New York: Oxford University Press.

Hynd, G. W., & Willis, W. G. (1988). *Pediatric neuropsychology*. New York: Grune & Stratton.

Ireton, H., & Twang, E. (1992). *Manual for the Minnesota Child Development Inventory*. Minneapolis: University of Minnesota Press.

Jastak, S., & Wilkinson, G. (1984). *Wide Range Achievement Test* (Revised). Wilmington, DE: Jastak Associates.

Kail, R. (1985). *The development of memory in children* (2nd ed.). San Francisco: W. H. Freeman.

Kolb, B. (1989). Brain development, plasticity and behavior. *The American Psychologist, 44*, 1203–1212.

Kolb, B., & Whishaw, I. Q. (1990). *Fundamentals of human neuropsychology* (3rd ed.). San Francisco: W. H. Freeman.

Koppitz, E. M. (1964). *The Bender Gestalt Test for Young Children*. New York: Grune & Stratton.

Kovacs, M. (1992). *The Childhood Depression Inventory*. North Tonowanda, NY: Multi Health Systems.

Lyons, G. R., Moats, L., & Flynn, J. M. (1988). From assessment to treatment: Linkage to interventions with children. In M. Tramontana & S. R. Hooper (Eds.), *Assessment issues in child neuropsychology* (pp. 113–144). New York: Plenum Press.

McCarthy, D. (1972). *McCarthy Scales of Children's Abilities*. New York: The Psychological Corporation.

Menkes, J. H. (1990). *Textbook of child neurology* (4th ed.). Philadelphia: Lea & Febiger.

Reitan, R. M. (1984). *Aphasia and sensory-perceptual deficits in children.* Tucson, AZ: Neuropsychology Press.

Reitan, R. M., & Davison, L. A. (Eds.). (1974). *Clinical neuropsychology: Current status and applications.* New York: Wiley.

Reitan, R. M., & Wolfson, D. (1992a). *Neuropsychological evaluation of young children.* Tucson, AZ: Neuropsychology Press.

Reitan, R. M., & Wolfson, D. (1992b). *Neuropsychological evaluation of older children.* Tucson, AZ: Neuropsychology Press.

Reynolds, C. R., & Fletcher-Janzen, E. (1989). *Handbook of clinical child neuropsychology.* New York: Plenum Press.

Rourke, B. P. (1982). Central processing deficiencies in children: Toward a developmental neuropsychological model. *Journal of Clinical Neuropsychology, 4,* 1–18.

Rourke, B. P., Bakker, D. J., Fisk, J. L., & Strange, J. D. (1983). *Child neuropsychology: An introduction to theory, research and practice.* New York: Guilford Press.

Rourke, B. P., Fisk, J. L., & Strange, J. D. (1986). *Neuropsychological assessment of children: A treatment-oriented approach.* New York: Guilford Press.

Routh, D. K. (Ed.). (1988). *Handbook of pediatric psychology.* New York: Plenum Press.

Rutter, M. (Ed.). (1983). *Developmental neuropsychiatry.* New York: Guilford Press.

Ryan, C., & Morrow, L. A. (1987). Neuropsychological characteristics of children with diabetes. In M. L. Wolraich & D. K. Routh (Eds.), *Advance in developmental and behavioral pediatrics* (Vol. III). Greenwich, CT: JAI Press.

Sattler, J. M. (1988). *Assessment of children's intelligence* (3rd ed.). San Diego: Jerome M. Sattler.

Satz, P., & Morris, R. (1981). Learning disability subtypes: A review. In F. J. Perozzolo & M. Wittrock (Eds.), *Neuropsychological and cognitive processes in reading* (pp. 109–141). New York: Academic Press.

Schmahmann, J. D. (1991). An emerging concept: The cerebellar contribution to higher cortical function. *Archives of Neurology, 48,* 1178–1187.

Schneider, G. E. (1979). Is it really better to have your brain lesion early? A revision of the "Kennard principle." *Neuropsychologia, 17,* 557–583.

Schneider, W., & Pressley, M. (1990). *Memory development between 2 to 20 years.* New York: Springer-Verlag.

Selz, M., & Reitan, R. M. (1979a). Neuropsychological performance of normal, learning-disabled and brain-damaged older children. *Journal of Nervous and Mental Disease, 167,* 298–302.

Selz, M., & Reitan, R. M. (1979b). Rules for neuropsychological diagnosis: Classification of brain function in older children. *Journal of Clinical and Consulting Psychology, 47,* 258–264.

Semel, E., Wiig, E., & Secord, W. (1987). *Manual for the Clinical Evaluation of Language Fundamentals—Revised.* New York: The Psychological Corporation.

Sheslow, D., & Adams, W. (1990). *Manual for the Wide Range Assessment of Memory and Learning.* Wilmington, DE: Jastak Associates.

Sparrow, S., Balla, D. A., & Cicchetti, D. V. (1984). *Vineland Adaptive Behavior Scales.* Circle Pines, MN: American Guidance Services.

Spielberger, C. D. (1973). *Manual for the State–Trait Anxiety Scale for Children.* Palo Alto, CA: Consulting Psychologists Press.

Spreen, O., Tupper, D., Risser, A., Tuokko, H., & Edgell, D. (1984). *Human developmental neuropsychology.* New York: Oxford.

Stringer, A. V., & Fennell, E. B. (1987). Hemispheric compensation in a child with left cerebral hypoplasia. *The Clinical Neuropsychologist, 1,* 124–138.

Talley, J. (1990). *Manual for the Children's Auditory Verbal Learning Test*. Odessa, FL: Psychological Assessment Resources.

Tartar, R. E., Van Thiel, D. H., & Edwards, K. L. (1988). *Medical neuropsychology*. New York: Plenum Press.

Thorndike, R., Hagen, E., & Sattler, J. (1986). *Stanford–Binet Intelligence Scale* (4th ed.). Chicago: Riverside.

Tramontana, M., & Hooper, S. R. (1988). *Assessment issues in child neuropsychology*. New York: Plenum Press.

Tramontana, M. G., & Hooper, S. R. (1992). *Advances in child neuropsychology* (Vol. 1). New York: Springer-Verlag.

Tranel, D. (1992). Functional neuroanatomy: Neuropsychological correlates of cortical and subcortical damage. In S. C. Yudosky & R. E. Hales (Eds.), *American Psychiatric Press textbook of neuropsychiatry* (2nd ed., pp. 57–88). American Psychiatric Press.

Walker, C. E., & Roberts, M. C. (1992). *Handbook of clinical child psychology* (2nd ed.). New York: Wiley.

Wechsler, D. (1960). *Manual for the Wechsler Intelligence Scale for Children*. New York: The Psychological Corporation.

Wechsler, D. (1981). *Manual for the Wechsler Adult Intelligence Scale—Revised*. New York: The Psychological Corporation.

Wechsler, D. (1989). *Manual for the Wechsler Preschool and Primary Scale of Intelligence—Revised*. New York: The Psychological Corporation.

Wechsler, D. (1991). *Manual for the Wechsler Intelligence Scale for Children—III*. New York: The Psychological Corporation.

Williams, H. G. (1983). *Perceptual and motor development*. Englewood Cliffs, NJ: Prentice-Hall.

Woodcock, W., & Mather, N. (1989). *The Woodcock Johnson Psychoeducational Battery— Revised*. Allen, TX: DLM Teaching Resources.

Yakolev, P. I., & Lecours, A. R. (1967). The myelogenetic cycles of regional maturation of the brain. In A. Minkowski (Ed.), *Regional development of the brain* (pp. 3–70). Oxford, England: Blackwell.

CHAPTER SIX

Neuropsychometric Issues and Problems

Paul D. Retzlaff
*University of Northern Colorado
and
VA Medical Center, Cheyenne, Wyoming*

Michael Gibertini
*Midwest Research Institute,
Kansas City, Missouri*

The field of psychometrics is concerned with the study of the adequacy of measures of human behavior. Recognized since the late 1800s, the field has grown in complexity and scope to a point that it represents one of the most developed areas of measurement theory in all of science today. Practically all of its more recent advances have been a consequence of our great need to have accurate and fair appraisals of student and employee ability. Modern psychometrics is, in other words, a product of psychologists' efforts to improve and defend the tests that are now responsible for determining the educational and occupational fates of millions of Americans. Because there is great need, enormous pools of subjects, and large profits at stake, measurement technology kept pace with the demands of consumers and politicians that tests be defensible against all attacks on their accuracy. Statistical and mathematical models not usually studied by psychology graduate students have been pressed into service for this defense and advancement of what is now a very large testing industry. For better or worse, the sum of the older and newer technologies sets the standard for all related disciplines. The result is that today the practicing psychologist is more likely than not to have inadequate and even obsolete training in test usage and evaluation. Obsolescence of graduate training is a situation, no doubt, common to all rapidly advancing sciences.

More troubling than the educational deficiencies of practicing psychologists, however, is the extremely uneven quality of data underlying the psychometric clinical instruments. Industry is at work here no less than in the educational or personnel arenas. Publishers of clinical and neuropsychological tests are expanding their libraries greatly. But the data required to meet the highest measurement technology standards typically are not collected. Nevertheless, clinical psychological and neuropsychological tests published today must meet higher standards of accuracy, representativeness, and fairness than ever before. But rarely are sufficient data available or published in test manuals to allow the user to evaluate the test against modern standards. Without high need, enormous subject pools, and huge profits at stake, the data necessary for evaluation according to classical reliability, generalizability, item response, or operating characteristics theories are too expensive to collect.

Neuropsychology has high need in the sense that the consequences of the evaluation are extremely powerful for individual patients. But the number of patients is relatively small and patients are dispersed among thousands of practitioners who are rarely organized for collaborative data gathering. Profits are also dispersed so that the individual test builder or publisher has little incentive for putting investment of time and money into modern comprehensive psychometric study of the test. And, because the consumer (i.e., the psychologist using the test) will not demand what he or she cannot interpret, there is no press for publishers or authors to update established instruments according to the latest advances in measurement technology. Clinical and clinical neuropsychological testing is a mere cottage industry, lagging far behind educational or personnel testing in measurement precision, sophistication, and technology use.

The intent of this chapter is to provide a practical framework for understanding psychometrics as they apply to neuropsychology. Initially, traditional psychometric concepts are reviewed, including reliability, validity, test referencing, and test theories. Secondly, the specific psychometric challenges that neuropsychologists face are placed in perspective. Thirdly, validity is re-examined through a discussion of operating and sampling distribution characteristics of tests.

Readers interested in the psychometric properties of specific tests are referred to Spreen and Straus (1991) and Franzen (1989). Those who would like an accessible mathematical perspective of psychometrics are encouraged to read Suen (1990). And, of course, the classic on psychometrics is Nunnally (1978).

TRADITIONAL PSYCHOMETRICS: CONCEPTS AND APPLICATIONS

Reliability

In using tests to sample and quantify behavior, variations in test performance may occur due to true differences in examinees' behavior or error. The reliability of a test is the estimate of what proportion of variance in performance can be attributed to true differences in behavior. Because many factors can contribute to error, a variety of procedures for estimating reliability have been developed, each of which identifies somewhat different variables as components of error.

Although reliability is probably one of the most central constructs to psychometrics, indeed, the term reliability should probably not be used. It is used to connote three differing concepts: internal consistency, stability, and interjudge concordance.

From a behavioral sampling perspective, the most important of these concepts is *internal consistency*. Internal consistency refers to the homogeneity of the test and items within it and is grounded in the problems of error in the sampling of behavior. Classically, some different types of internal consistency can be calculated. Alternative forms is when two tests built at the same time seeking to assess the same behavioral functions are correlated. The fact of the matter is that these days most test developers only develop one version of a test. Therefore, in practice rarely will alternative forms be available, although in many clinical situations there should be. The second method of calculating internal consistency is the *split-half method*. Here, the first half is correlated with the second half of a test, or the sum of odd items is correlated with the sum of even-numbered items. In essence, this is a more primitive form of the third and final method, which is the *Cronbach Alpha method* (Nunnally, 1978). The Cronbach Alpha method of internal consistency estimation relies on the intercorrelations of all items with each other. Indeed, in this way we get around the problem of alternative forms or split half; the homogeneity of items are judged on the basis of their intercorrelation. As such, under classical theory all multisampled behavioral tests have a reliability, and the best estimate of that reliability is the Cronbach Alpha measure of internal consistency.

Stability is often mistermed test–retest reliability. Stability is the performance on a test across time. To determine test–retest stability (reliability), a test is given to a sample twice within several weeks or months and the two scores are correlated. This is an appropriate statistic to reflect the generalizability of a patient's score to another point in time that is often of interest in neuropsychology. As such, it is useful when a clinician is interested in determining if a patient's scores represent a true and significant change in performance across time. Difficulties with this particular method include the fact that stability is not an interchangeable measurement with internal consistency. Therefore, it cannot be used to estimate true score, standard error of measurement, or most standard errors of estimation. This is because differences across time are related to both the internal consistency of a test and true and natural changes in people's scores across time. Additionally, different domains, constructs, and content behave differently in the face of a stability study. There are some constructs, such as certain aspects of intelligence, which are highly stable for 20 or 30 years of a person's life. Other constructs, such as attention, anxiety, or motivation, may be very situationally variable. Therefore, within stability studies the design of the study must be consistent with the underlying theoretical assumptions of that particular behavioral domain or disorder.

The final type of "reliability" is *interjudge reliability*. Again here, reliability is probably a poor term, and perhaps a better one would be interjudge concordance. In essence here, one is looking at the degree to which two judges make a similar diagnosis regarding a particular neuropsychological deficit in a single patient. There are fairly specific statistical calculations for this including the Kappa statistic (Cicchetti, 1991). The Kappa statistic very importantly deducts from the observed consistency of judgments that which is specific to chance. Indeed, if two judges tend to find 90% of a particular sample as having a particular disorder, at least 81% of the time they will be in agreement simply on the basis of chance. Therefore, the prevalence of a particular disorder or the prevalence of normality within a particular sample highly affects apparently concordant judgments.

Power Versus Speed Tests

Although the calculation of internal consistency through a Cronbach alpha is the preferred method of reliability estimation, tests that include speed as a component are inappropriate for the use of this technique. Power tests that have no time limit are well served by the Cronbach alpha, but speed tests will have artificially high alphas. In the case of tests where speed is central to the construct such as the time score on a Trails B, the split half or alternate-forms methods of reliability estimation should be used. The alternate-forms method is preferable as more items are available, but it is rare in neuropsychology for alternate forms to be available either due to construction cost or because the entire domain of possible items has already been exhausted. Many neuropsychological tests are timed, yet speed may not play a significant role in the underlying construct. The cost of speeding tests is the inability to properly estimate internal consistency and the loss of important measurement concepts such as the standard error of measurement that depend on proper estimation of reliability.

Test Theories

Test theory is a highly complex and difficult-to-understand area of psychometrics and psychology. Often, unfortunately, test theory is relegated to mathematical psychologists. Largely, there are two major schools of thought in test theory, and under each there are two subschools. The first school is primarily concerned with the test as a whole. The first such theory is that of classical test theory (Nunnally, 1978). Classical test theory is probably the most widely taught type of test theory in current American graduate schools. The second type concerned with the test as a whole is an extension of classical test theory brought to us by Lee Cronbach, that is generalizability theory (Cronbach, Gleser, Nanda, & Rajaratnam, 1972). The other major school is concerned more at an item level. First, this includes conventional item analysis; and second, the relatively sophisticated item response theory (Rasch, 1980). For the purposes of this chapter only the applications of classical test theory are discussed. It should be understood, however, that due to the inherent heterogeneity and complexity of neuropsychological work, classical test theory has serious limitations. Generalizability theory, conventional item analysis, and item response theory will undoubtedly play major roles in neuropsychological assessment in the decades to come.

Classical Test Theory

Classical test theory has been with us since the 1920s. In classical theory a particular score for a particular patient is composed of a true score and some amount of error variance. The attempt of classical test theory is to come as close as possible to the "true score." To this end, confidence intervals around obtained scores can be calculated with varying degrees of probability that the true score falls within that interval.

The important lessons that can be learned from classical test theory is first that the obtained score is not necessarily the "true score." Indeed, the estimation of the true score is based on the internal consistency of the test. It is calculated by multiplying the reliability times the deviation score of a particular patient. For example, with a test internal consistency of .50 and an obtained T score of 70 (a 20-point deviation), the estimated true score is very different from the 70. When the observed deviation is multiplied by the reliability, an estimated true T score of 60 results (a 10-point drop from the obtained T score). At this point the second intent of classical test theory is to develop confidence limits around that estimated true score. The formula for this "Standard Error of Measurement" is the test's standard deviation multiplied by the square root of 1 minus the test's reliability. If a neuropsychological test has a reliability of .50, we then have the square root of 1 minus .50, which is .71. Multiplying that by the test's standard deviation (10 points for a T metric) results in a Standard Error of Measurement of 7. Therefore, there is a 68% level of confidence that the patient's true score is a T score of 60 plus or minus 7 points. So, whereas a patient on a particular test with a reliability of .50 may have attained a T score of 70, according to classical test theory there is only 68% degree of certainty that the true score is between 53 and 67. The importance of this example (showing regressions to the true score and banding of confidence intervals) is to illustrate how imprecise neuropsychological testing can be; and more generally how imprecise tests are that are not reliable.

An additional use of true score theory and its confidence intervals is in the determination of the significant differences between two tests for a single patient. Often in the case of learning disabilities it is important to see if a child's ability is different from a child's achievement. Reynolds (1990) does a good job of providing the rationale and various formulae for such differences. A more common example, however, may be from the WAIS-R and the clinical practice of interpreting differences between scale scores. A clinician may be interested in seeing if the Vocabulary score of a patient (viewed as a good premorbid intelligence predictor) is statistically different from Digit Symbol (perhaps seen as a current global functioning indicator). Table 13 of the WAIS-R manual (Wechsler, 1981, p. 35) provides the requisite difference at a 15% level of confidence. In this case, Vocabulary must be 2.02 scale score units above Digit Symbol for the clinician to conclude that there is a good chance that current functioning is significantly below premorbid level.

These levels of significant difference are derived from the internal consistency of each subtest via a calculation of standard error of measurement formulae. As evidence of this, note that the two most internally consistent WAIS-R subscales are Vocabulary at 0.96 and Information at 0.89. These have standard errors of measurement of 0.61 and 0.93, respectively. The two subscales with the lowest internal consistency are Object Assembly at 0.68 and Picture Arrangement at 0.74. These have standard errors of estimate of 1.54 and 1.41, respectively. Using the data as calculated in the manual for a 15% confidence interval, a difference of only 1.60 is required for a significant difference between Vocabulary and Information, whereas a 3.01 is required for the less internally consistent Object Assembly and Picture Arrangement.

Whereas this is appropriate for determining if two scores are statistically different during one testing session, stability coefficients may be used to calculate the analogous standard error of estimate for comparing a patient's scores on a single test at two different times.

A problem with classical test theory is that the reliability calculation methods allow for only one source of true and one source of error variance within a score. Classical test theory does not deny multiple sources of true and error variance but can account or control for only one at a time. It is obvious that when tests are complex there may be multiple sources of true variance (different behaviors, all of which are essential to completing a test). Additionally, error variance may occur due to many factors such as fatigue, malingering, or the traditional error of the sampling of the items of behavior.

It is often tempting in a new field of psychology to presume that it is somehow immune to the psychometric and statistical requirements of other domains of psychology. However, all areas of psychology, including neuropsychology, require internally consistent measures to make highly confident inferences regarding patients' behavior and functioning.

Test Referencing

Test referencing is briefly discussed as preface to the next major issue, validity. There are three types of tests that can be developed, norm-referenced and two types of criterion-referenced tests.

The *norm-referenced test* is probably the most typical test within psychology. In it, a person's score is interpreted and inferences are made based on that individual's position in the distribution of all scores—how many standard deviations they may be above or below the mean. It is in this context that standard scores such as T scores and z scores, or percentile scores, are typically discussed. For some psychological constructs, norm referencing is an important and relevant method of inference (e.g., constructs such as intelligence). Knowing at what percentile against the norm reference an individual is contributes to our understanding of that individual's intellectual functioning. Norm referencing is also useful in the determination of change within an individual, through the determination of estimated true score changes as already discussed.

There are other cases within neuropsychology, however, where norm referencing is clearly inappropriate. For instance, in the case of aphasia, if a person is 2 standard deviations above or below the mean for nonaphasics on an aphasia test is not a particularly good indication of whether the individual has had a stroke or whether the individual has a receptive or expressive aphasia. In these types of situations, *criterion-referenced tests* are much more useful. There are two types of criterion-referenced tests, content and prediction (or expectancy).

In content-referenced tests the measure of performance is the amount of content material that an individual has successfully accomplished. This type of test is probably most common within academic settings where a professor will construct a test of 50 items based upon the lectures and readings for a particular class; students are graded upon the percentage of that information that they know. Within neuropsychology, such content referencing is probably highly appropriate for some things such as competency. If patients are unaware of their income, their bills, the status of their bank accounts, and the signatory authority over their bank accounts, it is highly probable that they are not competent for financial purposes. There is no need to reference their performance against a norm, nor do we need to predict individuals' ability and future behavior because those patients are unable to impress us with their understanding of their present fiscal condition. We and the courts recommend that these individuals are financially incompetent.

The second type of criterion-reference test is predictive or expectancy criterion referencing. Here the reference is the score or performance on, or classification made by some criterion measure. For example, a neuropsychological test may be referenced to findings on neuroimaging studies (CT or MRI scans). Thus, a poor performance on some measure of visuospatial ability may be referenced to the probability of finding demonstrable lesions in the right-parietal region. The criterion is not one of content, but an external criterion that, hopefully, properly categorizes individuals into "normals" or "brain impaired."

Validity

Validity is second in importance, only to reliability, as a psychometric variable. You can have the most reliable test in the world, but if it is not valid it is of little utility to the clinician. In fact, *validity* refers to a test's usefulness; validity is the degree to which a test fulfills the purposes for which it was intended. There are three traditional types of validity: content validity, construct validity, and predictive (or criterion-related) validity. These obviously often parallel the test-referencing approaches just discussed.

Content validity is the most primitive of the validities. With content validity through rational, logical analysis, experts judge the content of a particular test and infer its ability to tap a particular domain. Obviously, different judges may view the content in vastly different ways, and there may be little unanimity of agreement on the validity of a particular test when viewed from a content prospective. Indeed, there is no statistic that can operationalize content validity. Therefore, it should be viewed as the most primitive and minimally necessary form of validity. The unfortunate case within neuropsychology is, however, that many of our tests have no more than content validity. Face validity is often erroneously used interchangeably with content validity. However, face validity technically is not a type of validity at all and refers simply to whether or not a test appears to assess what it was designed to measure regardless of what expert judges may think.

Construct validity is a far more sophisticated method. Campbell and Fisk (1959) in the late 1950s presented the model of the multitrait, multimethod matrix. The intent of the multitrait, multimethod matrix was to assess some underlying domains through a number of different methods. Within neuropsychology, this may take the form of assessing intelligence, language, and executive processes through paper and pencil tests and report of significant others. Determination of construct validity is accomplished through examination of a triangular intertest, intermethod correlation matrix in which on the diagonals are the reliabilities of the particular measures. Through an analysis of this intercorrelation matrix, one could determine the degree to which a particular trait or domain held up across different methods and assess the amount of variance accounted for by differing measurement methods.

This multitrait, multimethod matrix came under fire, however, because it involves a large number of univariate analyses. Currently, factor analysis is commonly viewed as the most appropriate multivariate method of determining the actual underlying dimensions of such a matrix. Indeed, at this point it is common in neuropsychology to attempt to validate a construct underlying a particular test through factor analysis. The construct validity of a measure is examined by including in a factor analysis a number of "marker" variables of specific abilities. This serves to determine the extent to which abilities such as intelligence, memory, or attention play a role. In more homogeneous tests (high internal consistency), factor analysis often is used to determine how specific a particular test is to a focal domain. With proper sampling, a new memory scale should have high loadings on the same factor as two or three well-known memory scales. It should not necessarily load on intellectual, language, or visuospatial factors. Construct validity is critically necessary within neuropsychology, particularly due to the idiosyncratic construction techniques often used.

The final major type of validity is criterion-related validity, which reflects the relationship between performance on the test and on a criterion measure. There are two types of criterion-related validity, predictive and concurrent. The difference between them is related to the timing of the administrations of the test and the criterion measure. However, for all practical purposes both reflect the predictive relationship between the test and the criterion measure and establish the statistical relationship between them. In neuropsychology the criterion variable may be a known pathological factor. The test may be correlated with known diagnostic groupings, anatomical lesions as evidenced by CT or MRI scans, or other biological variables. Predictive validity within neuropsychology is probably the most important method of determining validity. Whereas there are many different assessment approaches to neuropsychology, including anatomical, cognitive domain, and neurobehavioral syndromes, all have standards of outcome. Therefore, it should be the goal of all neuropsychological tests to withstand criterion-related or predictive validity.

These three types of validity are not mutually exclusive; ideally, a test should stand up to all three. The content of a test should logically be associated with the ability, the disorder, or anatomical considerations. Additionally, the construct validity should be established through formal and sophisticated factor-analytic techniques. Finally, and most importantly, these tests should actually predict external behaviors/criteria. Neuropsychological tests that contain content, construct, and predictive validities will prove to be the best tests available.

NEUROPSYCHOMETRICS: PUTTING THE CLASSICS IN PERSPECTIVE

Every measurement context is composed of two parts, the measurement procedure and the object of measurement. Both components have aspects that influence the final interpretation of the data. Psychometrics is concerned exclusively with aspects of the measurement procedure and leaves alone aspects of the object of measurement. Psychometrics grew up in an environment where aspects of the object of measurement could be readily controlled, categorized, or measured separately (and thereafter "controlled statistically"). Educational, personnel, and, to some extent, personality psychologists have had the ability to isolate that part of their subjects' functioning that they intended to measure. The object of measurement, in other words, brought no serious confounds to the procedures of measurement. Neuropsychologists have no such luck.

The object of measurement for clinical neuropsychologists is the function, not the structure, of a damaged or diseased brain. To infer structural changes from data on function may be a reason for undertaking the measurement procedure, but the reason for testing and the object of testing are not to be confused. The object of measurement in neuropsychological testing is always the same, but the reasons can be many: Infer structure changes, aid in treatment planning, chart the course of a disease, educate the patient on his disabilities, and so on. The function of the damaged brain may be decomposed into as many parts as the investigator can imagine, and all are presumably measurable. Each function may be measured by a test that has the same properties of measurement as any other psychological test, namely, adequate reliability and validity.

To illustrate, in neuropsychological assessment intelligence is decomposed into verbal versus nonverbal, and these may be further decomposed into problem solving, reasoning, sequencing abilities, and so on. Memory is decomposed to immediate span, short-term register, and long-term store. These are divided into verbal and visual domains. The decomposition of brain function into smaller units is not a problem because each is merely a target at which the neuropsychologist aims assessment procedures. In fact, the decomposition of brain function into smaller units is a part of the measurement procedure and not, strictly speaking, a part of the object of measurement. Breaking brain functioning down or building it up for measurement purposes is what is meant by developing psychological constructs. The relationship of the construct to the object of measurement can never be more than theoretical, and so construct development belongs to the measurement side of our original dichotomy.

Decomposition of the object of measurement into smaller units is part of the measurement procedure and does not interfere with the psychometric purity of the neuropsychological situation. The special problems that neuropsychologists have are not in the realm of psychometrics, per se; they are not related to measurement procedures. Tests are tests and there is no technical reason why adequate psychometric statistics could not be generated for every neuropsychological procedure from finger tapping to the Wisconsin Card Sort. Adequate statistics do not exist, not because the tests are different, but because the population on which they are used is ill suited to classical test theory or any other psychometric theory yet devised. Neuropsychologists have trouble not with their measurement procedures but with their object of measurement.

Specifically, the object of measurement in neuropsychology is unstable. In psychometrics, the metaphor of the archer is used to illustrate the concepts of and relationship between reliability and validity. If the archer places all the arrows in a small radius anywhere on the target, it is said to be reliable. If a tight radius of arrows is placed in the bulls-eye, it is said to be reliable and valid. A neuropsychologist is shooting at a moving target that is moving at an unknown velocity and in unknown directions. The functions of a damaged brain are unstable, and from a strictly technical standpoint this makes the psychometrics of the measurement procedure unassessable. If the archer hits the bulls-eye with the first arrow and misses the entire target with the second, was the archer unreliable, was the archer–target relationship invalid, did the target move, or was there some combination of these possibilities? Without an external vantage that could separate these possibilities, the question is unanswerable. The neuropsychologist does not have any vantage but what is given in feedback from the test scores. Data from the test procedure are confounded with this unfortunate aspect of the object of measurement, and the two cannot be separated in the usual case. For most neuropsychological tests, the psychometric statistics that are available have been generated with normal populations and are not useful in estimating the reliability, validity, or errors of measurement and estimate of test results in the clinical situation.

Now that the Medusa has been named, it can be made more terrifying by describing its several heads. The problem of instability of the functions of the damaged brain can be divided into two major types. From the perspective of the measurement procedure, these are (a) changing foreground functions and (b) short- and long-term fluctuations in background conditions.

The Foreground

Changing foreground functions refers to the instability of the specific object of measurement. The neuropsychologist seeks to measure the patient's memory, for example. Is the obtained score the same today as what would have been obtained yesterday or what may be obtained tomorrow? From a psychometric standpoint, this a simple question of stability. But for the neuropsychologist, it is also a question about the functional state of the brain and thus part of the object of measurement. Each question is usually answered in terms of the known properties of the other. If both are unknown (the stability of the test and the stability of the function), then, as the mathematicians say, the system is indeterminate. Unfortunately, problems do not end with this indeterminacy. There is also a validity problem caused by the nonunitary nature of the object of measurement. Is memory a single functional unit? In truth, it should be remembered that memory does not exist; it is a construct that can be decomposed to simpler constructs. All of these may be changing and at different rates. Which of the many subcomponents of memory is the test measuring: attention, perception, encoding, transfer efficiency, storage, retrieval, others?

The changing foreground functions compound three problems for the neuropsychologist: (a) estimation of premorbid status, (b) construction of premorbid profiles, and (c) discernment of interactions among subcomponent processes of cognitive functions.

Issues related to premorbid functioning have been discussed in detail in chapter 2. Discussion included both approaches to estimating premorbid functioning, as well as difficulties in that regard due to variability in premorbid profiles of abilities. However, for the purposes of this discussion it is important to emphasize that current ability measures that may be used to estimate premorbid functioning should have demonstrably high reliability (internal consistency) and stability coefficients. There can be no substitute for reliability when trying to estimate the past in the face of a changing present.

Uncoupling Cognitive Subcomponents

All cognitive behavior involves the coordinated execution of many individual component processes. For example, it is current practice to divide memory assessment into verbal and visual domains. The clinician attempts to measure verbal memory independent of visual memory and vice versa. Is this possible? Verbal memory may be assessed by collecting the subject's store of remembered items from a list of verbally presented words after some time interval. If the subject used an intensely image-dependent mnemonic to transfer the words from immediate register to short-term storage, is that purely "verbal memory"? And what about other functions that are necessary for this type of test such as the ability to maintain attention, the ability to hear, the ability to understand language, the ability to follow instructions, or the ability to speak? Tests of verbal memory assume that these abilities are intact; to the extent that they are not, they influence the test score and detract from the test's reliability (if the collateral ability is changing), its construct validity (if the collateral ability is impaired to the point that the obtained score is very far off from where it would be if the collateral ability were intact), or both. Cognitive functions are interconnected and to some extent hierarchically organized (you cannot measure verbal memory in an inattentive or aphasic patient). Reliability suffers in this situation because the test sometimes measures more of the higher order function (e.g., memory) and sometimes more of the lower order function (e.g., attention). Can an archer shoot a single arrow at two targets? A correction that can be made is to arrange the evaluation in a way that assesses the lower order functions first and then uses data from this initial assessment to inform the choice of tests for the higher order evaluation. However, this is a clinical solution and does not address threats to the psychometric properties of the tests due to the interconnection among cognitive abilities.

The Background Conditions

The foreground is the foreground because the tests illuminate the cognitive components that are the focus of concern. But these selected functions are merely part of a vast cognitive landscape that is more like an undifferentiated prairie than the neatly quartered garden the examiner attempts to describe. Any function that is "lifted" out for examination carries with it connections to the whole brain and all its energies and fluctuations. The background that envelopes the artificially defined foreground cannot be ignored. There are many ways of attending to the background effects. For our purposes, four varieties of background effects are described, two short-term fluctuations (fatigue and motivation) and two long-term fluctuations (learning and maturation).

Short-Term Fluctuations

Cognitive tests require work. Ironically, brain-damaged patients, who eventually may be declared unfit to work, are often required to sit through 4 to 6 hours of intense and often intimidating mental tasks that would fatigue anyone. Fatigue leads to mistakes and mental slowing that increases the error of the test scores. We may expect less error in the tests given at the beginning of the session and more in those administered at the end of the session. Motivation works in the same way. Interestingly, motivation may increase during the session owing to rapport-building efforts of the examiner and then drop off precipitously when fatigue sets in. Aspects of both fatigue and motivation may be functions of the disease state, as well as of premorbid personality. This very complicated picture demands that the examiner be constantly aware of the patient's level of arousal and engagement. The point to be made is that the reliability and validity of a test depend on the administration context every bit as much as on the actual items of the test. When the context changes, so do the reliability and validity of the test. Neither of these indices is fixed at values given in the manuals; these values are upper bounds at best. And, because background conditions can be so volatile, reliability and validity can change during the course of an evaluation.

Long-Term Fluctuations

Some neuropsychological tests are eminently learnable. Memory tests are obvious examples. Many clinicians have had an opportunity to reassess supposedly amnesic patients 1 and 2 years after the initial assessment only to be told Wechsler Memory Scale—Revised stories before they are administered. In addition, Amelia Earhart has been getting a lot of press lately, a truly unfortunate development for Information Item Number 14 of the WAIS-R. The clinician who has opportunity to collect multiple assessments over time can obviate many of the threats to reliability and validity just outlined. But multiple testing brings the threat of artifacts due to learning the material and maturation of the individual. These changes may be independent of the disease state that precipitated the original referral and thereby threaten the reliability and validity of the tests. The solution to problems caused by learning is the use of multiple equivalent forms of the test, rarely available in neuropsychological assessment. The solution to problems caused by maturation and historical changes is to include them in the interpretation of the test score. Obviously, the available solutions are not satisfactory.

OPERATING CHARACTERISTICS AND SAMPLING: TOWARD USEFUL VALIDITIES

Operating Characteristics

Having conceptually discussed the traditional concepts of validity, including content, construct, and predictive validity, it becomes apparent that these approaches often do little to help the clinician in the N of one clinical situation. As evidenced by the preceding discussion, patients present changing foregrounds and backgrounds.

Traditionally, to examine whether or not a test is valid an empirical study is conducted. To that end, 50 normals and 50 patients may be selected and given the test. The problem with this is, however, that rarely are we faced with a clinical situation where we have 50 normals and 50 pathological patients and have to determine whether the groups are different. Indeed, in most clinical settings we have one patient and must determine whether she or he is normal or brain impaired. As such, many of the validity statistics used in neuropsychology are not ecologically useful.

Such group studies are attempts to model the means and variances and determine whether groups are different. However, a significant t or F statistic at .05 does little to tell us whether or not the individual case before us is a patient or a normal. Indeed, an ANOVA statistic's probability value may be as small as .00001, and we may feel more confident in the use of that particular test but have little information to tell us whether or not we are making an accurate diagnosis, inference, or prediction.

Alternatively, with regression approaches not only is there a test of whether or not the overall R squared is statistically significant, but also the appearance of having more information because the correlation has far more continuity to it. Therefore, a test having a correlation with the outcome criterion of 0.76 is viewed as a better test than one with a correlation of 0.21. Here again, however, we may be very good at predicting what one group may be vis-à-vis another or one variable vis-à-vis another, but at a loss with our $N = 1$ case.

Within experimental and industrial–organizational psychology, signal detection theory is often used to represent hit rates. Within signal detection theory, true positives are analyzed as well as true negatives, and over-all efficiency is gleaned through a *d*-prime statistic. Within medicine, these concepts are called operating characteristics. Operating characteristics arose largely from laboratory tests in which there is a need to determine whether or not tests are valid. If, for example, there is a blood marker for a cancer and that marker comes back positive, it is necessary to know what the chances are that indeed that patient actually has cancer. And conversely, if that blood test comes back negative, what are the chances that the patient actually does not have the cancer. Obviously, in this case both of those types of validity or hit rates are critically necessary. To tell a patient and his or her physician that he or she has cancer will set that patient along a long road of remediative therapies and very definitely change that patient's life. Conversely, should the test come back indicating no cancer, a patient would not be afforded the therapies necessary to perhaps save his or her life. An error of that type would result in a premature demise.

Psychology only recently has adopted the concept of operating characteristics. Indeed, relatively few tests use them. However, it is only operating characteristics that can allow a clinician to understand what the probabilities are that a patient has or does not have a disorder, has an anatomical lesion or not, or has a significant decrement in functioning or not. Operating characteristics take into account the prevalence of a disorder and the a priori probability that a patient may or may not have a disorder.

Getting back to the aforementioned example of 50 normal subjects and 50 clinical patients, what are the chances that a test properly identified the normals and properly identified the pathological subjects? If hit rates are given, other than a *t* test or an ANOVA, a typical finding may be that the test identified perhaps 30% of the normals and 95% of the patients as having the disorder. Such a finding suggests that the test is good at identifying patients with the disorder but tends to overinclude normals. There may be situations, also, where a test does not identify a great number of normals but then also does not identify most of the patients.

Within the framework of operating characteristics, these two statistics are known as sensitivity and specificity. Sensitivity is the concept of how sensitive a test is to a specific ability, disorder, or anatomical condition. If a person has a disorder, what are the chances the test will pick it up? Table 6.1 is adapted from Table 4.8 in *Contributions to Neuropsychological Assessment: A Clinical Manual* (Benton, Hamsher, Varney, & Spreen, 1983, p. 41) regarding performance on the Facial Recognition Test. Notice that 53% of patients with right-posterior lesions are identified by their scores on the facial recognition test. In this particular case, pathological scores are viewed as scores of less than 38. With 19 of the

TABLE 6.1
Operating Characteristics of the Facial Recognition Test
at a Prevalence of .11

	Pathology		
	Present	*Absent*	
Test			
Positive	19	10	29
Negative	17	276	293
Totals	36	286	322
Prevalence		36/322 =	.11
Sensitivity		19/36 =	.53
Specificity		276/286 =	.965
Positive Predictive Power		19/29 =	.66
Negative Predictive Power		276/293 =	.94
Overall Predictive Power		(19 + 276)/322 =	.92

36 patients properly identified, the test has a sensitivity to the disorder (right-posterior lesions) of 0.53. This answers the question, "Knowing that the patient has the disorder, what are the chances that the test will identify it?"

Specificity answers the question of how specific a test is to that disorder alone versus its tendency to identify others who do not have the disorder. In the Facial Recognition Test example, 276 of 286 normals are properly identified. This gives us a specificity of .965. Indeed, only 3.5% of normals are misidentified by the test as having the disorder. Specificity answers the question, "Knowing that this patient does not have this disorder, what are the chances that the test will not identify him or her as having the disorder?"

Although a sensitivity of .53 and a specificity of .965 appear to be very good, one must be cognizant of the fact that the group membership of these individuals was known a priori. The fact is, however, that when a patient is in your office rarely do you know whether he or she is a member of the control or the experimental group. It is the true positives and the true negatives divided by the *other* marginals that identify this information for us. It is positive predictive power and negative predictive power that allow us to understand the $N = 1$ patient in front of us.

Table 6.1 reveals that 29 individuals were identified by the test as having the lesion, whereas only 19 actually had the lesion. The ratio of 19 over 29 is the positive predictive power. Positive predictive power answers the question, "Only knowing that this person has a positive test score, what are the chances he or she actually has the disorder?" Notice that the dependent clause within that sentence is far more typical of the clinical situation. We never know whether he or she is a control or an experimental group member. All we know is whether he or she has a positive result on the test or has a negative result on the test. In the case of Benton's Facial Recognition Test, there is a positive predictive power of .66, which indicates that should a patient of yours have a positive test with this particular prevalence rate there is a two-thirds chance that the patient indeed has a right-posterior lesion.

The flip side of positive predictive power is negative predictive power. One would think that this should be 1 minus the positive predictive power, and that if you are correct 66% of the time in one direction you ought to be wrong perhaps 33% of the time in the other direction. This is not actually true because within operating characteristics varying prevalences are taken into account. Indeed, should a patient score fairly well on Benton's Facial Recognition Test, above or equal to a 38, what we find is that 276 individuals are properly identified out of the 293 who are identified as being "normal." This proportion, .94, is the negative predictive power. In this case what we can say is, "My patient had a good score on the Facial Recognition Test; I am 94% positive that he or she does not have a right-posterior lesion."

Finally, as in the case of other hit rate statistics, overall predictive power is in essence the true positives plus the true negatives over the total number of cases. In this case we have 19 plus 276 over 322, giving us an overall diagnostic efficiency of .92. If this statistic alone were presented, it would appear that this is a very good test. However, one must realize that the positive predictive power is only a moderately strong .66.

What makes operating characteristics more powerful than other psychometric statistics is their ability to adapt to varying prevalences. Again, in group research studies we usually have a .50 prevalence rate because we have 50 in one group and 50 in the other group. Taking Benton's hit rate statistics as an example, and only varying the number of patients having right-posterior lesions, important changes can be seen. Table 6.2 shows the effects of changing the prevalence rate from .11 (as in Table 6.1) down to 0.02. In this case, out of the 322 subjects only 6 have the disorder. Whereas the original example had 53% positively identified through sensitivity, here this becomes a 0.50 because of rounding. We have 3 patients identified by the test, 3 patients not identified by the test, for a total of 6 patients. Specificity remains the same with .965 of the 316 being identified as not having the disorder by the test, or 305 of them. This leaves 11 false positives. Here, although sensitivity and specificity remain constant from the prior example, prevalence has dropped from .11 to .02. The dramatic effects of the change of prevalence are primarily seen in positive predictive power. Calculating positive predictive power (3 over 14), we discover that it drops to .21. If

TABLE 6.2
Operating Characteristics of the Facial Recognition Test
at a Prevalence of .02

	Pathology		
	Present	Absent	
Test			
Positive	3	11	14
Negative	3	305	308
Totals	6	316	322
Prevalence		6/322 =	.02
Sensitivity		3/6 =	.50
Specificity		305/316 =	.965
Positive Predictive Power		3/14 =	.21
Negative Predictive Power		305/308 =	.99
Overall Predictive Power		(3 + 305)/322 =	.96

you were a clinician with this scenario, you would only be one-fifth positive that the patient had a right-posterior lesion.

Negative predictive power also changes, but because negative predictive power capitalizes on the great preponderance of people who do not have the focal disorder, it does not change as dramatically. This calculation of 305 over 308 shows us a negative predictive power of .99.

Overall predictive power in this example actually rises to 0.96. Again, should only overall predictive power be provided, we would believe that this example showed the test to be a stronger, better, and more valid test than the .92 of the prior example. However, within a clinical setting, positive predictive power is the most critical statistic. And, in low prevalence situations, this statistic drops precipitously.

What should be taken from the foregoing examples are two things. One, operating characteristics are by and large the best statistical mechanism for the representation of the validity of a test in neuropsychology when that validity is a dichotomous decision placing a patient into a group such as disordered, impaired, improved, or significantly changed. Specifically, positive predictive power should and must be calculated for all dichotomous predictions of brain abnormality and specific neurological disease. Second, it should be noted that as prevalence and the base rate of a pathology within a specific clinical practice drop, positive predictive power is forced down. Attempting to predict any low base-rate behavior is difficult. Operating characteristics are not as useful when a clinician is interested in multifactorial information such as interaction with psychological variables or other continuous variables.

Data and Its Distribution

Classically, we are trained that psychological and neuropsychological behaviors are normally distributed, and that if a behavioral sample is not
normally distributed we must make it so. Indeed, the normal distribution serves as a model. Unfortunately, the single largest threat to the
proper determination of reliabilities, validities, and operating characteristics is poor modeling of our samples. This includes an over-reliance on
the normal distribution, the lack of true test-specific distributions, and
poor subject selections for sampling.

Why the normal curve is used is both a behavioral assumption and a
matter of statistical convenience. There is a general consensus within the
physical, biological, and psychological communities that a great many
of their variables are normally distributed. From a statistical perspective,
there is the assumption that errors of measurement and errors made in
estimating population values are normally distributed.

The strengths of the normal curve model are that it allows us to model
our data in such a way as to limitedly interpret individual cases, to compare the means of populations, and through regression models to predict
with certain degrees of confidence other behavioral data. The weaknesses
of the normal distribution, however, are that some phenomena and some
behaviors do not fit the normal distribution. An argument is made here
that a great many neuropsychological variables (or at least performance
on neuropsychological tests) are either heavily skewed or have heavy kurtosis to the point where the normal distribution does a very poor job of
modeling them. This is particularly problematic in the $N = 1$ case.

Modeling of Data

Much behavioral research involves the modeling of means and standard deviations for the purposes of finding differences between groups
or for analyzing one variable's effect on another variable. A t test using
data from brain-damaged individuals and normals compares the two
means. Additionally, within regression models the modeling of the
means and the standard deviations is a necessary aspect with which to
quantify covariance and predict the variable of interest.

Uses of the normal curve include a number of widely popular linear
transformations of the sample's test scores. The most basic form of the
normal distribution can be viewed as a z-score distribution with a mean
of zero and standard deviation of 1. A patient 2 standard deviations below the mean would have a z score of -2. Transformations of this type
also include the T score that is probably most popularly found in the
MMPI. Here, a linear transformation occurs where the mean is made to

be 50 and standard deviations become 10. This is simply done by adding 50 to the z scores after multiplying the deviations by 10. Further, within the WAIS-R, the mean is 100 and the standard deviations are 15. There are no differences among any of these scores other than arbitrary metric.

It is important to realize that such transformations are done because of an underlying assumption that the construct is normally distributed (and so the data should actually be normally distributed). If the obtained data are not normally distributed, this must be due to sampling error. Therefore, normalizing the data transforms the "biased" sample distribution to the "correct" normal distribution. This, however, is probably rarely the case.

At times within neuropsychology, researchers and clinicians utilized percentile scores to model data. Normalized percentiles are simply a further transformation of a normal distribution; someone 2 standard deviations above the mean would be assigned a percentile score of 97.5. This approach is deceptive in that actual or "cumulative" percentile scores may differ widely from "normalized" percentile scores. The use of cumulative percentile scores is most appropriate with large samples because the actual data drive the assigned percentiles. The 190th person out of 200 falls at the 95th percentile. It is important when looking at neuropsychological norms and data to determine whether the percentiles are based on the actual population parameters, or whether they are simply normalized transformations from means and standard deviations of a sampling distribution that was not normally distributed in the first place. If the latter is the case, the percentile scores will not reflect reality, particularly toward the distribution tails.

Recently, with the advent of the MMPI-II, blind use of normal distributions and their assumptions have come under revision. With the MMPI-II, the authors used a uniform T score. The uniform T score adjusts for the problem of skewed distributions. What was discovered with the MMPI-I was that the percentage of scores above a T score of 70 on each of the 10 scales varied widely. With a normal distribution, exactly 2½% should be above that cut score. In the MMPI-II, uniform T scores have been used to correct that problem by adjusting in a nonlinear fashion the T statistics so that exactly 2½% of the population is above 70 on all scales. The problem with this of course is that 2½% of the population does not necessarily have a particular psychopathology (e.g., major depression). In some areas it may be greater, in other areas it may be less.

Skewed Distributions

If with the MMPI we find skewed distributions of data, it is highly likely that within other psychopathologies we will find similar types of distributions. Indeed, this is the case in neuropsychology. There is very little neuropsychological data, whether due to measurement problems or the underlying cognitive domain, which are clearly, normally distributed data. More often, it is skewed and has kurtosis.

Skew refers to how asymmetrical the two sides of the distribution are. For a normal bell-shaped curve, the two sides are perfectly symmetrical. However, within a skewed distribution, one of the two sides goes out in a long tail. In a positively skewed distribution, this extends to the right or in a positive direction. In a negatively skewed distribution, this tail drops well below the mean for some distance and to the left. Kurtosis is viewed as a parameter of the flatness or peakness of the distribution. All bells are not created equally. Some are very tall and narrow. This would be a form of high positive kurtosis. Other bells and distributions are relatively flat, and this flatness is negative kurtosis.

Much of the data in the neuropsychological literature is skewed and has kurtosis. In fact, both may exist on the same variable depending on the population sampled. For example, on Benton's Visual Form Discrimination Test (Benton et al., 1983, p. 60), the normal control group had a highly negatively skewed distribution, with the bulk of subjects attaining near-perfect scores of 30 to 32, but a number of subjects obtaining scores down to 23. Examination of the "brain disease group" reveals a very flat distribution, with patients attaining scores ranging from a perfect score (32) all the way down to scores in the single digits. Here there are no peaks; it is a flat distribution almost rectangular in nature. The same variable in the normal sample is skewed and in the clinical sample has negative kurtosis.

Some domains and/or measurement techniques do not lend themselves to a normal distribution. The Visual Form Discrimination Test does not allow scores above 32. For normals, therefore, we find no right side to the distribution. The modal score of the control group is the maximum score of 32. No one can achieve a 33 or greater. However, one can achieve less. Theoretically, it is possible that some people have a superior ability to discriminate forms that cannot be assessed utilizing this particular instrument.

It is obvious from these examples that the normal distribution does not properly model either the control group or the pathological group. Many researchers simply calculate means and standard deviations and present these in the literature. But in so doing they are implying an underlying normal distribution and lose most of the important information in the original data.

Sitting in your office diagnosing an individual patient requires models that allow that patient to be properly placed along the data's continuum and to determine whether or not he or she has an impairment. We need models that more properly model the skew and at times the kurtosis of the distribution. A good example of such a model is the Millon Clinical Multiaxial Inventory (Millon, 1987), a broad-range test of noncognitive psychopathology. The author of this particular test made nonlinear transformations from raw scores to develop what he calls a "base-rate" score. An arbitrary base-rate score of 85 was set for the lower boundary of those individuals manifesting each disorder of interest (e.g., major depression). A base-rate score of 30 was used for the mean of a normal sample. To accomplish this, he came down from the top of each distribution until the percentage of interest was found. For instance, there may have been 17% with major depression. At that point they placed the 85 base-rate score. In this way, an individual clinician can actually look at an individual patient's score and determine whether or not he or she is within the normal group or within the pathological group. This also forms the basis of the operating characteristics of this test.

The MMPI on the other hand indicates that all patients who are above a 70 have a significant score on the 2 scale, which is depression, but this supposes that 2½% of patients and individuals in the general population have major depression. This is inappropriate. To advance the psychometrics in neuropsychology, the N of 1 case must be the object of interest, and that case's position on a skewed tail must be maintained in the data transformation procedure.

Whereas base-rate scores may more clearly delineate the group membership of an individual patient, they must be creatively used to apply to other questions of interest. Neuropsychology is no longer answering the simple question, "Is this patient organic?" Instead, it attempts to answer a series of questions including: (a) Is some unusual or abnormal finding present?; (b) if so, does this represent a neurological, or psychological, or other disorder?; (c) if it is a neurological disorder, what is its nature?; (d) perhaps, what are its anatomical correlates?; (e) how severe is the disorder?; (e) what are the prognostic implications of the disorder?; (f) what are the functional limitations of the disorder in this particular patient? Here difference scores between tests or administrations may need to be modeled. Because neuropsychology is not answering only simple dichotomous questions, obviously the data on and between tests must be viewed in many different ways to answer the many different questions. To date, these modeling procedures have not been done.

Sampling Considerations

An advantage of using the normal distribution and the assumptions therein is that relatively small sample sizes of about 30 or so will accurately model the mean and the standard deviation. Errors in the assumption of the mean can be calculated and similar confidence statistics for the standard deviation can be developed. With sample sizes as small as 30, the mean will be fairly stable and, surprisingly, the standard deviation will actually be even more stable. The problem with small sample sizes is dealing with skewed and kurtosed distributions. Attempting to model the lower 5% of a skewed distribution because that portion of the sample consists of those subjects who have a disorder of some kind results in highly unstable findings or models with small sample sizes. For instance, with 30 subjects only one would fall within the lowest 5%. It is impossible to model the tail of a distribution based on 1 or 2 subjects. Even increasing the sample size to 100 results in only 5 subjects falling within the distribution tail of interest. Depending on sampling techniques and the populations being used, performance of this tail of the distribution may vary widely. Small samples result in unstable and unreliable distribution tails. Therefore, neuropsychology must get away from small sample sizes and utilize large-scale sampling techniques to begin to understand and accurately predict criterion measures.

It will be important to develop large samples not only for normals on our neuropsychological tests but also for our pathological samples. Obviously, operating characteristics and the accurate differentiation of our patients require samples from both populations. Increasingly, therefore, we should utilize and demand tests that have good norms for both normals and pathological cases. As indicated before, very often the shape of these distributions differs widely, and, aside from sophisticated operating characteristics, it is clinically necessary to know where a patient is on each of those distributions.

SUMMARY

Neuropsychology is not immune to psychometric problems. The intent of this chapter was to review some of the psychometric concepts within psychology in general and neuropsychology in specific. Psychometrically, these disciplines differ only in the level of complexity of procedures and patients. The complexities inherent in neuropsychological assessment require greater, not less, understanding of psychometric theory and application.

Many specific issues and principles were emphasized in this chapter. An understanding of the reliability and validity of tests is essential to appreciating the limits to inferences that can be made from test performances. In neuropsychology traditional concepts of normal curve performance distributions must be questioned because at times highly skewed distributions are found. Additionally, it was argued that neuropsychology should not be bound by traditional norm-referenced tests and should move toward the modeling of the tails of sample distributions through operating characteristics. The reader should also understand that there is no way to get around the problem of collecting large samples to build norms to be able to appropriately interpret test performances. Without large samples, the tails of the distributions will be poorly modeled. Much hard psychometric work lies ahead for the field of neuropsychological assessment.

REFERENCES

Benton, A. L., Hamsher, K., Varney, N. R., & Spreen, O. (1983). *Contributions to neuropsychological assessment*. New York: Oxford University Press.

Campbell, D. T., & Fiske, D. W. (1959). Convergent and discriminant validation by the multitrait–multimethod matrix. *Psychological Bulletin, 56*, 81–105.

Cicchetti, D. V. (1991). When diagnostic agreement is high, but reliability is low: Some paradoxes occurring in joint independent neuropsychological assessment. In B. P. Rourke, L. Costa, D. V. Cicchetti, K. M. Adams, & K. J. Plasterk (Eds.), *Methodological and biostatistical foundations of clinical neuropsychology* (pp. 417–434). Berwyn, PA: Swets & Zeitlinger.

Cronbach, L. J., Gleser, G. C., Nanda, H., & Rajaratnam, N. (1972). *The dependability of behavioral measurements: Theory of generalizability for scores and profiles*. New York: Wiley.

Franzen, M. D. (1989). *Reliability and validity in neuropsychological assessment*. New York: Plenum Press.

Millon, T. (1987). *Manual for the MCMI-II*. Minneapolis: National Computer Systems.

Nunnally, J. C. (1978). *Psychometric theory*. New York: McGraw-Hill.

Rasch, G. (1980). *Probabilistic models for some intelligence and attainment tests*. Chicago: The University of Chicago Press.

Reynolds, C. R. (1990). Conceptual and technical problems in learning disability diagnosis. In C. R. Reynolds & R. W. Kamphaus (Eds.), *Handbook of psychological and educational assessment of children: Intelligence and achievement*. New York: Guilford Press.

Spreen, O., & Straus, E. (1991). *A compendium of neuropsychological tests*. New York: Oxford University Press.

Suen, H. K. (1990). *Test theories*. Hillsdale, NJ: Lawrence Erlbaum Associates.

Wechsler, D. (1981). *Manual for the Wechsler Adult Intelligence Scale—Revised (WAIS-R)*. New York: The Psychological Corporation.

CHAPTER SEVEN

The Cognitive–Metric, Fixed Battery Approach to Neuropsychological Assessment

Elbert W. Russell
VA Medical Center
Miami, Florida

This chapter presents an approach to neuropsychological assessment that combines cognitive science with traditional psychometrics to form a type of assessment called the cognitive–metric approach. It attempts to apply the scientific rigor found in experimental neuropsychology to neuropsychological assessment.

A secondary related theme is the application of objective scientific methods to test batteries and to individual tests. Objective psychometric methods related to individual tests have been well developed in psychology (Anastasi, 1988; Kline, 1986). By contrast, almost no effort in psychology has been devoted to the study of how tests are integrated in a battery. Some beginnings of such a study are presented. As illustrative material, two computerized methods of scoring neuropsychological test batteries are examined.

HISTORY OF NEUROPSYCHOLOGICAL BATTERY ASSESSMENT METHODS

The cognitive–metric approach has developed out of the advances and controversies in neuropsychology as well as cognitive psychology. From the inception of neuropsychology assessment, the primary controversy has been between the qualitative, now championed by the process approach, and the quantitative or psychometric approach.

The Qualitative Period

In the early part of the 20th century the primary advocates of the qualitative approach were Kirk Goldstein, a neurologist, and Martin Scheerer, a psychologist. Goldstein and Scheerer (1941) developed the first group of tests that were used extensively in neuropsychological assessment. Their concept was that the level of functioning demonstrated by a test did not indicate brain damage as much as how the particular patient dealt with the test materials. They were concerned with why a patient obtained a score. Goldstein and Scheerer felt that the brain-damaged patient lost the abstract attitude and developed a more concrete approach to solving problems (Walsh, 1978). This was essentially the same concept that Werner (1956) called microgenesis.

In describing the process approach, Kaplan (1988) referred to H. Werner (1937, 1956) as an advocate of the process approach. Werner was one of a group of holistic neuropsychologists in the early part of the 20th century who were opposed to psychometric methods. In this regard the process approach has changed little in its method for 50 years. The primary change that has occurred since the 1930s is that the process approach is no longer holistic.

Recently, Kaplan (1988) and her colleagues made attempts to quantify the processes of the process approach. Such tests as the California Verbal Learning Test (CVLT: Delis, Kramer, Kaplan, & Ober, 1987) have been developed with elaborate scoring systems and a normative database that allows for a careful quantitative analysis of cognitive subcomponent processes. In so doing the CVLT is a carefully constructed psychometric test.

Psychometric Developments

In regard to batteries of tests, the most commonly used batteries in neuropsychology are the Wechsler intelligence scales. The first of these was the Wechsler–Bellevue Intelligence Scale, which was introduced in 1939 (Wechsler, 1939). The general form and theory of the Wechsler tests have remained the same since the Wechsler–Bellevue. Thus the major test of cognitive functions has not changed in any essential fashion for 53 years.

The Wechsler subtests were all normed simultaneously. This is coordinated norming, and it permits the comparison of one subtest directly with another. The Wechsler tests are the only set of tests that are universally used throughout neuropsychology (Butler, Retzlaff, & Vanderploeg, 1991). The irony is that they were not designed as neuropsychological tests but measures of normal intellectual ability.

The psychometric approach, which had been developing outside of neuropsychology since the beginning of the 20th century, was introduced into neuropsychology by Halstead and Reitan in the late 1940s and 1950s as the Halstead–Reitan Battery (HRB). It was originally designed as a group of tests by Halstead (1947). Reitan (1955a) added new tests, including the Wechsler-Bellevue, and transformed the original group into a set that was specifically designed to examine neurological conditions. Although he did not use scale scores, the particular selection of tests was designed to cover all areas of brain functioning. Reitan introduced the idea, adopted from neurology, that tests should be balanced between the right and left hemispheres. In many cases, the same measures, such as the tapping test, could be used to compare the two sides of the body.

The Boston Diagnostic Aphasia Examination (BDAE; Goodglass & Kaplan, 1972, 1983) is one of the best designed neuropsychological sets of tests that has yet been developed. As such, it can be used as a model for newer sets of tests. It was designed on the basis of a specific theory of aphasia, the Wernicke-Geschwind theory (Goodglass & Kaplan, 1972, 1983). The tests were designed to cover all aspects of aphasia, both brain areas and cognitive functions that were represented in the theory. A coordinated norming system was undertaken, such that all the tests were normed together. The primary difficulty with the battery was that the subtests were not anchored in the normal range because the subtests were primarily designed for subjects with explicit aphasia. Thus, there is difficulty in using this aphasia battery with subjects that have a very mild aphasia or in comparing the aphasic impairment with other types of impairment.

Recent Developments

After the creation of the HRB about 1955, no major developments related to neuropsychological batteries occurred for almost 35 years, other than the BDAE, its counterpart, the Western Aphasia Examination (Kertesz, 1979), and the Luria–Nebraska Neuropsychological Battery (LNNB; Golden, Hammeke, & Purisch, 1980). Luria developed a qualitative, flexible approach to assessment based on his theoretical formulations of brain functioning (Luria, 1973, 1980). Christensen (1979, 1984) compiled and described many of these procedures, which Golden and his colleagues subsequently attempted to standardize and quantify in the LNNB. The LNNB has been criticized for its psychometric development (Adams, 1980), its overemphasis on verbal functions (Russell, 1980b), and its failure to assess high-order cognitive functions. Because this chapter is primarily concerned with the HRB, the LNNB is not discussed further.

Recently, two batteries have been developed that demonstrate a considerable improvement over previous neuropsychological sets of tests. In 1988, the Halstead Rennick Russell Battery (HRRB) was published by a small company, Scientific Psychology (Russell, Starkey, Fernandez, & Starkey, 1988). It introduced many new applications into neuropsychological testing. This battery is composed of the HRB, the WAIS-R, and 12 other tests that were added to the HRB. The base sample was normed on 200 subjects, whereas another 576 were used in the procedure to construct the scale scores. The N for the tests that were added to the HRB varies. Subsequently, Western Psychological Services further developed this battery (Russell & Starkey, 1993) under the name of the Halstead Russell Neuropsychological Evaluation System (HRNES). This battery was published early in 1993.

The second recently published set of neuropsychological tests is The Comprehensive Norms for an Expanded Halstead-Reitan Battery (CNHRB). The CNHRB was published in 1991 by Psychological Assessment Resources (Heaton, Grant, & Matthews, 1991). This battery is composed of the HRB, with 14 other tests and the WAIS or WAIS-R. The base sample was normed on 378 subjects, whereas another 108 were used to validate the norms but do not contribute to the norming. The N for the additional tests varies.

This chapter uses the CNHRB and the HRNES as examples of the cognitive-metric approach to neuropsychological assessment because they have dealt more thoroughly with the problems of a set battery than any other test batteries. However, before these problems can be examined, the nature of a psychometrically designed set of tests must be discussed.

FOUNDATIONS OF THE COGNITIVE–METRIC APPROACH

The primary principle of the cognitive-metric approach is the belief that the same scientific rigor found in experimental methodology should characterize neuropsychological assessment. In research, this is hypothesis testing and validation of theories. In assessment, the scientific approach includes demonstrating the reliability and validity of the instruments. The cognitive-metric approach insists that assessment must be as able to demonstrate the accuracy of its methodological basis. In the cognitive–metric approach to neuropsychological assessment, these methodological bases include: (a) adequate instrumentation and measurement methodology, (b) development of tests that adequately represent brain functioning, (c) a set of tests that models all aspects of brain functioning, and (d) an interpretive approach that allows for an understanding of test data and its relationship to brain functioning.

Instrumentation and Measurement

An indispensable aspect of any scientific field is its instrumentation. Science has progressed as much through the development of new instruments as the creation of new theories. Instrumentation includes methods of measurement. In many cases the development of new instruments permits the use of more accurate measurement. In neuropsychology, the primary instruments are tests. The test measurement system, embodied in a neuropsychological battery, applies quantitative methods to examination procedures.

Necessity of Tests

There is a paramount principal of testing that applies to all neuropsychological approaches. The principle is that one cannot determine whether a function is impaired unless that function is evaluated; that is, unless you apply some form of test to a particular function, you cannot determine whether there is an existing deficit. There are, of course, a few exceptions in regard to gross phenomena, such as frank aphasia or hemiparesis. However, to determine the type of aphasia, the neuropsychologist requests the patient to perform different tasks to test various aspects of language. Many of these methods are represented more formally in the Boston Diagnostic Aphasia Examination (Goodglass & Kaplan, 1983). When an expert simply listens to a patient's speech, the expert is listening for certain deficits, and these specific observations represent rudimentary testing. Such structured observations are *informal qualitative testing*.

Established Psychometric Standards

For over a century psychology has been developing the methods and standards related to testing. These are established and are set forth in books and in the American Psychological Association's (1988) *Standards for Educational and Psychological Testing*. There is no ambiguity in the stance of the cognitive-metric approach. It accepts psychology's standards of validity and reliability. Wherever possible, interpretations are based on tests that meet these standards.

The use of clinical lore and qualitative methods is justified when no tests are available that provide the needed information for an interpretation. Lore and qualitative observations, whereas often necessary at this point in the development of neuropsychology, do not constitute solid knowledge. Science represents a gradual accumulation of knowledge. The candid position of the cognitive–metric approach is that we do not know everything. An advanced science is aware of what it does not know.

Assessment Versus Research

Although the cognitive-metric approach applies scientific rigor to assessment, it accepts the condition that assessment follows a different procedure than does scientific research. Although this should be obvious, some of the implications of the difference are not so obvious. Many neuropsychologists transfer research methods uncritically to assessment procedures. Unfortunately, statistically significant findings that discriminate in the research setting between groups of subjects may be totally ineffective in the clinical setting with individual patients.

The primary difference between research and assessment is that in scientific research one proceeds from data to theory, whereas in an assessment one goes from theory to data. For instance, instead of attempting to determine what functions are related to particular areas (i.e., constructing theory), assessment interpretations are derived from previously constructed theory that specifies which tests are related to different brain regions and cognitive abilities; that is, the examiner interprets a particular patient's behavior on the basis of the examiner's knowledge of the entire body of neuropsychology theory and lore.

The Nature of Neuropsychological Tests

A second set of principles in the cognitive-metric approach concerns the theoretical nature of tests. Until there is some understanding of how tests are related to the brain, attempts to design and utilize neuropsychological tests are at best mere groping in the dark. In neuropsychological theory this relationship of brain to tests is now in a preliminary stage.

Representation

Testing is a representational activity. A test is a procedure designed to represent some aspect of brain functioning in a public form. A brain function may be represented by the results of the particular task required by a test, and the ability to perform the task represents the effectiveness of the function.

To the extent that they are represented by test scores, mental processes can be observed and recorded. Through the use of tests the functioning of the brain becomes manifest as test scores and the contents of the "black box" (i.e., brain functioning) become observable. In fact, functions are discovered and generally, named by what they do, the type of task.

As early as 1922 Tolman had redefined the "behavioral response" as the *behavioral act* (Kimble, 1985), that is, behavior was what the behavior accomplishes in performing a task, not specific movements. This molar behaviorism was accepted by almost all behaviorists (Kimble, 1985). However, in effect, this redefinition of behaviorism nullifies the emphasis on behavior. It attaches the primary emphasis to the results of a task rather than to the behavior of the organism; that is, the emphasis is on the effect the person accomplished on an objective task, not the subject's behavior. The effect is recorded publicly as the test result. This emphasis on the task results, which are external to the person, is especially appropriate for neuropsychology. Except for motor behavior, the specific behavior of the organism is largely irrelevant. To demonstrate that one has an intact calculation function, the behavioral manner in which the answer is presented is largely inconsequential; that is, one can answer the question what is 2 plus 3 by writing 5, or V. One can show 5 fingers or 5 toes, can knock 5 times on a table, or put 5 objects into a container. There are almost an infinite number of different behaviors that can signify the answer. In cognitive psychology, one is testing the use of a symbolic system in the brain, not a behavior. The left-parietal aspect of the brain (and probably other areas as well) is being tested, not the motor strip.

Aspects of Cognitive Functions

There are two aspects of a brain function, form and proficiency. *Form* refers to an activity, how the brain accomplishes a task to produce a result. The form of the test (e.g., linguistic or spatial relations) represents the nature of the brain function. *Proficiency of brain function* refers to how well the function is performed. Proficiency is termed the ability of the person. Form is examined in a qualitative or process study, whereas ability is examined in a quantitative result. Any test of a function will contain both aspects, even though it specifically measures proficiency or ability.

Tests Represent Functions

A *function* is made manifest through performing a task. A *test* is a specified task and tasks must be specific in form. The type of task that is required by the parameters of the test determines the function that is being measured. Thus, there is a specificity between testing and function. This is true of both qualitative and quantitative testing.

The form of a test is derived from the function. Tests must be delineated through experimental procedures that design test characteristics to match the characteristics of the function. Thus, the test is designed to represent a function by building into the test characteristics of the function. The aim of neuropsychological research is to determine both the existence and characteristics of brain functions. When correctly designed tests will represent the content of a function, what function it is, and the formal aspects of the function, such as gradations in ability.

An "amount" of ability is measured by specific procedures incorporated into the test that are quantified in the results (i.e., test score). Traditionally, ability is measured in two general ways, speed and power. These measure how effective a person is in performing a function.

Modeling Brain Functions

A model is an abstract representational form in which each component has a specified relationship to the entity being modeled. It is standard practice for engineers and scientists to employ physical and mathematical models to represent complex structures and processes. In psychology, mental models have been used to represent aspects of cognition (Pellegrino, 1988).

Just as a single test represents a specific brain function, so an integrated set of tests represents either an area of brain functioning, such as language (aphasia batteries), or the functioning of the entire brain. Most neuropsychology batteries are attempts to represent the entire functioning of the brain; as such, they are brain function models.

The brain acts in a closely integrated manner. Every activity that is directed by the brain is produced by a system of functions (Luria, 1973, 1980). Because the brain acts through systems of functions, a single test cannot represent brain functioning. An adequate model of brain functioning will employ multiple measures to represent multiple functions. An examination should use a particular combination of tests representing, as much as possible, the functions of the brain. A full neuropsychological examination, using a well-designed, integrated set of tests, would be a *brain function model* that represents the whole functioning of the brain. Thus, the patterns of impairment may be represented by patterns of tests' results.

A "Set" of Tests

Since Halstead's (1947) work and the development of the Wechsler–Bellevue in the late 1930s (Wechsler, 1939), cognitive and neuropsychological tests have generally been given in sets, called batteries. Utilization of groups of tests has become the standard practice in neuropsychology. The scientific criteria and theory related to individual tests have been well developed in psychology (Anastasi, 1988; Kline, 1986). The literature is full of the psychometric requirements for individual tests such as reliability and validity (Franzen, 1989). However, there has been little psychometric discussion of the requirements for a set of tests composing a battery, fixed or flexible. Nunnally (1978) stated: ". . . ultimately psychometrics is concerned not only with such individual variables, but with the way that they relate to one another" (p. 329). To date, almost no effort has been devoted in neuropsychology to the study of how tests should function in a battery.

A set of tests is an integrated group of tests that is designed to be used as a unit. It is designed to represent quantitatively the complex functioning of the brain. The term *set* emphasizes the integration of a group of tests, rather than a group in which tests are selected in a haphazard manner. A *battery* may be either a set of tests or an unintegrated group of tests. The tests are integrated through systematic coverage and through structural considerations, such as coordinated norming and uniform scoring methods that increase accuracy and provide a complete and constant background. The set of tests may be selected to represent the entire brain, a specific area of the brain, or a system of functions.

Constant Background

A central concept related to the brain function model is that of a *constant background*. In a constant background the set of tests remains constant within a battery and from one subject to another. With the background of tests as a constant, any variation that occurs on or between the tests is due to the variation within the subject and not to differences between tests. An analogy may be made with a mirror. In a sense a set of tests is a mirror of a person's functioning. If the mirror is constant in that the glass does not vary from one point to another and the complete mirror is used each time, the reflected image is true and can be trusted. However, if the different parts of the glass vary in angle so that the surface is uneven, then one does not know whether the shape of the perceived image is due to variations in the object or variations in the medium, the mirror.

In neuropsychology there are two major aspects to a constant background. These are constancy between tests within a battery and constancy from one examination to another. The formal structure of the tests within a battery provides internal constancy, and a consistent set of tests (i.e., a fixed battery) provides an external or content constancy.

Internal Constancy

Internal consistency is produced by the formal structure or characteristics of a set of tests, including the norms, types of scales, and correction factors (e.g., age and education adjustments). The integration of a set battery of tests is primarily obtained by coordinated norming so that all the tests are, in effect, normed on the same population sample. Consequently, the norming does not vary from one test to another. This enables one to compare the results of one test to another and one subject to another.

A norm is a constant background against which one can compare an individual's behavior or an individual's test score; that is, when an examiner says "This behavior is abnormal or unusual," he or she is comparing that behavior against a fixed background of what is normal or usual behavior. In the qualitative approach, the individual compares a patient's performance against his or her understanding of what is normal. These norms may be experiential or learned or part of clinical lore; nevertheless, they represent a background for comparison. In a qualitative neuropsychological approach, because the background is subjective (clinical experience or lore) it may or may not be constant.

The concept of a constant background is related to that of a control group in research. The control group is used to compare the results of experimental procedures against normal functioning or against selected criteria. The control group, which remains unchanged, acts as a constant background against which the effects of the treatment can be observed and measured.

In assessment, the individual case results are compared against the scientifically established norms derived from a normal control group. In this case, a constant background is derived from the undamaged or normal group against which the effects of a particular form of damage can be perceived.

External or Content Constancy

External or content constancy occurs when a fixed battery is employed. The content of the battery remains constant from one testing to another. Thus, a fixed battery of tests forms a constant background against which a person's particular strengths and weaknesses become evident. If the background is not constant, the differences that are found may be due to the differences between the various tests that are used and the various norming methods employed with the various tests. In a flexible battery, the results may be due to the particular tests that happen to be selected at a particular time. In a fixed battery, the relationships between tests and the functions that those tests represent can be studied across many different neurological conditions, so that patterns can be discovered and verified.

Advocates of a flexible battery assert that the primary advantage of a flexible battery is that this approach takes the individual patient into consideration, and because patients vary the tests should vary (Lezak, 1984). There is a problem with this concept. Testing is designed to discover how an individual varies from other persons. Except for obvious things like hemiparesis, how does the examiner know that the subject is varying without some form of a constant background? It is the fixed battery that provides the constant background against which the patient's variation can be observed. A clearer picture of the whole person is obtained if the same background is retained rather than changing the background each time a different person is tested. A fixed battery permits more accurate observation of a person's individuality than does an individualized battery of tests. This is the reason that most advocates of a flexible battery eventually settle down to administering a fixed core of tests.

Even when individual problems such as hemiparesis do not permit the administration of the entire battery, a large coordinated fixed battery has an advantage in that when necessary tests may be selected from the battery and will retain their coordination. As such, the examiner can still compare the tests with each other. If they had been selected from various norming procedures, the advantage of coordinated norming would not exist.

Methods of Interpretation

The methods of interpretation in an assessment are related to the question of whether one uses a cognitive–metric or a more qualitative flexible approach. In the flexible and qualitative approach to interpretation, a method that is often used has been called "ongoing hypotheses testing." In addition to hypothesis testing, at least two other methods are known. These are algorithms and pattern analysis. In an algorithmic approach there is a series of alternative questions. Answering each question leads to another that further elaborates the assessment. Alternatively, in a pattern analysis approach the neuropsychologist examines the data for particular patterns without necessarily any hypothesis or question ahead of time.

Ongoing Hypothesis Testing

In ongoing hypothesis testing, the neuropsychologist has a particular hypothesis about a patient (Luria & Majovski, 1977), and tests are selected to determine whether the hypothesis is true. After confirming or disconfirming the first hypothesis, the examiner then selects another hypothesis to disconfirm until the assessment is completed. This method is modeled on the experimental method. However, as was pointed out earlier, assessment is a different procedure than research, and methods that work well in one setting may not be applicable to the other.

To a certain extent all neuropsychologists, regardless of their persuasion, use some hypotheses testing, or at least they answer questions, which is the same procedure; that is, it is merely a matter of terminology whether one calls something hypothesis testing or answering a question. For instance, a question may be, "Does the patient have brain damage?" This is stated in hypothesis testing as "The patient does not have brain damage—disprove this." The testing method will be the same whichever way the question is framed.

In ongoing hypotheses testing, as soon as the examiner disconfirms one hypothesis, this leads to another hypothesis. The difficulty with such ongoing hypotheses testing is that, in its pure form, it is quite limited. The limitation involves obtaining the new hypothesis. For instance, after the patient is assessed to have brain damage, how is the next hypothesis selected because there are hundreds of kinds of brain damage, dozens of locations, and many types and amounts of deficits? To obtain a new hypothesis or question, the neuropsychologist must either look for patterns on the tests that have already been administered or follow a loose logical progression based on experience and knowledge (i.e., an informal algorithm). In doing so, the neuropsychologist has abandoned the pure hypothesis-testing approach and moved to other interpretive strategies.

In practice, another major problem that may occur with the hypothesis-testing approach when using a flexible battery is related to coverage. When one simply selects tests based on a hypothesis, many areas and functions of the brain may not be examined. Rourke and Brown (1986) thoroughly discussed this problem with hypothesis testing. They consider it the most serious flaw in the flexible or hypothesis-testing method.

Algorithms

The primary methods of analysis used in the cognitive-metric approach are algorithms and pattern analysis. The algorithm method has been called a decision approach (Tarter & Edwards, 1986). In the algorithm method there are a series of questions that are formed ahead of time. In practice, these are usually not formalized but are implicit in that the examiner simply knows neurology well enough to be able to ask the appropriate question at each step. Each question will lead to a second group of questions, depending on the answer to the first one. For instance, the first question may be, "Is there brain damage?" If the test results indicate that there is no brain damage, that is the end of the process. However, if there is brain damage, the next question might be, "Is the damage lateralized to the right or the left hemisphere?," and so forth.

The algorithm method may use either a fixed or a flexible battery.

The examination is directed by a series of interlocking questions that have been formed prior to an examination. At each step these questions cull information from the test results to answer the particular question in the algorithm.

To some extent, this is the way all neuropsychologists analyze a protocol; that is, they begin the examination with a series of questions derived from their experience and knowledge. The answer to each question leads to another series of questions until the assessment questions (including questions unexpressed by the referral) are answered. In fact, this is what neuropsychologists who claim to use the ongoing hypothesis-testing method actually do. They do not begin the examination with a formal hypothesis (i.e., This patient has no brain damage). Rather they ask, "Does this patient have brain damage?" If the patient does have damage, they already have one or several questions in mind to ask next. This is what is meant by the word "ongoing." The difference between hypothesis testing and an algorithm is that in an algorithm the next set of questions is already preselected, based on a person's knowledge, whereas, in pure hypothesis testing, it is not.

Pattern Analysis

The third major method used in assessment is pattern recognition or pattern analysis. An experienced neuropsychologist using a set battery such as the WAIS-R or the HRB will recognize certain patterns of test results in the test matrix. To a large extent, the examiner who utilizes pattern identification does the opposite of hypotheses testing. Instead of beginning with a conception of the problem, the hypothesis, the examiner systematically explores the data with minimal preconceptions to discover the patterns in the data. Most of the patterns that have been identified in the literature to date have been related to the Wechsler tests because they are set batteries. Some of these patterns are familiar. Lateralization of brain damage is indicated by the difference between verbal and performance tests (Matarazzo, 1972; Russell, 1984). This may be confused with a fluidity pattern that has also been identified (Barron & Russell, 1992; Russell, 1979, 1980a)

Reitan's Four Methods of Pattern Analysis. Reitan (1964; Reitan & Wolfson, 1985, 1986) was one of the first neuropsychologists to propose a theory for methods of assessment. He delineated four methods of interpretive inference: (a) level of performance, (b) differential patterns of ability, (c) comparisons between the two sides of the body, and (d) pathognomonic signs. It is clear that the first three interpretive methods are forms of pattern analysis, whereas the fourth is a form of the qualitative approach.

Level of performance is the beginning of pattern analysis. When an index is used, such as the Halstead Index, it is an average level of performance, which in itself is a type of pattern. The second method is the pattern of performance. Patterns are simply combinations of levels of performance for several tests. In Reitan's actual practice the patterns appear to be largely confined to the WAIS, at least on the variables presented in the General Neuropsychological Deficit Scale (GNDS; Reitan, 1991). On examination, the third method, comparison of right and left sides of the body, is also a type of pattern analysis. It is the pattern of test results that occurs when the tests that are related to each side of the body are compared to each other. Finally, this leaves pathognomonic signs as the only method that does not involve pattern analysis. The signs themselves are actually qualitative signs that indicate types of brain damage. In practice, as demonstrated by the GNDS, Reitan utilized signs only in regard to the Aphasia Screening Test (Reitan, 1991). Many of the answers on the aphasia examination are written or drawn. Consequently, they can be examined qualitatively without testing the patient oneself. Reitan has been able to derive a large amount of data from a small number of items on this test using this sign approach.

In the Russell version of the Halstead tests, the HRNES (Russell & Starkey, 1993), instead of examining signs as related to particular pathologies, the number of items that are failed are counted and therefore quantified. Hence, this sign approach itself has been quantified and the score for the Aphasia Screening Examination becomes part of the patterns used in the total test battery. Of course, one can still use the Aphasia Screening Test qualitatively.

Comparisons.   The foundation of pattern analysis is comparison. In fact, almost all of neuropsychological interpretation is based on comparisons. Even in the qualitative approach, the examiner compares a particular abnormal performance against a normal performance. Also the examiner may compare the patient's performance against knowledge of a particular type of abnormal performance to assess or diagnose the particular type of problem. Other types of comparisons are right–left comparisons and comparisons with different forms of disease patterns. To determine whether a person is improving in rehabilitation, one must compare previous test results with the new results.

In an article advocating a qualitative approach, Luria and Majovski (1977) stated that they do not quantify the results. However, in describing a particular impairment, they stated that the type of impairment is very different from what you would normally expect. In this regard, they are not only making a comparison between what the patient did and a normal performance but also are making a quantitative nomothetic comparison, abnormal versus normal ability.

In the cognitive-metric approach, comparisons are based on the concept of a constant background. There must be equivalence of all test scale scores that are used before reliable comparisons can be made. In isolating a pattern, the individual's particular performance is compared against an array of other theoretical patterns to determine which form the individual resembles. Such a series of comparisons is only possible when the test scores are equivalent, thus creating a constant background.

Dissociation. In neuropsychology the basis for reliable comparisons is a modification of the concept that Teuber (1955, 1975) proposed called double dissociation. Double dissociation is a dissociation between both two tests and two areas of the brain. It also can be applied to other conditions than areas of the brain. For illustrative purposes, however, we use areas. Teuber's method primarily applies to research, although with the modification called multiple dissociation, it also applies to assessment.

Double dissociation. Double dissociation is concerned with research. To understand double dissociation refer to Table 7.1. At the top of Table 7.1 are three different forms of damage: right hemisphere, left hemisphere, and no damage (control). Along the side are possible methods of research, numbered 1 to 4, for the use of two tests, A and B. Patterns of test findings can be related to particular areas of the brain.

Method 1: Impairment of Test A is thought to indicate impairment in the right hemisphere, because patients with right-hemisphere damage performed more poorly than normals. Obviously, the problem here is that almost any kind of brain damage, not just right-hemisphere damage, could produce impairment on Test A. Amazingly, there are still a few research studies being published in which the procedure is no more complicated or informative than this.

Method 2: Comparing patients with right- and left-hemisphere damage with one test finds that Test A is more impaired with right-hemisphere damage than with left-hemisphere damage. The researcher states that impaired performance on Test A indicates right-hemisphere damage. Although this is a somewhat better procedure, the average amount of damage may be greater for the subjects with right hemisphere than the left in this sample.

Method 3: Two tests, A and B, are used, and A is more impaired for right-hemisphere damage than B. The researcher states that A is more of a right-hemisphere test and so indicates a function in the right hemisphere. However, the problem here is that A may simply be more sensitive to

TABLE 7.1
Double and Multiple Dissociation

Double Dissociation			
	Brain Damage Type		
Methods	*Right Hemisphere*	*Left Hemisphere*	*Control*
1. Test A	impaired	—	not impaired
2. Test A	more impaired	less impaired	not impaired
3. Test A	more impaired	—	not impaired
Test B	less impaired	—	not impaired
4. Test A	more impaired	less impaired	not impaired
Test B	less impaired	more impaired	not impaired

Multiple Dissociation[a]				
Tests	*R Frontal*	*R Parietal*	*L Frontal*	*L Parietal*
Test A	XXX			
Test B		XXX		
Test C			XXX	
Test D				XXX

Note: [a]Tests are related to the area of the brain marked with "XXX."
For multiple dissociations, possible combinations indicating locations of brain damage.
1. Tests A, B, C, D not impaired = No Damage.
2. Tests A, B, C, D impaired = Diffuse.
3. Tests A and B more impaired; Tests C, D less impaired = R hemisphere.
4. Tests C and D more impaired; Tests A, B less impaired = L hemisphere.
5. Tests A and C more impaired; Tests B, D less impaired = Bifrontal damage.
5. Tests B and D more impaired; Tests A, C less impaired = Biparietal damage.
6. Test A more impaired, Tests B, C, D less impaired = R Frontal
7. Test B more impaired, Tests A, C, D less impaired = R Parietal
8. Test C more impaired, Tests A, B, D less impaired = L Frontal
9. Test D more impaired, Tests A, B, C less impaired = L Parietal

damage in general than B. This has occurred in regard to fluid and crystallized intelligence (Barron & Russell, 1992; Russell, 1979, 1980a). The entire issue of whether alcoholism produces more right-hemisphere damage than left was apparently due to the situation that the WAIS subtests, which were thought to indicate right-hemisphere damage, were also more sensitive to brain damage in general (Barron & Russell, 1992); that is, they were fluid tests, whereas those related to the left hemisphere were crystallized.

Method 4: The procedure that most unequivocally demonstrates lateralization is double dissociation. This is the finding that Test A is more impaired for right-hemisphere damage than Test B, and Test B is more impaired for left-hemisphere damage than Test A. Under these circumstances, one can be fairly confident that A is related to the right hemisphere and B is related to the left hemisphere. It is only this finding that definitely indicates lateralization or localization of damage (Teuber, 1955, 1975). This kind of procedure also applies to types of disease entities and rehabilitation treatments.

Multiple dissociation. An extension of the double dissociation method is the basis for assessment. In assessment many tests are used in a process of multiple dissociation. The assessment procedure proceeds from theory, concerning the relation of tests or functions to certain areas of the brain, to interpretation. Individual test results are evaluated in accordance with the accepted theory.

As an example, in Table 7.1, there are four tests, A, B, C, and D. Theory based on previous research has related A to right-frontal lobe functioning. This is indicated by the Xs in the table. Test B is related to the right-parietal lobe, C to the left-frontal lobe, and D to the left-parietal lobe. The patterns that can be seen are fairly obvious. They are presented below the table. If none of the tests are impaired, there is no brain damage. If all the tests are impaired, there is diffuse brain damage. If only Test A is impaired, there is evidence for damage in the right-frontal area and nowhere else. If A and B are impaired and C and D are not, the damage is right-hemisphere damage. If A and C are more impaired, bilateral-frontal damage is indicated.

Consequently, the various possible patterns that will occur among these tests indicate where the damage is located. Obviously, the more tests that are in a battery, the more possible combinations exist. This table was limited to frontal and parietal lobes for simplicity. Also, it is desirable to have more than one test of each one of the areas or of abilities. Redundancy is required to verify that a pattern does exist.

This process of multiple dissociation applies to all areas of interpretation, not just to location. It is the method of determining chronicity, type of pathology, as well as the assets and deficits of the patient related to activities of daily living.

Both double and multiple dissociation presume a constant background. The multiple comparisons used in assessment, especially pattern analysis, require a constant background. The individual is not just being compared one function at a time against a normal background, but all functions are being compared against each other using a total constant background made up of all the tests in the battery.

Formulas and Indices. An index or formula are formalized ways of quantifying a particular empirical pattern. The formula, if correctly constructed, will select out of all the tests results those that are particularly important for a certain diagnosis or assessment pattern. It then, using quantitative methods, determines whether the battery results contain this particular pattern. Formulas have been isolated for Alzheimer's disease (Russell & Polakoff, 1993) and left-hemisphere damage (Dobbins & Russell, 1990; Russell & Russell, 1993).

An index method is equivalent to a complex formula in that it is a formalized way of quantifying a particular empirical pattern. Many indices such as the Halstead Impairment Index (Halstead, 1947) and the Average Impairment Rating (Russell, Neuringer, & Goldstein, 1970) have been developed. These have been found to be as accurate as clinical assessment (Heaton, Grant, Anthony, & Lehman, 1981). An index to assess lateralization and diffuse brain damage (Russell, 1984; Russell & Starkey, 1993) also has been developed and found to be quite accurate. Many other indices and programs for determining lateralization have been developed (Adams, Kvale, & Keegan, 1984; Reitan, 1991; Swiercinsky, 1978). Obviously, many proposed formulas and indices are variable in their accuracy. However, they have a major advantage in that they can be disproved or shown to be accurate in a certain proportion of cases. No such exactness is possible with any other interpretation method.

Mixed Method

In the practical situation, most neuropsychologists use a combination of the interpretive methods just described. In regard to the cognitive-metric fixed battery approach, all methods are utilized. The person may initially look for particular tests to determine whether there is or is not brain damage following an algorithm. Each step in the algorithm may be conceptualized as a hypothesis, but, based on knowledge, the hypotheses are ordered ahead of time so that one leads to another. Observation of patterns is something that can be done with a fixed battery. Here, after one or two of the original questions in the algorithms are examined, the examiner may simply look over the test data for certain patterns.

In what is probably one of the most informative descriptions of how neuropsychologists examine test data in the literature, Reitan and Wolfson (1986, pp. 142–144) described their method in some detail. They use the mixed method. In this description the examiner systematically explores the test data looking for patterns while being guided by knowledge of what each test contributes to the picture of the whole person. Certain questions guide the process such as "What is the course of the lesion?" It is evident that this method begins with minimal preconceptions concerning the patient and only gradually builds a picture of the person. To a great extent this method was derived from Reitan's practice of examining the data blind. In such a situation it is difficult to obtain any hypothesis before seeing the data, and the initial question would not be any more extensive than "Does this person have brain damage?"

REQUIREMENTS FOR A COGNITIVE–METRIC SET OF TESTS

Unless there is accurate representation of brain functions by a set of tests, there is no possibility of an adequate assessment. Accurate representation is obtained through a set of representative tests and a consistent background. Any battery has both a formal structure and content.

Content refers to the particular tests that compose the battery. How thoroughly the functions are represented is referred to as coverage. Coverage applies to both areas of the brain and types of functions. The coverage must be complete enough to represent the functioning of the brain. Adequate coverage is a major requirement for an integrated battery.

Formal structural characteristics are general features that all tests have in common. These include characteristics such as gradation, range, and norms. In this discussion of an integrated battery, the additional structural requirements of accuracy and equivalence are addressed.

Coverage

If the set of tests in a battery is to be an adequate representation of the brain, then coverage is an essential concern. Coverage follows the principle that one cannot tell whether a function is impaired unless that function is tested. As a brain model, a set of tests should be designed to cover all areas of the brain and all cognitive functions, in as much depth as efficiency allows. The exceptions to this are the special purpose batteries such as aphasia batteries. The principles provided here also apply to these special batteries within their domain.

Types of Coverage

There are two types of coverage important in neuropsychological assessment, areas of the brain and types of cognitive functioning.

Anatomic Area. Neuropsychological test batteries have traditionally attempted to fashion complete coverage by anatomic area; that is, an attempt is made to select tests that cover all the various areas of the brain. This approach has been utilized from the time that it was realized that different areas of the brain have different functions. A proper selection of tests helps determine the localization of the damage (Reitan, 1964).

Also, to some extent the diagnosis of a pathology is dependent upon what areas are impaired.

The most well-recognized division of functions related to area is that of lateralization (Matarazzo, 1972; Russell, 1972, 1974, 1979). Any well-organized test battery today will have tests that are related to both hemispheres of the brain, usually in a balanced or equal amount (Russell, 1980b). Because coverage by area is well known, in that there are large areas of textbooks devoted to it (Kolb & Whishaw, 1985), little more need be said concerning this subject.

Cognitive Function.   In recent years, there has been a tendency for neuropsychologists to downplay coverage by area and emphasize coverage by function. This change in emphasis has occurred since the mid 1970s when the CAT scan began to localize lesions more exactly than was possible using neuropsychological tests. Some neuropsychologists have argued that the detection of brain damage is passé (Mapou, 1988), and that neuropsychologists should concentrate on assessing cognitive functions. Ironically, studying cognitive functions does not require brain-damaged subjects at all. When neuropsychologists deal only with function, neuropsychology loses its distinctive aspect and it becomes a branch of normal psychometrics or cognitive psychology that has studied intellectual abilities and individual differences for a century. The problem is that neuropsychologists are not as sophisticated in these areas as cognitive and psychometric psychologists or even psychologists in vocational guidance.

Nevertheless, there is a contribution that neuropsychology can make in both the research and applied fields. In research, neuropsychology is in a unique position to study the differential effects that brain damage produces. In fact, one of the major concerns should be to determine what the human cognitive functions are and to categorize them (Rourke, 1991). In the clinical setting neuropsychologists understand the effect of specific lesions and brain conditions on human functions. This is important to medical and legal, as well as psychological, activities.

Principles of Coverage

There are several principles that must be kept in mind when designing a battery of tests that has adequate coverage. Some of these principles are fairly obvious and should be common sense for a knowledgeable practicing neuropsychologist. Nevertheless, they should be expressly stated so that they can be treated in theoretical discussions.

Completeness.   The first of these may be called completeness or thoroughness. As much as possible, a battery of tests, except specialized batteries, should contain tests related to all areas of the brain and all known functions. An integrated set battery is designed to have as adequate coverage as possible for both area and function. In regard to area, all areas of the brain should be represented. At present, this subdivision of the brain by area may be refined to the level of lobes and in some cases to parts of a lobe. The same thoroughness is required for functions. All major types of functions such as memory, verbal abilities, and spatial relations should be represented in a battery. This is especially important if the purpose of the battery is to determine the amount of impairment produced by brain damage to a person's total functioning.

It appears that a huge battery would be required to cover both areas of the brain and cognitive functions. However, this is not as difficult as one might imagine because generally different areas have different functions, and the same tests may simultaneously cover both aspects. A set battery should have been designed carefully over a period of time to contain thorough coverage for both area and function. A flexible battery, which is put together for each new patient, may very well have lacunae in different areas of coverage. Thus, problems may be missed that a fixed battery would discover (Rourke & Brown, 1986).

Balance.   A second principle is that of balance. *Balance* simply means that there are an equal number of tests devoted to each area of the brain and to each major type of function. Balance related to area is best understood in terms of right- versus left-hemisphere functions. One of the criticisms of the Luria–Nebraska Neuropsychological Battery is that it lacks balance (Russell, 1980b). As with all of Luria's work, the emphasis was primarily on verbal functions. Consequently, the Luria-Nebraska is very heavily weighted in the verbal area. Alternately, the Halstead-Reitan Battery is quite well balanced in regard to lateralization (Russell, 1980b).

Balance also should apply to the difference between anterior and posterior parts of the brain, as well as to localized areas. Balance can be applied to smaller areas such as lobes or even parts of lobes. The principle is that every area should be represented by tests but not over represented. In constructing a battery it is preferable to add a test related to an uncovered area rather than duplicate tests within areas even when the duplicated tests are well known.

Balance also concerns different types of functions and "crystallized" versus "fluid" abilities (Barron & Russell, 1992; Horn, 1976; Russell, 1979, 1980a). For instance, one should not overload a battery with verbal as opposed to spatial relations tests (Russell, 1980b). Our lack of understanding of the function of areas and the difficulty in finding tests related to various areas often has meant that balance is not only lacking, but that we may not even know it is lacking. For instance, most neuropsychological batteries lack tests of social intelligence or what Guilford (1967) called behavioral abilities.

Redundancy. A third principle related to coverage, that is somewhat less known, is redundancy (Russell, 1984). One of the characteristics of any cognitive test is that the scores for the same person are somewhat variable over time; that is, there is normal variability. This variability can lead to false identification of the existence of brain damage or descriptions of impaired functions simply because a subject was not paying attention or because something else interfered with his or her functioning on a particular test. The seasoned neuropsychologist does not trust a single incidence of a particular phenomenon. *Redundancy* means that the same functions or areas are covered by more than one test. It is important to add redundancy to a battery to "cross check" the results that are obtained from any test. When you have several tests that are all impaired related to the same area or function, one has more confidence that there is indeed an impairment in that area.

The more basic the decision, such as separation of brain damage from normality, the greater should be the redundancy. This overlapping often occurs in the Halstead-Reitan battery. Many of the tests in this battery are highly sensitive to brain damage; consequently, one can compare these sensitive tests to each other to insure that there is damage. The utilization of an index rather than a single score to determine brain damage is in large part based on the concept of redundancy.

Efficiency. An additional principle is that of *efficiency*. In some ways, this is the opposite of coverage as well as redundancy. It is obvious that a test battery cannot be infinitely long. At the present time, there are so many tests available that one could presumably test a person for 100 hours without running out of tests. Consequently, the number of tests must be limited at some point. To some extent efficiency may be retained even though there is redundancy. This is accomplished by using overlapping tests. Efficiency means that within the limits imposed by both thoroughness of coverage and redundancy, the length of the battery must be as short as possible. This subject is discussed at greater length under the heading of practical considerations.

Known Tests. The final principle in determining the nature of a fixed battery is that known tests are preferable to unknown tests. Known tests have known reliability, validity, and information concerning their actions. One's understanding of the effects of damage on known tests is greater than on unknown tests. It is only when there is an obvious lack in a particular area of coverage and no known tests are adequate that a new test should be added to an otherwise well-designed battery.

Another reason for using known tests is that information can be more readily transmitted to other clinicians. When one reads a report based on a set of unknown tests, the clinician will not be able to determine how well the testing has been done or how well it has been interpreted. In fact, the clinician may not be able to follow the interpretation to any great extent.

Coverage Solutions

To some extent, the problems that are raised related to coverage have been addressed in the development of two new neuropsychological batteries, the CNHRB and the HRNES. Both of these batteries recognize the need for coverage and also recognize that the traditional Halstead–Reitan Battery even with the inclusion of the WAIS or WAIS-R, whereas better than any previous battery of tests in terms of coverage, had rather large holes in the coverage of both functions and areas.

This section attempts to show how each one of these batteries has dealt with the various problems related to coverage. Both the CNHRB and the HRNES utilize the HRB and Wechsler intelligence tests as a core to which other measures have been added. The batteries are discussed more in terms of function than brain area. A comparison of the coverage by these two batteries is provided in Table 7.2.

Executive Functions.   *Attention* is probably the best known among the executive functions. Whereas an understanding of attention is still rudimentary, there have been a number of tests that are particularly designed to measure aspects of attention. These specialized measures of attention have been incorporated in computer-administered batteries (e.g., Kane & Kay, 1992). The CNHRB also contains a test that is specifically designed to measure attention, Digit Vigilance (Lewis & Rennick, 1979). In addition, it has the Digit Span, Speech Perception, and Rhythm tests, all of which measure aspects of attention as well as other functions. The HRNES uses Digit Span, Speech Perception, and Rhythm as measures of attention.

The second type of executive function may be called *mental flexibility*, which is the opposite of perseveration. The CNHRB has the Wisconsin Card Sort (Heaton, 1980) that measures this function. It was considered to be a frontal test. However, some recent research (Anderson, Damasio, Jones, & Tranel, 1991) tends to throw this into doubt. The Trail Making Tests, particularly Trails B, also appear to measure this function. Both the CNHRB and the HRNES contain Trails B.

As a test of *reasoning and problem solving*, both the CNHRB and the HRNES utilized the Category Test, a largely nonverbal test. In addition,

TABLE 7.2
Comparison of Halstead Russell Neuropsychology Evaluation System
and Comprehensive Norms for the Halstead Reitan Battery
for Various Functions[1]

Functions	HRNES	CNHRB
Executive		
Attention	Digit Span	Digit Span
	Speech Perception	Speech Perception
	Rhythm Test	Rhythm Test
		Digit Vigilance
Mental flexibility	Trails B	Trails B
	Category Test	Category Test
		Wisconsin Card Sort
Problem Solving	Category Test	Category Test
	Block Design	Block Design
		Wisconsin Card Sort
Fluency	*H-Words*	
	Design Fluency	
		Thurstone Word Fluency
Memory		
Immediate	Digit Span	Digit Span
		Tonal Memory Test
	Corsi Board	
	MSLT Immediate Rcl.	
Recent Memory	*WMS Logical Memory*	
	WMS Figural Memory	
Learning		*Story Memory Test*
		Figure Memory Test
	MSLT LTM	
	MSLT 1/2 hour	
	TPT Memory	TPT Memory
	TPT Location	TPT Location
Recognition	*MSLT Recognition*	
Verbal Abilities		
Reasoning	Similarities	Similarities
	Comprehension	Comprehension
	Arithmetic	Arithmetic
	Analogies Test	*Complex Ideational Test*
Academic Abilities	*WRAT-R Reading*	
		PAIT Reading Recognition
		PAIT Reading Comprehen.
		PAIT Spelling
	Arithmetic	Arithmetic
Verbal Recognition	Vocabulary	Vocabulary
	Information	Information
	PPVT-R	
Verbal Naming	*Boston Naming Test*	*Boston Naming Test*
Nonverbal Abilities		
Spatial Relations	Block Design	Block Design
	Object Assembly	Object Assembly
Visual reasoning	Picture Completion	Picture Completion
Social Intelligence	Picture Arrangement	Picture Arrangement

(Continued)

234

TABLE 7.2
(Continued)

Functions	HRNES	CNHRB
Motor Abilities		
Pure motor	Grip Strength	Grip Strength
	Finger Tapping	Finger Tapping
	Grooved Pegboard	Grooved Pegboard
Psychomotor Speed	Digit Symbol	Digit Symbol
	Trails Speed	
Perceptual Abilities		
Sensory	Perceptual Disorders	Perceptual Disorders
Perceptual	*Gestalt Id. Words*	
	Gestalt Id. Objects	
Body Schema	TPT Time	TPT Time

[1]Italicized tests are not part of the HRB. Tests may be repeated.
Abbreviations
MSLT: Miami Selective Learning Test
LTM: Long-Term Memory
PAIT: Peabody Individual Achievement Test
PPVT-R: Peabody Picture Vocabulary Test—Revised
Gestalt Id: Gestalt Identification Test
WRAT-R: Wide Range Achievement Test—Revised

the HRNES has a verbal reasoning test, the Analogies Test (Russell & Starkey, 1993). This test is utilized throughout the country as a major test of thinking and problem solving.

Another function that is generally accepted as an executive function is called *fluency*. This is the ability to rapidly produce new or novel ideas. In this regard, the CNHRB has the Thurstone Word Fluency Test (Pendleton, Heaton, Lehman, & Hulihan, 1982). The HRNES has the H-Words (Russell et al., 1970) and Design Fluency (Russell & Starkey, 1993). Thus, in the HRNES the Fluency tests are balanced. The H-Words, as a word fluency test, is a left-hemisphere measure, whereas Design Fluency is nonverbal and more right hemisphere.

Memory.   Probably in no other area of neuropsychology has so much work been done as in the area of memory. In this regard, it is quite evident that the original Halstead–Reitan Battery lacked the usual type of memory tests. The only specific memory tests that it contained were the memory and location tests related to the Tactual Performance Test (TPT). Even today, these memory tests have not been well studied, and their relationship to tests of other kinds of memory is not well known. Consequently, it became obvious that more usual memory tests should be added to the HRB. Two principles could be used to select additional memory tests. One of these would be completeness of memory coverage whereas the second principle would be to utilize known tests where possible.

In regard to immediate memory, the CNHRB has the Seashore Tonal Memory (Seashore, Lewis, & Saetveit, 1960) and the Digit Span tests. Digit Span is a left-hemisphere verbal test, whereas the tonal memory test seems to be a right-hemisphere test (Heaton et al., 1991). Its parameters are not well known at this time. To cover recent memory and learning, the CNHRB has two learning tests, the Story Memory test and the Figure Memory Test (Heaton et al., 1991). In each of these the material, a story or designs, is repeated until the person learns the material to a criterion. Then the subjects are tested for recall of the material after 4 hours. In addition, the CNHRB retains the TPT memory and location.

The HRNES has a large number of tests in the area of memory (Russell & Starkey, 1993). In regard to immediate memory, in addition to Digit Span the HRNES has incorporated the Corsi Board (Russell & Starkey, 1993), in which blocks are remembered in a spatial arrangement. It is a spatial analogue to the Digit Span. Thus the HRNES has both an immediate verbal and an immediate nonverbal test. In reference to recent memory, a half-hour recall for the Logical Memory and Figural Reproduction were added to the original Wechsler Memory Scale (Russell, 1975, 1988). Thus, recent memory, that is, the ability to put new information into memory, is covered in both the verbal and nonverbal areas. It should be noted that at least in regard to verbal memory the stories are semantic memory, that is, they represent memory for meaningful material.

There was also a need for a learning test. The HRNES added a version of the Buschke test (Buschke, 1973) called the Miami Selective Learning Test (Russell & Starkey, 1993). This test is relatively short compared to the original Buschke test and contains half-hour memory and recognition measures. The HRNES also contains the TPT Memory and Location tests, which provide measures of figural incidental memory. Long-term or remote memory is not covered in either battery unless one considers Information and Vocabulary of the WAIS as measures of this type of ability.

Verbal Abilities. Both batteries utilize either the WAIS or the WAIS-R. The verbal section of the WAIS-R is well known and need not be discussed. Both batteries added a test of word naming, the Boston Naming Test. This was lacking in most test batteries and is recognized as a very important verbal test, especially for assessing aphasia. The CNHRB uses the experimental form of the Boston Naming Test (Kaplan, Goodglass, & Weintraub, 1983), whereas the HRNES uses the commercial version. In addition to the Boston Naming Test, the HRNES added the Peabody Picture Vocabulary Test—Revised (Dunn & Dunn, 1981) to be able to measure recognition vocabulary. This test does not require the type of verbalization that the WAIS-R Vocabulary does. It is also a very crystallized ability. An unpublished research study has indicated that there is practically no drop in ability with age until late adulthood, over 80 years old.

Reasoning. Both batteries have added tests related to reasoning or comprehension. The CNHRB added the Complex Ideational Test, whereas the HRNES added the Analogies Test (Russell & Starkey, 1993).

Academic Abilities. In regard to academic abilities, the CNHRB has added the Peabody Individual Achievement Test, Reading Recognition, Reading Comprehension, and Spelling subtests (Dunn & Markwardt, 1970). These tests measure comprehension of reading rather than simply the ability to read. The HRNES uses the WRAT-R Reading Test. This test is both a crystallized test of ability and provides a measure of dyslexia. The WAIS-R Arithmetic Test is included in both batteries and apparently involves both reasoning and calculation functions.

Nonverbal Abilities. Nonverbal abilities are more poorly understood than are verbal abilities. Spatial relations is probably one of the best understood. Block Design and Object Assembly measure this function and are included in both batteries. Picture Completion apparently measures a kind of visual reasoning. Another function that is as important but often overlooked is that of social intelligence. Guilford (1967; Guilford & Hoepfner, 1971) called it Behavioral Abilities. This function enables us to get along with other people. Only the Picture Arrangement measures this function for both batteries and it apparently does not do this very well.

Motor Abilities. In regard to motor abilities, both the HRNES and the CNHRB retain the Grip strength and Finger Tapping tests from the HRB. They both added the Grooved Pegboard Test as a measure of complex movement. In regard to psychomotor speed, both batteries contain the Digit Symbol Test. In addition, the HRNES has a Trails Speed Test (Russell & Starkey, 1993), which is similar to Trails A except that the person knows ahead of time where all the positions are to which she or he is going. This means Trails Speed does not contain the elements of search present in Trails A. Consequently, it would be a fairly pure measure of psychomotor speed.

Perceptual Abilities. Both batteries contain the Sensory-perceptual Examination from the HRB. The CNHRB has added an auditory test, Tonal Memory, which was discussed previously. On the other hand, the HRNES added a Visual Gestalt Identification Test (Russell & Starkey, 1993). This is a test of the occipital area of the brain, and it has both a verbal and a visual form (Russell, Hendrickson, & VanEaton, 1988). Thus, it should be able to cover the lesions that occur in either the right- or left-occipital areas of the brain. Clinical experience indicates that it is a fairly crystallized ability; as such, it is not sensitive to brain damage in general, but it is sensitive to focal lesions. The Word section of the Gestalt Identification Test may well be related to problems in dyslexia.

Body Schema. The cognitive function related to the TPT has been rather a mystery to neuropsychology. It was known that the TPT was one of the most sensitive tests to brain damage, and that it involved stereognosis and some motor ability but little else. Clinical observation indicates that the TPT appears to be related to body schema. This function is not well understood (Kolb & Whishaw, 1985), but right-parietal damage impairs the TPT for both hands (Russell, 1974), and this impairment appears to accompany neglect.

Accuracy

Accuracy, as the second general requirement for a set of tests, constitutes part of the formal structure of an integrated battery. *Accuracy* signifies how closely a test corresponds to the characteristics of the function that it represents. Unless the individual tests are accurate, a constant background is not possible; that is, the accuracy of the constant background is dependent on the accuracy of the individual tests. The more accurate the scales, the more ability they have for assessment and diagnosis.

Standard Requirements

All the standard traditional requirements for individual test construction apply to tests in an integrated battery. These requirements include item analysis, reliability, and validity (Kline, 1986; Nunnally, 1978). Although there is not time in this chapter to discuss these requirements, there are differences between validating individual tests and validating an entire battery. As in many things, Nunnally (1978, pp. 327–497) appeared to be ahead of his time in being aware of the problems related to sets of tests. In the past a battery of tests has not usually been validated as a whole, but rather each individual test has been validated separately. When a set of tests such as the WAIS or WMS has been validated, typically it has been treated as a single test with a single result, such as an IQ score. It is this summary score that is usually validated against a criterion such as academic ability.

Neuropsychology batteries, such as the HRB, have begun to be validated as a set of tests. They have been validated in at least two ways. First, piecemeal studies demonstrate that the tests in a battery will predict many individual conditions. This has been the most common procedure. Second, patterns derived from the battery may be validated. Neuropsychologists such as Reitan have demonstrated that using the HRB as a whole they can predict many different conditions such as damage in different areas of the brain (Reitan, 1964). More formalized methods such as computer programs can demonstrate the ability of a battery to also assess different conditions (Goldstein & Shelly, 1982; Russell et al., 1970; Wedding, 1983a, 1983b). Finally, a battery is validated when formulas utilizing different groups of tests in the battery are found to identify different conditions, such as Alzheimer's disease (Russell & Polakoff, 1993) or left-temporal lobe damage (Dobbins & Russell, 1990; Russell & Russell, 1993). If patterns using different tests work for many conditions, the battery becomes increasingly valid in terms of construct validity.

Scale Development

In this chapter the primary problems concerning accuracy that are addressed are the requirements of scales. There are several questions related to scales that become critical when tests are used in a set. These questions are dealt with through examining the solutions that the HRNES and CNHRB have utilized. The problem of scale direction is particularly critical in neuropsychology.

Scale Direction.   In neuropsychology some scales are impairment scales such as the Category Test, and some are attainment such as the Finger Tapping Test. When neuropsychologists intuitively deal with scales, particularly raw score scales, they are able to make mental corrections for the different directions in which scales run so that it is possible to mix attainment and impairment scales in a battery. However, this becomes a problem when one applies statistics to the test scores. For example, in a factor-analytic study, if a factor is primarily dominated by impairment scales so that impairment scales are positive, the attainment scales will be negative. Ultimately, to understand the factor structure the psychologist must decide which direction the tests in a factor proceed and then reverse the signs for all the tests that go in the other direction. The same problem occurs when an examiner is exploring patterns among a great many scale scores. Thus, to improve the ease of dealing with large sets of tests, scales should run in the same direction. The direction may be either impairment or attainment.

Although it is clear that scales should all run in the same direction in a battery, the question is whether the scales should be impairment or attainment scales. Neuropsychological scales are basically cognitive-ability measures, and in psychology, ability scales almost always run in the attainment direction. It seems appropriate for larger numbers to indicate better performance. By mathematical convention, scales increase on going to the right and up. In neuropsychology, it appears that the direction has been decided because both the CNHRB and the HRNES have chosen to use attainment scales. This convention is accepted by both batteries and will undoubtedly become standard for neuropsychology as it has for other ability tests.

Type of Scale.   Many different types of scales exist in neuropsychology and in psychology in general (Anastasi, 1988; Lezak, 1983). There are two major groupings of scales: percentiles and standard score scales. *Percentiles*, which are utilized fairly commonly for educational tests, have the psychometric disadvantage that the size of the interval varies depending on the distance the scores are from the group mean. Percentile scales are difficult to interpret or to use psychometrically. Consequently, percentile scales are not utilized to any great extent, except for descriptive purposes.

Standard score scales are derived from z scores in which the mean is zero and the standard deviation is 1. In a z score scale, the numbers below the mean are negative. This is a difficult situation for scaling, and consequently there is general agreement that z scores themselves are not utilized as a scale in tests. Over the years there have been a number of methods of transforming z scores into different types of standard scores (Lezak, 1983).

The Wechsler intelligence tests utilized an approach where for intelligence the mean is 100 and the standard deviation is 15. However, for the subtests making up the Wechsler measures the mean is 10 and the standard deviation is 3. This makes it difficult to mentally transform subtest-scaled scores into IQ-score equivalents or vice versa, a process that is essential for comparative purposes. In addition, other neuropsychological measures do not tend to use this standard score method. Interpretation of a large set of tests requires the ability to easily compare level of performance across all measures.

An alternative standard score to z scores or the Wechsler scores are *T* scores. *T* scores utilized 10 as a standard deviation and 50 to indicate the mean. Apparently, 50 was originally used as the mean to prevent the scale scores from having more than three digits in them; that is, it was thought that the scales would never run above 100. However, as we see in the MMPI, scales do run above 100, and so there is no advantage to setting the mean at 50. Additionally, 50 is mathematically more awkward than 100 if you want to combine scales.

An alternative method is to use decimal scales. This type of scale has been utilized throughout science in almost all areas except the human sciences. In a decimal scale, the intervals are set at 10. Applying this to psychology, one would set the mean at 10 and have a standard deviation of 1. There are two advantages to this. One is that it is easy to compare scales with each other or to index scales. The average for any group of scales is approximately the same as the score for any individual scale in the index. Exact combinations require minimal mathematical manipulation (Russell & Starkey, 1993). Secondly, the scale can be subdivided into an infinite number of subdivisions. For instance, in regard to measure of length, a meter can be divided into centimeters or expanded into kilometers. There is nothing equivalent to this in psychology.

Decimal scales, in which the mean is 10 and the standard deviation is 1, could be applied to psychological measurement. If one needs to increase the finesse of the scale, decimal points can be used. Also, the scales could be increased and decimals removed by multiplying by 10. This would create scales that may be called C scores (centile scores). Then the mean becomes 100 and the SD 10. The scale is now quite flexible, without requiring complex calculations for conversions.

Solution to Scale Selection

The types of scales selected by the HRNES and CNHRB are different. The CNHRB chose T scores running in an attainment direction. The HRNES chose a form of decimal scale. However, in order to increase the number of possible intervals and also to make the mean (but not the SD) equivalent to the already accepted standard of the Wechsler tests, the decimal scales were multiplied by 10. This is the C scale or centile scale. The mean is 100 and each standard deviation is 10. Consequently, there is the possibility of 10 points within each standard deviation. As a matter of fact, the HRNES utilizes only 4 points for a standard deviation; that is, it divides the standard deviation into quarters.

Transformation of Raw Scores to Scale Scores.
Whereas both the HRNES and CNHRB have chosen the attainment direction for the scales to run, the method of transforming the raw scores into scale score units is different for each battery. The CNHRB transforms raw scores into attainment scale scores by using the same approach that the WAIS does for its subscales; that is, the mean for the scale is set at 10 and the standard deviation at 3, as with the WAIS subscales. This means that a limit is set on the accuracy of every scale; at most 3 points can be used to represent a standard deviation. Thus, it is impossible for the CNHRB to use a finer or more accurate system than 3 points for a standard devia-

tion. These scale scores are subsequently transformed to age- and education-adjusted T scores (discussed in more detail later). However, it should be noted that no matter how many points are in the T scores, the initial transformation limits the accuracy to 3 points per standard deviation.

The method used by the HRNES is to subtract the raw score from the highest possible score. This applies to impairment scales. Thus, if the highest possible score is 15 errors as it is in the Rhythm Test, the error score that the patient actually obtains is subtracted from 15. This reverses the raw score scale but retains the number of points in the original scale. In some cases such as time tests (i.e., the Trail Making Test), a limit had to be set on the length of time that a person is allowed to work on the test. The scale is again reversed by subtracting the time the person actually took from the total possible length of time. This method retains the number of points or accuracy of the raw score. The scale scores for the HRNES contain 4 points per SD. This sets the limit on the accuracy of the scale even if the raw score contains more than 4 points per SD.

It should be mentioned that some raw scores have insufficient range to be highly accurate. On the Digit Span, for instance, the average for the population is about 6 digits. The WAIS-R increased the length of the scale by counting two trials for each length of digits. Whereas improved, this is still not long enough for a test that is used to measure brain damage in which the impairment is often much greater than that found in the normal range of abilities.

Index of Brain Damage.   Since the development of the Halstead Index for brain damage (Halstead, 1947), there have been several other types of indices proposed. Early studies by Reitan (1955a) indicated that the Halstead Index was more accurate than any single test for brain damage. Studies have continued to support the greater accuracy of a group of tests than a single test in distinguishing brain damage from nonbrain damage.

Halstead Index.   *The Halstead Index* (1947) is basically the proportion of the tests in the index that are in the brain-damage range; that is, if half the tests are in the brain-damage range, the index would be .5. Over the years, the number of tests in the Halstead Index have been reduced from 10 to 7 (Reitan & Wolfson, 1985). The cutting point for assessing brain damage still remains at half of the tests or .5.

Average Impairment Rating (AIR).   Since the development of the Halstead Index, several other indices have been proposed. The most commonly utilized index other than the Halstead Index is the AIR proposed by Russell, Neuringer, and Goldstein (1970). This index simply averages the scale scores of the component subtests that constitute the index. This, of course, requires scale scores as the basis for the measure. The Halstead Index, instead, utilizes raw score cutting point for each scale. Studies have shown that the AIR is approximately as accurate as the Halstead Index in determining the existence of brain damage (Anthony, Heaton, & Lehman, 1980; Russell, 1984). However, it has the advantage of providing a measure of the amount of impairment as well as providing a simple cutting point for damage. In the same book that proposed the AIR (Russell et al., 1970), a second index was proposed that was similar to the Halstead Index. This was the percentage of index tests that were in the brain-damage range. This was called the percentage of damage index or the Rennick Index. It should also be noted that the AIR and the percentage of damage index contained additional tests than those used in the Halstead Index. Following Rennick's method the index utilized 12 tests rather than the 7 tests, which are used in the Halstead Index. The CNHRB utilizes the AIR and the Halstead Index.

Average Impairment Scale (AIS).   The HRNES has created a new scale, namely the AIS. The term *AIR* was always a misnomer. The scale even in its initial form was not a rating scale because it used objective scaling throughout. The term AIR was derived from Rennick's original index in which parts of the index were ratings. When the book, *Assessment of Brain Damage* (Russell et al., 1970), was published, the earlier term was retained even though the scales that had previously been ratings had been converted into objective scales.

There are some other changes in the AIS. It utilizes 10 tests rather than either 7 or 12. Some of the tests in the AIR and the Halstead Index were eliminated. These were the Cross Drawing (Spatial Relations) from the Aphasia Screening Test, Rhythm, and TPT location. Unpublished studies indicated that they were not as accurate as the other tests in the Index. The Cross was replaced by Block Design. Although the Aphasia and the Perceptual Disorders tests are not highly accurate for determining brain damage, they extend the range of the AIS. Many of the other tests in the index have a restricted floor.

Equivalence

The third general characteristic and requirement for an integrated set of tests is equivalence of scales. In regard to the formal structure of an integrated battery, the most important requirement of a set of tests is that the scores of all the tests are equivalent. In order to make multiple comparisons, the set must contain a constant background. An internal constant background is created when all the scales are equivalent so that the same scores indicate the same amount of ability or impairment. Equivalency requires that all the scales either be normed on the same sample of subjects or that samples are equated by some statistical method.

Norming Problems

There are some critical problems concerned with norming that are related to a set of tests. A primary problem is obtaining enough subjects. Normal adult subjects are difficult to obtain especially when the battery is long. One solution is to utilize subjects from what is called a negative neurological sample or medical sample. These are subjects that were sent to a neuropsychological laboratory to be tested because they were suspected of having brain damage, and then a neurological examination found that they did not have an organic condition. This type of sample has been criticized. The critics assert that because brain damage was suspected the subjects must have had something wrong, and consequently they are not representative of a normal sample. The irony here is that, whereas the standard criterion for the existence of brain damage is the neurological diagnosis obtained using methods such as the CT or MRI, this same criterion is rejected as the criterion for the nonexistence of brain damage.

Russell (1990; Russell & Starkey, 1993) examined the type of problems that a negative neurological sample contained and found that it was largely composed of subjects with a diagnosis of mild depression or some form of neurosis accompanied by memory or somatic complaints, and mild personality disorders.

The nonmedical samples that have been obtained to date are also faulted. These "normal" subjects, that have been obtained "off of the street," have not had a neurological examination and so they may be abnormal. In fact, these "normal" samples have not been normal in the sense of being an unbiased random sample of the total population of a country. First, they are volunteers and in many cases they were paid. An example of such a volunteer sample is the Fromm-Auch and Yeudall sample (1983). The mean WAIS FSIQ of this sample was 119 with a mean age of 25.4 years. Thus, the sample was both young and considerably above average in regard to intellectual ability.

In all the major studies (Fromm-Auch & Yeudall, 1983; Pauker, 1977), subjects have answered a "structured interview" in which they denied the existence of various types of organic problems. When the interview criteria were quite strict, so as to eliminate any condition that indicated possible organic damage, neurosis, psychosis, and mental retardation, the sample appeared to be "supernormal" (Fromm-Auch & Yeudall, 1983;

Heaton et al., 1991; Pauker, 1977). Obviously, a random sample of a normal population will have some subjects with emotional or organic problems.

Another aspect of the situation with normals is that a fairly high proportion of people over 50 will have some undiagnosed neurological problems that reduce their mental ability, such as cerebral arteriosclerosis (Russell, 1990). In a normative study of older people for Russell's version of the WMS, Haaland, Linn, Hunt, and Goodwin (1983) found lower ability than would be expected from direct extrapolation of the decrease in ability at the earlier ages. Thus a screened voluntary sample may be too "normal" at the younger range and too impaired due to undiagnosed cerebral arteriosclerosis at the older age range.

HRNES and CNHRB Norms. The HRNES sample included negative neurological subjects who were screened for vascular problems using a structured interview, as well as clinic records that indicated a negative neurological examination. Subjects hospitalized for depression, or with a history of alcoholism, significant head trauma, or schizophrenia were eliminated.

The CNHRB (Heaton et al., 1991) used structured interviews to screen for a learning disability, neurological disease, significant head trauma, psychiatric disorder, alcoholism, drug use, and other illnesses that affect brain functioning. They did not disclaim the inclusion of negative neurological or medical patients. Consequently, they evidently included negative neurological subjects; however, the proportion cannot be determined.

A study by Russell (1990; Russell & Starkey, 1993) that compared data used for the HRNES with four other major norming groups (Dodrill, 1988; Fromm-Auch & Yeudall, 1983; Heaton et al., 1986; Pauker, 1977) found no significant difference between them. However, a preliminary examination indicates that the HRNES norms will probably be a little more conservative than the CNHRB norms. In this regard, a study of the memory section of the HRNES, which is the Russell version of the Wechsler Memory Scale (WMS; Russell, 1988), found these norms to be equivalent to the typical norms found in many other studies of the WMS (Crosson, Hughes, Roth, & Monkowski, 1984).

Equalization of Scores

Another major problem concerning the equalization of scales is the use of different populations for norming. When different populations are utilized, the means and standard deviations will vary from population to population. Consequently, the performance represented by a scaled score may vary from scale to scale. There is no constant background.

This can be observed in a review of various studies using the Halstead–Reitan Battery (e.g., Fromm-Auch & Yeudall, 1983). Comparison of these studies demonstrates that the means and standard deviations vary greatly from one population to another. Consequently, if the norms for different tests had been derived from these different samples, a discrepancy in scores might only reflect a difference in norms. Note that any comparison of tests in a flexible battery assumes that the means and the standard deviations of the tests are equivalent, whereas in reality they are usually different.

Coordinated Norming. A solution to the norming problem, which is utilized by all developed sets of tests, is that of coordinated norming. Coordinated norming means that all the subtests in a battery were normed on the same population. Consequently, any difference between scale scores represents a difference within the subject and not between population norms. The first popular test that used coordinated norming was the Wechsler–Bellevue (Wechsler, 1939), in which the subtests were all normed on the same sample. Consequently, one could accurately and legitimately compare the scores from one subtest to another. Both the CNHRB and the HRNES utilize coordinated norming.

Adding Tests During Norming. Although coordinated norming equates the original total group of tests, a problem remains if new tests are added to the battery later in the collection of data. Obviously, the new tests will not be normed on all the subjects used for the original tests. The problem is to produce norms for the new tests that are equivalent to the norms for the entire battery.

The CNHRB and the HRNES dealt with this problem in a somewhat different manner. The CNHRB simply added the new tests to the core battery of tests (Heaton et al., 1991). The presumption was that the means and standard deviations of the total group of tests did not change over time. In the case of the Boston Naming Test, apparently the subtests were not coordinated with the rest of the CNHRB.

The HRNES used a somewhat different method of developing coordinated norms for tests that were added to the total group of tests at a later time (Russell & Starkey, 1993). The HRNES does not derive its scores directly from the means and standard deviations of the entire battery. The subtest scores are derived by predicting them from an index, which was composed of the z scores from the AIS index tests. This index remains the same even though new tests are added because the new tests do not contribute to the index. The scores for the new tests were predicted from the index that provides much of the consistency of completely coordinated norms. Although there may be slight variations, this method ensures that added tests are much closer in their scores to the overall test battery scores than if they had been derived from an entirely new population of subjects.

Adding Tests to a Normed Battery. With the advance of neuropsychology there will be the development of new tests. The problem then becomes one of adding new tests to a battery that has been normed. Two methods may be suggested. First, the method used to add tests while norming a battery may be used. Second, if the new test is a version of the old test, a test–new test correlation study may be utilized. Both versions of the test are given in a counterbalanced manner (i.e., for half the subjects give the new test first, and for half give the old test first). There is a refinement of this procedure that is extremely helpful. For a third group of subjects that is equal in size with each of the other two groups, give the old test twice so that a test–retest correlation is obtained. If the variance of the test–new test correlation is not much greater than the test–retest variance, the new test may be substituted for the old test. In some cases conversion scores may need to be predicted from linear regression to equate the scores of the new with the old test norms.

Age and Education Correction

Since the 1970s it has been known that both age (Reitan, 1955b) and IQ affect performance on neuropsychological tests (Heaton, Grant, & Matthews, 1986; Pauker, 1977). People are better at doing tests when they are in their 20s than when they are in their 60s or 70s, and for many tests they do better when their intelligence is higher (Gade & Mortensen, 1984; Gade, Mortensen, Udesen, & Jonsson, 1985; Heaton et al., 1986; Pauker, 1977; Reitan, 1955b). Because of this, neuropsychological tests should be corrected for age and IQ level. Age is obviously not affected by brain damage, but IQ is affected so that some other indication of premorbid ability is needed. Education level is the simplest indication of premorbid ability.

Standard Method of Correction. Although there are norms with formal age and intelligence corrections (Beardsley, Matthews, Cleeland, & Harley, 1978; Bornstein, 1985; Dodrill, 1988; Fromm-Auch & Yeudall, 1983; Pauker, 1977), there were problems with each of these sets of norms. The standard way in which a correction is made for age or IQ is to obtain subjects at every age and IQ level. This means that one must obtain a sufficient number of subjects to create stable norms at each age/IQ level. It has been extremely difficult in the past to obtain enough subjects for the extremes of such a matrix. Probably the best normed sample until recently was collected by Pauker (1977). However, he evidently never completed his subject collection, presumably due to the difficulty of obtaining the extreme cases. For instance, in his interim norms he had only 6 subjects for the WAIS IQ level of 84 to 109 at the age of 58 to 76.

Linear Regression.   Both the CNHRB and the HRNES have used linear regression to cope with this problem. The scores at all levels of age and IQ are simply predicted from the scores that were obtained using multiple linear regression. Not only does this procedure produce adequate norms at all age and IQ levels but it "smooths" the transition from one level to another. The assumption, of course, is that there is a linear relationship between ability and both age and IQ. This is somewhat questionable based on a number of studies that have apparently found more rapid deterioration of ability at older ages than at younger ages (Gade & Mortensen, 1984; Gade et al., 1985; Heaton et al., 1986). However, there is at present no alternative because a nonlinear regression line has not been determined. Also, there is the possibility that the nonlinearity of ability loss in older ages may be due to an artifact; people at the older ages tend to have more neurological diseases such as cerebroarteriosclerosis. Without these diseases, the rate of deterioration may be linear.

The first use of linear regression to produce correction tables was employed by the HRRB (Russell, Starkey, et al., 1988). Subsequently, both the CNHRB and the HRNES used linear regression to predict scores. The CNHRB simply predicts scores on the basis of a multiple regression formula. Consequently, it can predict them in exact age- and education-level segments. The precision of its prediction is limited only by its method of transformation, which is 3 scores per *SD*.

The HRNES, on the other hand, divides the ages into decades and uses only four levels of education. An unpublished study at Russell's laboratory indicated that there is no major improvement between 12 years of education and 15 years of education. Unless the person graduates from college, ability level is essentially the same as that of high school students. Consequently, the only breaks are below high school, high school, college graduation, and graduation from graduate school. There is also a question as to whether educational levels far below high school represent a lower level of ability because many factors can prevent people from attaining a high school education.

In addition, the HRNES does not directly correct for education level as does the CNHRB. Rather, the HRNES corrects for IQ directly and for education level indirectly. The procedure adjusts raw scores of four FSIQ levels to be equivalent to the mean high school level. The four levels are the mean FSIQ scores for below high school, graduation from high school, college, and graduate school. The mean IQ for the entire sample is the high school level so that, if the person has a high school education, no correction is made. If the person has a college degree, the difference between college and high school IQs are subtracted from the person's test scores. This corrects the test score so that it is equivalent to the mean high school FSIQ level. The same type of correction is made for people having a graduate degree.

Distribution Problems

A problem that has only recently become obvious with neuropsychological testing (Russell, 1987, 1991) but was previously recognized with regard to the MMPI is that different tests have different performance distributions. Brain damage tests in almost all cases do not have a normal distribution. They are skewed and, in some cases, severely skewed. For instance, in one study (Russell, 1987, 1991), the Aphasia Test with brain-damaged subjects had a skew in which the tests stretch out for 16 standard deviations from the mean in the impaired direction, whereas the mean for the test was within one standard deviation of the top of the distribution.

Not only are brain-damaged subjects' distributions abnormal, but the distributions vary widely from test to test. As long as one is measuring abilities near the normal mean, this difference in distribution does not affect the test results to any great extent. However, when measuring fairly severe brain damage, the difference in distributions may produce a pattern that looks as if a particular type of damage exists, whereas it actually reflects a difference in distributions (Russell, 1987, 1991).

CNHRB and HRNES Solutions. In regard to this problem, the CNHRB utilized no distribution correction for its *T* scores. In contrast and by way of illustration, the MMPI-2 recognized this problem and set up a method called the Uniform *T* scores (Graham, 1990). In brief, the *T* scores for the eight clinical scales on the MMPI-2 were averaged to produce a composite scale. Then, the distribution of each scale was adjusted to match the percentile distribution of the composite scale.

The HRNES utilized linear regression based on an index score, the Average *z*-score Index (AZI; Russell, 1987, 1991). (The AZI is not the same as the AIS.) Like the MMPI-2, the HRNES established an index made up of those tests that are the most sensitive to brain damage. The AZI was based on both normal and brain-damaged subjects, although the *z*-score formulas that were utilized were derived from only normal controls. This meant that the scale scores in the AZI were equivalent to normal control scale scores, with normal means and standard deviations. All the scales utilized in the HRNES were then derived from this index score using linear regression. Thus, the scores for each one of the tests on the HRNES are equivalent to the AZI tests. The equivalence was not absolute because there were some differences in the samples utilized, but the scales were certainly more equivalent than uncorrected scores.

Practical Considerations in Set Design

Although the major structural problems in designing an integrated set of tests have been discussed, there are some other issues that are related to practical aspects of a battery. These include efficiency, good design, adaptability, use of technicians, and crafting a battery for research purposes.

Efficiency

The primary practical problem in designing a test battery is the efficiency of the battery. It is obvious that a battery cannot be too long. There is a paradox in regard to efficiency (Russell, 1986) that is that a test battery cannot simultaneously have adequate coverage, accuracy, and brevity. In a short or brief battery the number of tests is reduced, but adequate coverage, of course, requires many tests. The more tests, the longer the battery. An alternative to brevity is to reduce the length of the individual tests. However, when one reduces the length of the tests, the accuracy of each individual test is reduced. Consequently, it is not possible to have all three of these attributes simultaneously.

Whereas a compromise must be made at some point, there are some methods of increasing efficiency. A method that requires establishing basal and ceiling scores reduces the administrative length of a long test such as the PPVT-R (Dunn & Dunn, 1981) or the Boston Naming Test (Kaplan et al., 1983). The reliability is not reduced.

A test should be as short as possible, while retaining its accuracy (Russell, 1986). Statistical studies have demonstrated that as tests grow longer they become more accurate, but that the increase in accuracy decreases with the length of the test. Consequently, there is a point at which you obtain the maximum accuracy with the least length. It has been advised (Nunnally, 1978) that with tests for normals that have a normal distribution of scores, tests should be at least 20 items long.

Obviously, there are many tests in neuropsychology that are either too short or too long. The Digit Span, even in the revised WAIS-R, is too short, whereas the Category Test is too long. It is relatively easy for a test that is too long to be reduced to a useful length. This has been done with the Category Test a number of times (Russell & Levy, 1987). Interestingly, in this regard, the first reduction in the length of the Category Test was accomplished by Reitan (Reitan & Wolfson, 1985).

Another method of increasing efficiency concerns scoring. The more complex the scoring procedures, such as obtaining age and education corrections, the longer the time and the greater the possibility of making errors. At least in this area there is a definite solution, which is to use computer-scoring programs. Both the CNHRB and the HRNES use computer-scoring programs.

Good Design

Another attribute of a good test battery is what might be called good design. It is difficult to state the nature of good design because it is related to such things as ease of administration, whether the patient and examiner like a particular test, and certain aesthetic qualities. It is possible that a test that a subject may enjoy is one that an examiner does not. However, in most cases, if the patient finds a test difficult or unenjoyable, it is also unpleasant for the examiner, who to a certain extent empathizes with the patient. One of the problems with very long tests, such as the original Category Test, is that they may be unpleasant to take. The term *interest* is important in a good design. A test that is designed well will maintain the interest of the subject. An advantage of the Wechsler intelligence tests is that they tend to maintain the interest of the subject.

In some cases a test may be retained that is somewhat unpleasant if it produces a great deal of information. The TPT may be an example of a test that is sometimes found to be disagreeable for the subject but that is worth giving because it produces much information. Interestingly, the TPT is often more disagreeable to the examiner than to the subject because it is difficult to watch a patient struggling with the test, but when blindfolded and taking the test for the first time one is less aware of the time.

Use of a Technician

Another consideration in designing a fixed battery is that one can utilize the services of a technician (Russell, 1984). Much of the testing done in neuropsychology is routine and, with a correctly designed battery, can be well administered by a trained, bright technician (DeLuca, 1989; Division 40 Task Force on Education, 1991). Lezak uses clerical or nursing staff to administer part of her basic battery (1983, pp. 107–109).

Technicians should be trained so that if any unusual occurrences are found, they will notify the neuropsychologist and she or he can then examine the patient. As a practical matter, the technician who continually does testing is probably a much better examiner than the neuropsychologist. Consequently, use of technicians may provide a combination of the administration skill of the technician and the knowledge of the neuropsychologist.

The use of a technician obviously saves a great deal of time for neuropsychologists. When an examiner uses a technician, his or her own time can be devoted to analysis of the test battery data, interpretation, and report writing. The length of time utilized by the neuropsychologist on interpretation and report writing of a case may be only an hour or 2, whereas the total amount of testing time may run 8 to 10 hours.

Another problem with neuropsychological testing is that it tends to become routine, and consequently it is relatively easy to "burn out." In a personal communication Reitan once stated that his technicians lasted for approximately 2 years. This would mean that it would take only about 2 years for neuropsychologists who do all their own testing to begin to burn out. When that occurs, not only is one's livelihood no longer any fun, but also one begins to cut corners and the testing tends to deteriorate.

Research

The fixed battery has a great advantage over a flexible battery in regard to research. With a fixed battery data can be gathered while the battery is being administered for clinical purposes. If you need to do a study on a new test or combination of new tests, you simply add those tests to the battery and in a year or 2 you have collected enough data for analysis and publication. Because most psychologists will "try out" new tests, this adding of tests only systemizes an existing process so that it becomes a research study.

The amount of research that has been done on fixed batteries is far greater than on flexible batteries, primarily because the same tests are administered across many types of subjects during clinical practice. This creates a pool of subjects from which specific types of subjects can be selected. From the point of view of research methodology, selecting subjects from a pool to test a hypothesis is no different than selecting them from hospital wards. As such, an active clinician can also be a researcher. It is no accident that almost all the factor-analytic studies that have been done in neuropsychology have utilized the Halstead-Reitan Battery or the Luria-Nebraska Neuropsychological Battery. These are the primary fixed batteries.

CHAPTER SUMMARY AND CONCLUSIONS

In this chapter, the outlines of a theory of cognitive–metric neuropsychology and of test sets or an integrated battery have been explicated. This led to a discussion of instrumentation, the brain function model, multiple dissociation, and a constant background. The nature and requirements for an integrated set of tests were proposed. These concepts were illustrated through examination of two new neuropsychology batteries, the CNHRB and the HRNES.

As a scientific approach to neuropsychological assessment, one would expect progressive cognitive-metric development. Overall, the great advantage of a metric approach to neuropsychology is that psychometric measurement makes possible assessment methods that are public, objective, and accurate. This permits research that will continually improve assessment procedures, not just the knowledge base of assessment. Thus, an unlimited development exists for a neuropsychology that adheres to the cognitive–metric approach.

There are especially two areas where progress may be expected, set theory and computer processing. In regard to the development of test set theory, a better understanding of the nature of representation is being acquired. Theoretical and experimental studies may soon examine the relationship of brain functioning to test construction in greater detail. Certainly, emphasis will be placed on increasing the accuracy of tests.

In regard to the concept of a test battery as a brain function model, greater efforts will be made to obtain a constant background for assessment through coverage and methods of equivalence. Coverage is already one of the guiding principles in neuropsychology. Methods designed to obtain equivalence were used to create both the CNHRB and the HRNES. Future studies will certainly increase both the development and the use of methods to obtain equivalence.

Progress in assessment will undoubtedly continue to move from a qualitative, intuitive approach that makes great use of clinical lore to the use of more formally reliable and validated methods. Here, computer processing is clearly the wave of the future. Although computer processing does not guarantee any of the requirements for valid scientific assessment, except perhaps consistency, it does provide programs that are open to correction with further research. Various methods of administration can be examined, and the best method for a particular test can be selected. Scoring procedures that increase accuracy but that are costly in time and expertise can be computerized and made almost as rapid as the use of raw scores. The use of computer scoring in neuropsychology already includes the Wechsler intelligence tests, the CNHRB, the HRNES, some children's tests, and some individual tests such as the CVLT (Delis et al., 1987).

Finally, computer interpretation will soon become part of mainstream neuropsychology as it is in other areas of psychology. The computer is capable of almost any cognitive processing in assessment that humans can accomplish (Kleinmuntz, 1968, 1987). The slower development of computer interpretation in neuropsychology than in other areas of psychology will certainly be overcome as neuropsychologists accept a more objective approach to assessment.

REFERENCES

Adams, K. M. (1980). In search of Luria's battery: A false start. *Journal of Consulting and Clinical Psychology, 48*, 511–516.

Adams, K. M., Kvale, V. I., & Keegan, J. F. (1984). Relative accuracy of three automated systems for neuropsychological interpretation. *Journal of Clinical Neuropsychology, 6*, 413–431.

American Psychological Association. (1988). *Standards for educational and psychological testing.* Washington, DC: APA Press.

Anastasi, A. (1988). *Psychological testing* (6th ed.). New York: Macmillan.

Anderson, S. W., Damasio, H., Jones, R. D., & Tranel, D. (1991). Wisconsin Card Sorting Test performance as a measure of frontal lobe damage. *Journal of Clinical and Experimental Neuropsychology, 13*, 909–922.

Anthony, W. Z., Heaton, R. K., & Lehman, R. A. W. (1980). An attempt to cross-validate two actuarial systems for neuropsychological test interpretation. *Journal of Consulting and Clinical Psychology, 48*, 317–326.

Barron, J. H., & Russell, E. W. (1992). Fluidity theory and the neuropsychological impairment in alcoholism. *Archives of Clinical Neuropsychology, 7*, 175–188.

Beardsley, J. V., Matthews, C. G., Cleeland, C. S., & Harley, J. P. (1978). *Experimental T-Score norms for CA 34- on the Wisconsin Neuropsychological Test Battery.* (Available from Klove-Matthews Psychological Test Equipment, 2768 Marshall Parkway, Madison, WI 53713).

Bornstein, R. A. (1985). Normative data on selected neuropsychological measures from a nonclinical sample. *Journal of Clinical Psychology, 41*, 651–659.

Buschke, H. (1973). Selective reminding for analysis of memory and learning. *Journal of Verbal Learning Behavior, 12*, 543–550.

Butler, M., Retzlaff, P., & Vanderploeg, R. (1991). Neuropsychological test usage. *Professional Psychology: Research and Practice, 22*, 510–512.

Christensen, A. L. (1979). *Luria's neuropsychological investigation. Text* (2nd ed.). Copenhagen: Munksgaard.

Christensen, A. L. (1984). The Luria method of examination of the brain-impaired patient. In P. E. Logue & J. M. Shear (Eds.), *Clinical neuropsychology: A multidisciplinary approach* (pp. 5–28). Springfield, IL: Charles C. Thomas.

Crosson, B., Hughes, C. W., Roth, D. L., & Monkowski, P. G. (1984). Review of Russell's norms for the Logical Memory and Visual Reproduction subtests of the Wechsler Memory Scale. *Journal of Consulting and Clinical Psychology, 52*, 635–641.

Delis, D. C., Kramer, J. H., Kaplan, E., & Ober, B. (1987). *CVLT: California Verbal Learning Test - Research edition.* New York: Psychological Corporation.

DeLuca, J. W. (1989). Neuropsychology technicians in clinical practice: Precedents, rationale, and current deployment. *The Clinical Neuropsychologist, 3*, 3–21.

Division 40 Task Force on Education (1991). Report of the Division 40 Task Force on Education, Accreditation and Credentialing. Recommendations for education and training of nondoctoral personnel in clinical neuropsychology. *The Clinical Neuropsychologist, 5*, 20–23.

Dobbins, C., & Russell, E. W. (1990). Left temporal lobe damage pattern on the Wechsler Adult Intelligence Scale. *Journal of Clinical Psychology, 46*, 863–868.

Dodrill, C. B. (1988, August). *What constitutes normal performance in clinical neuropsychology?*. Paper presented at the 97th Annual Convention of the American Psychological Association, Atlanta.

Dunn, L. M., & Dunn, L. M. (1981). *Peabody, Picture Vocabulary Test - Revised, Manual.* Circle Pines, MN: American Guidance Service.

Dunn, L. M., & Markwardt, F. C. (1970). *Manual for the Peabody Individual Achievement Test.* Minneapolis: American Guidance Service.

Franzen, M. D. (1989). *Reliability and validity in neuropsychological assessment.* New York: Plenum Press.

Fromm-Auch, D., & Yeudall, L. T. (1983). Normative data for the Halstead-Reitan neuropsychological tests. *Journal of Clinical Neuropsychology, 5,* 221–238.

Gade, A., & Mortensen, E. L. (1984, December). *The influence of age, education, and intelligence on neuropsychological test performance.* Paper presented at the 3rd Nordic Conference in Behavioral Toxicology, Arhus, Denmark.

Gade, A., Mortensen, E. L., Udesen, H., & Jonsson, A. (1985, June). *Predictors of cognitive performance: Age, education, and intelligence.* Paper presented at the 8th INS European Conference, Copenhagen.

Golden, C. J., Hammeke, T. A., & Purisch, A. D. (1980). *Manual for the Luria-Nebraska Neuropsychological Battery.* Los Angeles: Western Psychological Services.

Goldstein, K., & Scheerer, M. (1941). Abstract and concrete behavior, An experimental study with special tests. *Psychological Monographs, 53*(2, Whole No. 239).

Goldstein, G., & Shelly, C. (1982). A further attempt to cross-validate the Russell, Neuringer, and Goldstein Neuropsychological Keys. *Journal of Consulting and Clinical Psychology, 50,* 721–726.

Goodglass, H., & Kaplan, E. (1972). *Assessment of aphasia and related disorders.* Philadelphia: Lea & Febiger.

Goodglass, H., & Kaplan, E. (1983). *The assessment of aphasia and related disorders* (rev. ed.). Philadelphia: Lea & Febiger.

Graham, J. R. (1990). *MMPI-2: Assessing personality and psychopathology.* New York: Oxford University Press.

Guilford, J. P. (1967). *The nature of human intelligence.* New York: McGraw-Hill.

Guilford, J. P., & Hoepfner, R. (1971). *The analysis of intelligence.* New York: McGraw-Hill.

Haaland, K. Y., Linn, R. T., Hunt, W. C., & Goodwin, J. S. (1983). A normative study of Russell's variant of the Wechsler Memory Scale in a healthy elderly population. *Journal of Consulting and Clinical Psychology, 51,* 878–881.

Halstead, W. C. (1947). *Brain and intelligence.* Chicago: University of Chicago Press.

Heaton, R. K. (1980). *A manual for the Wisconsin Card Sorting Test.* Odessa, FL: Psychological Assessment Resources.

Heaton, R. K., Grant, I., Anthony, W. Z., & Lehman, A. W. (1981). A comparison of clinical and automated interpretation of the Halstead–Reitan Battery. *Journal of Clinical Neuropsychology, 3,* 121–141.

Heaton, R. K., Grant, I., & Matthews, C. G. (1986). Differences in neuropsychological test performance associated with age, education and sex. In I. Grant & K. M. Adams (Eds.), *Neuropsychological assessment of neuropsychiatric disorders* (pp. 100–120). New York: Oxford University Press.

Heaton, R. K., Grant, I., & Matthews, C. G. (1991). *Comprehensive norms for an expanded Halstead–Reitan Battery.* Odessa, FL: Psychological Assessment Resources.

Horn, J. L. (1976). Human abilities: A review of research and theory in the early 1970's. In M. Rosenzweig & L. Porter (Eds.), *Annual review of psychology* (Vol. 27). Palo Alto, CA: Annual Reviews.

Kane, R. L., & Kay, G. G. (1992). Computerized assessment in neuropsychology: A review of tests and test batteries. *Neuropsychology Review, 3,* 1–117.

Kaplan, E. (1988). A process approach to neuropsychological assessment. In T. Boll & B. K. Bryant (Eds.), *Clinical neuropsychology and brain function: Research, measurement, and practice* (pp. 129–167). Washington, DC: American Psychological Association.

Kaplan, E., Goodglass, H., & Weintraub, S. (1983). *Boston Naming Test.* Philadelphia: Lea & Febiger.

Kertesz, A. (1979). *Aphasia and associated disorders: Taxonomy, localization, and recovery.* New York: Grune & Stratton.

Kimbel, G. A. (1985). Conditioning and learning. In S. Koch & D. E. Leary (Eds.), *A century of psychology as science* (pp. 284–335). New York: McGraw–Hill.

Kleinmuntz, B. (Ed.). (1968). *Formal representation of human judgement.* New York: Wiley.

Kleinmuntz, B. (1987). Automated interpretation of neuropsychological test data: Comments on Adams and Heaton. *Journal of Consulting and Clinical Psychology, 55,* 266–267.

Kline, P. (1986). *A handbook of test construction.* New York: Methuen.

Kolb, B., & Whishaw, I. Q. (1985). *Fundamentals of human neuropsychology* (2nd ed.). New York: W. H. Freeman.

Lewis, R. F., & Rennick, P. M. (1979). *Manual for the Repeatable Cognitive–Motor Battery.* Grosse Pointe Park, MI: Axon.

Lezak, M. D. (1983). *Neuropsychological assessment* (2nd ed.). New York: Oxford University Press.

Lezak, M. D. (1984). An individualized approach to neuropsychological assessment. In P. E. Logue & J. M. Shear (Eds.), *Clinical neuropsychology: A multidisciplinary approach* (pp. 29–49). Springfield, IL: Charles C. Thomas.

Luria, A. R. (1973). *The working brain.* New York: Basic Books.

Luria, A. R. (1980). *Higher cortical functions in man* (rev. ed.). New York: Basic Books.

Luria, A. R., & Majovski, L. V. (1977). Basic approaches used in American and Soviet clinical neuropsychology. *American Psychologist, 32,* 959–968.

Mapou, R. L. (1988). Testing to detect brain damage: An alternative to what may no longer be useful. *Journal of Clinical and Experimental Neurology, 10,* 271–278.

Matarazzo, J. D. (1972). *Measurement and appraisal of adult intelligence* (5th ed.). Baltimore: Williams & Wilkins.

Nunnally, J. C. (1978). *Psychometric theory* (2nd ed.). New York: McGraw–Hill.

Pauker, J. D. (1977, February). *Adult norms for the Halstead–Reitan Neuropsychological Test Battery: Preliminary data.* Paper presented at the Annual Meeting of the International Neuropsychological Society, Santa Fe, NM.

Pellegrino, J. W. (1988). Mental models and mental tests. In H. Wainer & H. I. Braun (Eds.), *Test validity* (pp. 49–59). Hillsdale, NJ: Lawrence Erlbaum Associates.

Pendleton, M. G., Heaton, R. K., Lehman, R. W., & Hulihan, D. (1982). The diagnostic utility of the Thurstone Word Fluency Test in neuropsychological evaluations. *Journal of Clinical Neuropsychology, 4,* 307–317.

Reitan, R. M. (1955a). An investigation of the validity of Halstead's measures of biological intelligence. *Archives of Neurology and Psychiatry, 73,* 28–35.

Reitan, R. M. (1955b). The distribution according to age of a psychologic measure dependent upon organic brain functions. *Journal of Gerontology, 10,* 338–340.

Reitan, R. M. (1964). Psychological deficits resulting from cerebral lesions in men. In J. M. Warren & K. Akert (Eds.), *The frontal granular cortex and behavior* (pp. 295–312). New York: McGraw–Hill.

Reitan, R. M. (1991). *The Neuropsychological Deficit Scale for adults, computer program, users manual.* Tucson, AZ: Neuropsychology Press.

Reitan, R. M., & Wolfson, D. (1985). *The Halstead-Reitan Neuropsychological Test Battery; Theory and clinical interpretation.* Tucson, AZ: Neuropsychology Press.

Reitan, R. M., & Wolfson, D. (1986). The Halstead-Reitan Neuropsychological Test Battery. In D. Wedding, A. M. Horton, & J. Webster (Eds.), *The neuropsychology handbook* (pp. 134–160). New York: Springer.

Rourke, B. P. (1991). Human neuropsychology in the 1990's. *Archives of Clinical Neuropsychology, 6*, 1–14.

Rourke, B. P., & Brown, G. G. (1986). Clinical neuropsychology and behavioral neurology: Similarities and differences. In S. B. Filskov & T. J. Boll (Eds.), *Handbook of clinical neuropsychology* (Vol. 2, pp. 3–18). New York: Wiley.

Russell, E. W. (1972). The effect of acute lateralized brain damage on a factor analysis of the Wechsler-Bellevue Intelligence Test. *Proceedings, 80th Annual Convention of the American Psychological Association*, Honolulu.

Russell, E. W. (1974). The effect of acute lateralized brain damage on Halstead's Biological Intelligence Factors. *Journal of General Psychology, 90*, 101–107.

Russell, E. W. (1975). A multiple scoring method for the assessment of complex memory functions. *Journal of Consulting and Clinical Psychology, 43*, 800–809.

Russell, E. W. (1979). Three patterns of brain damage on the WAIS. *Journal of Clinical Psychology, 37*, 246–253.

Russell, E. W. (1980a). Fluid and crystallized intelligence: Effects of diffuse brain damage on the WAIS. *Perceptual and Motor Skills, 51*, 121–122.

Russell, E. W. (1980b). *Theoretical bases of the Luria-Nebraska and the Halstead-Reitan Battery.* Paper presented at the 88th Annual Convention of the American Psychological Association, Montreal.

Russell, E. W. (1984). Theory and developments of pattern analysis methods related to the Halstead–Reitan battery. In P. E. Logue & J. M. Shear (Eds.), *Clinical neuropsychology: A multidisciplinary approach* (pp. 50–98). Springfield, IL: Charles C. Thomas.

Russell, E. W. (1986). The psychometric foundation of clinical neuropsychology. In S. B. Filskov & T. J. Boll (Eds.), *Handbook of clinical neuropsychology* (Vol. 2, pp. 45–80). New York: Wiley.

Russell, E. W. (1987). A reference scale method for constructing neuropsychological test batteries. *Journal of Clinical and Experimental Neuropsychology, 9*, 376–392.

Russell, E. W. (1988). Renorming Russell's version of the Wechsler Memory Scale. *Journal of Clinical and Experimental Neuropsychology, 10*, 235–249.

Russell, E. W. (1990, August). *Three validity studies for negative neurological criterion norming.* Paper presented at the 98th Annual Convention of the American Psychological Association, Boston.

Russell, E. W. (1991). A reference scale method for constructing neuropsychological test batteries. In B. P. Rourke, L. Costa, D. V. Cicchetti, K. M. Adams, & J. Plasterk (Eds.), *Methodological and biostatistical foundations of clinical neuropsychology* (pp. 399–415). Berwyn, PA: Swets & Zeitlinger.

Russell, E. W., Hendrickson, M. E., & VanEaton, E. (1988). Verbal and figural Gestalt Completion Tests with lateralized occipital area brain damage. *Journal of Clinical Psychology, 44*, 217–225.

Russell, E. W., & Levy, M. (1987). A revision of the Halstead Category Test. *Journal of Consulting and Clinical Psychology, 55*, 898–901.

Russell, E. W., Neuringer, C., & Goldstein, G. (1970). *Assessment of brain damage: A neuropsychological approach.* New York: Wiley.

Russell, E. W., & Polakoff, D. (1993). Neuropsychological test patterns in men for Alzheimer's and multi-infarct dementia. *Archives of Clinical Neuropsychology, 8*, 327–343.

Russell, E. W., & Russell, S. L. K. (1993). Left temporal lobe damage pattern on the Wechsler Adult Intelligence Scale: An addendum. *Journal of Clinical Psychology, 49*, 241–244.

Russell, E. W., & Starkey, R. I. (1993). *Halstead, Russell Neuropsychological Evaluation System* [Manual and Computer program]. Los Angeles: Western Psychological Services.

Russell, E. W., Starkey, R. I., Fernandez, C. D., & Starkey, T. W. (1988). *Halstead, Rennick, Russell Battery* [Manual and Computer program]. Miami: Scientific Psychology.

Seashore, C. B., Lewis, C., & Saetveit, J. G. (1960). *Seashore Measure of Musical Talent: Manual.* New York: Psychological Corporation.

Swiercinsky, D. P. (1978). *Computerized SAINT: System for analysis and interpretation of neuropsychological tests.* Presented at the annual meeting of the American Psychological Association, Toronto.

Tarter, R. E., & Edwards, K. L. (1986). Neuropsychological batteries. In T. Incagnoli, G. Goldstein, & C. J. Golden (Eds.), *Clinical application of neuropsychological test batteries* (pp. 135–153). New York: Plenum Press.

Teuber, H. L. (1955). Physiological psychology. *Annual Review of Psychology, 6,* 267–296.

Teuber, H. L. (1975). Recovery of function after brain injury. In Ciba Foundation Symposium 34, *Outcome of severe damage to the central nervous system* (pp. 159–190). Amsterdam: Elsevier.

Walsh, K. W. (1978). *Neuropsychology, a clinical approach.* New York: Churchill Livingstone.

Wechsler, D. (1939). *The measurement of adult intelligence.* Baltimore: Williams & Wilkins.

Wedding, D. (1983a). Clinical and statistical prediction. *Clinical Neuropsychology, 5,* 49–55.

Wedding, D. (1983b). Comparison of statistical and actuarial models for predicting lateralization of brain damage. *Clinical Neuropsychology, 4,* 15–20.

Werner, H. (1937). Process and achievement: A basic problem of education and developmental psychology. *Harvard Educational Review, 7,* 353–368.

Werner, H. (1956). Microgenesis and aphasia. *Journal of Abnormal and Social Psychology, 52,* 347–353.

CHAPTER EIGHT

The Flexible Battery Approach to Neuropsychological Assessment

Russell M. Bauer
University of Florida

Clinical neuropsychology represents an increasingly well-defined and well-respected specialty within the neuroscientific community. The field has enjoyed great success not only in contributing to scientific knowledge about brain–behavior relationships, but also in applying such knowledge through the provision of humane and effective assessment, treatment, and advocacy services for persons with CNS impairment. Of all these activities, *assessment* of the behavioral and cognitive effects of brain disease has been by far the most common applied task performed by neuropsychologists (Meier, 1974), and a great number of testing instruments has emerged over the past few decades. These instruments, known as neuropsychological tests, represent formal observation-measurement systems in which behavior is examined under certain specified conditions and evaluated against normative or individual comparison standards (cf. Lezak, 1983).

Despite the fact that most neuropsychologists would agree as to the major purposes of the discipline, there is great diversity of opinion about which procedures best achieve the goals of clinical assessment (Kane, 1991). Even when basic psychometric yardsticks such as test reliability and validity are considered, there is a wide range of opinion about the stability or accuracy of neuropsychological measures and about the relative importance of criterion-oriented versus construct-validity considerations in test development. Because of this diversity, there are no consensually agreed-upon "acid tests" or even empirical criteria (other than basic standards of reliability and validity) for including or excluding particular tests in one's neuropsychological toolbox. The selection of specific neuropsychological tests thus remains an individual professional decision.

Most modern neuropsychological test procedures derive either from the psychometric tradition within clinical psychology (cf. Russell, 1986) or from the information-processing tradition in cognitive psychology (Neisser, 1967) and experimental neuropsychology (Ellis & Young, 1986; McCarthy & Warrington, 1990). Most contemporary neuropsychologists are sufficiently familiar with these two great traditions to be confronted by literally hundreds of instruments having potential diagnostic utility in the neuropsychological setting. As a result, every practicing neuropsychologist must make fundamental decisions about which tests to use, which cognitive abilities to sample, how to balance breadth and depth, and how to relate behavioral test data to the underlying (physical) neurological substrate.

The issue of test selection can be illustrated by considering the following two case scenarios:

Case 1: A 62-year-old patient is referred from the Inpatient Psychiatry unit with a 9-month history of depression and progressive intellectual decline. Over the past 9 months, she has gradually withdrawn from family and social activities and has neglected personal finances and self-care. She is hospitalized for evaluation of recent well-formed visual hallucinations of "strangers in her house," and of her belief that her dead husband has sent these individuals to harass her. She has adapted well to the ward milieu, except that she needs prompting to perform even the most simple activities. She has not learned the names of her doctors and seems occasionally disoriented and lost when she attempts to return to her room from the dayroom.

Case 2: A 21-year-old college sophomore is referred for evaluation of the effects of a well-documented closed head injury in an alcohol-related automobile accident 18 months prior to the evaluation. The accident occurred in the early morning hours when the car the patient was driving crossed the center line on a rural highway and struck an oncoming truck. His best friend, a front-seat passenger in the car, was killed instantly. The patient was comatose at the scene of the accident and has an extensive period of post-traumatic amnesia. Although the parents deny any preinjury problems, academic records indicate that he was a C-D student before his injury, and that he had not yet picked a major field. Current problems include memory impairment, aggression and irritability toward family and friends, and poor academic performance since his return to school 6 months ago. The evaluation is requested by the patient's law firm. The patient himself seems disinterested in the evaluation and generally minimizes or denies having any significant postaccident problems.

The clinical issues faced by these two patients are quite different and, although both consultations may contain only minor variations on the simple request to "please evaluate," the referring professionals are likely to have very different questions in mind when they refer their patients for neuropsychological consultation. Whereas examination of Case 1 might require a detailed evaluation of intellectual and neuropsychological functioning and may incorporate formal evaluation of psychiatric symptomatology, the evaluation of Case 2 might focus more specifically on academic achievement, learning ability, and the capacity for behavioral self-control. The results of neuropsychological assessment may have different treatment relevance in the two cases. Especially in Case 2, specific impairments that exist in memory and attention/concentration might be used to help plan rehabilitation efforts or to design appropriate educational experiences. In contrast, neuropsychological test performance in Case 1 might be used to assist a differential diagnosis between depression and dementia, and repeated testing over time might be used to chart the course of the disease or to assess the effects of an intervening treatment.

It is important to ask whether such differences in purpose or focus will be reflected in the neuropsychological assessment plan. Some clinicians take the point of view that, despite such differences, both referrals require, as a starting point, a comprehensive assessment of neuropsychological skills. For others, the tests selected in response to these two referrals will be quite different and will reflect the different goals of assessment in these two instances. The previous chapter described the "fixed battery approach," in which the clinician gives the same tests to every patient regardless of the specific referral question. This chapter describes another approach, the "flexible battery approach," in which the nature of the patient's neuropsychological deficits helps determine the direction the evaluation will take.

Before discussing the distinctive characteristics of the flexible battery approach, it should be noted that *flexibility* as a dimension in neuropsychological assessment refers more directly to a way of thinking about the neuropsychological assessment process than to the specific tests or assessment protocols that are used in the course of case evaluation. As we see later, many flexible battery clinicians do, in fact, utilize a limited "core" battery of neuropsychological tests (Milberg, Hebben, & Kaplan, 1986). However, such a core is used primarily to provide a basis for generating pertinent clinical hypotheses about the patient's neuropsychological status; the subsequent course of the evaluation and the manner in which such tests are used will depend on the strengths and weaknesses of the individual patient, and on the dimensions of performance that are important in describing the patient's problem (Goodglass, 1986).

The flexible battery approach is different, both pragmatically and conceptually, from the more prevalent fixed battery strategy. Such differences are discussed in the next section, after which an intermediate position between fixed and flexible approaches (the "multiple fixed battery") is defined. Most flexible battery approaches emanate from a preferred theoretical position regarding (a) the manner in which behavioral impairment reflects underlying brain pathology, and (b) the focus and methodology of the neuropsychological examination. Three such positions, the neuropsychological investigative program of Luria, the European cognitive neuropsychology approach, and the Boston process approach, are highlighted. The specific skills and knowledge required of a flexible battery proponent are then described, and advantages and limitations of the flexible battery approach are outlined. The chapter concludes with an assertion that both fixed and flexible battery approaches reflect an important part of our heritage, and that effective clinical practice typically utilizes elements of both.

DISTINGUISHING "FIXED" AND "FLEXIBLE" BATTERIES

"Fixed" and "flexible" battery approaches have been distinguished in three ways. Important differences exist in (a) the nature and timing of test-selection decisions, (b) the relative reliance on psychometric versus neurologic concepts in conceptualizing the process and goals of neuropsychological assessment, and (c) the relative emphasis placed on quantitative versus qualitative performance criteria in case formulations and interpretations. Each of these distinctions is briefly discussed.

Nature and Timing of Test-Selection Decisions

In the fixed battery approach, decisions regarding test selection are made a priori, whereas in the flexible battery approach, decision making occurs "on line" in a Markovian (decision-tree-oriented) manner. Implementation of the flexible battery approach involves a process of selection, hypothesis testing, and selective attention to relevant subsets of data (Rourke & Brown, 1986). Data collection is selective in the sense that decisions made early in the assessment focus the specific direction the evaluation will take and thus limit the domains of behavior assessed (Rourke & Brown, 1986). Whether such selectivity clarifies the relevant issues or blinds the examiner to other possibilities depends largely on whether correct decisions are made early in the process.

The flexible battery clinician views the neuropsychological examination as an "experiment-in-evolution" in that both the methods used, and the results obtained, change as a function of early data returns. For the most part, flexible batteries represent clinical applications of the classic hypothetico–deductive method, the purpose of which is to uncover meaningful cause–effect relationships between independent and dependent variables. Quantitative and qualitative performance measures comprise the relevant dependent measures. Three sets of independent variables (dimensions of brain function, organismic variables [age, education, pre-illness abilities, etc.], and task factors) combine interactively to produce the complex behavioral outcomes observed on neuropsychological tests.

One important feature of the hypothetico–deductive method is that possible accounts of a phenomenon (e.g., a test performance) are phrased in the form of experimental hypotheses that can be tested empirically. Attention is gradually focused on those hypotheses that survive experimental disconfirmation (Platt, 1966; Popper, 1959). The virtues of this approach to neuropsychological assessment are apparent when it is considered that most neuropsychological tests impose diverse input, processing, and output demands on the patient. That is, most neuropsychological tests are multifactorial; in addition to the more obvious "face valid" ways of describing neuropsychological tests as measures of memory, language, attention, and so forth, a more microgenetic analysis suggests that such tests can be described and classified in terms of input (task), processing (solution), and output (response) requirements.

On the input side, most conventional neuropsychological tests provide stimuli to one sensory–perceptual channel (visual, auditory, tactile), so that hypotheses related to a pattern of deficits across tasks can be evaluated in terms of whether a specific sensory modality is involved. Second, tasks can be grouped in terms of whether they impose the same, or similar, information-processing requirements on subjects. Although no comprehensive classification of such requirements is available, tests can be easily classified in terms of their reliance on certain "levels" of processing (e.g., phonological, orthographic, semantic, etc.; see Craik & Lockhart, 1972) and in terms of their relative demands on data-driven versus conceptually driven processes (Jacoby, 1983). Finally, tasks can be described and classified in terms of the output demands (e.g., verbal, graphomotor, pointing, naming, etc.) imposed on the patient. Whereas this descriptive analysis of neuropsychological tests is intended to be heuristic, hypothesis disconfirmation is often threatened by the fact that most neuropsychological tests are not "pure" in terms of their input, processing, and output demands. Because of this, most tests can be failed (or passed) for many different reasons. Thus, simply knowing a patient's score on such a test may reveal little about the why or how such a score was achieved. A flexible process of hypothesis formulation and hypothesis testing is frequently needed to more precisely characterize the nature of the impairment. This is why the flexible battery approach has sometimes been referred to as the *hypothesis-testing approach* (cf. Lezak, 1983).

The fundamentals of the flexible approach can be illustrated by considering a common clinical example. WAIS-R Digit Symbol is one of the most sensitive tests to neurologic damage (Kaplan, Fein, Morris, & Delis, 1991; Lezak, 1983). It is a complex test that requires graphomotor speed, symbol manipulation, short-term memory, visual acuity, and manual dexterity. If Digit Symbol is impaired, a deficit in any or all of these skills might be implicated. Determining the cause of such impairment requires treating these dimensions as independent variables and then performing subsequent testing in which the potential influence of each variable is manipulated and the resulting effects on behaviors are observed. For example, the influence of unfamiliar symbol manipulation can be evaluated by presenting the patient with symbols, and requiring him or her to respond with more familiar numbers (this is one basis of the Symbol Digit Modalities Test; Smith, 1973). If the patient's performance level is improved by this maneuver, then a difficulty with processing of unfamiliar symbols remains as a viable explanation of the defect because its manipulation resulted in task improvement. If not, then other factors remain alive as rival explanations of the deficit in Digit Symbol. Subsequent testing would then attempt to evaluate the potential contribution of all potential factors that survived disconfirmation. In some cases, the examiner must create new tests or modify existing instruments for purposes of more precisely zeroing in on which input, processing, or output dimension is responsible for the patient's deficit. Neuropsychological modifications of existing psychometric tests have been a particularly important contribution of the Boston "process approach" to neuropsychological assessment (Kaplan, 1983, 1990; Kaplan et al., 1991; Milberg et al., 1986).

Reliance on "Psychometric" Versus "Neurologic" Concepts

Russell (1986) distinguished between psychometric versus behavioral–neurologic approaches to neuropsychology, and the fixed versus flexible battery distinction reflects this dichotomy in a general way. The best historical example of the fixed battery approach, the Halstead-Reitan Neuropsychological Battery (cf. Parsons, 1986, for review), arose directly from the parent field of "mental abilities testing" and flourished largely because of its formidable psychometric strengths. Among the most important of these was criterion-oriented validity; the HRNB has, in many studies, been shown to have proven utility in detecting the presence, lateralization, and localization of brain dysfunction as defined by neurologic criteria such as clinical examination and neuroradiological findings (e.g., Boll, 1981; Filskov & Goldstein, 1974; Kløve, 1974). The focus on statistical prediction gave rise to a general reliance on a broad, fixed battery of tests as the fundamental basis of neuropsychological assessment. A broad, comprehensive battery was favored because of its perceived sensitivity and because of its ability to evaluate patients for general indications of brain dysfunction (Goldstein, 1986; Kane, 1991; Russell, 1986), and a "fixed" battery was favored because it encouraged rapid proliferation of a database necessary for establishing stable normative comparison standards.

Whereas psychometric approaches have focused on statistical prediction of brain damage from psychological tests, the neurologic approach has historically emphasized the examination of brain-behavior relationships through analysis of behavioral syndromes and pathognomic signs on the single-case level (cf. Rourke & Brown, 1986). This intensive "case-analytic" method has been particularly favored in settings in which neuropsychological assessment is conducted for purposes of qualifying, rather than identifying, the behavioral effects of brain damage. With recent advances in clinical and radiologic diagnosis in neurology (cf. Mazziotta & Gilman, 1992), neuropsychologists are consulted less frequently to detect or localize brain impairment. Instead, they are more likely to be asked to evaluate the nature or underlying cause of a neuropsychological complaint (e.g., in memory, perception, or attention) or to attempt to elicit behavioral signs that might help differentiate between two behaviorally similar disorders (e.g., organic dementia vs. dementia syndrome of depression; cf. Caine, 1986; LaRue, D'Elia, Clark, Spar, & Jarvik, 1986; Richards & Ruff, 1989). Because of this, it is increasingly important to discover the specific character of the observed defect and the causes or factors responsible for its appearance. This is what Luria (1980), Vygotsky, and others have called "qualification of the symptom."

Recognition of the fundamental importance of this latter goal has led to the use of flexible batteries designed to be more specifically responsive to the deficits with which the individual patient presents. In describing the rationale underlying such flexibility, Luria (1980) wrote:

> the neuropsychologist who has the task of diagnosing a patient's condition does not know which process or which aspect of the patient's mental activity should be the focal point for subsequent investigation. He must first make preliminary studies of the patient's mental processes, and from these preliminary results he must single out the crucial changes and then subject them to further scrutiny. (p. 388)

Luria's flexible approach is based on the idea that the neuropsychological examination should be constructed to result in a qualitative, structural analysis of the patient's symptoms, rather than to binary statements regarding whether an ability is "spared" or "impaired."

Reliance on "Quantitative" Versus "Qualitative" Data

Although the psychometric tradition has been primarily concerned with the quantification and measurement of cognitive and mental abilities, neurology has been more concerned with (a) eliciting characteristic signs and symptoms of brain disease, and (b) linking behavioral syndromes to regional brain function through a process of anatomico–clinical correlation. This distinction reflects a relative reliance on quantitative versus qualitative data, and some have argued that fixed battery clinicians rely more heavily on quantitative criteria, whereas flexible battery clinicians are more interested in qualitative data. While this argument is generally correct, it is important to note that adopting a flexible battery approach does not in any way require the clinician to neglect or de-emphasize quantitative data, nor is it necessarily true (as some have asserted) that fixed battery proponents are unconcerned with qualitative aspects of performance. As Incagnoli (1986) indicated, the quantitative/qualitative distinction refers more directly to the manner in which neuropsychological test data are evaluated rather than to the method of administration by which the data are obtained.

One of the most important contributions of psychometrics to neuropsychological assessment has been the introduction of a variety of neuropsychological tests that are comprised of a series of relatively homogeneous items and that involve at least interval-level measurement and that meet appropriate standards of reliability and validity (Rourke & Brown, 1986). Such tests yield numerical scores (e.g., number of items passed) that can be evaluated by comparing the subject's performance to appropriate normative standards. Numerical scores can reflect the extent to which an ability is affected in the individual case. Scores on individual tests are often combined in complex (multivariate) ways to form the basis for interpreting the results of the battery (cf. discussion of "pattern analysis" in the previous chapter). For example, decades of research with the HRNB have yielded quantitative criteria for inferring presence–absence of brain impairment, laterality, lesion size/type (e.g., diffuse vs. focal; acute vs. chronic), and intrahemispheric locus of damage (Boll, 1981; Russell, 1986; Russell, Neuringer, & Goldstein, 1970). It is important to recognize that strong reliance on quantitative indicators almost always implies a fixed battery approach because such indicators depend on full, balanced data sets.

In contrast to a quantitative performance analysis, a qualitative analysis is primarily intended to reveal the factors responsible for failure or success on neuropsychological tests, rather than to indicate nominal success or failure. Concern with the reasons for impairment rather than the presence of impairment often requires adjustive testing procedures because most neuropsychological tests can be failed (or passed) in a number of different ways. Thus, attempts to elicit qualitative signs of brain impairment have tended to involve a flexible battery approach. In the literature, the term *qualitative* has been used to describe analyses based either on the patient's approach to a cognitively complex task (the distinction between *process* and *achievement*; cf. Kaplan, 1983) or to refer to an analytic method designed to isolate the functional basis of a neuropsychological deficit in information-processing terms (Luria, 1980; McCarthy & Warrington, 1990). These two meanings of the term are discussed more fully in the next section.

Although I have aligned "fixed" with "quantitative" and "flexible" with "qualitative", it is not accurate to say that fixed battery proponents are unconcerned with qualitative data or that flexible battery practitioners neglect quantitative criteria. Evidence to the contrary can be found in the writings of fixed (Reitan & Davison, 1974) and flexible (McKenna & Warrington, 1986) proponents alike, and the recent process modification of the WAIS-R (WAIS-R-NI; Kaplan et al., 1991) is a practical tour de force in how so called qualitative performance features can be measured and analyzed in quantitative terms. Lezak (1983) expressed the dominant opinion that "to do justice to the complexity, variability, and subtleties of patient behavior, the neuropsychologist . . . needs to consider quantitative and qualitative data together" (p. 131). The main difference between fixed and flexible battery proponents appears to be in the relative weight given to quantitative and qualitative test data.

Rourke and Brown (1986) provided a convincing argument that quantitative and qualitative data are more closely related than they may seem at first glance. In fact, most qualitative performance dimensions can be, and have been, quantified in meaningful ways (e.g., Goldberg & Costa, 1986; Kaplan et al., 1991). For example, Kaplan et al. (1991) advocated the use of a "scatter score" that characterizes performance variability within several of the WAIS-R subtests. Each time the patient passes one item and fails the next (or vice versa), a scatter score of 1 is recorded (otherwise, a 0 is registered). Because items within each of these tests are difficulty graded, it is frequently the case that a patient will pass earlier items and will then reach a threshold beyond which failure will occur relatively consistently. Such a pattern will result in a relatively low scatter score. Large scatter results from the situation in which there is inconsistent responding from item to item and may reflect variable effort, waxing and waning attention, or some other "state" variable. Quantitative evidence of such problems, derived from what is essentially a qualitative variable, may be important in the differential diagnosis of a variety of conditions, including epilepsy, attention-deficit disorder, closed head injury, major depressive disorder, or other forms of serious psychopathology.

AN INTERMEDIATE APPROACH:
MULTIPLE FIXED BATTERIES

In many settings, the referral base is sufficiently varied, and the ability of the neuropsychologist sufficiently sophisticated, to result in the implementation of distinct protocols for different diagnoses, referral questions, or referral sources. Here, the clinician makes an a priori decision to tailor the assessment approach to the individual case by subjecting each homogeneous patient group to a different subset of available tests. Such decisions may be based on predictive validity considerations (e.g., what best predicts outcome or clinical status in a given population), or on a more informal assessment of what is meaningful and useful for a given question or referral source. This approach represents an intermediate position between *fixed* and *flexible* batteries in that it combines a priori test selection with a recognition that the neuropsychological test protocol should directly target the unique problems presented by different patient groups.

Three types of multiple fixed batteries can be distinguished: the general "screening" battery, the "population-specific" battery, and the "domain-specific" battery. General screening batteries contain a wide variety of maximally sensitive items designed to elicit clinically relevant abnormalities worthy of more detailed, follow-up testing. Population-specific batteries provide more extensive guidelines for the evaluation of individual patient populations or disease entities (e.g., epilepsy, HIV seropositive status, neurotoxic exposure, multiple sclerosis, etc.) and are widely used in clinical research settings where the goal is to provide a selective but standardized evaluation of cognitive domains judged to be most relevant to diagnosis or treatment outcome. The domain-specific batteries contain procedures designed to provide a detailed assessment of a particular cognitive domain (e.g., language, memory, visuospatial/perceptual skill). Examples of each of these types of batteries are provided in Table 8.1.

The multiple fixed battery approach is, like the flexible battery, designed to be "problem specific." The specific cognitive skills that are sampled in such problem-specific batteries are based on empirical as well as clinical considerations. Available clinical and research literature serves

TABLE 8.1

Some Examples of Screening, Population-Specific, and Domain-Specific Batteries

Battery Name	Reference	Domains Assessed
A. Screening Batteries		
Dementia Rating Scale (DRS)	Mattis, 1988	attention, initiation, perseveration, memory, construction, language
Pittsburgh Initial Neuropsychological Test System (PINTS)	Goldstein, Tarter, Shelly, & Hegedus, 1983	intelligence, memory, motor and constructional skill
Neurobehavioral Cognitive Status Examination (NCSE)	Kiernan, Mueller, Langston, & Van Dyke, 1987 Mysiw, Beegan, & Gatens, 1989	consciousness, orientation, attention, language (comprehension, naming), construction, memory, calculation, reasoning (similarities, judgment)
B. Population-Specific Batteries		
NIMH AIDS Battery	Butters et al., 1990	attention, speed of processing, memory, abstraction, language, visual perception, construction, motor functions, psychiatric symptoms
WHO Neurotoxicology Battery	World Health Organization & Nordic Council of Ministers Working Group, 1985	visuomotor skill, reaction time, visual memory, mental tracking, mood
Epilepsy Battery	Dodrill, 1978	intelligence, verbal and nonverbal memory, language screening, visuomotor skill, abstraction, attention, motor speed, sensory–perceptual
Multiple Sclerosis Battery	Peyser, Rao, LaRocca, & Kaplan, 1990	global dementia screening, fund of information, attention–concentration, memory, language, visuospatial skills, abstract reasoning, concept formation

(Continued)

269

TABLE 8.1
(Continued)

Battery Name	Reference	Domains Assessed
C. Domain-Specific Batteries		
Boston Diagnostic Aphasia Examination	Goodglass & Kaplan, 1972	34 subtests in 9 defined areas of language (fluency, auditory comprehension, naming, oral reading, repetition, paraphasia, automatic speech, reading comprehension, writing); 2 tests of musical competence; 7 subtests in the spatial-quantitative battery (drawing to command, stick memory, 3-D blocks, finger agnosia, right–left orientation, map orientation, arithmetic, clock setting)
Boston Spatial-Quantitative Battery (BDAE and "Parietal Lobe Battery")		
Western Aphasia Battery (WAB)	Kertesz, 1979	similar to Boston Diagnostic Aphasia Examination
Multilingual Aphasia Examination (MAE)	Benton & Hamsher, 1989	visual naming, oral word productivity, auditory comprehension, repetition (memory span for words), spelling, reading comprehension, ratings of articulation and writing praxis
Memory Assessment Clinics Memory Battery	Crook, Salama, & Gobert, 1986 Crook & Larrabee, 1988	facial recognition, paired-associate memory, facial memory (delayed nonmatch to sample), memory for object location, digit memory (telephone dialing), recall of TV news broadcast, reaction time in simulated automobile driving task; attempts to make memory testing more 'ecologically valid'; computer-assisted

as the basis for determining which clinical procedures (a) most likely differentiate target patients from those without the target deficit and (b) yield information most relevant to clinical decision making. Such an approach requires a clinician who is experienced in dealing with the target population, and who is attuned to the diagnostic and prescriptive contributions that neuropsychological evaluation can make to patient care.

Although the decision to adopt a multiple fixed battery approach is often theory-driven, such an approach may emerge for purely practical reasons. For example, the clinician may become aware that an individual referral source (e.g., an agency, a physician, a school system) makes use of a specific set of assessment instruments, so a decision is made to administer these instruments to any individual, regardless of specific diagnosis, referred from that source. For example, tests of intellectual ability and academic achievement might be included in any learning-disability referral from the local school system, regardless of their apparent relevance for each individual case. The decision to employ such tests might be based primarily on statutory definitions of learning disability (e.g., a significant IQ-achievement split) and only secondarily on a theoretical model of learning disability. Similarly, a multiple fixed battery approach might informally evolve as a way of handling different referral questions. For example, a specific set of tests (including learning capacity, interpersonal adaptation and motivation, and vigilance) might be employed in a battery designed to assess rehabilitation potential, while a different set of tests might be employed in the evaluation of effects of seizure surgery. Decisions about which tests to include in the protocol should, of course, be based on a measured evaluation of the kinds of information needed to make important diagnostic or treatment decisions in the clinical environment.

Multiple fixed batteries can also be used sequentially in the form of a "tiered" approach to neuropsychological assessment. Here, increasingly stringent, or restricted, criteria are placed on neuropsychological test performances such that patients who meet certain criteria are subjected to further testing. Such an approach has been described as a *step battery* (Tarter & Edwards, 1986) and has been characterized as a method of "successive hurdles" (Rourke & Brown, 1986). Here, an initial "screening" battery is given to all patients, followed by specific tests designed to pursue potentially significant findings. Based on results of the initial screening battery, a decision is made to expose the patient to one of several available "sub-batteries" designed to evaluate specific domains of neuropsychological performance. The decision to admit the patient for further testing is largely made on the basis of quantitative criteria (i.e., whether tests within the screening battery were passed or failed; Tarter & Edwards, 1986).

The screening tier usually addresses a broad range of neuropsychological functions (e.g., intellectual performance, attention, memory, language, visuoperceptual, and psychomotor processes). It is designed to be maximally sensitive and minimally specific to neuropsychological impairment. Depending on the results obtained, a more restricted and in-depth battery of tests follows. For example, a more specific battery of memory tests would be given to a patient who, on the basis of the screening examination, has an apparent memory disorder. Similar domain-specific batteries would be available for patients with disorders of language, attention, problem solving, and so forth. Several such domain-specific batteries might be employed by the clinician who wants to implement a more exhaustive evaluation of a neuropsychological deficit. The domain-specific batteries are populated by tests capable of yielding increasingly specific information about the patient's pattern of strengths and weaknesses within the specific cognitive domain being assessed.

Tarter and Edwards (1986) provided a clear three-stage example of this approach. The first stage involves a screening battery that measures a broad variety of skills including intellect, memory, language, perceptual skill, problem solving, and attention. Because of the nature of the screening battery, only a limited number of maximally sensitive tests are included. If the patient does well on the screening battery, assessment is terminated. If she or he fails a particular area, she or he is admitted to the second stage, which involves either intensive assessment of specific modalities (e.g., vision) or a specialized set of tests designed to provide a more in-depth evaluation of one or more of the major categories of neuropsychological skill (e.g., memory, language, etc.). Based on the results of this stage, assessment is either terminated or the patient is admitted for what Tarter and Edwards call "idiographic testing." They state that this phase of the evaluation is appropriate when specific aspects of the case call for more specialized assessment than would normally be afforded by the fixed battery. Tarter and Edwards (1986) cautioned against a formalized decision tree in this phase, suggesting that, "at this stage of the assessment, clinician judgement and experience are crucial for selecting the most appropriate measures and for obtaining maximal information . . . from the client" (p. 146).

THREE FLEXIBLE APPROACHES

Having described the basic features of the flexible battery approach, it now becomes important to review the basic conceptual models that most flexible battery clinicians employ in interpreting neuropsychological test data. In addition to the distinguishing features I described in a previous section, flexible batteries are different from fixed batteries in that they typically are conducted from the point of view of a theoretical model of brain function. Because of this, most flexible battery clinicians construct their assessments in a way that will conform to theoretical assumptions about the manner in which specific kinds of brain damage will affect cognitive abilities. These models guide clinicians in understanding and conceptualizing the ways in which cognitive abilities are affected by neurological disease and provide a basis for test selection.

One of the distinctive characteristics of the flexible battery approach to neuropsychological assessment is its hypothesis-testing orientation. The specific hypotheses that are tested in a given patient are largely dependent on the clinician's theoretical preferences. Three conceptual frameworks that commonly drive hypothesis formulation in the flexible battery framework include the neuropsychological investigative program of Luria (1973), the analytic strategy within European cognitive neuropsychology (Ellis & Young, 1986; McCarthy & Warrington, 1990; McKenna & Warrington, 1986), and the Boston "process" approach to neuropsychological assessment (Kaplan, 1983, 1990; Kaplan et al., 1991; Milberg et al., 1986). Each of these frameworks is briefly described next.

Luria's Neuropsychological Investigation

Luria's (1980) neuropsychological investigation is most widely known in the United States through Christensen's (1979) compilation of his qualitative techniques into a coherent battery. Luria's assessment approach is based on an integrated theory of brain function and his neuropsychological assessment techniques flow directly from specific aspects of his theory. The key relevance of Luria's views for neuropsychological assessment lies in his belief that the fundamental purpose of neuropsychological assessment is to describe the functional nature of neuropsychological symptoms, rather than their presence or absence in a given case. Luria's approach is thus essentially "qualitative" and is designed to describe the conditions under which a patient's problem becomes "clinically significant."

One of Luria's most important contributions was the introduction and formalization of the notion of a *functional system* in the brain. In Luria's terms, a functional system in the brain consists of a collection of brain regions and their interconnections. According to Luria, the system operates in an integrated, dynamic way to form the substrate for a complex psychological function. In the normal brain, for example, complex skills such as memory or perceptual ability are not discretely localized; instead, such processes depend on the integrated activity of diverse brain areas.

Taking memory as an example, several decades of research have implicated mesial temporal, diencephalic, and basal forebrain structures as the neural substrate for different forms of memory and learning (cf. Squire, 1987). It makes sense to speak of this distributed anatomic substrate as a functional system because such diverse regions appear to function in an integrated fashion to support complex mnestic skills. For neuropsychological assessment, the most important aspect of the functional systems view is the idea that the nature of the patient's cognitive deficit (i.e., the specific symptoms the patient exhibits) will differ depending on the specific location of the damage within the functional system, and on the response of the other (undamaged) system components to the loss. As indicated before, Luria believed that the neuropsychological investigation should be patient- and problem-centered and was particularly strong in his point of view that the examiner <u>could not know</u> what tests to give without first conducting preliminary evaluation of the patient's symptoms. Based on this preliminary analysis, specialized procedures designed to systematically explore the role of specific cognitive demands and input–output factors ensue. For Luria, the properly constructed examination includes tests of simple, complex, and integrative skill. Examination increasingly focuses on the manner in which problems are solved, rather than on whether they are solved.

Luria (1980) specifically rejected the use of a fixed battery, which he saw as useful only in providing general indications of brain impairment. He wrote:

> in order to gain a better understanding of the nature of the defects interfering with the performance of a particular task and to identify as precisely as possible the factor(s) responsible for the difficulties, it is not enough to merely carry out a particular experiment in the standard manner. The experiment must be suitably modified so that the conditions . . . . making the performance of the test more difficult, as well as those enabling compensation to take place, can be taken into account. (p. 392)

In addition to formalizing the notion of a functional system and describing pioneering assessment methods, Luria's approach is important for neuropsychology because it emphasizes the need to understand complex patterns of symptom presentation (the so-called "syndrome analysis" that is central to behavioral neurology) and their clinicopathological correlations with regional brain impairments. Because various brain regions potentially participate in a number of functional systems, localized brain lesions frequently lead to disturbances in a group of functional systems. The result is what Luria (1980) called a "symptom-complex" or syndrome, made up of "externally heterogeneous, but, in fact, internally interconnected symptoms'' (p. 83). Thus, for example, large lesions in the left-parieto-temporal-occipital junction may be associated with disturbances of language, praxis, visual object processing, naming, and other cognitive skills. Discovering and analyzing the basis of such symptom co-occurrence is, for Luria, an essential goal of the neuropsychological examination. As we see later, this means that clinicians practicing within this kind of flexible-battery framework must have basic familiarity with such syndromes if they are to appropriately plan and interpret a neuropsychological examination.

Cognitive Neuropsychology

The test-analytic strategy of European cognitive neuropsychology provides another example of the use of flexible-adjustive assessment methods. The cognitive neuropsychology approach is a relatively new approach that represents a hybrid between syndrome analysis in classical behavioral neurology and the information-processing tradition in cognitive psychology (Ellis & Young, 1986; McCarthy & Warrington, 1990). The major goal of cognitive neuropsychology as a discipline is to explain patterns of impaired and intact cognitive performance seen in brain-injured patients in terms of damage to one or more of the components of a *theory or model of normal cognitive functioning* (Coltheart, 1985; Ellis & Young, 1986). It is assumed that neurologic diseases produce orderly patterns of breakdown that reflect the way in which cognitive abilities are normally organized in the brain. Thus, an underlying model of normal function not only informs the clinical evaluation but also must account for selective neuropsychological disturbances seen in the clinic. In other words, the relationship between the underlying model and the appearance of selective behavioral deficit is bidirectional. Excellent examples of this bidirectionality are evident in the manner in which recent cognitive neuropsychological models of face recognition (e.g., Bruce & Young, 1986) or reading (e.g., Marshall & Newcombe, 1973) resulted in the introduction of new, highly specific, neuropsychological tests. As Shallice (1988) pointed out, the cognitive neuropsychology approach dates back at least to Wernicke's (1874) description of behavioral subtypes of aphasia, and his introduction of a model of language function that actually predicted the existence of patients who at that point had not yet been clinically discovered.

Flexible assessment procedures are important to the cognitive neuropsychology approach because different patients will suffer impairment at different points in the model. Observing behavioral dissociations (selective impairments in some skills, but not in others) is centrally important in drawing inferences about cognitive structure from neuropsychological test data, because they reveal something about how such skills are normally organized in the brain and help localize the deficit within the overall organizational schcme (McCarthy & Warrington, 1990; Shallice, 1988; Teuber, 1955).

For example, suppose a patient presents to the clinic with a specific inability to decipher the meaning of emotional facial expressions but is able to recognize facial identity and can extract age, gender, and other information from visual analysis of faces. The selectivity of this deficit serves as preliminary evidence that "emotion recognition" represents a discrete component in the overall organization of face-recognition abilities. This possibility will be strengthened if another patient can be found who shows the opposite pattern of performance. This is what is called a "double dissociation" and constitutes the strongest evidence of underlying cognitive structure because it rules out the possibility that the first patient's problem arose simply because emotion recognition was more difficult than recognizing age, gender, or identity.

Because the cognitive neuropsychology approach is driven by an underlying theory of information processing, research within this tradition has resulted in the discovery of new patients and in the creation of new tests of highly specific neuropsychological skill. Often, the cognitive basis for such new tests rests in theory, not in clinical data, and might not have been anticipated by even the most astute clinical observer. As indicated before, this was a striking characteristic of Wernicke's (1874) model of language disturbances. One good contemporary example comes from British work on visual object recognition (Humphreys & Riddoch, 1987; McCarthy & Warrington, 1990). Impairment in the ability to visually identify objects may result from significant primary visual sensory impairment, higher order perceptual difficulty, or from a failure in relating normal perception to stored memories of what familiar objects look like. To distinguish these possibilities, specific tests have been constructed at each of these three levels. At the first level, it is important to determine whether the patient has sufficient visual field, acuity, and shape-discrimination abilities to allow object recognition. At the second level, it is important to determine whether the patient is capable of forming an integrated visual percept of an object, and to ascertain whether the patient is able to perceptually categorize objects as belonging to the same functional or semantic class. Patients have been described, for example, who are capable of identifying the broad category to which a viewed object belongs but who fail to appreciate the object's specific identity (Warrington, 1975). The ability to form an integrated percept might be tested by requiring the subject to match familiar objects across different views (Warrington & James, 1986), whereas tests of perceptual categorization might require the subject to determine whether two objects belong together (McCarthy &

Warrington, 1986). It is important to recognize that such tests are not widely available on the commercial market and are usually constructed in the course of evaluating a single patient or a homogeneous group. For this reason, formal clinical application of the cognitive neuropsychology approach has not been widespread.

The Boston "Process" Approach

A third example of a flexible battery framework is the Boston process approach to neuropsychological assessment (Kaplan, 1983, 1990; Milberg et al., 1986). Drawing on the seminal contributions of Werner (1937), the process approach is based on the assumption that observing and reporting the manner in which a patient solves a problem (task "process") is more important in understanding his or her neuropsychological status than is simply observing and reporting success or failure (task "achievement"). The emphasis on the problem-solving approach itself is thought to be more useful than global summary scores to rehabilitation professionals who must have sufficient information about the nature of a patient's problem to be able to design an intervention strategy. Such knowledge is also potentially useful in monitoring recovery from brain injury.

The process approach asserts that performance on neuropsychological tests is importantly determined by the information-processing requirements of each task, and that a systematic analysis of the nature of a patient's deficits requires a Markovian approach in which patient-centered deficits are followed up with increasingly specific, or "process-pure," tests. In the process approach, an emphasis is placed on qualitative performance variables (e.g., how an item is passed or failed) in addition to whether it is passed or failed. For example, a patient who gets eight of nine blocks correct on the more difficult trials of block design will earn the same 0 score as a patient who eats or throws the blocks (Kaplan, personal communication). However, it is important to distinguish these two performances, because they might mean something different as regards the cognitive status of the patient.

As classically stated, the process approach involves increasingly fine-grained analysis of a patient's cognitive deficit by (a) systematically exploring and exploiting the information-processing requirements of otherwise standard tasks by attempting to control the input, processing, and output demands, and (b) requiring the subject to perform increasingly sensitive, or process-pure, measures until the specific nature of a cognitive deficit can be determined.

Proponents of the process approach contend that the strategy employed by the patient in attempting to solve problems must be examined if the patient is to be properly understood. Such strategies reflect a complex mix of variables related to premorbid status (e.g., educational and occupational history, handedness, specific talents) and to the patient's neurologic disease itself (e.g., lesion laterality, intrahemispheric focus, etiology). Because each patient will be characterized by a unique combination of these variables, the specific approach and testing procedures employed to elucidate the nature of a neuropsychological deficit may differ substantially from patient to patient.

Although the process approach utilizes many of the same clinical tests that are found in common fixed batteries, standardized tests are frequently modified to answer specific questions that arise during initial aspects of testing. The examiner may choose to "test the limits" by allowing the subject more time to complete the problem or by providing specific structure or cuing not present in the standard administration format. Importantly, such modifications are not random attempts to provide more data but are motivated by a knowledge of the neuropsychological demands imposed by each task and by an understanding of how specific neuropathological processes can affect response strategy. Two specific examples of strategic variables that have received recent attention illustrate this basic point.

1. Featural Versus Configurational Processing

Most common neuropsychological tests consist of a series of elements or basic stimuli arranged together within a spatial, temporal, or conceptual framework (Milberg et al., 1986). Therefore, one important strategic variable is the extent to which the patients differentially respond to low-level detail ("features") versus higher level configural or contextual information. According to proponents of the process approach, the "featural" versus "configural" dichotomy becomes particularly important in light of recent evidence that the left and right hemispheres may differ in their reliance on featural (left) versus configurational (right) processing. If this is true, then qualitatively different patterns of performance deficit might be expected to result from unilateral lesions of the right versus left hemisphere. This has been demonstrated in studies of Block Design performance in unilateral stroke patients (cf. Kaplan et al., 1991). Patients with right-hemisphere strokes (who suffer a relative impairment in configurational processing) more often break the 2×2 or 3×3 configuration, whereas patients with left-hemisphere damage (who are relatively impaired in the ability to process features) preserve the overall configuration but have specific difficulty correctly reproducing internal details (Kaplan, 1990; Kaplan et al., 1991). According to Milberg et al. (1986), the featural–configural distinction is not restricted to Block

Design but is a relatively stable variable that can manifest itself in numerous neuropsychological tests.

2. Hemispatial Priority

The two cerebral hemispheres differ not only in terms of their specific information-processing contributions to complex tasks but also in their contribution to overall deployment of attention across visual space. Although the attentional capacities of the two hemispheres are probably not equal, it is generally true, given the contralateral organization of sensory and motor skills, that each hemisphere "prefers" to process information and to direct activity in contralateral hemispace; that is, the right hemisphere likely is dominant in mediating activity taking place in the left side of personal space, and vice versa.

These considerations have led Kaplan (1990; Kaplan et al., 1991) to formulate a general rule that can be used to qualitatively evaluate performance on any task that takes place on both sides of the midline. This general rule states that the patient will prefer to work, or will perform better, in the side of space contralateral to the more intact hemisphere. Again using a Block Design example, the patient with a unilateral right-hemisphere lesion will be more likely to begin block construction on the right side of the design (contralateral to the more intact left hemisphere) and will construct the design in an unusual right-to-left manner. Because most individuals in Western cultures adopt a left-to-right strategy (because of the bias imposed by reading), perturbations of this dominant approach may have implications for diagnosing lesion laterality.

Because of its emphasis on the patient's problem-solving strategy, the process approach focuses on qualitative performance variables in addition to standard quantitative scores. As indicated earlier, however, such variables *can* be quantified and subjected to the same type of normative process as more traditional achievement measures. This, in fact, has been accomplished for selected tests and is a major feature of the WAIS-R-NI (WAIS-R as a Neuropsychological Instrument), a process-oriented approach to intellectual testing (Kaplan et al., 1991). In this context, it should be noted that adopting a process approach does not require the examiner to forfeit the usual quantitative scores; where possible, modifications to test administration have been designed in such a way as to allow the usual scores to be calculated. The reader is directed to the WAIS-R-NI manual for further details.

These three examples of the flexible battery approach share a basic belief that the goal of neuropsychological assessment should be to discover the specific nature of the patient's cognitive deficits. Although they emphasize different aspects of the overall picture, all seek to uncover the "structure" of such deficits, and all go beyond provision of quantitative summary scores or indices. One additional feature common to all three approaches is that the clinician practicing the flexible battery must have certain skills and knowledge about brain–behavior relationships to implement them effectively. It is to this topic that we now turn.

SKILLS REQUIRED OF THE FLEXIBLE BATTERY CLINICIAN

One of the primary goals of the flexible battery approach is to provide neuropsychological assessments that are responsive to the specific questions contained within a professional consultation or to the specific problems presented by an individual patient or patient population. To be effective in pursuing this goal, the neuropsychologist must be able to integrate various sources of information in formulating a neuropsychological assessment plan that is maximally useful to the patient and other health care professionals. In the medical area, the neuropsychologist must possess basic knowledge of neurology, internal medicine, psychiatry, and other specialties, and in particular must understand neuropsychological implications of those neurologic, systemic, and psychiatric diseases that are likely to present in the neuropsychologist's setting. Because the neuropsychologist functions within an interdisciplinary environment, she or he must also have a basic understanding of major diagnostic tools within clinical medicine that are relevant for functional localization or differential diagnosis of brain disease. The neuropsychologist is likely to frequently encounter information derived from the clinical neurologic exam and from diagnostic procedures such as CT, MRI, EEG, or functional neuroimaging. Because of this, the neuropsychologist should have at least a basic understanding of the goals, technological basis, and possible outcomes of each of these procedures (see DeMyer, 1974; Mazziotta & Gilman, 1992).

The neuropsychologist practicing within a flexible battery framework normally, through training and experience, possesses basic knowledge in the behavioral manifestations of major neurologic syndromes. Thus, basic biomedical, neurologic, neuroradiologic, and behavioral manifestations of the major neurologic syndromes (stroke, dementia, epilepsy, closed head injury, degenerative disorders, congenital and developmental disorders, neoplastic disorders, substance abuse, and psychopathological states [e.g., depression, schizophrenia]) will guide initial differential diagnostic decisions regarding which tests are likely to be fruitful in describing the nature of a patient's cognitive deficits.

One of the primary issues facing the clinician who uses a flexible battery concerns the manner in which decisions are made regarding test selection. If such rules are not articulated, or if they are not based on neurobehaviorally sound principles, the resulting approach can, at best, be subjective, difficult to teach, and impossible to replicate. (This problem has, in fact, been a major criticism by advocates of the fixed battery approach who argue that such decision rules have never been explicitly articulated and that, as a result, practice within a flexible battery approach is more a matter of art than of applied neuropsychological science.) Certainly, the experience of the clinician appears to play an important role in determining the efficiency and accuracy of decision-tree-oriented approaches to clinical assessment (Kleinmuntz, 1968), but this in itself does not convincingly argue for or against a particular approach.

The flexible battery clinician generally selects tests that satisfy certain specific criteria thought to be important either for functional localization or for characterizing the nature of a neuropsychological deficit in information-processing terms. To intelligently select tests, the flexible battery clinician needs to be generally familiar with both of these general areas.

With regard to functional localization, the past two decades of neuropsychological research, together with advances in neuroanatomic analysis, have revealed numerous orderly relationships between damage to specific neural systems and appearance of specific neuropsychological syndromes and deficits (cf. Tranel, 1992, for an excellent review). Such findings permit unprecedented correlation of specific psychological processes with damage to localized brain regions. Various symptoms and syndromes resulting from damage to frontal, temporal, parietal, and occipital regions are widely known within the behavioral neurology literature and have been delineated with sufficient specificity to have meaningful impact on neuropsychological test selection. Furthermore, our understanding of the neuroanatomic correlates of specific neurologic diseases (e.g., Alzheimer's disease, closed head injury, viral infections of the CNS, anoxia, AIDS, specific stroke syndromes, to name a few) has advanced to the point where distinctive patterns of neuropsychological presentation, couched in information-processing terms, are proving useful in differential diagnosis.

One specific example of how advancements in functional localization can help inform neuropsychological test selection concerns the differential diagnosis of dementia versus depression. It is known, for example, that an early neuropathological signature of Alzheimer's disease involves damage to the medial temporal-hippocampal region (Hyman, Van Hoesen, Damasio, & Barnes, 1984), and that, as the disease progresses, it likely spreads to include parietal and frontal association cortices. An early behavioral feature of Alzheimer's disease is a marked anterograde memory impairment, and, as the disease progresses, the gradual involvement of association cortex is likely responsible for the increasingly severe fallout in premorbidly acquired knowledge and semantic memory, and for the disturbances in language that become so prominent later in the disease. The cognitive symptoms of Alzheimer's disease may be difficult to distinguish from the memory dysfunction and cognitive slowing characteristic of the "dementia syndrome of depression" (Caine, 1986), particularly during early stages of the illness. However, an understanding of the neural substrate underlying depressive illness may yield important clues for differential diagnosis if the neuropsychological examination is planned accordingly.

Recent evidence suggests that subcortical white matter changes and an increased ventricle-to-brain ratio are two neurobehavioral markers that may predispose to depression in geriatric populations (Jeste, Lohr, & Goodwin, 1988; Morris & Rapoport, 1990), but little if any data exist to suggest specific involvement of either the medial temporal–hippocampal system or of association cortex. Thus, neuropsychological tests of new learning and of semantic memory might be useful in distinguishing between depression and dementia. Indeed, there is some evidence that depressives, but not demented individuals, can make use of categorical cuing in list learning (Weingartner et al., 1982). Independent studies suggest that demented, but not depressed, individuals frequently show language impairment including prominent naming defects (Bayles & Tomoeda, 1983; Cummings & Benson, 1992; Whitworth & Larson, 1989) and an increased category/exemplar ratio (increased production of categorical designations like "furniture," "fruit," and "clothes" relative to specific exemplars like "chair," "orange," and "sweatshirt") in verbal fluency tasks, suggesting a disruption of semantic memory organization (cf. Rosen, 1980). This data makes it clear that including a detailed, qualitative evaluation of semantic memory, language, and new learning are essential to this specific differential diagnosis. Importantly, different domains of functioning might be more important evaluative foci in other diagnostic contexts, and it is thus important for the flexible battery clinician to be aware of the manner of presentation of the major forms of neurologic disease.

The flexible-battery proponent must also be aware of the information-processing characteristics of a formidable number of neuropsychological tests. It is customary to describe neuropsychological tests in terms of the overall cognitive skill they are intended to measure. Thus, it is common to describe a test as measuring short-term memory, naming, constructional skill, abstract concept formation, and so on. However, most commonly used neuropsychological tests are multifactorial and can be analyzed in terms of the input, processing, and output demands they impose on the patient. Understanding neuropsychological tests at this "microgenetic" level allows the clinician to evaluate resulting patterns of failure and success in light of the possibility that specific aspects of the patient's information-processing capacity have been disturbed.

The flexible battery clinician must be prepared to consider such microgenetic task demands in evaluating patterns of neuropsychological deficit and must be concerned about whether performances on various tasks that share input, processing, or output demands lead to convergent conclusions about the locus of impairment. Suppose a patient displays significant deficits on a variety of neuropsychological tests including WAIS-R Digit Symbol, WMS-R Visual Reproduction, the Rey–Osterrieth Complex Figure, Grooved Pegboard, Luria Recursive Writing Sequences, and Thurstone (written) Verbal Fluency. Such a pattern of deficits could mean that the patient has diffuse brain disease manifested by defects in psychomotor speed, visual memory, language, and complex motor sequencing. However, this pattern of deficits can be explained more simply by noting that all these tests require either graphomotor or fine motor output. Understanding such commonalities makes it less likely that a clinician will simply accept the "face valid" explanation of what each test measures (e.g., Digit Symbol measures psychomotor ability, Visual Reproduction measures visual memory, etc.) and makes it more likely that she or he will seek to explain deficit patterns in more parsimonious ways. It should be pointed out that such considerations are firmly rooted in the widely accepted notion (cf. Campbell & Fiske, 1959) that most measures of psychologically meaningful constructs should be evaluated in terms of both *trait variance* (the neuropsychological function[s] tapped by the test) and *method variance* (the manner in which such function[s] are affected by the specific assessment method).

Thus, effective practice within the flexible battery approach requires a knowledge base that includes method and theory in behavioral neurology, cognitive psychology, psychometrics, and clinical psychology. How does one get this knowledge? The answer to this question is somewhat controversial, although recent recommendations on training experiences necessary and sufficient to obtain this level of expertise have been published by the APA Division 40 Task Force on Education, Accreditation, and Credentialing (Bornstein, 1988) and should provide useful guidelines.[1]

---

[1]This statement should not be construed to mean that adopting a flexible battery approach requires training and experience additional to that required for clinicians adopting a more fixed battery approach. Instead, this statement is simply meant to convey that practice within a flexible battery approach normally requires a level of clinical expertise that is likely to result only from a formalized, supervised training program in neuropsychology such as that described in the APA Division 40 Guidelines. Such a background is also, by APA standards, reasonably effective in producing a clinician capable, by training and experience, of practicing within a fixed battery framework.

Such guidelines (see also Costa, Matarazzo, & Bornstein, 1986) outline competency-based criteria and minimal training experiences to be obtained in formal graduate and/or postdoctoral programs and specifically reject workshop experience as a sole means of achieving competency in neuropsychological practice.

ADVANTAGES AND LIMITATIONS
OF THE FLEXIBLE BATTERY APPROACH

When compared to the more prevalent use of a fixed battery, the flexible battery approach has certain clear advantages and limitations (Kane, 1991). As can be seen from preceding sections, a major advantage in the use of flexible batteries is that a precise description of the patient's deficits from the viewpoint of some specific neuropsychological model is an achievable goal. Because the course of the examination is problem dependent, proponents argue that the flexible battery is more economical and time efficient (Kane, 1991). Thus, it is argued, a specific, focused referral question might be answered by giving only a few procedures rather than a full battery of tests. Although this is generally true, it is sometimes the case that precise characterization of the nature of a neuropsychological deficit may involve follow-up testing that is actually more time consuming and exacting than if a standard battery had been used.

The flexible battery is easy to alter based either on the introduction of new tests or on advancements in research. Fixed batteries are, by their nature, more difficult to revise, and there is a practical limit as to how many new tests can be added.

A fixed battery that assays a number of cognitive functions is sometimes seen as more clinically sensitive than a highly selective flexible battery, particularly if, in selecting a battery, there has been insufficient sampling of cognitive domains relevant to the patient's problem. The counterargument is that the knowledgeable flexible battery clinician will rarely make such an error because test selection is guided by an understanding of the domains of functioning that are relevant in the individual context. In a related argument, some fixed battery proponents have argued that, by using a standard battery, unsuspected strengths and weaknesses can be evaluated (Kane, 1991).

Proponents of the fixed battery approach have sometimes depicted the flexible battery approach as too "deficit centered" and have suggested that the flexible approach gives short shrift to the patient's cognitive strengths. This argument seems inconsistent with the fact that one of the goals of a flexible approach is to reveal circumstances under which the requirements of a task allow the patient to compensate effectively for the deficit (Luria, 1980).

One clear advantage of the fixed battery approach is that the repeated administration of a standard corpus of tests permits the development of a normative base against which patient performance can be evaluated, whereas the use of a flexible, changeable battery makes the building of a normative database more difficult. However, it should be emphasized that the process of test standardization and norms collection is not the exclusive ballywick of the fixed battery clinician. For example, most practitioners of the Boston process approach do, in fact, rely on a "core" set of tests that have proven useful in generating the kinds of clinical hypotheses on which the flexible battery depends (Milberg et al., 1986), and recent publication of norms for both quantitative (Borod, Goodglass, & Kaplan, 1980) and qualitative (Kaplan et al., 1991) aspects of this battery will narrow the gap between fixed and flexible batteries on this issue.

Because a fixed battery involves the standard administration of a predetermined series of tests, it can be administered by a trained technician or psychometrician who can collect and score the data for later interpretation by the neuropsychologist. Thus, the fixed battery approach might be considered more cost effective because it does not require large amounts of professional administration time. Although this may, in principle, be possible within the flexible battery framework, effective use of a flexible battery often requires the examiner to have more advanced knowledge of neurologic syndromes, functional anatomy, and psychopathology. Also, use of a technician seems somewhat inconsistent with the general view among flexible battery proponents that direct interaction with the patient and observation of microgenetic aspects of behavior are important sources of information in interpreting test results that require a professional level of competence.

A final issue has to do with comparative strengths and weaknesses of these two approaches when it comes to training of clinical neuropsychologists. In my view, students should learn the fundamentals of both fixed and flexible approaches, because such learning almost assuredly requires the student to understand neuropsychological assessment in historical perspective. In practicum training, initial training within a fixed battery approach has certain benefits for the beginning student. The opportunity to master a standard, comprehensive battery may be an effective way to learn how to administer neuropsychological tests, to gain an appropriate understanding of psychometric issues, and to acquire basic skills in test interpretation (e.g., the use of appropriate comparison standards, see Lezak, 1983). After students gain experience with actual clinical application, they can then learn to vary procedures, generate and test idiographic hypotheses, and more precisely examine the compensatory strategies that patients attempt to use in response to their cognitive impairment. Because flexible battery approaches flow directly from underlying models of brain function, they provide a conceptual framework within which students can begin to understand how complex skills are functionally organized in the brain. This conceptual framework provides a rational basis for acquiring skills in neuropsychological interviewing and behavioral observation and provides the foundation on which test-selection decisions are made. Training within a flexible battery approach more firmly grounds the student in behavioral neuroscience and seems a particularly effective method for helping students acquire an appreciation of construct validity in neuropsychological assessment, because it focuses centrally on the underlying skills and abilities responsible for success and failure on specific tests.

SUMMARY AND CONCLUSIONS

The flexible battery approach to neuropsychological assessment represents a measured attempt to systematically adopt a decision-tree-oriented approach to clinical evaluation. Proponents of this approach contend that it involves a process of assessment and yields the kind of results that are most relevant to what Luria and Vygotsky described as "qualification of the symptom." All flexible battery approaches attempt to provide a functional description of the patient's neuropsychological status and depend upon a priori models of brain function and dysfunction as guides to clinical decision making during assessment. Major examples of this approach include Luria's investigative program, the European cognitive neuropsychology tradition, and the Boston process approach to neuropsychological assessment.

Because the flexible battery approach is Markovian in nature, the clinician must possess certain background information so that the decision tree is implemented systematically, and so that decisions are based on sound neuroscientific and psychological principles. Such information includes knowledge of etiologic factors in brain disease, neurologic signs and symptoms, and an understanding of clinical diagnostic tests employed by other medical and nonmedical disciplines. It further includes advanced knowledge about the quantitative and qualitative bases of a formidable array of available neuropsychological tests and about how to creatively apply and modify such tests in response to the needs of the individual patient.

From time to time, proponents of the flexible approach have sparred with fixed battery proponents regarding which approach is more neurobehaviorally sound, relevant to the kinds of referral questions most commonly faced by contemporary neuropsychologists, or more likely to lead to advances in our understanding of brain-behavior relationships. Although such debates are interesting and entertaining, they have shed more heat than light on clinical practice because they have commonly assumed that "which is the better approach?" can be answered by considering the weight of evidence in favor of one or the other strategy. As I have argued, the fixed and flexible battery approaches are most strongly distinguished not by the adoption of particular procedures but by the manner in which the resulting data is collected and analyzed. The fixed battery approach most commonly appeals to concepts developed within the psychometric tradition, whereas the flexible battery approach most commonly utilizes neurologic and information-processing constructs. Because of their distinct roots, each approach plays an important role in the professional activity of neuropsychologists and in the training of new scientist practitioners. These two traditions provide alternative, but not mutually exclusive, frameworks for conceptualizing quantitative and qualitative data, and, as I have indicated, recent attempts have been made to bridge the quantitative–qualitative distinction. Althought this chapter emphasized the virtues of the flexible battery approach, it should be recognized that the most effective clinical practice will be one that recognizes, utilizes, and attempts to further our diverse heritage in psychometrics, neuroscience, and cognitive psychology.

REFERENCES

Bayles, K., & Tomoeda, C. K. (1983). Confrontation naming impairment in dementia. *Brain and Language, 19*, 98–114.

Benton, A. L., & Hamsher, K. deS. (1989). *Multilingual aphasia examination* (2nd ed.). Iowa City: University of Iowa.

Boll, T. J. (1981). The Halstead–Reitan Neuropsychology Battery. In S. B. Filskov & T. J. Boll (Eds.), *Handbook of clinical neuropsychology* (Vol. 1, pp. 577–608). New York: Wiley.

Bornstein, R. A. (1988). Reports of the Division 40 Task Force on Education, Accreditation, and Credentialing. *The Clinical Neuropsychologist, 2*, 25–29.

Borod, J. C., Goodglass, H., & Kaplan, E. (1980). Normative data on the Boston Diagnostic Aphasia Examination, Parietal Lobe Battery, and the Boston Naming Test. *Journal of Clinical Neuropsychology, 2*, 209–216.

Bruce, V., & Young, A. W. (1986). Understanding face recognition. *British Journal of Psychology, 77*, 305–327.

Butters, N., Grant, I., Haxby, J., Judd, L. J., Martin, A., McClelland, J., Pequegnat, W., Schacter, D., & Stover, E. (1990). Assessment of AIDS-related cognitive changes: Recommendations of the NIMH Workgroup on neuropsychological assessment approaches. *Journal of Clinical and Experimental Neuropsychology, 12*, 963–978.

Caine, E. D. (1986). The neuropsychology of depression: The pseudodementia syndrome. In I. Grant & K. M. Adams (Eds.), *Neuropsychological assessment of neuropsychiatric disorders* (pp. 221–243). New York: Oxford University Press.

Campbell, D. T., & Fiske, D. W. (1959). Convergent and discriminant validation by the multitrait–multimethod matrix. *Psychological Bulletin, 56*, 81–105.

Christensen, A.-L. (1979). *Luria's neuropsychological investigation. Text* (2nd ed.). Copenhagen: Munksgaard.

Coltheart, M. (1985). Cognitive neuropsychology and the study of reading. In M. I. Posner & O. S. M. Marin (Eds.), *Attention and performance* (Vol. 11, pp. 3–37). Hillsdale, NJ: Lawrence Erlbaum Associates.

Costa, L. D., Matarazzo, J. D., & Bornstein, R. A. (1986). Issues in graduate and postgraduate training in clinical neuropsychology. In S. B. Filskov & T. J. Boll (Eds.), *Handbook of clinical neuropsychology* (Vol. 2, pp. 652–668). New York: Wiley.

Craik, F. I. M., & Lockhart, R. S. (1972). Levels of processing: A framework for memory research. *Journal of Verbal Learning and Verbal Behavior, 11*, 671–684.

Crook, T. H., & Larrabee, G. J. (1988). Interrelationships among everyday memory tests: Stability of factor structure with age. *Neuropsychology, 2*, 1–12.

Crook, T. H., Salama, M., & Gobert, J. (1986). A computerized test battery for detecting and assessing memory disorders. In A. Bes, J. Cohn, S. Hoyer, J. P. Marc-Vergenes, & H. M. Wisniewski (Eds.), *Senile dementias: Early detection* (pp. 79–85). London: John Libbey Eurotext.

Cummings, J. L., & Benson, D. F. (1992). *Dementia: A clinical approach* (2nd ed.). Boston: Butterworth-Heinemann.

DeMyer, W. (1974). *Technique of the neurologic examination.* New York: McGraw–Hill.

Dodrill, C. B. (1978). A neuropsychological battery for epilepsy. *Epilepsia, 19*, 611–623.

Ellis, A. W., & Young, A. W. (1986). *Human cognitive neuropsychology.* Hillsdale, NJ: Lawrence Erlbaum Associates.

Filskov, S. B., & Goldstein, S. G. (1974). Diagnostic validity of the Halstead–Reitan Neuropsychological Battery. *Journal of Consulting and Clinical Psychology, 42*, 419–423.

Goldberg, E., & Costa, L. D. (1986). Qualitative indices in neuropsychological assessment: An extension of Luria's approach to executive deficit following prefrontal lesions. In I. Grant & K. M. Adams (Eds.), *Neuropsychological assessment of neuropsychiatric disorders* (pp. 48–64). New York: Oxford University Press.

Goldstein, G. (1986). An overview of similarities and differences between the Halstead–Reitan and Luria–Nebraska neuropsychological batteries. In T. Incagnoli, G. Goldstein, & C. J. Golden (Eds.), *Clinical application of neuropsychological test batteries* (pp. 235–275). New York: Plenum Press.

Goldstein, G., Tarter, R., Shelly, C., & Hegedus, A. (1983). The Pittsburgh Initial Neuropsychological Testing System (PINTS): A neuropsychological screening battery for psychiatric patients. *Journal of Behavioral Assessment, 5*, 227–238.

Goodglass, H. (1986). The flexible battery in neuropsychological assessment. In T. Incagnoli, G. Goldstein, & C. J. Golden (Eds.), *Clinical application of neuropsychological test batteries* (pp. 121–134). New York: Plenum Press.

Goodglass, H., & Kaplan, E. (1972). *Assessment of aphasia and related disorders.* Philadelphia: Lea & Febiger.

Humphreys, G. W., & Riddoch, M. J. (1987). *To see but not to see: A case study of visual agnosia.* London: Lawrence Erlbaum Associates.

Hyman, B. T., Van Hoesen, G. W., Damasio, A. R., & Barnes, C. L. (1984). Alzheimer's disease: Cell-specific pathology isolates the hippocampal formation. *Science, 225*, 1288–1298.

Incagnoli, T. (1986). Current directions and future trends in clinical neuropsychology. In T. Incagnoli, G. Goldstein, & C. J. Golden (Eds.), *Clinical application of neuropsychological test batteries* (pp. 1–44). New York: Plenum Press.

Jacoby, L. L. (1983). Remembering the data: Analyzing interactive processes in reading. *Journal of Verbal Learning and Verbal Behavior, 22*, 485–508.

Jeste, D. V., Lohr, J. B., & Goodwin, F. K. (1988). Neuroanatomical studies of major affective disorders. *British Journal of Psychiatry, 153*, 444–459.

Kane, R. L. (1991). Standardized and flexible batteries in neuropsychology: An assessment update. *Neuropsychology Review, 2*, 281–339.

Kaplan, E. (1983). Process and achievement revisited. In S. Wapner & B. Kaplan (Eds.), *Towards a holistic developmental psychology* (pp. 143–156). Hillsdale, NJ: Lawrence Erlbaum Associates.

Kaplan, E. (1990). The process approach to neuropsychological assessment of psychiatric patients. *Journal of Neuropsychiatry, 2*, 72–87.

Kaplan, E., Fein, D., Morris, R., & Delis, D. C. (1991). *The WAIS-R as a neuropsychological instrument. Manual*. San Antonio, TX: The Psychological Corporation.

Kertesz, A. (1979). *Aphasia and associated disorders*. New York: Grune & Stratton.

Kiernan, R. J., Mueller, J., Langston, J. W., & Van Dyke, C. (1987). The Neurobehavioral Cognitive Status Examination: A brief but differentiated approach to cognitive assessment. *Annals of Internal Medicine, 107*, 481–485.

Kleinmuntz, B. (1968). Processing of clinical information by man and machine. In B. Kleinmuntz (Ed.), *Formal representation of human judgement*. New York: Wiley.

Kløve, H. (1974). Validation studies in adult clinical neuropsychology. In R. M. Reitan & L. A. Davison (Eds.), *Clinical neuropsychology: Current status and applications* (pp. 211–235). New York: Hemisphere Publishing Company.

LaRue, A., D'Elia, L. F., Clark, E. O., Spar, J. E., & Jarvik, L. F. (1986). Clinical tests of memory in dementia, depression, and healthy aging. *Psychology and Aging, 1*, 69–77.

Lezak, M. D. (1983). *Neuropsychological assessment* (2nd ed.). New York: Oxford University Press.

Luria, A. R. (1973). *The working brain: An introduction to neuropsychology* (B. Haigh, Trans.). New York: Basic Books.

Luria, A. R. (1980). *Higher cortical functions in man* (2nd ed.). New York: Basic Books.

Marshall, J. C., & Newcombe, F. (1973). Patterns of paralexia: A psycholinguistic approach. *Journal of Psycholinguistic Research, 2*, 175–199.

Mattis, S. (1988). *Dementia Rating Scale*. Odessa, FL: Psychological Assessment Resources.

Mazziotta, J. C., & Gilman, S. (1992). *Clinical brain imaging: Principles and applications*. Philadelphia: F. A. Davis.

McCarthy, R. A., & Warrington, E. K. (1986). Visual associative agnosia: A clinico-anatomical study of a single case. *Journal of Neurology, Neurosurgery, and Psychiatry, 49*, 1233–1240.

McCarthy, R. A., & Warrington, E. K. (1990). *Cognitive neuropsychology: A clinical introduction*. New York: Academic Press.

McKenna, P., & Warrington, E. K. (1986). The analytic approach to neuropsychological assessment. In I. Grant & K. M. Adams (Eds.), *Neuropsychological assessment of neuropsychiatric disorders* (pp. 31–47). New York: Oxford University Press.

Meier, M. (1974). Some challenges for clinical neuropsychology. In R. M. Reitan & L. A. Davison (Eds.), *Clinical neuropsychology: Current status and applications* (pp. 289–323). New York: Wiley.

Milberg, W. P., Hebben, N., & Kaplan, E. (1986). The Boston process approach to neuropsychological assessment. In I. Grant & K. M. Adams (Eds.), *Neuropsychological assessment of neuropsychiatric disorders* (pp. 65–86). New York: Oxford University Press.

Morris, P., & Rapoport, S. I. (1990). Neuroimaging and affective disorder in late life: A review. *Canadian Journal of Psychiatry, 35*, 347–354.

Mysiw, W. J., Beegan, J. G., & Gatens, P. F. (1989). Prospective cognitive assessment of stroke patients before inpatient rehabilitation: The relationship of the Neurobehavioral Cognitive Status Examination to functional improvement. *American Journal of Physical Medicine and Rehabilitation, 68*, 168–171.

Neisser, U. (1967). *Cognitive psychology*. New York: Appleton-Century-Crofts.

Parsons, O. A. (1986). Overview of the Halstead–Reitan Battery. In T. Incagnoli, G. Goldstein, & C. J. Golden (Eds.), *Clinical application of neuropsychological test batteries* (pp. 155–192). New York: Plenum Press.

Peyser, J. M., Rao, S. M., LaRocca, N. G., & Kaplan, E. F. (1990). Guidelines for neuropsychological research in multiple sclerosis. *Archives of Neurology, 47*, 94–97.

Platt, J. R. (1966). Strong inference. *Science, 146*, 347–353.

Popper, K. R. (1959). *The logic of scientific discovery*. New York: Harper.

Reitan, R. M., & Davison, L. A. (1974). *Clinical neuropsychology: Current status and applications*. New York: Hemisphere.

Richards, P. M., & Ruff, R. M. (1989). Motivational effects on neuropsychological functioning: Comparison of depressed vs. nondepressed individuals. *Journal of Consulting and Clinical Psychology, 57*, 396–402.

Rosen, W. (1980). Verbal fluency in aging and dementia. *Journal of Clinical Neuropsychology, 2*, 135–146.

Rourke, B. P., & Brown, G. G. (1986). Clinical neuropsychology and behavioral neurology: Similarities and differences. In S. B. Filskov & T. J. Boll (Eds.), *Handbook of clinical neuropsychology* (2nd ed., pp. 3–18). New York: Wiley.

Russell, E. W. (1986). The psychometric foundation of clinical neuropsychology. In S. B. Filskov & T. J. Boll (Eds.), *Handbook of clinical neuropsychology* (2nd ed., pp. 45–80). New York: Wiley.

Russell, E. W., Neuringer, C., & Goldstein, G. (1970). *Assessment of brain damage: A neuropsychological key approach*. New York: Wiley.

Shallice, T. (1988). *From neuropsychology to mental structure*. New York: Cambridge University Press.

Smith, A. (1973). *Symbol Digit Modalities Test. Manual*. Los Angeles: Western Psychological Services.

Squire, L. R. (1987). *Memory and brain*. New York: Oxford University Press.

Tarter, R. E., & Edwards, K. L. (1986). Neuropsychological batteries. In T. Incagnoli, G. Goldstein, & C. J. Golden (Eds.), *Clinical application of neuropsychological test batteries* (pp. 135–153). New York: Plenum Press.

Teuber, H.-L. (1955). Physiological psychology. *Annual Review of Psychology, 6*, 267–296.

Tranel, D. (1992). Functional neuroanatomy: Neuropsychological correlates of cortical and subcortical damage. In S. C. Yudofsky & R. E. Hales (Eds.), *The American Psychiatric Press textbook of neuropsychiatry* (2nd ed., pp. 57–88). Washington, DC: American Psychiatric Press.

Warrington, E. K. (1975). The selective impairment of semantic memory. *Quarterly Journal of Experimental Psychology, 27*, 187–199.

Warrington, E. K., & James, M. (1986). Visual object recognition in patients with right hemisphere lesions: Axes or features? *Perception, 15*, 355–366.

Weingartner, H., Kaye, W., Smallberg, S., Cohen, R., Ebert, M. H., Gillin, J. C., & Gold, P. (1982). Determinants of memory failures in dementia. In S. Corkin, K. L. Davis, J. H. Growdon, E. Usdin, & R. J. Wurtman (Eds.), *Alzheimer's disease: A report of progress in research* (pp. 171–176). New York: Raven Press.

Werner, H. (1937). Process and achievement: A basic problem of education and developmental psychology. *Harvard Educational Review, 7*, 353–368.

Wernicke, C. (1874). *Der aphasische symptomenkomplex* [The Aphasia Symptom Complex]. Breslau, Poland: M. Cohn & Weigert.

Whitworth, R. H., & Larson, C. M. (1989). Differential diagnosis and staging of Alzheimer's disease with an aphasia battery. *Neuropsychiatry, Neuropsychology, and Behavioral Neurology, 1*, 255–265.

World Health Organization & Nordic Council of Ministers Working Group (1985). *Environmental health 5: Organic solvents and the central nervous system*. Copenhagen: WHO and Nordic Council of Ministers.

Author Index

A

Achenbach, T. M., 173, 181
Adams, K. M., 109, 110, 111, 209, 213, 228, 254, 255, 257, 287, 288, 289
Adams, R. L., 19, 40, 60, 66, 144, 145, 146, 151, 162
Adams, W., 176, 179, 183
Akert, K., 256
Alberts, M. S., 123, 135, 160
Alexander, G. E., 77, 108
Alexopoulos, G. S., 101, 112
Alfano, D. P., 115, 160
Allan, K. M., 54, 65
Alliger, R. J., 124, 160
Altman, I. M., 49, 68
Amadeo, M., 101, 103, 111
Amatruda, C. S., 170, 182
American Psychiatric Association, 84, 108, 130, 160
American Psychological Association, 30, 39, 113, 152, 160, 254
Anastasi, A., 2, 19, 30, 39, 104, 109, 211, 218, 240, 254
Anderson, H. R., 178, 181
Anderson, S. W., 233, 254
Andreasen, N. C., 124, 160, 161

Annett, M., 81, 109
Anthony, W. Z., 228, 243, 254, 255
Aram, D. M., 178, 181
Archer, R. P., 173, 181
Arsdell, G. V., 178, 181
Axelrod, B. N., 27, 39

B

Baddeley, A., 150, 163
Baikie, E. M., 53, 67
Bailey, L. L., 178, 181
Bakker, D. J., 167, 183
Balla, D. A., 172, 183
Barclay, L. L., 83, 109
Barco, P. P., 135, 138, 142, 160
Barkley, R. A., 180, 181
Barnes, C. L., 281, 288
Barona, A., 50, 58, 59, 61, 62, 63, 65
Barr, W. B., 124, 160
Barron, J. H., 223, 226, 231, 254
Barth, J. T., 19, 39, 122, 145, 150, 160, 162, 169, 181
Bauer, R. M., 125, 160, 170, 172, 178, 182
Baumgardner, M. H., 6, 39

291

Bayles, K., 282, 287
Bayley, N., 177, 181
Beardsley, J. V., 247, 254
Beegan, J. G., 269, 289
Beery, K., 179, 181
Behner, G., 106, 109
Ben-Porath, Y. F., 173, 181
Ben-Shachar, G., 178, 181
Benson, D. F., 76, 109, 111, 282, 288
Benton, A. L., 73, 74, 95, 109, 110, 128,
    137, 160, 161, 162, 177, 179, 181,
    200, 206, 209, 270, 287
Berg, E. A., 19, 27, 39
Berg, R. A., 39, 167, 178, 181
Berman, K. F., 124, 163
Bernard, B. A., 53, 54, 68
Bernstein, F. B., 106, 112
Berthier, M. L., 125, 162
Besson, J. A. O., 53, 54, 65
Bickart, W. T., 146, 160
Bigler, E., 13, 40
Bilder, R. M., 124, 160
Binder, L. M., 98, 109, 123, 135, 145,
    160
Black, F. W., 47, 65
Blackmore, L., 54, 65
Blair, J. R., 55, 65
Blaney, P. H., 103, 109
Blass, J. P., 83, 109
Blau, T. H., 144, 146, 160
Blumberg, E., 116, 161
Bogerts, B., 124, 160
Bolesta, M. M., 135, 160
Boll, T. J., 27, 39, 41, 122, 161, 162,
    169, 181, 256, 257, 265, 266, 287,
    288, 290
Bolter, J., 60, 62, 65, 66
Bond, O., 83, 109
Bond, M. R., 134, 161
Boone, K. B., 73, 111
Bornstein, R. A., 86, 109, 247, 254, 283,
    284, 287, 288
Borod, J. C., 285, 287
Bowers, D., 91, 111
Bowman, W. P., 178, 181
Branch, C., 81, 109
Braun, P., 49, 65
Braun, H. I., , 256
Bremner, M., 53, 65
Briggs, G. G., 81, 109
Brinkman, S. D., 49, 65

Brobeck, T. C., 135, 160
Brooks, D. N., 129, 162
Brooks, N., 134, 161
Brown, G. G., 59, 68, 222, 231, 257,
    262, 265, 266, 267, 271, 290
Bruce, V., 275, 287
Bryant, B. K., 110, 256
Buschke, H., 236, 254
Butcher, J. N., 173, 181
Butler, M., 17, 39, 212, 254
Butters, N., 77, 78, 94, 109, 123, 160,
    269, 287

C

Caflin, R., 106, 112
Caine, E. D., 100, 102, 109, 110, 124,
    161, 265, 282, 287
Calsyn, D. A., 27, 39
Campbell, D. T., 193, 209, 283, 288
Carlin, A. S., 144, 161
Carotte, R. M., 13, 39
Cattarin, J., 106, 109
Celinski, M. J., 49, 66
Cermak, L. S., 94, 109
Ch'ien, L. T., 178, 181
Chaney, E. F., 27, 39
Chastain, R. L., 50, 57, 59, 65, 67
Chatman, S. P., 46, 65
Christensen, A. L., 213, 254, 273, 288
Cicchetti, D. V., 172, 183, 188, 209, 257
Cimino, C. R., 91, 99, 106, 109, 111
Clark, E. O., 265, 289
Cleeland, C. S., 247, 254
Coburn, T. H., 122, 162
Cochrane, R. H. B., 53, 54, 65
Cockburn, J., 150, 163
Cohen, B., 124, 160
Cohen, R., 282, 290
Coltheart, M., 275, 288
Connell, D. K., 146, 160
Connor, R., 49, 67
Cooper, P. V., 135, 160
Cope, D. N., 123, 161
Corwin, J., 101, 109
Costa, L. D., 209, 257, 267, 284, 288
Craig, P. L., 60, 66
Craik, F. I. M., 263, 288
Crawford, J. R., 53, 54, 55, 60, 65
Cronbach, L. J., 189, 209

Crook, T. H., 270, 288
Crosson, B., 115, 134, 135, 138, 160, 168, 181, 245, 254
Crowley, T. J., 124, 130, 161
Cummings, J. L., 76, 109, 110, 161, 282, 288

D

D'Elia, L., 49, 67
Damasio, A. R., 78, 107, 109, 110, 115, 160, 161, 281, 288
Damasio, H., 78, 110, 233, 254
Daniel, M. H., 45, 46, 67
Davison, L. A., 166, 168, 169, 171, 179, 183, 267, 289, 290
De'Elia, L. F., 265, 289
DeFilippis, N. A., 27, 39
DeLacey, G., 53, 65
Delis, D. C., 21, 39, 90, 110, 120, 137, 161, 178, 181, 212, 253, 254, 264, 273, 289
DeLuca, J. W., 251, 254
DeMyer, W., 280, 288
Denburg, J. A., 13, 39
Denburg, S. D., 13, 39
Denckla, M. B., 179, 181
Dhawan, M., 124, 162
Diller, L., 66, 162
Division 40 Task Force on Education, 251, 254
Dobbins, C., 228, 239, 254
Dodrill, C. B., 245, 247, 255, 269, 288
Doehring, D. G., 47, 66
Doerr, H. O., 144, 161
Dolinskas, C. A., 129, 163
Drachman, D. A., 83, 109
Dunn, L. M., 18, 39, 91, 109, 236, 237, 250, 255

E

Early, T. S., 124, 162
Ebert, M. H., 282, 290
Ebmeier, K. P., 53, 65
Edelbrock, C., 173, 181
Edgell, D., 167, 183
Edwards, K. L., 13, 40, 83, 112, 167, 184, 222, 258, 271, 272, 290

Ehrhardt, J. C., 124, 160
Eichman, P. L., 166, 181
Eisenberg, H. M., 161, 162, 171, 181
Ekelman, B. L., 178, 181
Ellis, A. W., 260, 273, 275, 288
Eppinger, M. G., 60, 61, 62, 66
Ernhart, C. B., 166, 181
Eslinger, P. J., 78, 107, 109, 110, 115, 161
Evans, M. E., 107, 111
Ewings-Cobb, L., 171, 181

F

Faust, D., 145, 150, 161
Fausti, S. A., 145, 162
Feenan, K., 101, 109
Fein, D., 21, 39, 90, 110, 120, 161, 264, 273, 289
Fenichel, G. M., 168, 181
Fennell, E. B., 168, 169, 170, 172, 173, 180, 181, 183
Fennell, R. S., 178, 182
Fernandez, C. D., 214, 258
Fieve, R., 101, 109
Filley, C. M., 49, 66
Filskov, S. B., 39, 161, 181, 257, 265, 287, 288, 290
Finlayson, M. A. J., 115, 160
Fisher, L., 60, 66
Fishman, M. A., 168, 182
Fisk, J. L., 167, 183
Fiske, D. W., 193, 209, 283, 288
Fletcher, J. M., 170, 171, 181, 182
Fletcher-Janzen, E., 167, 181, 182, 183
Flynn, J. M., 180, 182
Fogel, M., 56, 66
Forster, A. A., 26, 39
Fox, J. H., 53, 54, 68
Franzen, M. D., 74, 109, 186, 209, 218, 255
Fromm-Auch, D., 244, 245, 247, 255
Fuld, P. A., 49, 66
Funkenstein, H. H., 106, 112
Fuster, J. M., 77, 108

G

Gaddes, W. H., 26, 40
Gade, A., 47, 67, 247, 248, 255

Gainer, C., 13, 40
Galkin, T. M., 182
Gardner, E. F., 155, 161
Gardner, H., 45, 66
Gary, H. E., 61, 66
Gatens, P. F., 269, 289
Gentilini, M., 122, 161
Gesell, A. L., 170, 182
Gfeller, J. D., 49, 66
Gill, M., 116, 162
Gilleard, C. J., 53, 67
Gillette, J., 132, 161
Gilley, D. W., 53, 54, 68
Gillin, J. C., 282, 290
Gilman, S., 265, 280, 289
Giordani, B., 122, 162
Gleser, G. C., 189, 209
Gobert, J., 270, 288
Goethals, G. R., 163
Goff, J. R., 178, 181
Gold, P., 282, 290
Goldberg, E., 124, 160, 267, 288
Golden, C. J., 19, 39, 40, 53, 67, 171,
        178, 182, 213, 255, 258, 288, 290
Goldman, H., 13, 27, 40
Goldman, J. R., 173, 182
Goldman, P. S., 169, 170
Goldstein, F. C., 61, 62, 66
Goldstein, G., 13, 40, 228, 239, 243,
        255, 257, 258, 265, 266, 269, 288,
        290
Goldstein, K., 212, 255
Goldstein, S. G., 265, 288
Gollin, E. S., 95, 109
Goodglass, H., 74, 79, 109, 110, 120,
        148, 161, 213, 215, 236, 250, 255,
        256, 261, 270, 285, 287, 288
Goodwin, F. K., 282, 289
Goodwin, J. S., 245, 255
Gouvier, W., 60, 62, 65, 66
Graff-Radford, N., 78, 110
Graham, F. K., 166, 181
Graham, J. R., 173, 181, 249, 255
Granholm, E., 94, 109
Grant, I., 61, 66, 80, 81, 109, 110, 111,
        214, 228, 247, 255, 287, 288, 289
Greene, R. L., 36, 39
Greenwald, A. G., 6, 39
Gregory, R. J., 27, 39
Grek, A., 99, 110
Grober, E., 54, 66

Gronwall, D., 122, 161
Grossman, R. G., 73, 110, 128, 161
Grove, W. M., 124, 161
Guerry, S., 173, 182
Guilford, J. P., 232, 237, 255
Gundry, S., 178, 181
Gutkin, T. B., 46, 67

H

Haaland, K. Y., 245, 255
Haas, J. F., 123, 161
Hagen, E., 177, 184
Hall, K., 123, 161
Halstead, W. C., 213, 218, 228, 242, 255
Hammeke, T. A., 213, 255
Hampton, J. R., 8, 39
Hamsher, K. deS., 74, 109, 137, 160,
        177, 179, 181, 200, 209, 270, 287
Hannay, H. J., 95, 109
Harkins, S. W., 102, 110
Harley, J. P., 247, 254
Harrison, M. J. G., 8, 39
Hart, R. P., 102, 110
Hart, S., 53, 66
Harter, S., 173, 182
Hawk, G. L., 145, 160
Haxby, J. V., 132, 161, 287
Heaton, R. K., 27, 28, 39, 49, 61, 66, 80,
        81, 110, 124, 130, 161, 214, 228,
        233, 235, 236, 243, 245, 246, 247,
        248, 254, 255, 256
Heaton, S. R., 28, 39
Hebben, N., 79, 111, 261, 273, 277, 278,
        285, 289
Hegedus, A., 269, 288
Heilman, K. M., 76, 78, 91, 105, 110,
        111, 112, 160, 169, 182
Heinrichs, R. W., 49, 66
Hendrickson, M. E., 238, 257
Henry, R. R., 27, 39
Herman, D. O., 45, 46, 67, 87, 88, 111
High, W. M., 128, 162
Hinrichs, J. V., 103, 111
Hiscock, C. K., 98, 110
Hiscock, M., 98, 110
Hoepfner, R., 237, 255
Hoffman, R. E., 124, 161
Hooper, H. E., 92, 95, 110, 161
Hooper, S. R., 166, 167, 172, 182, 184

Horgan, P. A., 106, 112
Horn, J. L., 231, 255
Horn, L. C. 53, 67
Horton, A. M., 257
Hughes, C. W., 245, 254
Hulihan, D., 235, 256
Humphreys, G. W., 276, 288
Hunt, W. C., 245, 255
Hyman, B. T., 281, 288
Hynd, G. W., 30, 39, 67, 167, 169, 178, 182

I

Incagnoli, T., 40, 258, 266, 288, 290
INS-Division 40 Task Force on Education, Accreditation and Credentialing, 74, 110, 151
Ireton, H., 172, 182

J

Jacoby, L. L., 263, 288
James, M., 276, 290
Jane, J. A., 122, 162
Jarvis, P. E., 19, 39
Jastak, S., 155, 161, 173, 182
Jennett, B., 128, 134, 161
Jeste, D. V., 282, 289
Jones, R. D., 233, 254
Jonsson, A., 247, 255
Judd, L. J., 269, 287

K

Kaemmer, B., 173, 181
Kail, R., 169, 176, 182
Kamphaus, R. W., 209
Kane, R. L., 233, 255, 259, 265, 284, 289
Kaplan, B., 110,
Kaplan, E., 21, 39, 74, 78, 79, 90, 109, 110, 111, 112, 120, 124, 137, 148, 160, 161, 178, 181, 212, 213, 215, 236, 250, 254, 255, 256, 261, 264, 267, 270, 273, 277, 278, 279, 285, 287, 288, 289, 290
Karlsen, B., 155, 161

Karzmark, P., 61, 62, 63, 66
Kaszniak, A. W., 103, 110
Kaufman, A. S., 39, 45, 46, 48, 57, 66, 67, 86, 87, 88, 110
Kay, G. G., 233, 255
Kaye, W., 282, 290
Keegan, J. F., 228, 254
Keen, P. L., 53, 65
Kertesz, A., 74, 110, 213, 256, 270, 289
Kiernan, R. J., 269, 289
Kimble, G. A., 216, 256
King, D. A., 102, 110, 124, 161
Kirkwood, K., 53, 65
Kitzinger, H., 116, 161
Kleinman, K. M., 13, 27, 40
Kleinmuntz, B., 253, 256, 281, 289
Klesges, R. C., 53, 60, 62, 66, 67
Kline, P., 211, 218, 238, 256
Klonoff, H., 26, 39
Kløve, H., 47, 66, 254, 265, 289
Knights, R. M., 26, 39
Kobayashi, J., 49, 66
Kohout, F. J., 103, 111
Kolb, B., 165, 168, 169, 182, 230, 238, 256
Koppitz, E. M., 166, 182
Kovacs, M., 173, 182
Kramer, J. H., 137, 161, 178, 181, 212, 254
Kreutzer, J. S., 160
Kubos, K. L., 124, 162
Kvale, V. I., 228, 254
Kwentus, J. A., 102, 110

L

L'Engle-Stein, C., 173, 182
Ladd, C., 56, 67
Lancaster, W., 178, 181
Langston, J. W., 269, 289
Largen, J. W., 53, 67
LaRocca, N. G., 269, 290
Larrabee, G. J., 53, 67, 94, 105, 110, 270, 288
Larson, C. M., 282, 290
LaRue, A., 265, 289
Leavitt, J., 27, 40, 83, 109
Leckliter, I. N., 26, 39, 80, 110
Lecours, A. R., 169, 184
Lehman, R. A. W., 228, 235, 243, 254, 255, 256

Leippe, M. R., 6, 39
Lemke, J. H., 103, 111
Levin, H. S., 53, 61, 66, 67, 72, 73, 75, 110, 128, 135, 161, 162, 171, 181
Levine, D., 99, 110
Levy, M., 27, 40, 250, 257
Lewinsohn, M. W., 178, 181
Lewis, C., 236, 258
Lewis, R. F., 233, 256
Lezak, M. D., 2, 3, 6, 20, 28, 29, 30, 39, 44, 56, 67, 71, 73, 74, 82, 86, 89, 100, 107, 110, 111, 114, 115, 134, 135, 136, 145, 162, 220, 240, 251, 256, 259, 264, 267, 285, 289
Linn, R. L., 67
Linn, R. T., 245, 255
Linton, J. C., 167, 181
Lockhart, R. S., 263, 288
Logan, S. G., 27, 40
Lohr, J. B., 282, 289
Long, C., 60, 65, 66
Luria, A. R., 6, 39, 72, 111, 213, 218, 221, 224, 256, 265, 267, 273, 274, 275, 284, 289
Lyons, G. R., 180, 182

M

Macko, K., 72, 111
Madden, R., 155, 161
Malloy, P., 99, 111
Maloney, M. P., 2, 7, 40
Mandleberg, I. A., 129, 162
Manley, M. W., 101, 112
Mapou, R. L., 230, 256
Marin, O. S. M., 288
Marshall, J. C., 275, 289
Marshall, J. M., 166, 181
Martin, A., 269, 287
Martin, D. C., 53, 67
Martone, M., 94, 109
Matarazzo, J. D., 2, 40, 45, 46, 47, 56, 67, 80, 87, 88, 110, 111, 223, 230, 256, 284, 288
Mateer, C. A., 116, 123, 134, 142, 162
Mather, N., 173, 184
Matthews, C. G., 61, 66, 80, 81, 110, 214, 247, 254, 255
Mattis, S., 83, 109, 269, 289
Mazziotta, J. C., 265, 280, 289

McCampbell, E., 27, 39
McCarthy, D., 174, 182
McCarthy, R. A., 260, 267, 273, 275, 276, 289
McClelland, J., 269, 287
McFie, J., 52, 53, 67
McKenna, P., 53, 67, 267, 273, 289
McLean, J. E., 48, 57, 67
Meertz, E., 124, 160
Meier, M. J., 66, 162, 259, 289
Melendez, F., 12, 40
Melton, G. B., 143, 144, 146, 162
Menkes, J. H., 167, 168, 173, 178, 183
Messick, S., 43, 67
Mesulam, M. M., 76, 94, 105, 111, 112
Meyer, R. G., 146, 160
Mickle, J. P., 173, 182
Milberg, W. P., 79, 111, 261, 264, 273, 277, 278, 285, 289
Miller, E., 105, 111
Millon, T., 207, 209
Milner, B., 19, 40, 81, 107, 109, 111
Mings, E., 178, 182
Mishkin, M., 72, 111, 112, 169, 182
Mitchell, J. R. A., 8, 39
Moats, L., 180, 182
Moberg, P. J., 60, 68
Monkowski, P. G., 245, 254
Moore, R. Y., 78, 112
Morris, M. K., 178, 182
Morris, P., 282, 289
Morris, R., 21, 39, 90, 110, 120, 161, 180, 183, 264, 273, 289
Morrison, M. W., 27, 39
Morrow, L. A., 178, 183
Mortensen, E. L., 47, 56, 67, 247, 248, 255
Moses, J. A., 19, 39
Mueller, J., 269, 289
Mukherjee, S., 124, 160
Mysiw, W. J., 269, 289

N

Nanda, H., 189, 209
Nebes, R. D., 53, 67, 81, 109
Neilson, P. M., 115, 160
Neisser, U., 260, 290
Nelson, H. E., 27, 40, 53, 54, 55, 65, 67
Neuringer, C., 228, 243, 255, 257, 266, 290

Newcombe, F., 275, 289
Nichelli, P., 122, 161
Nixon, S. J., 19, 40
Nunnally, J. C., 186, 187, 189, 209, 219, 238, 250, 256

O

O'Boyle, M., 101, 103, 111
O'Carroll, R. E., 53, 67
O'Connell, A., 53, 67
O'Hara, M. W., 103, 111
O'Leary, M. R., 27, 39
Ober, B. A., 137, 161, 178, 181, 212, 254
Obrist, W. D., 129, 163
Ochs, J., 178, 181
Orsini, D. L., 73, 111
Osmon, D. C., 19, 39
Osterrieth, P. A., 90, 95, 111

P

Paniak, C. E., 115, 160
Pankratz, L., 98, 109, 145, 160, 162
Paolo, A. M., 49, 67
Pardo, P. J., 124, 162
Parikh, R. M., 125, 162
Parker, D. M., 53, 54, 65
Parker, K. C. H., , 45, 67
Parsons, O. A., 19, 40, 60, 66, 264, 290
Pauker, J. D., 244, 245, 247, 248, 256
Paul, J. J., 27, 39
Peed, S., 145, 162
Pellegrino, J. W., 218, 256
Pendleton, M. G., 235, 256
Pequegnat, W., 269, 287
Peselow, E. D., 101, 109
Petrides, M., 107, 111
Petrila, J., 143, 162
Peyser, J. M., 269, 290
Phay, A., 13, 40
Pheley, A., 60, 66
Plasterk, K. J., 209, 257
Platt, J. R., 263, 290
Polakoff, D., 228, 239, 257
Poon, L. W., 103, 110, 112
Popper, K. R., 263, 290
Porte, H. S., 106, 112

Porteus, S. D., 139, 162
Posner, M. I., 116, 124, 162, 288
Post, F., 101, 111
Povlishock, J. T., 122, 162
Powell, D. H., 106, 112
Powers, L., 37, 40
Poythress, N. G., 143, 162
Pratkanis, A. R., 6, 39
Pressley, M., 169, 176, 183
Price, T. R., 124, 125, 162, 163
Prifitera, A., 37, 40, 45, 46, 67
Prigatano, G. P., 115, 134, 142, 162
Pritchard, J. S., 8, 39
Purisch, A. D., 213, 255

R

Rafal, R. D., 116, 162
Raffaele, K., 132, 161
Rajaratnam, N., 189, 209
Rankin, E. J., 49, 66
Rao, K., 124, 162
Rao, S. M., 269, 290
Rapaport, D., 116, 162
Rapcsak, S. Z., 91, 111
Rapoport, S. I., 132, 161, 282, 289
Rasch, G., 189, 209
Rasmussen, T., 81, 109
Razzouk, A., 178, 181
Reiman, E. M., 124, 162
Reinisch, J. M., 47, 67
Reitan, R. M., 19, 23, 26, 40, 47, 66, 98, 111, 166, 168, 169, 170, 171, 179, 183, 213, 223, 224, 228, 229, 239, 242, 247, 250, 256, 257, 267, 289, 290
Rennick, P. M., 233, 256
Retzlaff, P., 17, 39, 212, 254
Rey, A., 90, 95, 111
Reynolds, C. R., 46, 48, 50, 57, 59, 65, 67, 167, 181, 182, 183, 190, 209
Richards, P. M., 265, 290
Richardson, R. E. L., 144, 145, 146, 151, 162
Riddoch, M. J., 276, 288
Ridgley, B. A., 49, 68
Riege, W., 103, 110
Rimel, R. W., 122, 162
Risser, A., 167, 183
Roberts, M. C., 165, 181, 184

Robinson, R. G., 124, 125, 162, 163
Rosen, W., 282, 290
Rosenbaum, G., 59, 68
Rosvold, H. E., 169, 182
Roth, D. L., 245, 254
Rothke, S., 150, 151, 162
Rotrosen, J., 101, 109
Rourke, B. P., 59, 68, 166, 167, 171,
        180, 183, 209, 222, 230, 231, 257,
        262, 265, 266, 267, 271, 290
Routh, D. K., 178, 183
Rowed, D., 49, 68
Rubens, A. B., 125, 160
Ruff, R. M., 265, 290
Russell, E. W., 27, 40, 52, 56, 67, 81,
        111, 213, 214, 223, 224, 226, 228,
        230, 231, 232, 235, 236, 237, 238,
        239, 241, 243, 244, 245, 246, 248,
        249, 250, 251, 254, 255, 257, 258,
        260, 264, 265, 266, 290
Russell, S. L. K., 228, 239, 257
Rutter, M., 167, 183
Ryan, C., 178, 183
Ryan, J. J., 37, 40, 49, 67
Ryan, T. V., 145, 160

S

Saetveit, J. G., 236, 258
Saffran, E., 54, 66, 68
Salama, M., 270, 288
Salovey, P., 103, 111
Sattler, J. M., 3, 40, 177, 183, 184
Satz, P., 49, 67, 151, 162, 180, 183
Schacter, D., 287
Schafer, R., 116, 162
Schapiro, M. B., 132, 161
Scheerer, M., 212, 255
Schinka, J. A., 12, 40
Schmahmann, J. D., 168, 183
Schneider, W., 169, 176, 183
Schoenhuber, R., 122, 161
Schonfeldt-Bausch, R., 124, 160
Schwartz, M., 54, 66, 68
Seashore, C. B., 236, 258
Secord, W., 176, 183
Self, D., 103, 111
Selz, M., 169, 171, 183
Semel, E., 176, 183
Semrud-Clikeman, M., 30, 39
Seymour, C., 8, 39
Shallice, T., 107, 111, 275, 276, 290

Shelly, C., 239, 255, 288
Shelton, P. A., 91, 111
Sherer, M., 19, 40
Sheslow, D., 176, 179, 183
Simpson, C. D., 47, 68
Singer, J., 103, 111
Skenazy, J., 13, 40
Sliwinski, M., 54, 66
Slobogin, C., 143, 162
Smallberg, S., 282, 290
Smith, A., 264, 290
Smith, C. M., 53, 66
Snoek, J., 134, 161
Snow, W. G., 49, 68
Sohlberg, M. M., 116, 123, 134, 142, 162
Sparrow, S., 172, 183
Spearman, C., 45, 68
Speedie, L., 78, 105, 112
Spielberger, C. D., 173, 183
Spreen, O., 26, 40, 55, 65, 74, 109, 112, 149,
        162, 167, 169, 183, 186, 200, 209
Squire, L. R., 77, 78, 112, 274, 290
Starkey, R. I., 111, 214, 224, 228, 235,
        236, 237, 238, 241, 244, 245, 246,
        248, 257, 258
Starkey, T. W., 214, 258
Starkstein, S. E., 124, 125, 162, 163
Starr, L. B., 124, 162
Stebbins, G. T., 53, 54, 68
Stewart, L. E., 53, 54, 65
Stopek, S., 124, 161
Stout, R., 135, 160
Stover, E., 269, 287
Strange, J. D., 167, 183
Strauss, E., 74, 112, 149, 162, 186, 209
Strauss, J., 163
Stringer, A. V., 168, 169, 183
Stroop, J. R., 98, 112
Stuss, D. T., 77, 78, 109, 125, 163
Suen, H. K., 186, 209
Sutherland, K. M., 53, 65
Swash, M., 53, 66
Swayze, V. W., 124, 160
Sweet, J. J., 60, 61, 62, 68
Swiercinsky, D. P., 52, 68, 228, 258

T

Talley, J., 177, 184
Tantleff, S., 106, 109
Tarter, R. E., 13, 40, 83, 112, 167, 184,
        222, 258, 271, 272, 288, 290

Taylor, H. G., 170, 182
Taylor, J. M., 27, 40
Taylor, J. R., 102, 110
Teasdale, G., 128, 134, 161
Teuber, H. L., 27, 40, 225, 227, 258, 276, 290
Thorndike, R., 177, 184
Thurston, D., 166, 181
Thurstone, L. L., 45, 68
Todnem, K., 83, 112
Tollegen, A., 173, 181
Tomoeda, C. K., 282, 287
Tovian, S. M., 60, 68
Tramontana, M. G., 166, 167, 172, 182, 184
Tranel, D., 168, 184, 233, 254, 281, 290
Troster, A. I., 53, 60, 66
Tuokko, H., 167, 183
Tupper, D., 167, 183
Twang, E., 172, 182

U

Udesen, H., 247, 255
Ungerleider, L. G., 72, 111, 112
Uzzell, B. P., 129, 163

V

Valenstein, E., 76, 91, 110, 160, 169, 182
Van Allen, M., 95, 109
Van Gorp, W. G., 67, 73, 111
Van Hoesen, G. W., 281, 288
Van Thiel, D. H., 13, 40, 83, 112, 167, 184
Vanderploeg, R. D., 13, 17, 27, 39, 40, 123, 129, 212, 254
VanEaton, E., 238, 257
Varney, N. R., 74, 95, 109, 200, 209
Vasey, M., 60, 66
Vega, A., 47, 68
Velozo, C. A., 135, 160
Veneklasen, J., 60, 65, 66
Vik-Mo, H., 83, 112

W

Walker, C. E., 165, 181, 184
Wallace, R. B., 103, 111
Walsh, K. W., 32, 40, 70, 73, 105, 106, 107, 112, 212, 258

Wapner, S., 110, 289
Ward, M. P., 2, 7, 40
Ware, J., 106, 112
Warnock, J. K., 52, 68
Warren, J. M., 256
Warrington, E. K., 260, 267, 273, 275, 276, 277, 289, 290
Watson, R. T., 76, 91, 110
Webster, J., 257
Wechsler, D., 21, 22, 23, 29, 40, 45, 46, 52, 58, 59, 64, 68, 81, 86, 87, 92, 107, 112, 114, 128, 138, 163, 166, 174, 177, 184, 190, 209, 212, 218, 246, 258
Wedding, D., 144, 145, 163, 239, 257, 258
Wehman, P. H., 160
Weinberger, D. R., 124, 163
Weingartner, H., 102, 112, 282, 290
Weintraub, S., 74, 76, 94, 105, 106, 110, 112, 120, 161, 236, 250, 256
Weiss, E. M., 83, 109
Wells, C. E., 101, 112
Werner, H., 212, 258, 277, 290
Wernicke, C., 275, 276, 290
Werts, D., 135, 160
Westlake, R., 99, 111
Wetzel, L., 27, 41
Whipple, B. S., 106, 112
Whishaw, I. Q., 168, 169, 182, 230, 238, 256
White, T. G., 146, 163
Whitla, D. K., 106, 112
Whitman, D., 59, 68
Whittick, J. E., 53, 67
Whitworth, R. H., 282, 290
Wiig, E., 176, 183
Wilkening, G. N., 53, 67
Wilkinson, G. S., 155, 161, 173, 182
Williams, C. L., 173, 181
Williams, H. G., 169, 176, 184
Williams, J. M., 12, 29, 41
Williams, M., 20, 41
Willis, W. G., 167, 169, 178, 182
Willson, V. L., 46, 65
Wilson, B., 150, 163
Wilson, R. S., 53, 54, 58, 59, 61, 63, 68
Wolfe, J., 94, 109
Wolfson, D., 19, 40, 98, 111, 171, 183, 223, 228, 242, 250, 256, 257
Wolraich, M. L., 183

Wood, M., 178, 181
Woodard, J. L., 27, 39
Woodcock, W., 173, 184
World Health Organization & Nordic
    Council of Ministers Working
    Group, 269, 290

Y

Yakolev, P. I., 169, 184
Yamada, T., 78, 110

Yates, A., 52, 68
Yeudall, L. T., 244, 245, 246, 247, 255
Young, A. W., 260, 273, 275, 287, 288
Young, R. C., 101, 112,
Yuh, W. T. C., 124, 160

Z

Zec, R. F., 124, 163
Ziebell, S., 124, 160
Zimmerman, R. A., 129, 163

Subject Index

A

Adjustment reactions to brain injury, 134, 139, 153
Administration, *see* Test Administration
Age effects, *see* Individual differences, demographic factors
Age-adjustment, 36, 81, 247–249
Algorithms, 222–223
AMNART, *see* Premorbid functioning.
Amnesia, 77–78, *see also* Memory psychogenic, 125, 128–129
Analogies Test, 235, 237
Anosognosia, 125
Arousal, 25, 90, *see also* Attentional deficits
Assessment of Cognitive Skills test, 106
Attainment scales, 239–240
Attention, 90–91, 116, 233,
Attentional deficits, 32
Average Impairment Rating, 242–243
Average Impairment Scale, 243
Average z score Index, 249–250
Awareness, 142–143
  case example, 138–139
  emergent awareness, 135, 138

B

Base-rate, 77–78
Batteries, test, *see* Test batteries
Behavioral disturbances and brain damage, *see* Emotional disturbances
Behavioral observations, 14–16, 101–102, 119
Best performance method, *see* Premorbid functioning
Block Design, *see* Wechsler Adult Intelligence Scale—Revised
Boston Diagnostic Aphasia Examination, 213
Boston Naming Test, 74, 120, 236
Brain-behavior relationships, *see also* Cognitive functions
  functional organization, 71–72
  conceptual model, 70–71, 74–75
Brain damage, *see also* Amnesia, Dementia
  acute versus chronic, 72, 168, 169
  age at onset, 169–170
  diffuse effects, 72–73, 168
  emotional disturbance, *see* Emotional disturbances

Brain damage *(cont.)*
  focal effects, 72–73, 168
  index of, 242–243
  lesion type, 167–168
  lesion velocity, 168
  location, 168–169
  personality changes with, *see* Personality changes
  progressive, 72, 168
  severity, 242–243
  static, 168

C

C score, 241
Capgras syndrome, 99
Case history, 8–14, *see also* Interview
  elements of, 9–10, 130
  medical records, 13–14
  obtaining, 12–13
Category test, 23, 27, 33, 233
Calibration, *see* Test administration, calibration of instruments
Child Behavior Checklist, 173
Child Development Inventory, 172
Child neuropsychology, 165–180
  assessment approaches, 170–172
  elements of the examination, 174–177
  historical trends, 166–167
  interview, 173, 174–175
  medical populations, 178–180
  norms, 177–180
  psychometric issues, 177–178
Clinical Evaluation of Language Fundamentals—Revised, 176
Clinical interview, *see* Interview
Cognitive Behavior Rating Scale, 12
Cognitive functions, 217, 230, *see also* Brain-behavior relationships
Cognitive remediation, 180
Cognitive neuropsychology, 275–277
Comparison standards, 43–44, 49, 62, 65, *see also* Norms and Premorbid functioning
  individual-specific, 44
  self-standard, 44
Compensation,
  for attentional deficits during testing, 25, 32, 35
Complex Ideational Test, 237

Composite scores, 242–243
Comprehensive Norms for an Expanded Halstead-Reitan Battery, 214, 233–238, 241–242, 245, 246–247, 249–250
Computerized test interpretation, *see* Test interpretation
Configural processing, 278–279
Confirmatory bias, 6–7, 96
Confrontation, *see* Interview, confrontation.
Consistency
  brain dysfunction and performance, 30–32, 93–99
Contradictions, *see* Discrepancies.
Coordinated norming, 246
Corsi Board, 236
Crystallized abilities, 231

D

Decimal scales, 241
Delusions, 99
Dementia, 49, 77–78
  and depression, 102–103, 126, 281–282
Depression, *see also* Emotional disturbances
  and test performance, 100, 102–103, 124–125
Design fluency test, 235
Developmental critical periods, 169
Developmental inventories, 172
Diagnosis, 121–123
  overlapping conditions, 123, 124
  problems in, 123–129, 132
Digit Vigilance, 233
Discrepancies, *see also* Interview, discrepancies
  among test scores, 86–87
  between functional and testing behavior, 101–102, 141
  between WAIS-R subtests, 45–49
Dominance
  language, 81
Double dissociation, 225–227
Driving evaluations, 141

E

Education, *see* Individual differences, demographic factors

Education-adjustment, 81–82, 247–249
Emotional disturbances
  and test performance, 73, 84, 99, 100–101
  assessment of, 141–142
  case example, 139–140
  disinhibition, 117–118
  Ethical principles, 30, 113, 152
Evaluation
  questions, *see* Referral questions
  purpose, 3, 113
Examiner drift, 22, 25, 37
Executive abilities, 77–78, 233–235, *see also* Frontal lobe

F

Facial Recognition Test, 95
Fatigue, 32, 35, 84, 96
Featural processing, 278–279
Feedback to patients and families, 152–158
Figure Memory Test, 236
Finger tapping test, 237
  administration, 23
  calibration, 26
  handedness, 81
  norms, 26
Fluency, 235
Fluid abilities, 231
Forensic issues, 143–152
  case example, 147–149
  historically structured fact-based approach, 151
Frontal lobe, *see also* Executive abilities
  and awareness of deficits, 125
  dysfunction, 33,
  failure to detect pathology, 107
Fuld pattern, 49
Functional system, 273–274

G

General intelligence factor (*g*), 45
Gollin Figures, 95
Greek cross, 33–34
Grip strength, 26, 81, 237
Grooved Pegboard Test, 237

H

H-Words test, 235
Halstead Index, 242

Halstead-Reitan Battery, 213, 231, *see also* Comprehensive Norms for an Expanded Halstead-Reitan Battery
  validity, 239, 265
Halstead-Reitan Neuropsychological Test Battery for Children, 171
Halstead Rennick Russell Battery, 214
Halstead Russell Neuropsychological Evaluation System, 214, 233–238, 241–243, 245, 246–247, 249–250
Handedness, 81
Head injury
  and post-traumatic stress disorder, 126
Health status
  and performance, 13, 83
Hemispatial priority, 279–280
History, *see* Case history
Hooper Visual Organization Test, 92, 95
Huntington's disease and memory, 94
Hypothesis testing, 221–222

I

Ideographic approach to assessment, 171
Impairment scales, 239–240
Index of brain damage, *see* Brain damage, index of
Individual differences,
  demographic factors, 30–31, 80–83
  native language, 83
  sensitivity to, 30–32
  state factors, 83 84
  variability in level of performance, 44–49
  variables affecting performance, 30–32, 79–84
Intelligence-adjustment, 247, 248–249
Interpretation, *see* Test interpretation
Interview, 6–8, *see also* Case history
  confrontation, 7–8
  developmental history, 173
  discrepancies, 8
  open-ended questions, 7
  relatives as sources, 125–126, 131
  topics to cover, 9–10, 119, 140

J

Judgment of Line Orientation, 95

K

Kappa statistic, 188
Kennard principle, 170

L

Luria's Neuropsychological Investigation,
273–275
Luria-Nebraska Neuropsychological Test
Battery, 213, 231

M

Malingering, 95, 98–99, 145–146, 151
Markovian decision process, 262, 277
Maximum performance, 28–29, 32
Medical records, 13–14, see also Case
history
Medication effects, 83
Memory, 235–236
behavioral observations, 14, 97
disorders, 77–78
primary versus secondary deficit,
92–93
testing the limits, 20–21
Memory Assessment Scale, 29
Mental flexibility, 233
Mental status examination, 14–16
Method variance, 283
Miami Selective Learning Test, 236
Microgenesis, 212
MMPI, 36, 115
MMPI-2, 205, 249
MMPI-A, 173
Modeling brain functions, 218–221
Moderator variables, 30–31

N

NART, see Premorbid functioning
NART-R, see Premorbid functioning
Nebraska Neuropsychological Children's
Battery, 171
Neglect, 76–77, 91
Neighborhood signs, 76–77
Neuropsychological assessment, see also
Neuropsychological testing and
Test batteries

approaches, 17, 170–172, 211–214
cognitive-metric approach, 211, 214
domains of assessment, 17, 172–174
fixed approach, 262
flexible approach, 262
hypothesis testing approach, 263–264
multiple fixed batteries approach,
268–272
process approach, 211–212
versus testing, 2–3
Neuropsychological Questionnaire, 12
Neuropsychological Status Examination,
12
Neuropsychological testing, see also Test,
Testing, and Test administration,
and Test Interpretation,
constant background in test batteries,
219
internal consistency, 219–220
content constancy, 220–221
external constancy, 220–221
fixed battery, 17, 171
flexible battery, 17, 171
historical traditions, 114, 211–214
interpretation, see Test interpretation
relationship to functional abilities,
133–134
Nomothetic approach to assessment, 171
Norms, 26, 43–44, 80–81, 245, see also
Psychometric issues

O

Observations, see Behavioral observations
Occam's razor, 88
Operating Characteristics, 199–203
negative predictive power, 202–203
positive predictive power, 201–203
sensitivity, 200–203
specificity, 200–203

P

Parsimony, 88
Patient-centered approach to assessment,
171
Pattern of performance, see Test interpre-
tation
Pathognomonic signs, 44, 223

Peabody Individual Achievement Test, 237
Peabody Picture Vocabulary Test—
 Revised, 18, 91, 236
Percentiles, 205, 240
Personality changes
 and brain injury, 115, 134
Plasticity, 169–170
Practice effects on performance, 87–88
Premorbid functioning, 43–65
 AMNART, 54–56
 assumptions regarding, 44–45
 based on demographic factors, 56–63
 based on historical data, 49–52
 best performance method, 56
 clinician-based demographic method,
  57–58
 estimation of, 49–65
 hold measures, 52–56
 NART, 53–56
 NART-R, 55–56
 personality characteristics, 134–135
 psychiatric problems, 134–135
 recommendations, 63–65
 regression equation approaches, 58–63
 relationship to education and occupation, 50–51, 56–58
 WAIS/WAIS-R hold subtests, 52–53
 windows of performance, 63–65, 82
Problem-solving, 233–235
Process approach, 211–212, 277–280, see
 also Neuropsychological assessment
Prognostic predictions, 135, 141
 case examples, 137–138, 138–139
Pseudodementia, see also Depression,
 Emotional disturbances
 differentiating from dementia,
  100–101, 102
Psychiatric disturbances, see Emotional
 disturbances
Psychometric issues, 73–74, 177–180,
 185–209, see also Norms, Reliability, Validity
 accuracy, 238–243
 base-rate scores, 207
 distribution of data, 204–208, 249
 kurtosis, 206–207
 norming problems, 244–245, 246–247
 norms, 74, 177–180, 245
 operating characteristics, see Operating
  characteristics

power versus speed, 188–189
 reliability, 187–189
  Cronbach alpha, 187
  interjudge, 188
  internal consistency, 187
  Kappa statistic, 188
  split-half, 187
  test-retest, 187–188
 scale development, 239–241
 scale equivalence, 243–247
 scale types, 204–205, 240–241
 set of tests, 218–219, 238
 skew, 205–207
 stability, 187–188
 standard error of measurement, 188,
  190
 standard error of estimate, 188, 191
 test referencing, 191–192
  content-referenced, 192
  criterion-referenced, 192
  norm-referenced, 191
  predictive-referenced, 192
 transformation of scores, 204–205
 true score, 189–190
 validity, 192–194, 199–203

R

Reasoning, 233–235
Referral questions, 3–6
 useful evaluation questions, 4
Rehabilitation context in neuropsycholo-
 gy, 132–143
 utility of assessment, 132–133
Reitan-Indiana Neuropsychological Test
 Battery for Children, 171
Reliability, 3, 187–189, 238, see also Psy-
 chometric issues
Rey-Osterrieth Complex figure, 90, 95
Rivermead Behavioural Memory Test, 150

S

Schizophrenia, 124
Scales, see Psychometric issues
Scores, see Test scores
Scoring, see Testing, scoring errors
Seashore Tonal Memory test, 236, 237
Seashore Rhythm test, 120, 233

Sensitivity, *see* Operating characteristics
Sensory-perceptual Examination, 237
Session, *see* Testing, session
Signal detection theory, 199–200
Specificity, *see* Operating characteristics
Speech Sounds Perception test, 120, 233
Standard error of estimate, 188, 191, *see also* Psychometric issues
Standard error of measurement, 188, 190, *see also* Psychometric issues
Standard scores, 240
Standardization
   administration, 19–21
   de-emphasis of, 22–23
   unclear aspects, 21–22
   variations in, 23–24
State factors, *see* Individual differences
Stimulus bound, 33
Story Memory test, 236
Stroop task, 98
Subject-specific variables, *see* Individual differences
Symptom Validity testing, 98–99, 145–146
Syndrome analysis, 274

T

T score, 204–205, 240–242
Tactual Performance Test, 235, 236, 238
Tapping, *see* Finger tapping test
Technician, use of, 251–252
Test, 2, 215, 216–221, *see also* Test batteries, Neuropsychological testing
   multifactorial nature, 89, 115, 120, 195, 196–197, 263–264, 282–283
   representational nature, 216–217
   "sets" of tests, 218–221
   variations in, 27
Test administration, *see also* Standardization and Testing
   calibration of instruments, 26–27
   issues, 27–28
   phrasing instructions, 29–30
   recommendations, 24–25,
   timing, 22–23,
   variations in, 26
Test batteries, *see also* Neuropsychological testing and Neuropsychological Assessment

advantages and disadvantages of fixed versus flexible batteries, 284–286
distinguishing fixed and flexible approaches, 262–268
   psychometric versus neurologic, 264–266
   quantitative versus qualitative data, 266–268
   test selection, 262–264
fixed battery, 17, 171
   and research, 252
   battery requirements,
      coverage, 229–238
      accuracy, 238–243
      equivalence, 243–250
      practical, 250–252
   cognitive-metric approach, 211–254
flexible battery, 17, 171, 261–287
multiple fixed batteries, 268–272
Test interpretation, 43–44, 69–108, 221–229
algorithms, 222–223
avoiding erroneous assumptions, 103–107
change in performance, 87–88
comparisons, 224–228
computers, 253–254
conceptual model, 70–72, 74–75
consistency, 76, 93–99
data for interpretation, 69–70
dissociations, 225–228
expectations of performance, 75–78
fatigue, 32, 84, 198
formulas and indices, 227–228
hypothesis testing, 221–222
methods, 221–229
microgenetic analysis, 282–283
motivation, 198
multiple measures, 94–95
pattern analysis, 223–229
patterns of performance, 49, 78, 96–97
   diffuse versus specific effects, 89–90
   lower-order versus higher-order effects, 90–91
   primary versus secondary effects, 91–93, 95–96
profile analysis, 86
psychiatric/psychological factors, 84
qualitative analysis, 78–79
single-score interpretation, 85–86
variability and brain damage, 47

Test scores, 43, 56
  cutoff scores, 85–86
  transformation to scale scores,
    241–242
Test theory, 189–191
  classical test theory, 189–190
  generalizability theory, 189
  item analysis, 189
  item response theory, 189
Testing
  allowing deficits to emerge, 32–33
  approaches, 17
  behavior, 101
  breaks during, 35
  introduction to, 33–35
  maximal performance, 28–29
  ordering of tests, 35–36
  pacing, 35
  rapport, 29
  relationship, examiner–patient, 29–30
  scoring errors, 36–38
  session, 28, 33–36
  single versus multiple sessions, 36
  structure, 33–36
  test selection, 17–19
Testing the limits, 20, 25
Thalamus, 78
Thurstone Word Fluency test, 235
Tonal Memory test, see Seashore Tonal
    Memory test
Trail Making test, 23, 33, 98, 233
Trails Speed Test, 237
Training of neuropsychologists, 74,
    280–284
Trait variance, 283
True score, 189–190, see also Psycho-
    metric issues

V

Validity, 3, 192–194, 199–203, 238, see
    also Psychometric issues
  construct, 134, 193
  content, 192–193
  criterion-related
    concurrent, 193–194
    predictive, 134, 193–194
  face validity, 104–105, 193
Vineland Adaptive Behavior Scales, 172
Visual Gestalt Identification Test, 238

Visual Retention Test, 95
Visual system, 72
Visuospatial disorders, 72

W

WAIS-R as a Neuropsychological Test In-
    strument, 21, 90, 120, 267, 279
Wechsler Adult Intelligence Scale—
    Revised, 236
  Arithmetic, 21–22, 237
  Block design, 21, 79, 89–90, 120, 237
  Comprehension, 37
  Digit Span, 22, 116, 233, 236
  Digit Symbol, 81, 237
  Information, 236
  Object Assembly, 237
  Picture Arrangement, 237
  Picture Completion, 22, 25, 120, 237
  Similarities, 37
  variable performance, 44–49
  Vocabulary, 37, 236
Wechsler-Bellevue Intelligence Scale, 212,
    213
Wechsler Memory Scale,
  Logical Memory, 236
  Visual Reproduction, 236
Wechsler Memory Scale—Revised, 29
  Digit Span, 35, 233, 236
  Logical Memory, 22
    interpretation, 92–93
  Mental Control, 35
  scoring errors, 36–37
  Visual Reproduction, 23
    interpretation, 92–93
Western Aphasia Battery, 74
Wide Range Achievement Test—Revised,
    173, 237
  scoring errors, 37
Wide Range Assessment of Memory and
    Learning, 176
Wisconsin Card Sorting test, 23, 27, 33,
    233
Woodcock-Johnson Psychoeducational
    Battery—Revised, 173

Z

z score, 204–205, 240